CASES IN GENDER AND DIVERSITY IN ORGANIZATIONS

THE IVEY CASEBOOK SERIES

A SAGE Publications Series

Series Editor

Paul W. Beamish

Richard Ivey School of Business
The University of Western Ontario

Books in This Series

CASES IN BUSINESS ETHICS
Edited by David J. Sharp

CASES IN ENTREPRENEURSHIP
The Venture Creation Process
Edited by Eric A. Morse and Ronald K. Mitchell

CASES IN GENDER AND DIVERSITY IN ORGANIZATIONS
Edited by Alison M. Konrad

CASES IN OPERATIONS MANAGEMENT
Building Customer Value Through World-Class Operations
Edited by Robert D. Klassen and Larry J. Menor

CASES IN ORGANIZATIONAL BEHAVIOR
Edited by Gerard H. Seijts

CASES IN THE ENVIRONMENT OF BUSINESS
International Perspectives
Edited by David W. Conklin

ALISON M. KONRAD
The University of Western Ontario

CASES IN GENDER AND DIVERSITY IN ORGANIZATIONS

SAGE Publications
Thousand Oaks ▪ London ▪ New Delhi

For information:

Sage Publications, Inc.
2455 Teller Road
Thousand Oaks, California 91320
E-mail: order@sagepub.com

Sage Publications Ltd.
1 Oliver's Yard
55 City Road
London EC1Y 1SP
United Kingdom

Sage Publications India Pvt. Ltd.
B-42, Panchsheel Enclave
Post Box 4109
New Delhi 110 017 India

Printed in the United States of America

Library of Congress Cataloging-in-Publication Data

Cases in gender and diversity in organizations / [compiled by] Alison M. Konrad.
        p. cm.—(The Ivey Casebook Series)
Includes bibliographical references.
ISBN 1-4129-1804-9 (pbk.)
    1.   Diversity in the workplace—Case studies. 2.   Discrimination in employment—Case studies.
3.   Sex discrimination in employment—Case studies. 4.   Interpersonal relations—Case studies.
I. Konrad, Alison M. II. Series.
HF5549.5.M5C396 2006
658.3'008—dc22   2005019716

This book is printed on acid-free paper.

05   06   07   08   09   10   9   8   7   6   5   4   3   2   1

Acquisitions Editor:	Al Bruckner
Editorial Assistant:	MaryAnn Vail
Production Editor:	Laureen A. Shea
Copy Editor:	Gillian Dickens
Typesetter:	C&M Digitals (P) Ltd.
Proofreader:	Mary Meagher
Cover Designer:	Edgar Abarca

CONTENTS

Introduction to the Ivey Casebook Series   vii
Paul W. Beamish

Introduction   ix

1. Workplace Discrimination   1
    Avoiding Discrimination in Employment
        Selection and Retention: Some Legal Issues   11
    Staffing at Wal-Mart Stores, Inc. (A)   17
    NexTech Inc. (A)   25
    Stamford Machine Corporation: Allegations of Racism   37
    Ottawa Valley Food Products   39
    CTV Newsnet (A)   41

2. Sexual Harassment   47
    Sexual Harassment in the Workplace: Definition, Cases and Policy   53
    Rebecca Collier   60
    Ruth Jones (A)   64
    Telcom   70
    "Most Likely to Sleep With Her Boss . . . and
        the Winner Is . . . Gail Wilson" (A)   83

3. Work-Life Balance   87
    Anna Harris (A)   93

4. Organizational Diversity Programs   99
    Diversity: A Quota by Any Other Name?   108
    Women in Management at London Life (A)   109
    The Bank of Montreal—The Task Force on
        the Advancement of Women in the Bank (A)   118
    "Synergy" at City Hall (A)   126

5. Cross-Cultural Diversity   139
    Ellen Moore (A): Living and Working in Bahrain   146
    Ellen Moore (A): Living and Working in Korea   155
    Julie Dempster (A)   168
    The European Experience (A)   172

Being Different: Exchange Student Experiences   181
The Changing Face of Europe: A Note on Immigration and Societal Attitudes   184

6. Entrepreneurship   197
Marie Bohm and The Aspect Group   201
The Purchasing Co-Op   208
Rubenesque   212
Growth, Strategy and Slotting at No Pudge! Foods, Inc.   225
English Center for Newcomers   233

About the Editor   **245**

INTRODUCTION TO THE IVEY CASEBOOK SERIES

As the title of this series suggests, these books all draw from the Ivey Business School's case collection. Ivey has long had the world's second largest collection of decision-oriented, field-based business cases. Well more than a million copies of Ivey cases are studied every year. There are more than 2,000 cases in Ivey's current collection, with more than 6,000 in the total collection. Each year approximately 200 new titles are registered at Ivey Publishing (www.ivey.uwo.ca/cases), and a similar number are retired. Nearly all Ivey cases have teaching notes available to qualified instructors. The cases included in this volume are all from the current collection.

The vision for the series was a result of conversations I had with Sage's Senior Editor, Al Bruckner, starting in September 2002. Over the subsequent months, we were able to shape a model for the books in the series that we felt would meet a market need.

Each volume in the series contains text and cases. "Some" text was deemed essential in order to provide a basic overview of the particular field and to place the selected cases in an appropriate context. We made a conscious decision to not include hundreds of pages of text material in each volume in recognition of the fact that many professors prefer to supplement basic text material with readings or lectures customized to their interests and to those of their students.

The editors of the books in this series are all highly qualified experts in their respective fields. I was delighted when each agreed to prepare a volume. We very much welcome your comments on this casebook.

—Paul W. Beamish
Series Editor

INTRODUCTION

Workplace diversity can be defined as the set of individual, group, and cultural differences people bring to organizations. On the surface, people differ in their demographics, such as gender, race, age, disability status, and appearance. In addition to *surface-level differences*, people bring different sets of *achieved human capital,* such as abilities, skills, qualifications, and achievements, which they can choose to contribute to the organization fully or less so. Furthest from the surface and difficult to observe without regular interaction over time are the *deep-level* differences people bring in terms of values, beliefs, cultures, and cognitive and behavioral styles. As such, the variety of interpersonal differences that managers and other organizational members experience and navigate each day is substantial.

Workplaces are becoming more diverse for a number of reasons. Women's labor force participation rates have greatly increased in the past three to four decades. For instance, in 1970, 43% of women in the United States participated in the paid labor force, a figure that increased to 52% in 1980, 58% in 1990, and 60% in 2000, and is projected to increase to 62% by 2010 (U.S. Census Bureau, 2004). Figures are similar in Canada. In 1976, about 42% of Canadian women worked for pay, a figure that rose to about 58% in 2002 (Statistics Canada, 2003). Women have similarly moved into the European labor force, and in 2002, 56% of women in France, 65% of women in the United Kingdom, 73% of women in Sweden, and 74% of women in Norway worked for pay (Eurostat, 2004). A major cause of the increase in women's labor force participation has been that women no longer drop out of the labor force when they get married. Also, women are much more likely to continue working upon the arrival of children. In 1981, only about 42% of Canadian mothers with children younger than age 6 worked for pay, compared to about 65% in 2002 (Statistics Canada, 2003). Statistics are similar in the United States, where in 1980, 45% of married women with children younger than age 6 worked for pay, compared to 63% in 2001 (U.S. Census Bureau, 2004).

Another factor leading to greater workplace diversity is the growth of racial and ethnic minority populations in many industrialized countries. For instance, in the United States, the 1980 labor force was 88% White, 10% Black, and 6% Hispanic. In 2000, those figures had changed to 83% White, 12% Black, and 11% Hispanic, with projected figures of 81% White, 13% Black, and 13% Hispanic by 2010 (U.S. Census Bureau, 2004). The Canadian labor force is less diverse by race and ethnicity. In 1996, 11% of the Canadian population consisted of "visible minorities," which includes Asians, Blacks, and Hispanics. In 2001, visible minorities had increased to 13% of the total population (Statistics Canada, 2005a), and projections suggest that by 2017, about one in five Canadians will be visible minorities (Statistics Canada, 2005b). Much of this growth will come from immigration, and immigration will have a considerably greater impact on the Canadian than on the U.S. labor force. The United States, a country of more than 280 million people, admits slightly over 1 million immigrants annually (U.S. Census Bureau, 2004) compared to Canada, a country of about 31 million, which admits almost 250,000 immigrants each year (Statistics Canada, 2005b).

Beyond race and ethnicity, cultural differences, such as religion, are increasingly affecting North American workplaces. In 2001, about 2% of the Canadian population was Muslim, 1% was Jewish, 1% Buddhist, 1% Hindu, and 1% Sikh (Statistics Canada, 2005b). In the same year, the U.S. population was about 0.5% Muslim, 1.4% Jewish, 0.5% Buddhist, 0.4% Hindu, and 0.03% Sikh (U.S. Census Bureau, 2004). Although the percentages appear small, they are growing, and North American courts are increasingly recognizing the rights of religious minorities in the workplace (Cash, Gray, & Rood, 2000).

All three levels of diversity—surface-level differences, achieved human capital, and deep-level diversity—affect organizations and their members. Surface-level diversity is associated with immediate impressions that can stimulate stereotypical perceptions and expectations (Bargh, 1999). Achieved human capital has obvious effects on people's organizational experiences because most work organizations assign people to jobs on the basis of demonstrated qualifications and aptitude. People prefer to be judged on the basis of qualifications rather than surface-level demographics, and they rate meritocratic organizational practices very highly (Konrad & Linnehan, 1995b). Unfortunately, misunderstandings due to cultural differences and differences in assumptions based on divergence of life experiences make it more difficult for coworkers, supervisors, and mentors to build a rapport with dissimilar others, despite level of qualifications (Chattopadhyay, 1999; Ensher & Murphy, 1997; Ragins, 1997; Riordan, 2000; Thomas, 1993, 2001; Tsui, Egan, & O'Reilly, 1992). In addition, the automatic activation of stereotypes can pose a barrier to the recognition of people's qualifications and achievements, especially when performance is difficult to judge, such as the quality of a written essay, or when future rather than past performance is an important criterion (Fiske & Taylor, 1991; Nieva & Gutek, 1980; Tosi & Einbender, 1985). For example, Martin (1996) found that decision makers were more likely to promote men on the basis of the belief that they would grow and develop the skills needed for the job, while women were required to demonstrate the necessary job skills before they were promoted. Bell and Nkomo (2001) documented similar stories among Black female executives.

The deepest level of diversity concerns values, beliefs, cultures, cognitive style, and behavioral style. These factors are usually not apparent to coworkers until after regular interaction over a period of time, yet they have the potential to have the greatest impact on workplace relations. Indeed, Harrison and his colleagues demonstrated that over time, deep-level value differences were a better predictor of relationships among coworkers than surface-level demographic differences (Harrison, Price, & Bell, 1998; Harrison, Price, Gavin, & Florey, 2002). These findings suggest on the positive side that deep-level similarities can overcome surface-level differences, but on the negative side, they suggest that deep-level diversity can engender difficulties for developing good working relationships.

Writers have argued that diversity potentially constitutes a competitive advantage for organizations. For example, Cox and Blake (1991) as well as Robinson and Dechant

(1997) theorized that workplace diversity should be associated with better problem solving and more creativity, due to the availability of a greater variety of viewpoints to bring to bear on organizational issues. They also pointed out that workplace diversity provides organizations with better insights into the psychology of a more diverse consumer group, which should result in valuable market intelligence. Finally, these authors suggested that given the labor force is becoming globalized, with increased immigration as well as increased pressure from minority groups in many nations for full access to economic opportunities, organizations that are effective at recruiting a diverse workforce will have better access to top-quality talent among historically excluded groups.

Although the potential benefits of workplace diversity are clear and logically sound, research is needed to document the true effects on organizational performance. A number of studies show that workplace diversity is positively related to effectiveness. For example, in two studies examining 291 and 410 U.S. firms, respectively, Frink et al. (2003) demonstrated that organizations with about equal numbers of women and men showed better financial performance than organizations with either a predominantly male or a predominantly female workforce. Richard (2000) found that racial diversity was positively associated with the financial performance of 63 U.S. banks pursuing a growth strategy. Similarly, in a study of 177 U.S. banks, Richard, McMillan, Chadwick, and Dwyer (2003) found that racial diversity was positively related to financial performance for banks pursuing an innovation strategy.

Not all studies have shown positive effects of diversity, however. Richard, Barnett, Dwyer, and Chadwick (2004) found that the association between racial diversity in top-management teams and firm performance was curvilinear and complex. Kochan et al. (2003) conducted research at four major U.S. firms that were leaders in supporting workforce diversity. Comparing performance, group process, and financial results for comparable business units, the authors concluded that workforce diversity was unrelated to organizational performance. Combining the results of 24 studies of intact work groups, Webber and Donahue (2001) concluded that neither job-related human capital diversity nor surface-level demographic diversity was related to group cohesion or group performance. Finally, Williams and O'Reilly (1998) concluded from their review of the research literature that demographic diversity in work groups might be associated with *less* cohesion and *lower* performance.

Clearly, workplace diversity does not automatically result in positive performance, and it is likely that effective management is needed to overcome the initial barriers of surface-level stereotyping and longer term issues associated with deep-level differences in values, beliefs, and styles. Fortunately, organizations have found some solutions to these challenges. For example, in a study of 138 Philadelphia-area organizations, Konrad and Linnehan (1995a) found that formal practices designed to aggressively recruit and monitor the treatment of women and people of color were associated with having women at a higher management rank and more people of color in management. Goodman, Fields, and Blum (2003) found that organizations placing more emphasis on development and promotion of employees had more women in top-management positions in their study of 228 medium- to large-sized firms in Georgia. Wright, Ferris, Hiller, and Kroll (1995) found that the stock price of 34 firms rose after the announcement that they had been awarded an Exemplary Voluntary Effort (EVE) award for affirmative action from the U.S. federal government. In a study of 195 for-profit U.S. firms, Konrad and Mangel (2000) found that work-life benefits were associated with higher productivity for firms employing a higher percentage of women. In a study of 527 U.S. firms, Perry-Smith and Blum (2000) found that firms with more extensive work-life benefits were more likely to be perceived by their peers as high performers. In sum, human resource practices aimed at effective diversity management appear to be associated with moving a more diverse group into management as well as better firm financial performance.

Gender and diversity issues will continue to challenge organizations as the globalization of business and pressures from historically underrepresented identity groups increase. Effective organizations manage to embrace an ever-increasing diversity of identity groups while at the same time establishing and achieving appropriate organizational objectives. Research suggests that it is possible for organizations to achieve both diversity and fairness. Konrad and Linnehan (1995b) found that line managers had neutral to positive attitudes toward almost all affirmative action practices, and Parker, Baltes, and Christiansen (1997) found that White men did not associate their organization's support for affirmative action with a loss in career development opportunities, organizational injustice, or negative work attitudes.

Effective diversity management requires that managers have a rich awareness and understanding of contemporary identity group dynamics, an openness to continuous learning and development as new identity groups and issues emerge, and an exposure to a rich variety of organizational responses that can provide a foundation for developing the new management solutions that will become necessary in the future. The cases included in this volume are designed to provide a solid foundation for the diversity journey.

REFERENCES

Bargh, J. A. (1999). The cognitive monster: The case against the controllability of automatic stereotype effects. In S. Chaiken & Y. Trope (Eds.), *Dual-process theories in social psychology* (pp. 361–382). New York: Guilford.

Bell, E. L. J. E., & Nkomo, S. M. (2001). *Our separate ways: Black and White women and the struggle for professional identity.* Boston: Harvard Business School Press.

Cash, K. C., Gray, G. R., & Rood, S. A. (2000). A framework for accommodating religion and spirituality in the workplace. *Academy of Management Executive, 14*(3), 124–134.

Chattopadhyay, P. (1999). Beyond direct and symmetrical effects: The influence of demographic dissimilarity on organizational citizenship behaviors. *Academy of Management Journal, 42,* 273–287.

Cox, T., Jr., & Blake, S. (1991). Managing cultural diversity: Implications for organizational competitiveness. *Academy of Management Executive, 5*(3), 45–56.

Ensher, E. A., & Murphy, S. E. (1997). Effects of race, gender, perceived similarity, and contact on mentor relationships. *Journal of Vocational Behavior, 50,* 460–481.

Eurostat. (2004). *How Europeans spend their time: Everyday life of women and men.* Luxembourg: European Communities.

Fiske, S. T., & Taylor, S. E. (1991). *Social cognition* (2nd ed.). New York: McGraw-Hill.

Frink, D. D., Robinson, R. K., Reithel, B., Arthur, M. M., Ammeter, A. P., Ferris, G. R., et al. (2003). Gender demography and organization performance: A two-study investigation with convergence. *Group & Organization Management, 28,* 127–147.

Goodman, J. S., Fields, D. L., & Blum, T. C. (2003). Cracks in the glass ceiling: In what kinds of organizations do women make it to the top? *Group & Organization Management, 28,* 475–501.

Harrison, D. A., Price, K. H., & Bell, M. P. (1998). Beyond relational demography: Time and the effects of surface- and deep-level diversity on work group cohesion. *Academy of Management Journal, 41,* 96–107.

Harrison, D. A., Price, K. H., Gavin, J. H., & Florey, A. T. (2002). Time, teams, and task performance: Changing effects of surface- and deep-level diversity on group functioning. *Academy of Management Journal, 45,* 1029–1045.

Kochan, T., Bezrukova, K., Ely, R., Jackson, S. E., Joshi, A., Jehn, K. E., et al. (2003). The effects of diversity on business performance: Report of a feasibility study of the diversity research network. *Human Resource Management, 42,* 3–21.

Konrad, A. M., & Linnehan, F. (1995a). Formalized HRM structures: Coordinating equal employment opportunity or concealing organizational practices? *Academy of Management Journal, 38,* 787–820.

Konrad, A. M., & Linnehan, F. (1995b). Race and sex differences in line managers' reactions to equal employment opportunity and affirmative action interventions. *Group and Organization Management, 20,* 409–439.

Konrad, A. M., & Mangel, R. (2000). The impact of work-life programs on firm productivity. *Strategic Management Journal, 21,* 1225–1237.

Martin, P. Y. (1996). Gendering and evaluating dynamics: Men, masculinities, and managements. In D. L. Collinson & J. Hearn (Eds.), *Men as managers, managers as men: Critical perspectives on men, masculinities and managements* (pp. 186–209). Thousand Oaks, CA: Sage.

Nieva, V. F., & Gutek, B. A. (1980). Sex effects on evaluation. *Academy of Management Review, 5,* 267–276.

Parker, C. P., Baltes, B. B., & Christiansen, N. D. (1997). Support for affirmative action, justice perceptions, and work attitudes: A study of gender and racial-ethnic group differences. *Journal of Applied Psychology, 82,* 376–389.

Perry-Smith, J., & Blum, T. C. (2000). Work-family human resource bundles and perceived organizational performance. *Academy of Management Journal, 43,* 1107–1117.

Ragins, B. R. (1997). Diversified mentoring relationships in organizations: A power perspective. *Academy of Management Review, 22,* 482–521.

Richard, O. C. (2000). Racial diversity, business strategy, and firm performance: A resource-based view. *Academy of Management Journal, 43,* 164–177.

Richard, O. C., Barnett, T., Dwyer, S., & Chadwick, K. (2004). Cultural diversity in management, firm performance, and the moderating role of entrepreneurial orientation dimensions. *Academy of Management Journal, 47,* 255–266.

Richard, O. C., McMillan, A., Chadwick, K., & Dwyer, S. (2003). Employing an innovation strategy in racially diverse workforces: Effects on firm performance. *Group & Organization Management, 28,* 107–126.

Riordan, C. M. (2000). Relational demography within groups: Past developments, contradictions, and new directions. *Research in Personnel and Human Resources Management, 19,* 131–173.

Robinson, G., & Dechant, K. (1997). Building a business case for diversity. *Academy of Management Executive, 11*(3), 21–31.

Statistics Canada. (2003). *Women and men in Canada: A statistical glance.* Ottawa: Status of Women Canada.

Statistics Canada. (2005a). *Census of population.* Retrieved from http://www12.statcan.ca/english/census01/home/index.cfm

Statistics Canada. (2005b). *Population projections of visible minority groups, Canada, provinces, and regions* (Statistics Canada Product Number 91-541-XIE). Retrieved from http://www.statcan.ca/cgi-bin/downpub/freepub.cgi?subject=3867#3867

Thomas, D. A. (1993). Racial dynamics in cross-race developmental relationships. *Administrative Science Quarterly, 38,* 169–194.

Thomas, D. A. (2001). The truth about mentoring minorities: Race matters. *Harvard Business Review, 79*(4), 98–112.

Tosi, H. L., & Einbender, S. W. (1985). The effects of the type and amount of information in sex discrimination research: A meta-analysis. *Academy of Management Journal, 32,* 662–669.

Tsui, A. S., Egan, T. D., & O'Reilly, C. A. (1992). Being different: Relational demography and orga-nizational attachment. *Administrative Science Quarterly, 37,* 547–579.

U.S. Census Bureau. (2004). *Statistical abstract of the United States.* Washington, DC: Government Printing Office.

Webber, S. S., & Donahue, L. M. (2001). Impact of highly and less job-related diversity on work group cohesion and performance: A meta-analysis. *Journal of Management, 27,* 141–162.

Williams, K. Y., & O'Reilly, C. A., III. (1998). Demography and diversity in organizations: A review of 40 years of research. In B. M. Staw & L. L. Cummings (Eds.), *Research in organizational behavior* (Vol. 20, pp. 77–140). Greenwich, CT: JAI.

Wright, P., Ferris, S. P., Hiller, J. S., & Kroll, M. (1995). Competitiveness through management of diversity: Effects on stock price valuation. *Academy of Management Journal, 38,* 272–287.

1

WORKPLACE DISCRIMINATION

D iscrimination is a fact of life for members of historically excluded identity groups in many societies. Evidence of systematic discrimination is provided by sophisticated statistical studies of wages. For instance, on the basis of a national U.S. sample of wage data from recent male and female college graduates, Joy (2003) concluded that women's salaries would be 25% higher if they were treated equally to men in the labor market. In other words, a woman earned 25% less than a man with the same educational qualifications and the same job preferences. Canada also has a gender gap in earnings. Between 1993 and 2002, the wages of Canadian women working full-time and year-round ranged between 69% and 72% of the earnings of their male counterparts (Statistics Canada, 2004). These and many other studies document a substantial amount of gender discrimination in wages.

Studies also document wage discrimination on the basis of race or ethnicity. Darity, Guilkey, and Winfrey (1996) analyzed data from the 1980 and 1990 U.S. censuses and found that Black men earned less on the basis of their race compared to White men. Even among Hispanics, Black Hispanics with equal qualifications earned significantly less than White Hispanics in the United States. Another study showed that among Mexican Americans, those with Spanish accents earned less than their equally qualified nonaccented counterparts (Dávila, Bohara, & Saenz, 1993). Similarly, a study of the 1991 Canadian census data showed that immigrants who are visible minorities faced substantial earnings penalties, but the Canadian-born children of Asian, Latin American, and Middle Eastern immigrants earned as much as their White Canadian counterparts. Black men, however, experienced earnings discrimination even if they were native-born Canadians (Pendakur & Pendakur, 1998).

Studies also demonstrate wage discrimination on the basis of sexual orientation. Two U.S. studies showed that gay men experienced an earnings penalty of between 14% and 32% compared to equally qualified straight counterparts. Lesbians, however, had an earnings advantage of between 17% and 34% compared to equally qualified heterosexual women (Black, Makar, Sanders, & Taylor, 2003; Blandford, 2003).

Further evidence of systematic discrimination comes from studies of promotions. Maume (1999) found that in the United States, Black men, Black women, and White women waited longer than did White men with equal qualifications for the managerial promotions they received. Hultin (2003) found that Swedish men in typically female occupations were promoted significantly faster than equally qualified women. She also found that Swedish women and men in typically male occupations were promoted equally rapidly, however.

Even in the field of basketball, which is dominated by Black men in the United States, evidence of discrimination has been found. Hoang and Rascher (1999) found that White basketball players had a 36% lower risk of being cut from professional basketball teams than equally performing Black players. This difference in terminations translates into an expected career length of 7.5 seasons for a White player and 5.5 seasons for a similarly performing Black player, resulting in a career earnings loss of $808,000 on the basis of race.

The reasons for these differences in career outcomes are a matter of debate in the fields of economics and sociology, but most empirical studies show systematic differences in career outcomes favoring men and Whites over women, Blacks, and Hispanics in the United States. Psychologists have studied interpersonal discrimination to better understand the reasons behind these negative outcomes. The next section outlines the psychological research on discrimination.

DISCRIMINATION AND ATTITUDES

Discrimination can be blatant or subtle. Blatant discrimination has diminished in many societies over the past several decades. As societal members gain savvy about discrimination, they are less likely to express discriminatory attitudes directly. For example, most contemporary North Americans do not agree to blatantly racist statements that Blacks[1] are less intelligent, ambitious, or honest than Whites. However, they are more likely to agree with subtle statements of hostility toward Blacks, such as "over the past few years, Blacks have gotten more economically than they deserve," and "over the past few years, the government and news media have shown more respect for Blacks than they deserve" (McConahay, 1986). Similarly, although people are less likely to agree with blantantly sexist statements that women are inferior to men, they are more likely to concur with subtly hostile statements toward women, such as, "women make too big a deal out of sexual harassment issues in the workplace," "women interpret innocent remarks as sexist," or "once a man commits, she puts him on a tight leash" (Glick & Fiske, 1996; Ponterotto, Burkard, Rieger, & Grieger, 1995). People are also somewhat likely to express negative attitudes toward heavyset people, agreeing to statements such as, "I really don't like fat people much," or "one of the worst things that could happen to me would be if I gained 25 pounds" (Crandall, 1994). People also express negative attitudes toward gays and lesbians, with a 1998–1999 U.S. study showing 48% of male respondents saying that they felt "somewhat" or "very" uncomfortable around a gay man and 43% of women indicating they were "somewhat" or "very" uncomfortable around a lesbian woman (Herek, 2002).

People are unwilling to express discriminatory views explicitly because they know such views are not socially acceptable in contemporary society (Konrad & Spitz, 2003). For this reason, researchers examining discrimination have used unobtrusive measures that participants cannot consciously control to document the existence of discriminatory stereotypes and attitudes. One research paradigm that has generated sobering results is the Implicit Association Test (IAT; Greenwald, McGhee, & Schwartz, 1998). IAT research is conducted at a computer terminal, which presents participants with words and images. The goal is for participants to produce the correct answers to a set of simple questions as quickly as possible. For example, people may be asked to indicate whether a word on the computer screen represents something "good" or something "bad." Words such as *joy, happy,* or *pleasant* are "good," while words such as *pain, terrible,* or *harmful* are "bad." To indicate that a word represents "good," the participant presses the *f* key on the computer terminal, and to indicate a "bad" word, the participant presses the *j* key. The computer program measures how long it takes the person to press the correct key after each word is flashed on the screen, a measure called "response latency."

In addition, the computer program presents pictures along with the set of words—for example, a photo of a Black face or a White face. Implicit attitudes are assessed by comparing response latency when "good" and "bad" words are paired with each of the photographs. A substantial literature has demonstrated that people show a significantly longer response latency when "good" words are paired with a member of a lower status outgroup—for example, a Black face compared to a White face, a Jewish name compared to a Christian name, or an old person compared to a young person (Dovidio, Kawakami, Johnson, Johnson, & Howard, 1997; Fazio & Dunton, 1997; Rudman, Greenwald, Mellott, & Schwartz, 1999). They also show a significantly shorter response latency when "bad" words are paired with the out-group. Error rates show the same pattern—specifically, participants are more likely to hit the "bad" key in error when the out-group stimulus is shown on the computer screen. Researchers conclude from these studies that people have an automatic negative reaction to out-groups because it is more difficult for them to make the "good" response and easier for them to make the "bad" response in the presence of the out-group (Dunton & Fazio, 1997; Poehlman, Uhlmann, Greenwald, & Banaji, 2004; Wittenbrink, Judd, & Park, 1997).

Other research similarly indicates that stereotyping is quite automatic and may not be under the control of the individual. Bargh (1999) reports the result of a series of experiments demonstrating the automatic nature of stereotyping. For example, people made more stereotypic completions of word stems (e.g., *shy* for *s_y*) when an Asian woman presented those stems in a video presentation. As another example, in a "scrambled sentence test," people were presented with either words relating to age stereotypes (e.g., *conservative, gray, bingo*) or neutral words. After solving several puzzles, they were thanked and left the room, believing that the experiment was over. A confederate posing as the next participant timed how long it took them to walk down the hall. People presented with the age stereotypes walked more slowly, apparently acting out the stereotype. A third experiment showed that when people were asked to review paper credentials and then interview either a White or a Black candidate, they hired both candidates in equal proportions. One week later, however, they recalled the answers to the interview questions given by Black applicants as having been significantly less intelligent when, in fact, the actual interview content was identical (Frazer & Wiersma, 2001). On the basis of these results and many others, Bargh concludes that stereotyping is automatic, affecting both behavior and memory in ways that cannot be consciously controlled. The human cognitive limitations he identified and their implications for intergroup relationships troubled Bargh so much that he titled his article "The Cognitive Monster."

INTERPERSONAL DISCRIMINATION

Consistent with the view that unconscious stereotyping affects people's attitudes and behavior, Dovidio, Gaertner, Kawakami, and Hodson (2002) have argued that although many contemporary people truly wish to be egalitarian and free of racial prejudice, unconscious negative feelings toward out-groups remain. Hostile or stereotypical portrayals of out-groups in the media as well as parents' fearfulness or uneasiness around persons who are different teach children negative attitudes toward ethnic groups accorded lower status in their societies. In adulthood, people are capable of questioning these attitudes, but as studies of automatic stereotyping and prejudice demonstrate, it may not be possible to eradicate the negative information encoded in childhood.

Dovidio et al. (2002) argue that because people truly desire to be egalitarian, they will not intentionally discriminate against others. Unfortunately, people's unconscious negative feelings toward out-groups affect behavior that is not intentional. As a result, people do not act negatively toward out-groups when the discrimination would be obvious to themselves and others. Instead, discrimination primarily occurs in complicated and ambiguous situations where people can justify their behavior on the basis of factors other than race. For example, if choosing a White over a Black job candidate would clearly indicate racism, as would be the case if the Black candidate were substantially more qualified, most contemporary people will act in a nonracist way and choose the Black candidate. If, however, there is an alternative explanation other than racism—for example, if their qualifications are different, but it is unclear who is better qualified—many people will choose the White candidate and cite the difference in qualifications as their "nonracist" rationale (Dovidio et al., 2002).

Despite a sincere desire on the part of most contemporary people to be egalitarian and treat others fairly, continued feelings of prejudice, animosity, discomfort, fear, or simple uncertainty regarding how to deal with people who are dissimilar result in discriminatory behavior. Regardless of whether the behavior is intentional or unintentional, interpersonal discrimination has substantial social, psychological, and economic consequences for the recipients. Bell and Nkomo (2001) describe several discriminatory incidents reported by Black female professionals in corporate America. For example, one of their interviewees recalled,

> I remember at one site there was a guy who had an office right beside mine, separated only by glass. This White man could not part his lips. He walked by me every morning and afternoon to get coffee but he never spoke. The first couple of times I said, "Good morning." He said nothing. After a while I knew this man could not speak to me. I really knew it when I was walking down the hall with a White woman colleague, and he spoke to her but not me. It's stuff like that I carry with me, and it's hard to get rid of how it makes me feel. (p. 144)

Many of Bell and Nkomo's (2001) interviewees told stories of being subjected to offensive racial "jokes." For example,

> After a meeting, a small group from my work team went to the bar for drinks. There were four white males, all managers. They asked me if I wanted to join them. I thought it would be best to go to my room and not get involved in socializing, but then I figured it was important for me to act like I was part of the team. So I went. Everybody gathered around the bar for drinks. The five of us were standing in a circle. One of the guys said to me, "My this was a good year for you; you did like 187 percent for the year." I said, "Yes, I had a good year." Then one of the other guys looks me right in the face and jokingly says, "You little black bitch." I couldn't believe it was coming out of his mouth. It was very insulting. (pp. 141–142)

Although people who tell offensive jokes may often intend no harm, they make the workplace less welcoming for members of historically excluded or devalued groups. Also, people who do not build many friendships with dissimilar others may not intend to be discriminatory, but members of minority groups feel the social isolation keenly and are negatively affected by it.

STRUCTURAL DISCRIMINATION

In work organizations, some jobs are part of a career path offering opportunities for advancement, while others are not. Employees in jobs without a career path are considerably less likely to receive promotions and wage increases (DiPrete & Soule, 1986, 1988). Hence, being in a job without a career path has substantial consequences for people's labor market outcomes.

The development of career paths in organizations is determined by many factors, including the skill level of the job and the average education of the job incumbent. In addition, researchers have found that career paths are associated with the demographic composition of the jobholders, such that women and minorities are considerably more likely to be stuck in dead-end jobs without a career path (Baron, Davis-Blake, & Bielby, 1986; Reskin & Roos, 1990). Reskin and Roos (1990) provide an example from the insurance industry:

> Throughout the 1960s, "outside" adjusters—virtually all male—worked in the field, where they settled a few claims a day. They scheduled their own work, used company cars, and enjoyed reasonable prospects for promotion into managerial jobs. During the high-inflation 1970s, unstable interest rates and increased competition resulting from the deregulation of the financial industry prompted insurance companies to cut costs by standardizing work. Toward this end, they brought adjusting into the office, where "inside" adjusters handled a large number of claims, using telephones and video display terminals. In clericalizing adjusting . . . , firms robbed the job of its autonomy, bumped it from the career ladder to management, and subjected workers to quotas and electronic monitoring—all for lower pay. (pp. 43–44)

The workers found in dead-end jobs taken off the managerial career path tend to be women and visible minorities. As Reskin and Roos (1990) note, "With the clericalization of adjusting, the number of male adjusters dropped by 6,447 between 1970 and 1980, while the number of women increased by 73,744" (p. 44). Reskin and Roos's book provides similar stories for the occupations of bank teller, pharmacist, corporate public relations officer, real estate, and others. Even in the U.S. federal government, which is mandated to be a model employer, dead-end jobs are disproportionately filled by women and minorities (DiPrete & Soule, 1986, 1988).

Organizational structures instituted years or decades ago, sometimes with the deliberate intention of excluding certain groups from management positions, persist, often long after their discriminatory intent has been forgotten (Baron et al., 1986). The career consequences for women and minorities stuck in dead-end jobs are devastating.

MANAGERIAL RESPONSIBILITIES

In the face of ongoing blatant, subtle, and structural discrimination, managers have a responsibility to both understand the environment faced by their diverse employees and to ameliorate discriminatory conditions to the best of their ability. A large body of literature demonstrates that creating a workplace that is fair and welcoming to everyone is essential to positive employee attitudes and performance (Colquitt, Conlon, Wesson, Porter & Ng, 2001).

Managerial understanding begins with awareness that statistical, interpersonal, and structural discrimination may be occurring in the workplace. Knowledge of the employment statistics in the firm and industry provides a big-picture understanding of the environment faced by different groups of employees. If the firm is more progressive than the industry as a whole by, for example, hiring more women for historically male-dominated jobs or promoting more visible minorities into management, these statistics signal a positive environment demonstrating substantive progress away from historical patterns of exclusion and bias. If the firm is consistent with the industry, it is likely to be in compliance with nondiscrimination law and a fair corporate citizen. If the firm is less diverse than the industry average for the region, then the firm's employment statistics may indicate lack of effort to eradicate discrimination and promote fairness or even a problem with continuing discrimination and/or a hostile work environment.

Hence, examining employment statistics is an important tool for diagnosing the current firm environment for diversity. Failure to gather employment statistics by demographic group means that managers do not have an accurate picture of their current labor force. If the firm is doing well, managers who have not collected statistics cannot document that fact. If there are problems, managers who do not have statistics are likely to be unaware of their extent. Although identifying problems through statistical examination can be painful, failure to look at the data means management is not even willing to acknowledge that problems might exist, which communicates a lack of caring about fairness to all employees.

Understanding the dynamics of interpersonal discrimination, particularly social isolation and harassment of historically excluded groups, helps managers to both prevent negative events from occurring and to handle such events appropriately when they do occur. A clear statement from the manager that fairness and a welcoming environment for everyone is important lets employees know that professional behavior is expected of them. Managers can be role models for other employees by building diverse personal and business networks and including a diverse group in all social activities and important workplace decisions. Announcing the qualifications and achievements of all new hires when they are added to the workgroup, as well as communicating the achievements of all employees on an ongoing basis, lets employees understand that everyone is making valuable contributions to the firm. Managers can also coach employees about building a diverse business network and appreciating the contributions of all employees.

Even with the best prevention program in place, interpersonal discrimination can occur in any work environment. When these events happen, the manager needs to handle them appropriately and professionally. An unfortunate tendency is for managers and others to try to "explain away" interpersonal discrimination by attributing it to some other factor (Blank & Slipp, 1994). Bell and Nkomo (2001) provide an example of this response:

> The partner who ran one of the European offices and I were talking. He told me they had lunch every day in his office. I said, "That's a really nice perk." He asked, "Do you serve lunch here?" I said, "No, we don't do that." He said, "No, I mean do you serve the lunch to the consultants every day?" Again, I said, "No, we don't do that," and he asked me again. Then I realized that this man was asking me if I personally made lunch for the consultants. (p. 141)

When this Black female professional spoke with the head of her office about the incident, he told her, first, that the partner must not have meant the remark the way she was interpreting it. Then he said the man must have been joking. Then he said the man would probably have said it about his own wife. By coming up with a series of alternative explanations for the incident, this woman's manager made her feel even more unsupported and offended.

A better response is for the manager to listen to the employee's views actively and not to argue with the person (Blank & Slipp, 1994). Don't deny or try to explain away these issues; rather, treat them as a valuable learning opportunity to improve your organization's environment. You might start by thanking the employee. Feedback is a gift, and it is difficult for employees to raise diversity issues. Ask the employee what you can do to help, and develop a strategy together for dealing with the event. If appropriate for team development and learning, managers might even consider processing the event in a team meeting.

Finally, managers who are cognizant of structural discrimination can notice positions within their own firms that provide no career path. Building a diverse network within the firm can help managers identify talented people stuck in these dead-end jobs and nominate them for promotion to positions with more opportunities. Recognizing the human capital available in the firm enhances perceptions of fairness and allows diverse employees to contribute more fully to organizational effectiveness.

Understanding the discrimination dynamics arising from human cognitive limitations, uncertainty around dissimilar others, and structural barriers to advancement will help managers respond thoughtfully to organizational situations that will inevitably arise under their watch. Awareness of the statistical, interpersonal, and structural discrimination that can occur in the workplace is necessary for managers to develop solutions that will welcome an ever more diverse set of employees while at the same time maintaining a sense of fairness and justice among all identity groups, including the historical majority.

READING

Avoiding Discrimination in Employment Selection and Retention: Some Legal Issues

This note provides background information on legal issues in employment selection and retention. Presented are some of the restrictions that are placed on how employers conduct the recruitment process. The human rights legislation that governs the entire employment process is introduced. In addition, the issues of reasonable and bona fide job requirements, medical testing in preemployment, and current employment situations are discussed. Issues that interviewers need to be aware of to avoid discrimination during the hiring process are also highlighted.

CASES

Staffing at Wal-Mart Stores, Inc. (A)

Wal-Mart Stores, Inc. is a large *Fortune* 500 retail chain. The distinction of being the top-ranked company comes with intense scrutiny from the public and, especially, critics.

Wal-Mart, a company lauded for its rapid response capability and stated commitments to gender equality, is shown to be deficient in some glaring areas—the percentage of women compared to men at all levels of the company and the compensation paid to women versus men at all levels of the company, to cite two examples. An executive vice president must examine why these inequalities exist when the company seems to be doing everything else right. The company is the target of several gender discrimination lawsuits, and the executive vice president has the opportunity to obtain information that would be useful in the current situation and must determine what information is needed.

Assignment Questions:

1. Taking the role of executive vice president (EVP) of Wal-Mart's People Division, what kinds of data do you need to access to determine whether the gender discrimination lawsuits raised against your company have merit?

2. What kinds of statistical findings would provide a sound defense against a gender discrimination lawsuit? What kinds of statistical findings would suggest that gender discrimination may have occurred?

3. How important a priority is the gender discrimination lawsuit among your many duties as EVP of the People Division? Explain why it is important or unimportant.

4. If the statistics show that gender discrimination is a problem, what action steps should you take as EVP of the People Division?

NexTech Inc. (A)

A manager in a technology company must decide among a set of seven candidates (five male and two female) for a promotion. Examining Canada's employment equity act and the company's employment statistics, the manager considers each candidate's qualifications. The case provides brief biographical sketches of each candidate as seen through the manager's eyes. Students are asked to judge which person should receive the promotion and provide a rationale for their choice.

Assignment Questions:

1. Does Nextech have a gender discrimination problem? What do the company statistics tell you?

2. Take the role of Adam Blackburn and decide which of the seven candidates you will choose for the promotion. Justify your choice.

3. What are the implications of your decision for Nextech's human resource strategy?

4. What steps can Adam Blackburn take to ensure that women and men in his group have fair and equal career prospects?

Stamford Machine Corporation: Allegations of Racism

Stamford Machine Corporation is a market leader in the manufacturing of photocopiers and office equipment. The director of corporate business ethics and compliance has been notified that the company is being served with a discrimination lawsuit. A newspaper announcement was released to the public outlining details of the charges, and before the director could leave his office, he receives a call from a journalist asking for the company's comments. He must determine if there has been a breach in the company's policy on discrimination and plan how the company will deal with the media.

Assignment Questions:

1. Outline the steps that Douglas should take in the next 24 hours.

2. Suggest how Stamford Machine can resolve this issue without incurring further damage to its business and reputation.

Ottawa Valley Food Products

In response to the dismissal of a newly hired administrative assistant, all 10 of this company's executive assistants have vacated their posts and demanded that the plant's manager reverse the young woman's discharge.

Assignment Questions:

1. Trace the series of events in Mary Gregory's tenure at Ottawa Valley Food Products (OVFP) that ended in all of the executive assistants vacating their posts. At each step, explain the perceptions, feelings, motivations, and power struggles of the key players. At each step, did the key players act within appropriate limits? Explain.

2. What alternatives are available to Jennings? What are the consequences of each of his alternative courses of action?

3. What should Jennings do over the short term (the next 20 minutes) and over the longer term?

CTV Newsnet (A)

After showing the wrong take of a CTV broadcast, one filled with ethnic, gender, and social slurs intended to amuse studio technicians, the broadcaster must decide what to do to manage the situation. The on-air personality who had been caught making the remarks must also deal with the event. With her reputation and future uncertain, the on-air personality must devise a personal strategy for how to handle herself in the ensuing media spotlight.

Assignment Questions:

1. As Henry Kowalsky, what are the options available to you and their implications?

2. Which option would you choose? How would you present your decision in a press release?

3. Create Henry's communication plan for Monday morning.

NOTE

1. In this book, I use the term *Black* rather than the term *African American,* which is often preferred in the United States, because this book is targeted to Canadians and other English-speaking countries in addition to the United States.

REFERENCES

Bargh, J. A. (1999). The cognitive monster: The case against the controllability of automatic stereotype effects. In S. Chaiken & Y. Trope (Eds.), *Dual-process theories in social psychology* (pp. 361–382). New York: Guilford.

Baron, J. N., Davis-Blake, A., & Bielby, W. T. (1986). The structure of opportunity: How promotion ladders vary within and among organizations. *Administrative Science Quarterly, 31,* 248–273.

Bell, E. L. J. E., & Nkomo, S. M. (2001). *Our separate ways: Black and White women and the struggle for professional identity.* Boston: Harvard Business School Press.

Black, D. A., Makar, H. R., Sanders, S. G., & Taylor, L. J. (2003). The earnings effects of sexual orientation. *Industrial and Labor Relations Review, 56,* 449–469.

Blandford, J. M. (2003). The nexus of sexual orientation and gender in the determination of earnings. *Industrial and Labor Relations Review, 56,* 622–642.

Blank, R., & Slipp, S. (1994). *Voices of diversity: Real people talk about problems and solutions in a workplace where everyone is not alike.* New York: AMACOM.

Colquitt, J. A., Conlon, D. E., Wesson, M. J., Porter, C. O. L. H., & Ng, K. Y. (2001). Justice at the millennium: A meta-analytic review of 25 years of organizational justice research. *Journal of Applied Psychology, 86,* 425–445.

Crandall, C. S. (1994). Prejudice against fat people: Ideology and self-interest. *Journal of Personality and Social Psychology, 66,* 882–894.

Darity, W., Jr., Guilkey, D. K., & Winfrey, W. (1996). Explaining differences in economic performance among racial and ethnic groups in the USA: The data examined. *American Journal of Economics and Sociology, 55,* 411–425.

Dávila, A., Bohara, A. K., & Saenz, R. (1993). Accent penalties and the earnings of Mexican Americans. *Social Science Quarterly, 74,* 902–916.

DiPrete, T. A., & Soule, W. T. (1986). The organization of career lines: Equal employment opportunity and status advancement in a federal bureaucracy. *American Sociological Review, 51,* 295–309.

DiPrete, T. A., & Soule, W. T. (1988). Gender and promotion in segmented job ladder systems. *American Sociological Review, 53,* 26–40.

Dovidio, J. F., Gaertner, S. L., Kawakami, K., & Hodson, G. (2002). Why can't we just get along? Interpersonal biases and interracial distrust. *Cultural Diversity and Ethnic Minority Psychology, 8*(2), 88–102.

Dovidio, J. F., Kawakami, K., Johnson, C., Johnson, B., & Howard, A. (1997). On the nature of prejudice: Automatic and controlled processes. *Journal of Experimental Social Psychology, 33,* 510–540.

Dunton, B. C., & Fazio, R. H. (1997). An individual difference measure of motivation to control prejudiced reactions. *Personality and Social Psychology Bulletin, 23,* 316–326.

Fazio, R. H., & Dunton, B. C. (1997). Categorization by race: The impact of automatic and controlled components of racial prejudice. *Journal of Experimental Social Psychology, 33,* 451–470.

Frazer, R. A., & Wiersma, U. J. (2001). Prejudice versus discrimination in the employment interview: We may hire equally, but our memories harbour prejudice. *Human Relations, 54,* 173–191.

Glick, P., & Fiske, S. T. (1996). The Ambivalent Sexism Inventory: Differentiating hostile and benevolent sexism. *Journal of Personality and Social Psychology, 70,* 491–512.

Greenwald, A. G., McGhee, D. E., & Schwartz, J. L. K. (1998). Measuring individual differences in implicit cognition: The Implicit Association Test. *Journal of Personality and Social Psychology, 74,* 1464–1480.

Herek, G. M. (2002). Gender gaps in public opinion about lesbians and gay men. *Public Opinion Quarterly, 66,* 40–66.

Hoang, H., & Rascher, D. (1999). The NBA, exit discrimination, and career earnings. *Industrial Relations, 38,* 69–91.

Hultin, M. (2003). Some take the glass escalator, some hit the glass ceiling? *Work and Occupations, 30,* 30–61.

Joy, L. (2003). Salaries of recent male and female college graduates: Educational and labor market effects. *Industrial and Labor Relations Review, 56,* 606–621.

Konrad, A. M., & Spitz, J. (2003). Explaining demographic group differences in affirmative action attitudes. *Journal of Applied Social Psychology, 33,* 1618–1642.

Maume, D. J., Jr. (1999). Glass ceilings and glass escalators: Occupational segregation and race and sex differences in managerial promotions. *Work and Occupations, 26,* 483–509.

McConahay, J. B. (1986). Modern racism, ambivalence, and the Modern Racism Scale. In J. F. Dovidio & S. L. Gaertner (Eds.), *Prejudice, discrimination, and racism* (pp. 91–125). New York: Academic Press.

Pendakur, K., & Pendakur, R. (1998). The colour of money: Earnings differentials among ethnic groups in Canada. *Canadian Journal of Economics, 31,* 518–548.

Poehlman, T. A., Uhlmann, E., Greenwald, A. G., & Banaji, M. R. (2004). *Understanding and using the Implicit Association Test: Meta-analysis of predictive validity.* (Available from M. R. Banaji, Department of Psychology, 33 Kirkland Street, Harvard University, Cambridge, MA 02138)

Ponterotto, J. G., Burkard, A., Rieger, B. P., & Grieger, I. (1995). Development and initial validation of the Quick Discrimination Index (QDI). *Educational and Psychological Measurement, 55,* 1016–1031.

Reskin, B. R., & Roos, P. A. (1990). *Job queues, gender queues: Explaining women's inroads into male occupations.* Philadelphia: Temple University Press.

Rudman, L. A., Greenwald, A. G., Mellott, D. S., & Schwartz, J. L. K. (1999). Measuring the automatic components of prejudice: Flexibility and generality of the Implicit Association Test. *Social Cognition, 17,* 437–465.

Statistics Canada. (2004, November 3). *CANSIM, Table 202–0102.* Ottawa, Ontario: Author.

Wittenbrink, B., Judd, C. M., & Park, B. (1997). Evidence for racial prejudice at the implicit level and its relationship with questionnaire measures. *Journal of Personality and Social Psychology, 72,* 262–274.

AVOIDING DISCRIMINATION IN EMPLOYMENT SELECTION AND RETENTION: SOME LEGAL ISSUES[1]

Prepared by Paula Puddy under the supervision of Professor Lyn Purdy

Version: (A) 2001-08-08

INTRODUCTION

In Canada, extensive restrictions are placed on how employers conduct the recruitment process. Specifically, human rights legislation governs the entire employment process including recruiting, hiring, firing and retiring. Every advertisement for a position, every employment application, and every interview is governed by human rights legislation. It is important, therefore, that managers understand what they can and cannot do during the pre-employment process as well as throughout the entire employment cycle. Each province and the federal government have enacted similar human rights legislation that governs the employment process. For the purposes of brevity, this note will only refer to Ontario Human Rights Code.[2]

LEGISLATION

Section 5(1) of the Ontario Human Rights Code states that:[3]

> Every person has a right to equal treatment with respect to employment without discrimination because of race, ancestry, place of origin, colour, ethnic origin, citizenship, creed, sex, sexual orientation, age, record of offences, marital status, same-sex partnership status, family status, or handicap.

In addition, the Human Rights Code protects individuals from harassment in the workplace on any prohibited ground, similar to those listed above, including freedom from harassment because of sex, and freedom from any sexual solicitation by a person in a position to confer or deny a benefit.[3]

Section 23 of the Ontario Human Rights Code deals specifically with the pre-employment process. In particular, the right under section 5 to equal treatment with respect to employment is infringed where:

1. an invitation to apply for employment or an employment advertisement classifies qualifications by a prohibited ground of discrimination;

2. an employment application is used or a written or oral inquiry is made of an applicant that directly or indirectly classifies qualifications by a prohibited ground;

3. an employment agency discriminates against a person because of a prohibited ground in receiving, classifying, disposing of or acting upon applications for its services or in referring an applicant to an employer.

The Act also outlines circumstances where the right to equal treatment with respect to employment is *not* infringed. Religious, philanthropic, educational, or social organizations that are engaged in serving the interests of persons identified by a prohibited ground may give preference to applicants similarly identified, as long as the qualification is reasonable and bona fide (i.e., there is a legitimate reason why the qualification is in place). For example, when the separate school board advertises for a position within its organization, it requires that the person be Roman Catholic or that the person has knowledge of the tenets of the faith. These requirements are bona fide because of the nature of religious instruction that takes place in the schools.

Similarly, there is no infringement when discrimination in employment is for reasons of age, sex, record of offences, marital status or same-sex partnership status if it is a reasonable and bona fide qualification because of the nature of the employment. For example, if individuals are working with children, it is reasonable not to hire them if they have a record of offences involving children.

In addition, an individual may refuse to employ a person for any prohibited ground where the primary duty of the employment is attending to the medical or personal needs of the person or of an ill child or an aged, infirm or ill spouse, same-sex partner or relative of the person. Finally, an employer may grant or withhold employment or advancement in employment to a person who is the spouse, same-sex partner, child or parent of the employer or employee.[4]

It should be noted that even if there are reasonable and bona fide qualifications, employers should try to accommodate individuals in regards to these qualifications. It is only in circumstances of undue hardship where the employer can uphold the qualification or restriction. The court should consider any additional costs, sources of funding, and health and safety requirements when determining whether the qualification can or cannot be accommodated without undue hardship.[5] For example, in *Canada (Attorney General) v. Martin*,[6] the Federal Court of Canada held that the compulsory retirement age policy of the Canadian Armed Forces constituted discrimination in employment because they forced retirement without assessing or trying to accommodate aging employees. The Federal Court relied on the arbitrator's conclusions that individual testing to assess an employee's physical condition in this case was a reasonable expectation to be made of the employer and it was feasible to conduct such individualized tests without causing undue hardship on the employer. In particular, the court stated:

> The evidence indicates that testing in order to assess the level of fitness is feasible. It involves tailoring the standard exercise tests. . . . With respect to the cost of testing beyond the initial screening for symptoms, the evidence reveals that it is reasonable . . . .The cost of such a test in a physician's office ranges from $25 to $50. . . .

If an employer has discriminated on a prohibited ground, the employee or potential employee can file a complaint with the Ontario Human Rights Commission. If the employer is found to have discriminated, the Commission can provide numerous remedies to the complainant, which include, but are not limited to, the following: damages (money), an apology, staff training, requirements to advertise in minority newspapers.

There is a duty on the complainant to minimize damages by seeking alternative employment. The complainant's effort to find employment, and/or the length of time it took the individual to find employment, can be taken into account by the commission before awarding damages to the complainant.

DISCUSSION

General Requirements

When dealing with individuals throughout the employment process, the decision-making process should be fair, unbiased, comprehensive and objective. Furthermore, the decision making process should not have the effect of excluding any racial or ethnic group.[7] In *Wong v. Ottawa Board of Education,* the school principal placed Mr. Wong, one of two automotive mechanics teachers, on a list of surplus teachers (a transfer list). Of these two teachers, Mr. Wong had the most seniority and he was an excellent teacher. Mr. Wong also participated in extracurricular activities by staying in his classroom before school and during the lunch hour in order to assist students. Extracurricular activities were one of the criteria used by the principal to determine whom to transfer. He decided that the other teacher made a greater contribution to extracurricular activities. The Board of Inquiry determined that the principal placed a significant emphasis on committee work when considering extracurricular activities, rather than considering relevant extracurricular activities that members of a visible minority would be most likely to participate in. (Evidence was presented to indicate that persons of Chinese descent are more likely to participate in activities directly related to education such as spending extra time with students.) The Board of Inquiry stated that the decision-making process and the assessment of extracurricular activities excluded and discounted Mr. Wong's actual contributions. The Board of Inquiry concluded that the principal and the Ottawa Board of Education had infringed Mr. Wong's rights under the code.

Some Pre-Employment Issues

It is interesting to note that for the pre-employment process (s.23(2)) to be violated, there need not be any intention to discriminate. Also, there is no requirement that actual discrimination occurred as a result of obtaining information through the process of improper questioning.[8] A violation is deemed to have occurred even if the employer casually asks about any of the restricted areas. In *Lannin v. Ontario*, the applicant applied for a stenographer position with the Ontario Provincial Police (OPP) in Blind River, Ontario. During the interview, she was asked her age, whether she had children, and what her husband did for a living. The Board of Inquiry determined that these questions related to prohibited grounds and, therefore, were all violations of the Human Rights Code. As such, she was awarded $2,000 in damages, even though it was determined that there was no intention by the interviewer to discriminate against Ms. Lannin.

Furthermore, there is no requirement on the applicant to disclose information in the pre-employment process or while employed that would give rise to classification on a prohibited ground that does not impair work performance.[9] In *Rapson v. Stemms*, Rapson was employed as a bartender by Stemms Restaurants. Mr. Rapson had epilepsy, but he had never informed his employer about his medical condition. He had an epileptic seizure at work. No other employees were injured and nothing was broken. He returned to work the next day. Approximately one month later, Mr. Rapson was terminated. Rapson took his case to the Human Rights Commission where the Board of Inquiry considered the testimony of medical doctors. The Board concluded that Mr. Rapson had a low risk of suffering seizures, and if he did so, was unlikely to hurt himself or others. The board further concluded that he was capable of performing the duties of his employment safely and effectively and had been terminated without just cause. Mr. Rapson was awarded damages in the nature of $3,000.

Reasonable and Bona Fide Requirements

The leading case interpreting whether a job qualification is reasonable and bona fide was considered by the Supreme Court of Canada in *Ontario (Human Rights Commission) v. Etobicoke (Borough)*[10] ("Etobicoke"). In this case, the employer had imposed a mandatory retirement for all firefighters who were aged 60. The complainant was a 60-year-old firefighter who did not want to retire and filed a complaint against his employer on the basis of age discrimination. The Supreme Court of Canada held that the particular qualification would be seen as reasonable and bona fide only if both a subjective test and an objective test were satisfied. For the subjective test to be satisfied, the qualification or limitation must be imposed honestly, in good faith, and with the sincerely held belief that it is imposed in the interests of adequate performance of the work involved (i.e., for reasonable efficiency, safety and economy) and not for any extraneous purpose. Also, the qualification/limitation must be objectively

related to the performance of the work. In the *Etobicoke* case, the employer met the subjective test but failed to meet the objective test because it had not presented enough evidence that the qualification/limitation was reasonable.

Large v. *Stratford (City) Police Department*[11] also considered the objective and subjective elements of the bona fide occupational requirement. In *Large*, a mandatory retirement age of 60 was imposed on police officers through a collective agreement. Mr. Large fought his retirement on the basis of age discrimination. The Supreme Court of Canada clarified the elements required for establishing a reasonable and bona fide occupation requirement originally outlined in the *Etobicoke* case. The Supreme Court of Canada explained that the purpose of the subjective requirement was to ensure that a discriminatory occupational rule was adopted for a valid reason and not for a prohibited, discriminatory reason. As such, the employer must prove that the qualification requirement was necessary for safety or effective carrying out of work. To meet the objective test, scientific evidence was presented that indicated there was an increased risk of cardiovascular disease and lack of aerobic capacity in those over 60 years. It was acknowledged that the risk could be avoided by accommodation in the officer's duties; however, the employer established that individual testing of each officer for cardiovascular disease and decline of aerobic activity was not feasible. In this case, the court ruled that the employer had met its onus—the objective test had been met because reasonable alternatives had been considered and rejected.

In *British Columbia (Public Service Employee Relations Commissions v. B.C.G.S.E.U.)*, the British Columbia government established a minimum aerobic fitness standard for its forest firefighters. A female firefighter, an employee of 3 years, failed to meet the aerobic standard after four attempts. She was dismissed from her employment. On appeal to the Supreme Court of Canada, the firefighter (the union on her behalf) was successful. In order to succeed, a complainant must prove a prima facie case of discrimination (e.g., that the qualification discriminated against women). The onus then shifts to the employer to show that the test is a bona fide reasonable occupational requirement. The employer must show that the purpose of the standard is rationally connected to the performance of the job, the standard was adopted in a bona fide belief that it was necessary to fulfil a legitimate work-related purpose, and the standard is reasonably necessary to the accomplishment of that purpose. To satisfy this final requirement, the employer must show that it would be impossible to accommodate individual characteristics of the claimant without imposing undue hardship on the employer.

The firefighter established that she had been discriminated against because she was female. The Supreme Court relied on the arbitrator's comments, based on the evidence, that the aerobic requirement was one of the measures available to the employer, and that generally, there is a relationship between aerobic activity and the ability to perform the job. However, the employer failed to show that the aerobic standard was necessary for the safe and efficient performance of the work. In fact, it was concluded that men and women may require different levels of aerobic activity to perform a firefighter's job. Furthermore, the employer failed to discharge its burden of showing that it would experience undue hardship if a different standard were used (i.e., a different standard capable of identifying women who could perform the job safely and efficiently).

Medical Testing: Pre-Employment Examinations

Potential employers are permitted to ask questions about disabilities that would prevent performance of the essential duties of the job, or if they relate to genuine and reasonable qualifications for the position. Employers often require job applicants to submit to various tests of their health, aptitude, ability and intelligence as a pre-condition of being hired. However, pre-employment testing may give rise to pitfalls under human rights legislation.

Pre-employment medical tests or assessments of a person's medical capacity to do the job should only take place after a conditional offer of employment has been made. This ensures that every person could apply for the position regardless of disability. If a medical examination reveals a disability then it must be determined whether the disability constitutes a bona fide, reasonable occupational requirement and whether the employer has made efforts to reasonably accommodate the applicant's disability.

Every test administered by employers must be reliable and valid. Otherwise, for example, a test may have a statistical effect of excluding a disproportionate number of protected group members from being employed or promoted. Reliable means that the degree of error in measuring the required criteria must be within tolerable statistical limits (i.e., the correlation must be 0.3 or higher). Validity means that satisfactory performance in the criteria tested for will result in satisfactory job performance. The actual elements involved in performing the job must be delineated and tested.

Medical Testing: Current Employees

In situations where the medical test is a bona fide occupational requirement, it is possible to require annual physicals of employees that have the effect of discriminating on the basis of age. For example, in *Re Stelwire and United Steel Workers of America, Local 5328,*[12] every employee over 40 years of age was required to have a yearly physical examination. In *Stelwire*, the complainant had applied to be a tractor operator, but refused to have a medical examination, and was subsequently refused the position. It was ruled that the employer was allowed to ensure that the operators were physically fit. It was shown to be a reasonable and bona fide occupational requirement based on the nature of the employment.

In addition, if an employee has been ill, it is not necessarily required to provide an employer with a medical note or certificate if other employees, in similar circumstances, are not required to provide such a note or certificate. In *Decker v. K & G Pool Products Ltd.,*[13] the complainant, Decker, suffered from Crohn's disease, a bowel disorder. She sewed hot tub covers for her employer. Several months after being hired, she suffered from an episode of the disease and was hospitalized for 10 days. She was required to attend day surgery the following year, and was sent home when she returned to work the next day. Several days later, Decker's employment was terminated and she was informed that she could not return to work unless she provided her employer with a medical certificate. The Human Rights Council decided that her employer had discriminated against her for terminating her employment, and requiring a medical certificate from her before returning to work; this requirement did not apply to other employees. She was awarded more than $5,000 in damages for lost wages and suffering.

To justify a compulsory drug or alcohol test, an employer must provide objective evidence that clearly demonstrates an employee's alcohol or drug use will either impair job performance or pose a real risk to the health or safety of other workers, third parties or the environment.[14] In *National Gypsum (Canada) Ltd. V. I.U.O.E., Local 721*, the employer required an employee, an operator of a loader, to take a drug test, after suspecting that he was under the influence of marijuana. The alcohol and drug testing policy was a part of the collective agreement. In this case, the employer did not prove beyond a balance of probability that it had reasonable and probable grounds to suspect impairment—they had not collected the hard evidence to support their suspicions. Damages were not awarded in this case because the employer had acted in good faith.

Similarly, in *Provincial-American Truck Transporters v. Teamsters Union,*[15] unionized truck drivers were asked to provide periodic urine samples for drug and alcohol testing. The union grieved on behalf of the employees that the employer was not allowed to conduct drug testing as it was not a specific provision in their collective agreement. The Labour Relations Board decided that unless there was some evidence of drug problems in the workplace, on an individual or group basis, periodic drug testing could not be upheld.

In *Canadian Civil Liberties v. Toronto Dominion Bank,*[16] TD Bank attempted to justify a mandatory drug testing program for all newly-hired employees. (N.B. this was not a conditional offer, the employees had been hired.) Every employee entered into an agreement with TD Bank that permitted the testing. The tests checked for cannabis, cocaine and opiates. If the test was positive (i.e., drugs found in the system), then the employee was referred to rehabilitation, paid by the employer, and kept on the payroll. If the employee failed the test three times, then he or she could be terminated. The complainant argued that mandatory drug testing discriminated against employees on the basis of disability because an employee could be fired if he or she failed the drug testing three times or failed to co-operate with the test. The tribunal dismissed the complaint because the employee's dismissal resulted from the failure of the employee to participate in the drug testing, rather than based on drug dependence. Essentially, the employee had breached her employment contract. If, in other circumstances where the employee was terminated after taking three tests, it was for the persistent use of an illegal substance, rather than being terminated for a drug dependency.

In general, purely random drug testing is illegal. If a worker occupies a sensitive job, making periodic drug testing mandatory, it must be found that this is a bona fide occupational requirement. An employer would also be warranted in testing a specific employee who is suspected of having an abuse problem, based on hard evidence such as recurrent or unscheduled absences from work.

Other than the cases referred to above, there is limited case law on this subject. This implies that if testing is taking place, most employees are agreeing to the tests. If you are subjected to testing, and it does not offend you, make sure that you receive a copy of the test, and an interpretation of the test results. In addition, it may be wise to obtain a letter from the company conducting the testing stating that they will not disclose this information to anyone other than the current employer.

CONCLUSION

Because the entire employment process is governed by human rights legislation, managers should be aware of the particulars of the legislation when advertising for the position, revising employment application forms, and conducting employment interviews.

The right to equal treatment is infringed when advertisements, applications and interviews directly or indirectly classify or indicate qualifications by a prohibited ground of discrimination. The right to equal employment is also infringed where a requirement, qualification or factor exists which precludes certain groups of people from applying to, or qualifying for, the position.

In devising or reviewing advertisements or job applications or in conducting interviews, an employer should ask themselves:

1. Is this information necessary to determine an applicant's competence or qualification on the job?

2. Could the answers to this question have an unfair effect by screening out special groups or persons as defined by the Code?

3. If yes to question 2, is there a reasonable and bona fide reason for the exception because of the nature of the employment, and is it unreasonable to require the employer to accommodate that individual?

Certain questions are only appropriate after a conditional offer of employment has been made. For example, requests for medical examinations, health information, or age, which is necessary for pension, disability, or life insurance plans or policies.

Based on this discussion, it is evident that employers should be cognisant of human rights legislation when managing the employment process. There are serious consequences of discriminating that are best to be avoided.

NOTES

1. In no way is this note intended to provide legal advice. It should be recognized that the case law referred to in this note is extremely case specific and depends on the unique facts and circumstances.
2. R.S.O. 1990, c.H.19, as amended.
3. Sections 5(2), 7(2) and 7(3) of the Human Rights Code.
4. Section 24 of the Human Rights Code.
5. s.24(2) of the Human Rights Code.
6. (1994), 72 F.T.R. 249.
7. Wong v. Ottawa (City) Board of Education (No. 3) (1994), 23 C.H.R.R. D/41 (Ontario Board of Inquiry).
8. Lannin v. Ontario (Ministry of the Solicitor General) (1993), 26 C.H.R.R. D/58 (Ontario Bd. Of Inquiry).
9. Rapson v. Stemms Restaurant Ltd. (1991), 14 C.H.R.R. D/449 (Ont. Bd. Of Inquiry).
10. [1982] 1 S.C.R. 202.
11. (1995), 95 C.L.L.C. 230-033 (S.C.C.).
12. (1996), 54 L.A.C. (4th) 303 (Ont. Arb. Bd.).
13. (1990), 12 C.H.R.R. D/87 (B.C. Human Rights Council).
14. (1997) L.A.C. (4th) 360 (N.S. Arb. Bd.).
15. (1991), 18 L.A.C. (4th) 412 (Ont.).
16. (1994), C.L.L.C. 17026 (Ont. H.R.).

STAFFING WAL-MART STORES, INC. (A)[1]

Prepared by Ken Mark under the supervision of Professor Alison Konrad

Version: (A) 2004-01-20

INTRODUCTION

In 2003, an executive vice-president (EVP) at Wal-Mart Stores, Inc. (Wal-Mart), wondered about Wal-Mart's employment equity record. For the past few years, Wal-Mart consistently appeared on *Fortune*'s list of the 100 best companies to work for in the United States, most recently ranking 94 in 2002. Although the EVP was aware of several lawsuits against the company alleging gender discrimination, Wal-Mart's published practices indicated that the organization was committed to fair practices. The EVP wondered what employment-related information should be requested from the People Division.

WAL-MART STORES, INC.

In 2002, Wal-Mart was the world's largest employer and the world's largest company. With net income of US$8 billion on sales of US$247 billion, Wal-Mart was the subject of countless newspaper features and journal articles praising its dominance and success. For a look at Wal-Mart's selected financial information, see Exhibit 1. One of the many reasons for this success was that, unlike its retail counterparts in the grocery industry, Wal-Mart remained a non-unionized company, working incessantly to fend off organizing attempts in the United States and around the world.

Wal-Mart's Workforce

Available data showed that by 2001, Wal-Mart employed 930,000 people in its domestic U.S. stores, and this employment figure was up 50 per cent since 1996. But during the same

	1994	1995	1996	1997	1998	1999	2000	2001	2002	2003
Selected Financial Information										
Net revenues	67,977	83,398	94,765	106,152	119,248	139,025	166,628	193,116	219,671	246,525
Cost of sales	53,444	65,586	74,505	83,510	93,438	108,725	129,664	150,255	171,562	191,838
Operating, selling and general and administrative expenses	10,333	12,858	15,021	16,946	19,358	22,363	27,040	31,550	36,173	41,043
Net income	2,333	2,681	2,740	3,056	3,526	4,430	5,377	6,295	6,671	8,039
Shareholders' equity	10,753	12,726	14,756	17,143	18,503	21,112	25,834	31,343	35,102	39,337
Return on shareholders' equity	21.7%	21.1%	18.6%	17.8%	19.1%	21.0%	20.8%	20.1%	19.0%	20.4%
Total number of associates (000)	528	622	675	728	825	910	1,140	1,244	1,383	1,400
Shares outstanding (millions)	2,299	2,298	2,294	2,266	2,240	4,450	4,454	4,470	4,451	4,386
Book value per share	4.68	5.54	6.43	7.57	8.26	4.74	5.80	7.01	7.89	8.97

Exhibit 1   Wal-Mart Historical Financials (years ending January 31) (US$ millions, except per share data)

Source: Company files.

period, the percentage of women employed decreased from 67 per cent to 64 per cent. The number and composition of people at Wal-Mart was of keen interest to company officials because of the sheer size of their workforce and how employment costs affected the company's financials. Analysts who examined the company's stores and financial performance estimated that payroll expenses accounted for 50 per cent of Wal-Mart's total operating, selling, general and administrative expenses.

At Wal-Mart, there were retail store employees (including hourly and salaried workforce), the store management, and high-level managers such as district managers and regional vice-presidents (see Exhibit 2). In 2001, management

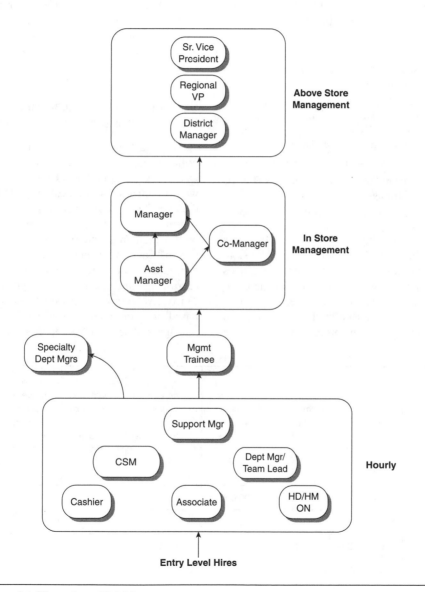

Exhibit 2   Job Hierarchy at Wal-Mart

employees earned about $50,000 on average while hourly employees earned $18,000.

Operations

There were four types of domestic retail stores at Wal-Mart in 2002: discount stores, supercentres, SAM's Club, and Neighborhood Markets. A quick overview of key 2001 store statistics is provided in Exhibit 3.

Level	Description
Corporate	Total Wal-Mart including domestic and international
Division	Division One stores (discount stores, supercentres, Neighborhood Markets) and SAM's Club make up Wal-Mart's two key domestic divisions
Region	There were 41 regions in the United States
District	Each region contained five to six Districts on average
Store	Each District contained 10 to 15 stores

Corporate-wide human resource policy was the responsibility of Wal-Mart's People Division. Primary and secondary people policy committees met with representatives from each of the company's operating divisions and representatives from home office in Bentonville, Arkansas, to formulate policies. This process was overseen by the EVP of the people division. The EVP described his duties as "overall responsibility for getting, keeping and developing Wal-Mart talent worldwide." He reported to Wal-Mart's president and chief executive officer (CEO) and sat on the corporate executive committee. The company's senior human resource executives all had "dotted-line" reporting relationships to the EVP of the People Division. For example, the senior vice-president of People for the SAM's Club division would report both to the president of that division and to the EVP of the People Division.

Human Resources Reporting Relationships for Domestic Divisions

Wal-Mart had similar human resources (HR) policies across its domestic divisions, i.e., Division One and SAM's Club. The HR function was organized hierarchically: in Division One, the over 2,600 stores were organized into five or six divisional areas, with five or six regions within each area, and 80 to 85 stores within each region. Each store had an hourly employee, the personnel manager, who co-ordinated hourly recruiting and performed payroll functions. Thirty-five regional personnel managers (RPM) based in Bentonville oversaw these personnel managers. These RPMs reported to one of three

Store Type	Division	Number of Domestic Stores	Average Size (in square feet)	Annual Sales per Store (US$ millions)	Operations Expense (% of store sales)	Average Number of Employees per Store (estimate)	% of Workforce Full-time
Discount Stores	Division One	1,736	125,000	39	15.0	207	85
Supercenters	Division One	888	200,000	75	15.7	540	85
SAM's Club	SAM's Club	475	135,000	60	14.5	172	85
Neighborhood Markets	Division One	19	30,000	14	16.0	81	85

Exhibit 3   2001 Store Statistics

Source: Company files.

People Directors in the home office; in turn, these People Directors reported to the vice-president of People at Division One.

The company had a computerized information system that made personnel policies and guidelines available to its staff. In addition to relying on information generated by reports at store, district, regional and divisional levels, store visits by district managers and RMP were frequent; district managers visited stores once every two weeks and RPMs visited stores weekly. Reports from each visit were immediately submitted to the regional vice-president.

Organizational Culture

Wal-Mart prided itself on its strong culture, with numerous references to Sam Walton's personal biography, the history of the company and how Walton's personal values became core beliefs for the company. Wal-Mart public information indicated that its customer-focused culture stemmed from the company's pursuit of everyday low prices (EDLP) and "genuine customer service." Founder Sam Walton had three basic beliefs on which the company was built: Respect for the individual; Service to Our Customers; and Strive for Excellence. In addition, there were two key "rules" at Wal-Mart that supported the three basic beliefs: the sundown rule (attending to requests the same day they were received); and the Ten-foot Rule (offering greetings whenever one was within 10 feet of a customer). In his autobiography, Walton outlined his Rules For Building A Business (see Exhibit 4).

Rule 1

Commit to your business. Believe in it more than anybody else. I think I overcame every single one of my personal shortcomings by the sheer passion I brought to my work. I don't know if you're born with this kind of passion or if you can learn it. But I do know you need it. If you love your work, you'll be out there every day trying to do it the best you possibly can, and pretty soon everybody around will catch the passion from you—like a fever.

Rule 2

Share your profits with all your Associates, and treat them as partners. In turn, they will treat you as a partner, and together you will all perform beyond your wildest expectations. Remain a corporation and retain control if you like, but behave as a servant leader in a partnership. Encourage your Associates to hold a stake in the company. Offer discounted stock, and grant them stock for their retirement. It's the single best thing we ever did.

Rule 3

Motivate your partners. Money and ownership alone aren't enough. Constantly, day-by-day, think of new and more interesting ways to motivate and challenge your partners. Set high goals, encourage competition, and then keep score. Make bets with outrageous payoffs. If things get stale, cross-pollinate; have managers switch jobs with one another to stay challenged. Keep everybody guessing as to what your next trick is going to be. Don't become too predictable.

Rule 4

Communicate everything you possibly can to your partners. The more they know, the more they'll understand. The more they understand, the more they'll care. Once they care, there's no stopping them. If you don't trust your Associates to know what's going on, they'll know you don't really consider them partners. Information is power, and the gain you get from empowering your Associates more than offsets the risk of informing your competitors.

Exhibit 4   Sam's Rules for Building a Business   *(Continued)*

Rule 5

Appreciate everything your Associates do for the business. A paycheck and a stock option will buy one kind of loyalty. But all of us like to be told how much somebody appreciates what we do for them. We like to hear it often, and especially when we have done something we're really proud of. Nothing else can quite substitute for a few well-chosen, well-timed, sincere words of praise. They're absolutely free—and worth a fortune.

Rule 6

Celebrate your successes. Find some humor in your failures. Don't take yourself so seriously. Loosen up, and everybody around you will loosen up. Have fun. Show enthusiasm—always. When all else fails, put on a costume and sing a silly song. Then make everybody else sing with you. Don't do a hula on Wall Street. It's been done. Think up your own stunt. All of this is more important, and more fun, than you think, and it really fools the competition. "Why should we take those cornballs at Wal-Mart seriously?"

Rule 7

Listen to everyone in your company. And figure out ways to get them talking. The folks on the front lines—the ones who actually talk to the customer—are the only ones who really know what's going on out there. You'd better find out what they know. This really is what total quality is all about. To push responsibility down in your organization, and to force good ideas to bubble up within it, you must listen to what your Associates are trying to tell you.

Rule 8

Exceed your customers' expectations. If you do, they'll come back over and over. Give them what they want—and a little more. Let them know you appreciate them. Make good on all your mistakes, and don't make excuses—apologize. Stand behind everything you do. The two most important words I ever wrote were on that first Wal-Mart sign, "Satisfaction Guaranteed." They're still up there, and they have made all the difference.

Rule 9

Control your expenses better than your competition. This is where you can always find the competitive advantage. For 25 years running—long before Wal-Mart was known as the nation's largest retailer—we ranked No. 1 in our industry for the lowest ratio of expenses to sales. You can make a lot of different mistakes and still recover if you run an efficient operation. Or you can be brilliant and still go out of business if you're too inefficient.

Rule 10

Swim upstream. Go the other way. Ignore the conventional wisdom. If everybody else is doing it one way, there's a good chance you can find your niche by going in exactly the opposite direction. But be prepared for a lot of folks to wave you down and tell you you're headed the wrong way. I guess in all my years, what I heard more often than anything was: a town of less than 50,000 population cannot support a discount store for very long.

Exhibit 4   Sam's Rules for Building a Business

Source: www.walmart.com, accessed June 5, 2003.

New employees learned the "Wal-Mart Way" by viewing videos about the company's history, completing computer-based learning modules about elements of the culture and reading the associate handbook. At each store, a daily meeting, held at shift changes, allowed managers to discuss company culture and encourage employees to perform the Wal-Mart cheer.

The company indicated in its promotional literature that it received letters from customers praising individual associates for exceptional service, citing examples of employees who had gone above and beyond the call of duty. Walton had once asked associates to practice what he called "aggressive hospitality"—striving to be the most friendly, giving better service over what customers expected, and generally exceeding customers' expectations. This hospitality also extended to the community in which Wal-Mart operated. The company frequently provided charitable assistance, raised funds for organizations and provided scholarships to students.

Ongoing training for store managers and home office employees consisted of weekly Saturday morning meetings (the first meeting of the month was devoted to a culture topic). In addition, instruction and orientation on the Wal-Mart culture was given to managers at all levels of the company.

Rewards and Promotions

Annual pay increases were tied to performance evaluation ratings, with a percentage increase guideline specified by the home office. Typically, an annual merit increase of four per cent or five per cent was the maximum given, although this amount could not be granted within 90 days of an annual performance increase or raise due to promotion.

Before 1998, higher-level jobs were not posted. In 2002, these and any other openings were typically posted at stores and were usually available online, but there were exceptions. Store managers could circumvent this process and rely on filling positions with lateral moves. In addition, store managers had the authority to waive minimum requirements regarding time in current position in order to promote employees.

When employees were promoted to higher-level jobs, there was an implicit expectation that they would be moved to other stores, districts or regions, as much as business need required. For example, a district manager in Northern California asked employees applying for the management training program to certify in writing that they were willing to transfer "to any location within the Wal-Mart trading area" to receive training and were willing to relocate post-training. A former regional vice-president required co-managers to be open to relocate "whenever and wherever we need them." See Exhibit 5 for relocation statistics by job type.

In the late 1980s, Wal-Mart implemented and formalized a policy of creating resident assistant manager positions for individuals who were eligible to be assistant managers but were not able to relocate. These resident assistant managers could move into co-manager positions without relocating. One company official stated that the program had been phased out by 2002. Another official stated that the program still existed but only on an "as requested" basis.

In his 1992 autobiography, Sam Walton discussed the changes he had made to his original management philosophy of requiring managers to be extremely flexible:

> Maybe that was necessary back in the old days (that one had to be ready to relocate on a moment's notice to move into management), and maybe it was more rigid than it needed to be. Now, though, it's not really appropriate anymore for several reasons. First, as the company grows bigger, we need to find more ways to stay in touch with the communities where we operate, and one of the best ways to do that is by hiring locally, developing mangers locally, and letting them have a career in their home community—if they perform. Second, the old way really put good, smart women at a disadvantage in our company because, at the time, they weren't as free to pick up and move as many men were. Now I've seen the light on the opportunities we missed out on with women.[2]

ADDRESSING DISPARITIES

Wal-Mart established the goal that the percentage of women employed should reflect the community—50 per cent of the workforce. This

Percent of Promotions Where Employee Changed Store, District, or Region 1996 and Later

Target Job	Changed Store	Changed District	Changed Region
Store Manager	91.2%	69.4%	35.6%
Co-Manager	81.3	57.0	32.6
Assistant Manager	63.3	40.2	22.0
Management Trainee	62.2	32.5	17.0
Area Manager, SAM's	17.4	5.4	2.8
Support Manager	4.8	7.6	6.0

Average Number of Changes in Store, District and Region After Entering Store Management Jobs

Target Job	Changed Store	Changed District	Changed Region
Store Manager	3.6	2.8	1.7
Co-Manager	3.0	2.2	1.3
Assistant Manager	2.8	2.0	1.2
Management Trainee	3.0	2.0	1.2
Area Manager, SAM's	1.2	0.6	0.5
Support Manager	0.8	0.6	0.4

Exhibit 5   Relocation Statistics by Job Type

Source: Richard Drogin, "Statistical Analysis of Gender Patterns in Wal-Mart Workforce," Drogi, Kakigi & Associates, February 2003.

was a well-known target throughout the organization, and all managers insisted they were aware of it and were striving to meet it. In fact, numerous company memos since 1999 had raised the issue of employment equity and urged managers to address inequalities if they existed.

The executive vice-president wanted to know what types of information should be requested to evaluate the state of Wal-Mart's employment practices. Simply asking for "everything" would be illogical as there were literally thousands of documents that could be retrieved, requiring months, if not years, to sift through.

NOTES

1. This case has been written on the basis of published sources only. Consequently, the interpretation and perspectives presented in this case are not necessarily those of Wal-Mart Stores, Inc. or any of its employees.

2. Sam Walton, "Sam Walton with John Huey" *Made in America*, Bantam Books, New York, 1992.

NexTech Inc. (A)

Prepared by Professor Gerard H. Seijts
(originally prepared by Eileen Watson and Professor James C. Rush)

  Version: (A) 2004-10-13

The date was October 24, 1997, and Adam Blackburn—second level manager in the Digital Switching Systems group of NexTech Inc.—was deep in thought. The information he and other NexTech managers had just received seemed directly related to a promotion recommendation he would be making the following day. He had been somewhat undecided before attending the meeting—now he was in a quandary. Given the company's new focus on equal opportunity for its female employees, which of his first-level managers (five male, two female) should receive his support?

Walking briskly back to his office, Adam mentally reviewed the facts he had just been given about some of the company's employment statistics and the Employment Equity Act. He understood that the Employment Equity Act differed from the concept of "equal pay for work of equal value," which was primarily concerned with eliminating gender bias from compensation and job evaluation systems. As well, Adam knew that both types of legislation (the Employment Equity Act, and pay equity legislation) related to and were governed by the Charter of Human Rights and Freedoms. What had been unfamiliar to him (and to most of the other managers who had attended the meeting) were actual details of the Employment Equity Act, and requirements for its enforcement.

The Employment Equity Act

The 1995 Employment Equity Act was implemented "in order to achieve equality of employment." The formally stated purpose of the legislation was:

> To achieve equality in the workplace so that no person shall be denied employment opportunities or benefits for reasons unrelated to ability and, in the fulfillment of that goal, to correct the condition of disadvantage in employment experienced by women, aboriginal peoples, persons with disabilities and members of visible minorities, by giving effect to the principle that employment equity means more than treating persons in the same way but also requires special measures and the accommodation of differences.

During the meeting, Adam learned that the Act updated the legislation that had actually been in effect for over a decade. The V.P. of Human Resources and Administration explained that progress toward the objective to achieve equality of employment in the Canadian workplace had been uneven and unacceptably slow, in part because the existing legislation "lacked the proverbial teeth of enforcement." The Act, he clarified, was about to change all that. For example, the Act stipulated that financial penalties may be imposed on organizations, and that organizations may be ordered to put in place quotas to increase the representation of members of the four designated groups, if organizations are in violation of the Act.

The Act required all federally regulated companies with over 100 employees (banks, airlines, telecommunication companies, interprovincial railway, trucking, and other industries governed by the Canada Labor Code) to implement employment equity, and report their results to the government. As well, federal government contractors with contracts worth over $200,000 would be required to adhere to employment equity guidelines under a contract compliance agreement. The Canadian Armed Forces and the Royal Canadian Mounted Police were also covered under the Act.

While no requirements were stipulated for establishing numerical targets, employers would have to develop specific employment equity plans, and provide statistical evidence of a change in the distribution of employees to include more members of designated groups (see Exhibit 1 for an example of a statistical summary sheet).

The implementation of employment equity would require employers to integrate equal employment concerns into their normal business practices. This would include the identification and removal of elements in existing employment systems, practices, and attitudes that might limit opportunities for women, native people, the disabled, and visible minorities. As well, special measures to facilitate the integration of previously under-represented groups into the organization's workforce would be introduced.

As a direct result of the Act, NexTech's human resources department had begun to collect detailed statistics on selection, promotion, performance evaluations, turnover and compensation. The human resources department quickly learned that there were striking imbalances in several areas. For example, it appeared that women in particular were under-represented in the NexTech's workforce, and that their salaries were generally lower as compared to those of their male counterparts.

The V.P. of Human Resources and Administration expressed his concerns about these statistics. He encouraged the managers that attended the meeting to be more sensitive to "the ease with which such discrepancies can creep into our employment system." In the meantime, he explained, the human resources department would work on specific policies and practices that could be implemented in the short term for the hiring, training, and promotion of persons in the designated groups.

Adam glanced at the printed information he had picked up at the meeting—a list of requirements under the Employment Equity Act:

Employer's Duty

- To identify and eliminate employment barriers against members of designated groups that result from the employer's employment system, policies and practices that are not authorized by law.
- To implement new policies and practices with the objective of positively encouraging and facilitating the participation of the excluded groups.
- To make appropriate accommodation for members of designated groups to enable their entry into areas or occupational groups from which they have previously been excluded.
- To set up a program to ensure that the composition of the employer's personnel reflects the composition of the relevant pool of available workers, that is, the workforce.

Reports

Reports must be submitted annually by industrial sector and location of the employer and its employees, providing data on:

• hires		• women
• promotions	for	• aboriginal people
• terminations		• disabled persons
• salary		• visible minorities

Employers were also expected to submit an additional narrative segment describing any activity in support of employment equity. For example, the employer was encouraged to describe the measures taken during the reporting period to rectify under-representation of designated group members, or explain the lack of progress toward the goal of facilitating a more equitable workplace.

Once submitted and reviewed, all reports will be available for public inspection.[1]

NOTE: See instructions
NOTA: Voir instructions

OCCUPATIONAL GROUPS: PERMANENT FULL-TIME EMPLOYEES*
CATÉGORIES PROFESSIONNELLES: SALARIÉS PERMANENTS À PLEIN TEMPS*

Form 2   Part A,
Formulaire   Partie A,   Page 1

Reporting Period:
Période de rapport: _____

Name of Business:
Nom de l'entreprise: _____

Industrial Sector:
Branche d'activité: _____

Location-Endroit

☐ National (Canada)
   National (Canada)

☐ Province/Territory (specify)
   Province/territoire (préciser) _____

☐ Designated CMA (specify)
   RMR désignée (préciser) _____

Occupational Groups Catégories professionnelles	Top and bottom of salary range Maximum et minimum de rémunération	** Quarter Quart	All Employees Tous les salariés			Aboriginal Peoples Autochtones			Persons with Disabilities Personnes handicapées			Members of Visible Minorities Membres des minorités visibles		
			Total Number Nombre total	Men Hommes	Women Femmes	Total Number Nombre total	Men Hommes	Women Femmes	Total Number Nombre total	Men Hommes	Women Femmes	Total Number Nombre total	Men Hommes	Women Femmes
	Col. 1		Col. 2	Col. 3	Col. 4	Col. 5	Col. 6	Col. 7	Col. 8	Col. 9	Col. 10	Col. 11	Col. 12	Col. 13
Senior Managers Cadres supérieurs		4 3 2 1												
Middle and Other Managers Cadres intermédiaires et autres administrateurs		4 3 2 1												
Professionals Professionnels		4 3 2 1												
Semi-Professionals and Technicians Personnel semi-professionnel et technique		4 3 2 1												
Supervisors Surveillants		4 3 2 1												
Supervisors: Crafts and Trades Contremaîtres		4 3 2 1												
Administrative and Senior Clerical Personnel Personnel administratif et de bureau principal		4 3 2 1												

LAB 1111 (07-97) P-1 B

* Use the other Parts for permanent part-time and temporary employees
  Utiliser les autres parties pour les salariés permanents à temps partiel et les salariés temporaires

** 1 refers to the lowest salary quarter; 4 refers to the highest salary quarter
   1 représente le quart le moins élevé de l'échelle de rémunération; 4 représente le plus élevé

Canada

(Continued)

Exhibit 1   Example Statistical Summary Sheet

■ Human Resources Development Canada   Développement des ressources humaines Canada

NOTE: See instructions
NOTA: Voir instructions

Form   2   Part A,
Formulaire   Partie A,   Page 2

OCCUPATIONAL GROUPS: PERMANENT FULL-TIME EMPLOYEES*
CATÉGORIES PROFESSIONNELLES: SALARIÉS PERMANENTS À PLEIN TEMPS*

Occupational Groups Catégories professionnelles	Top and bottom of salary range Maximum et minimum de l'échelle de rémunération	** Quarter Quart	All Employees Tous les salariés				Aboriginal Peoples Autochtones				Persons with Disabilities Personnes handicapées				Members of Visible Minorities Membres des minorités visibles		
			Total Number Nombre total	Men Hommes	Women Femmes	Total Number Nombre total	Men Hommes	Women Femmes	Total Number Nombre total	Men Hommes	Women Femmes	Total Number Nombre total	Men Hommes	Women Femmes
	Col. 1		Col. 2	Col. 3	Col. 4	Col. 5	Col. 6	Col. 7	Col. 8	Col. 9	Col. 10	Col. 11	Col. 12	Col. 13
Skilled Sales and Service Personnel Personnel spécialisé de la vente et des services		4 3 2 1												
Skilled Crafts and Trades Workers Travailleurs qualifiés et artisans		4 3 2 1												
Clerical Personnel Personnel de bureau		4 3 2 1												
Intermediate Sales and Service Personnel Personnel intermédiaire de la vente et des services		4 3 2 1												
Semi-Skilled Manual Workers Travailleurs manuels spécialisés		4 3 2 1												
Other Sales and Service Personnel Autre personnel de la vente et des services		4 3 2 1												
Other Manual Workers Autres travailleurs manuels		4 3 2 1												
TOTAL NUMBER OF EMPLOYEES NOMBRE TOTAL DE SALARIÉS														

LAB 1111 (07-97) P-2 B

* Use the other Parts for permanent part-time and temporary employees
* Utiliser les autres parties pour les salariés permanents à temps partiel et les salariés temporaires

** 1 refers to the lowest salary quarter; 4 refers to the highest salary quarter
** 1 représente le quart le moins élevé de l'échelle de rémunération; 4 représente le plus élevé

Canada

Exhibit 1   Example Statistical Summary Sheet

NEXTECH INC.

The origins of the company for which Adam worked stretched back nearly 25 years, when NexTech Research Corporation (NTRC), a high-profile employer in Calgary, established NexTech Inc. (NTI) in the same municipality. NTI was a research and development organization which specialized in designing advanced telecommunications and information management system products, primarily for the parent company. Later, NTI performed systems engineering, long-range network planning, and research and development for a variety of other clients as well, when the work complemented the overall direction of NTI's laboratories.

NTI's major client, however, continued to be its parent company, NTRC. NTRC represented the marketing, manufacturing, and service operations for products designed and developed at NTI. NTI's new product innovations and technologies contributed to NTRC's placement at the leading edge of the telecommunications equipment industry.

NTI was organized into two major areas— Network Products (60 per cent of the company's human resources) and Office Products (the remaining 40 per cent). (See Exhibit 2 for a partial organizational chart.) The Network Products area, organized into four divisions, was concerned with a great variety of activities related to the design of public and private telecommunication networks—for example, the development of new transmission, switching, and outside plant network products. The four divisions of the Office Products area were concerned with the design and development of such products as private switching systems and data products.

Currently more than 1,100 men and women were employed at NTI's Calgary location. Close to 60 per cent held university degrees (see Exhibit 3), the majority in electrical engineering. Computer scientists comprised the second-largest employee segment. One senior manager observed:

> Although the stereotypes are not as clear today as they once were, there seems to be a typical systems engineer—very methodical and systematic, someone who takes time to do processes such as performance evaluation, giving feedback, looking after people's training needs. That's because systems, even human systems, are this person's stock in trade.
>
> Electrical engineers are typically quite different— their motto is, if it works, don't fix it! They only pay attention to their people when they break down, just as they only pay attention to a system when it is not working.

Employees were broadly defined by two groupings—"technical" (computer scientists, engineers, and other responsible for designing and operating products and equipment) or "non-technical" (professionals, administrators, support staff, and others). New technical recruits were designated "MSS" (Member of Scientific Staff)[2] or "MTS" (Member of Technical Staff).[3] Technical employees outnumbered non-technical roughly three to one.

NTI's organizational structure, like that of other research and development companies, displayed a high degree of flexibility in response to constantly changing demands. One employee remarked, "In spite of its size, NexTech is more dynamic than most." Massive reorganizations could be expected two or three times a year in response to re-vectoring of projects, changes in divisional responsibilities, and so forth. For example, the recent promotion of an assistant vice-president triggered many shifts, promotions, and other changes, "for the purpose of consolidation and trying to get projects and people working together."

Individual employees found that their career mobility was affected not only by internal shifts but also by the transfers and promotions which were exchanged regularly between NTI and its parent. Career opportunities were available for most NTI employees in NTRC, and vice-versa.

RECRUITING

NTI had long prided itself on its non-discriminatory hiring practices, and on providing equal

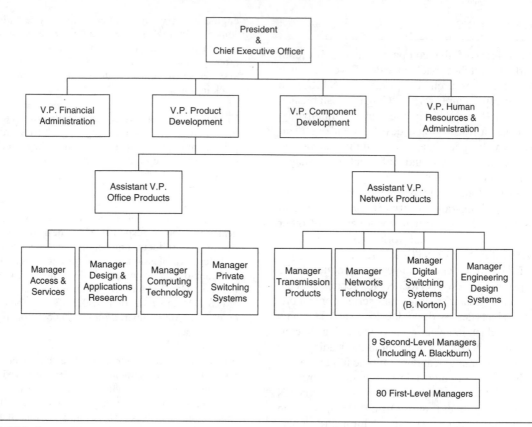

Exhibit 2 Nextech Inc.: Partial Organizational Chart (current)

Major	Bachelor	Master	PhD
	(number of employees)		
Physics, Physical Chemistry, Applied Science	25.0	7.0	10.0
Chemistry, Chemical Engineering	4.0	1.0	1.0
Electrical Engineering, Communications	177.0	125.0	31.0
Mechanical Engineering	10.0	3.0	0.0
Metallurgy, Metal Engineering	2.0	0.0	1.0
Engineering—Civil, Systems, Industrial, Structural, etc.	6.0	4.0	3.0
Math, Statistics, Information Theory	23.0	11.0	4.0
Computer Science	98.0	59.0	9.0
Business Administration, Law, P.R., Engineering Administration	8.0	18.0	1.0
Economics, Finance, Accounting	7.0	4.0	0.0
Psychology, General Arts, Library Arts, Human Factors	16.0	15.0	6.0
% of total population with degrees	32.6%	21.4%	5.7%
Current # of Employees: 1,155	Total Degrees:		689.0

Exhibit 3 NTI Employees—Education by Degree

opportunities to all it employees. As explained by a human resource manager at the meeting attended by Adam Blackburn:

> We are committed to attracting and retaining exceptionally talented people, regardless of race, sex, or physical disability. NTI employs several disabled people, as well as people from a wide variety of different cultures—a fact which is underlined by the approximately 40 languages spoken by our employees!

> But few women have chosen to pursue careers in technical areas such as electrical engineering and computer science; so women form a relatively small proportion of the technical employees at NTI. This is changing as more qualified women become available.

As Adam thought about what the V.P. of Human Resources and Administration had said, he recalled seeing some hiring statistics from the previous year in the company's recruiting office:

Female Graduate Recruiting		
	Electrical Engineering	*Computer Science*
Graduating Class	1,277	1,276
Females Graduating	94	372
Females Applied to NTI	41	105
Females Hired by NTI	4	25

Comparative figures for male applicants to NTI were 315 (electrical engineering) and 328 (computer science). Actually hired by NTI were 100 male electrical engineers and 83 male computer science grads.

JUNIOR MANAGEMENT

Different management tasks were performed at each of the two lowest management levels. First-level managers had to be able to organize and delegate work to others; but they also were expected to pitch in and help their people with their day-to-day assignments, whenever necessary. The essential ingredients of a second-level manager's job were mature, effective interpersonal skills, and superior integrative ability. A "second level" should be capable of assuming the role of integrator, going beyond established boundaries, making outside contacts, relating to work going on in other areas, and having a broad view of the organization.

DISCRIMINATION AT NTI?

As he considered his upcoming promotion decision, Adam carefully studied some statistical tables which had been distributed at the seminar. It was clear that women were not proportionally represented in management positions at NTI, as indicated in the following chart:

NTI Female Employees *(as a per cent of the same-level male/female population)*			
	Year Before Last (%)	*Last Year (%)*	*Current Year (%)*
Technical			
1st Level Managers	4.0	3.3	5.4
2nd Level Managers	2.6	3.0	3.6
Non-Management	14.8	15.9	17.0
Non-technical			
1st Level Managers	22.5	22.0	21.1
2nd Level Managers	11.4	10.8	10.0
Non-Management	54.8	54.1	53.4

Adam noted that, although there had been an increase in the percentage of women in technical positions over the past three years, this was offset somewhat by reductions in female participation in non-technical positions. He thought about remarks made by a colleague regarding promotions within NTI:

Our typical male promotee (for first-level management, at any rate) is the hot-shot, technical whiz-kid. But we sometimes recognize technical expertise by giving the title, "manager," simply as recognition of outstanding performance—a title bearing no actual management responsibilities along with it.

And we tend to create jobs that fit the people we have, not appoint someone for a specific position—the mandate changes with the person in the position. A second-level manager here, who has a dozen or so first-level managers working for him or her, is doing one kind of project . . . but when people change, so does the mandate.

Compensation statistics had been prepared, comparing salary distributions between male and female employees (see Exhibits 4 and 5). Possible explanations for discrepancies were implicit in another statistical table which indicated male-female differences in salary, length of service, and age (see Exhibit 6).

One second-level manager described his practical approach to salary raises, indicating that he gave no thought to the gender of the recipients:

Giving raises in my department is no problem for me. I allocate my "pot" of money after ranking my people, picking out the best producers and making adjustments for effort and merit. I also sort them according to year of graduation, ranking, age—after juggling the data for a while, names become meaningless!

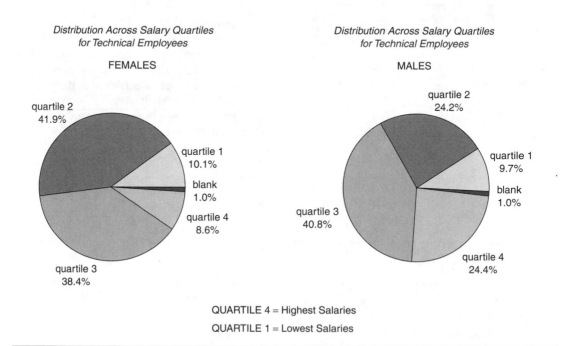

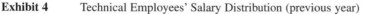

Exhibit 4   Technical Employees' Salary Distribution (previous year)

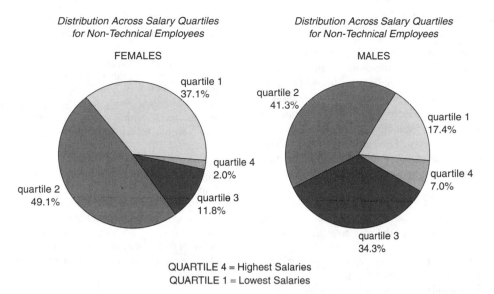

Distribution Across Salary Quartiles for Non-Technical Employees

FEMALES

quartile 1 37.1%
quartile 4 2.0%
quartile 3 11.8%
quartile 2 49.1%

Distribution Across Salary Quartiles for Non-Technical Employees

MALES

quartile 2 41.3%
quartile 1 17.4%
quartile 4 7.0%
quartile 3 34.3%

QUARTILE 4 = Highest Salaries
QUARTILE 1 = Lowest Salaries

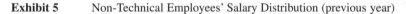

Exhibit 5   Non-Technical Employees' Salary Distribution (previous year)

	Number of Employees		Differences Between Males and Females: Median Data		
Level	*Male*	*Female*	*Salary ($1,000s) (M-F)*	*NTI Services (Yrs.) (M-F)*	*Age (Yrs.) (M-F)*
AVP	8	0	n/a	n/a	n/a
Division Manager	28	1	8.3	1.3	1.5
2nd Level Manager					
• Non-Technical	9	1	4.75	3.6	0.5
• Technical	53	2	1.2	2.8	5.8
1st Level Manager					
• Non-Technical	30	8	1.95	1.3	1.5
• Technical	122	7	3.45	0.8	3.3
MSS	411	54	5.7	0.5	3.1
MTS	89	5	5.5	1.8	6.6
Specialist	63	60	6.5	(0.8)	1.3
Support	76	128	3.16	0.5	(0.9)
Total	**889**	**266**			
	1,155				

Exhibit 6   Male/Female Differences by Level (current year)

PERFORMANCE APPRAISAL

A company-wide audit confirmed that performance reviews were being done regularly, manager with employee, twice a year, for 98 per cent of NTI employees. The format was a personal, one- to two-hour discussion mainly devoted to the subordinate's objectives, and the level of achievement of them. The audit discovered some individual expressions of dissatisfaction, written as comments on questionnaire forms:

- It is hard to know what you are being rated on.
- I'm given objectives, but there is no one-to-one correspondence of the objectives to my salary increases.
- I'm not sure how my set of responsibilities stacks up against other people.
- You should rate us on an absolute scale—or if it is a relative scale, then tell us what the relative rating is.
- The question is, are we being scored against stated objectives or unstated expectations?

A human resources manager explained:

Individual objectives are unequal due to individual differences in experience, skills, expertise, and so forth. For instance, managers will assign more difficult and far-reaching objectives to people they know have the capability of reaching those objectives. So, under "Critical Responsibilities" in the individual's performance review, the rating "Fully Satisfied" is really a judgment call on the managers' part regarding what they have assigned to their various people.

And goals are constantly set and revised. Any group can review what has changed in the project, what else needs to be done, what additional goals need to be set.

But there are various checks and balances so that no one is unjustly overlooked or over-criticized. There are very few operations in this company where you work one-to-one, only yourself with one manager—mostly you deal with other management people, other groups. There is a great deal of cross-checking among managers—frank discussions, typically fair. Employees never see that, and

are cynical. They commonly complain "My manager never stands up for me, never takes my part."

As a formal process, there is the regular managers' review, where a number of managers get together and talk about their ratings for their people, and their reasons for giving those ratings. A manager can be, and sometimes is, challenged to give reasons for his or her assessment of a particular person.

Discussions about placement also occur in this management group review—should this employee be retained on this particular assignment, or is he or she looking for a developmental move? Also, promotions are discussed . . . but some groups are different in the way they make promotions possible. There is no typical way with which promotions are dealt.

TRAINING AND DEVELOPMENT

In the complex technological environment of NTI, new hires were required to spend 14 to 16 weeks in an intensive training program to learn the systems with which they would be working. Many other training opportunities were offered on an ongoing basis. One manager stated:

We're provided with endless technical and management programs, both internal and external. Millions of dollars are spent each year on training and development. However, there is no required number of days for any individual laid down or prescribed. Each manager lays out what he or she feels necessary for the development of his or her employee, during the performance evaluation process. The follow-through by management can be spotty, unfortunately.

ADAM'S CHOICE

Adam Blackburn had worked at NexTech for six years. He had joined NTI as an MSS following his graduation with an M.Sc. (Electrical Engineering) degree. His career had followed a typical path—promotion to first-level manager after three years, where he supervised from six to 12 people in developing a new major product. When that particular project wound down two years later, Adam was promoted to a second-level manager's position reporting to the divisional manager, Digital Switching Systems.

The seven first-level managers and 38 MSS and MTS personnel of Adam's department were recognized as an effective, productive unit. When Adam was approached in June this year regarding the transfer (and promotion) of one of his first-level managers, he agreed somewhat regretfully to consider the request—any such change would cause a ripple effect throughout the department.

The "open" second-level position was located in the Software Development department, and required the supervision and coordination of seven or more project groups working toward the development of a complex new software product. Three of these projects groups were already in existence, having been recently formed through the efforts of three capable first-level managers. The remaining four (or five or six) groups were still to be established—no first-level managers had yet been designated, although the software to be developed was needed urgently in another NTI division.

Adam wondered which of his seven first-level managers should receive his strong recommendation for the promotion. He thought about the overall ratings he had given his subordinates (out of a possible five points) during their most recent performance evaluations: Gilles, Jozef and Natalie, four; Ashok and Laura, three; Todd, 2.5; and Barry, two. He described his criteria for high performance ratings as follows:

I evaluate people carefully, using NTI's rating range of one to five (five is the highest) for each task or category. If you give someone a job and they do it really well, that rates a three. For four or five, you must do *more* than just your immediate job. You must find things that need to be done, and do them—nobody ever gets promotions for just doing their job.

My biggest problem is forecasting how long a job will take. One person does a certain job in a week,

while another person might take two months to do the same work. After a job is done, I have to assess how difficult the job *really* was, and how innovative were the solutions that this particular person provided.

One way of judging effort is overtime slips . . . which seem to be turned in by more male than female employees, generally. But is that overtime necessary because the person's done a crummy job? Or is it because he or she is very dedicated to the work?

Above all, I appreciate, and look for, a positive attitude. I look for people who say, "Here's the deficiency—now here's how to go about fixing it."

I tell my first-level managers that my success hinges on their success. Anything I can do to help make them successful, I'll do.

Seeking an objective outside opinion about which manager to recommend for promotion, Adam arranged to meet with his divisional manager, Brent Norton. In response to Brent's suggestion, "Why not give me a brief summary of your perception of each manager?" Adam replied:

Technically, Gilles is probably my best manager. He is brilliant, and has bailed NTI out of deep trouble, many times; but he's deficient in people management skills. Gilles expects others to be as brilliant as he is, and doesn't realize they need coaching. When his people ask for help, he tells them, "This is how to do it!" He gives solutions, but doesn't describe the process. I've had to move some people who couldn't tolerate his style, out of his department. I don't consider Gilles promotable to second-level . . . unless, of course, he works on changing his management style.

Todd is my newest promotion, but the function of his department hasn't developed as fast as we had hoped, so he still has no staff. Todd tends to be very short, almost confrontational, with people in "outside" departments. My gut feeling is that he'll be OK with managing his own department. He's technically outstanding. Put him on a problem, and he'll work night and day to fix it. A bit demanding, no patience with small talk, Todd won't butter people up when asking them to do something.

Jozef is a man with a good mix of abilities. Technically, he's above average; but his real *forte* is management skills. Jozef's very good at organizing his department so everybody's working as a team, producing what's needed. All the jobs in his department are clearly defined—so when he's away, the department carries on as usual. When Gilles is away for a couple of weeks, everything's in disarray! But an AVP I used to work for favors promoting Gilles. He was surprised when I championed Jozef recently. However, he has been watching Jozef in operation, and I think he's changing his mind.

Laura's technical ability is above average. She is well organized and has her department perfectly coordinated, doing all the right things. However, I see her as personally not dedicated enough for the job she has to do. It's a particularly high-pressure job—requires an 18-hour-a-day commitment—she doesn't want to spend the time required. And Laura's not forceful enough. Her department has many demands placed on it, and she hasn't learned how to say "no." Also, a second-level manager has to be involved in a lot more than his or her immediate job—getting people to do things for you, doing things for them. Laura doesn't seem to be interested. If you give her a job, she does that job very well; but she doesn't look outside her immediate area of responsibility.

Barry is another man who is very strong technically, but who has some communication and management deficiencies. His work is usually successful, but he has a problem with slipped schedules. When a deadline is going to be missed, Barry doesn't recognize this soon enough; and he doesn't effectively drive the bad news up the line, to make sure everybody who needs this information, gets it!

Ashok is a good mix of managerial and technical abilities. He does a capable job of managing his own department. His deficiencies are his inability to work with people *outside* his department. Ashok's focus is too narrow. He forgets he's just one piece of a bigger picture, and he fights doing any extra thing which would benefit the total program but might cause problems for his group. But he works almost 24 hours a day—he has doubled the amount of legal overtime he's allowed to do.

Natalie's technical abilities are quite a bit above average—not at the same level as Gilles and Ashok, but high up there. Her best asset is probably in the effective way she interfaces with other people—not only inside the company, but outside, with our customers. She combines technical ability plus the ability to get her point across to others, and to get things coordinated. I'm not sure she's promotable right now—she's been with NTI only two years. But ultimately, yes . . . and in 10 years, she'll be higher on the ladder than I'll be!

My people are such a high-spirited team—I have to hold them back from all the things they'd like to do. But I don't want to discourage them, because they may come up with some great innovative things which will advance TRI tremendously.

I'm going to regret losing any one of them, though I don't want to stand in their way of advancement.

As his conversation with Brent continued, Adam was remembering the information he had received in the meeting where the emergent concern of employment equity (or the lack thereof) in the company was discussed. He told Brent:

I assume employment equity is a problem, although most NTI people really believe that they get ahead on their skills and merit alone. Maybe the company wants better statistics to show the government that it's serious about emphasizing equal opportunity for female employees. I think NTI is extremely fair, already—but there is definitely a smaller percentage of women managers than men, and certainly a small percentage of women managers who are promotable. Typically, there are not many aggressive women in this organization—Natalie is an exception. Guys who do what she does get ahead.

I recollect promoting Laura and Natalie to first-level management. Prior to promoting Laura, we gave her the informal position of team leader, still reporting to a manager. Because she hadn't previously been identified as promotable, we watched carefully to see how competent she really was, and if she liked the new position. We noticed that people started to look to her as a leader. She was seen as competent, bright—not super-bright, but she still did good, if not particularly innovative, work.

Compared with other managers, Laura was not as sociable. She was a lot older than the rest of her people, by 10 or 12 years. And she was not single—no beer after work, or long lunches. I am disappointed with my own performance managing her. When I took over this department, it was in a crisis mode and needed hours and hours of intensive managing. I didn't spend much time with Laura when she was a new manager. It's a credit to her that she didn't screw up . . . and so, I had no immediate concerns about her performance.

It was different with Natalie. I had reservations about her promotion, too, but mostly because she was so young. And she had only been here a couple of years—typically, the average first-level manager has been an MSS for four years or more. But I needn't have worried. When a promotion announcement is made, someone usually walks out in a huff from the meeting. It's to Natalie's credit that nobody walked out in a huff following her promotion! People acknowledged she was a good candidate for first-level—when Natalie sees a problem, she goes and fixes it herself, whether it is in her area or not. She's outgoing, and does what needs to be done.

DECISION TIME

Adam left Brent's office mentally comparing his choices for promotion to the second-level position. The fact that some were male and others female, caused him to think about the promotional issue more carefully than ever before—given the company's new focus on equal opportunity for its female employees, which person should receive his support? And what about the notion of merit? He realized that the choice for promotion posed a significant challenge.

NOTES

1. http://www19.hrdc-drhc.gc.ca/~eeisadmin/cgi-bin/INTRO.cgi.
2. MSS, or Member of Scientific Staff, was the designation given to a graduate of a four-year honors technical degree program.
3. MTS, or Member of Technical Staff, was the designation given to a graduate of a three-year university degree or community college diploma program.

STAMFORD MACHINE CORPORATION: ALLEGATIONS OF RACISM

*Prepared by Ken Mark under the
supervision of Professor Christina A. Cavanagh*

Version: (A) 2002-03-22

INTRODUCTION

It was May 2001, and Allen Douglas, director of corporate business ethics and compliance of Connecticut-based Stamford Machine Corporation (SMC), received a call from Michael Weisberg, senior partner in New York law firm Weisberg Coltin. Douglas was advised that SMC was being served with a racial discrimination lawsuit from current and former black sales representatives.

The lawsuit was filed on behalf of six salespeople from California, Georgia, New York and Texas, and alleged that white sales managers would routinely exclude black salespeople from opportunities that would allow them to earn higher commissions and promotions. Douglas requested full details from Weisberg, and then sat down to chart a course of action. He knew that Weisberg's next call was to the press.

STAMFORD MACHINE CORPORATION

Founded in 1925, Stamford Machine Corporation had a long history of prevailing against seemingly impossible odds in the office products market: surviving the Great Depression, technology change, entrance and dominance of Japanese and Taiwanese competitors.

SMC designed, manufactured and marketed a range of typewriters, photocopiers and overhead projectors to businesses. With sales approaching US$1 billion in 2000, Stamford senior management believed it had achieved a major milestone. In the 1980s, Asian competitors had entered the fray, changing the sedentary pace of the industry almost overnight. Faced with year after year of large losses, Stamford knew it had to reorganize its business practices.

Throughout the 1990s, Stamford embarked on an ambitious program to overhaul its sales force, rewarding successful salespeople with increasingly larger territories, and transferring or dismissing poor performers. The company avoided its competitor's strategies of promoting successful salespeople into management positions, where they were often ineffective. Rather, Stamford chose to richly compensate salespeople, keeping them in their preferred environment.

The program bore fruit in late 1999, when Stamford became the market leader in the U.S. copier market. With high positive cash flow and growth, Stamford looked poised to remain the leader for years to come.

THE PUBLIC ANNOUNCEMENT BY WEISBERG COLTIN

Weisberg announced in a press release:

> Our clients have described a system where Stamford Machine routinely assigns white salespeople to profitable territories and expeditiously promotes them through ranks, while assigning minority salespeople to traditionally less profitable territories. Our clients charge, furthermore, that no

matter how well minority salespeople perform in their territories, Stamford Machine rarely, if ever, promotes them to more profitable positions and territories.

In a press interview, another attorney in the case, James Fulton, continued:

> Basically, the company would send white salespeople to Wall Street and all the black salespeople to Harlem or the Bronx. The whites would sell 30 copiers at Morgan Stanley, and the black salesman was lucky if he sold one machine at a little mom-and-pop business. There was racial steering here, and there was an incredible difference in pay.

Before Douglas could even leave his office, the telephone rang again. It was the state newspaper's business affairs journalist, asking for comment. The journalist, who did not give his name, alluded to the fact that several employees had already voiced their opinion in separate interviews. Douglas was furious but tried not to show it. He calmly reserved comment and thanked the journalist for his interest. Out of concern, he asked the journalist what the employees had told him in their interviews:

- Cory Jameson, who sold for SMC in Atlanta, charged that the company took away his most lucrative accounts in late 1999 as part of a reorganization, giving the accounts to white salespeople. Jameson claimed that many of the representatives who gained control of his accounts not only had less tenure at SMC but also received commissions on several sales that were pending at the time. Jameson had filed charges with the Equal Employment Opportunity Commission in 1998 and received a notice from the commission earlier in 2001 that said he had enough of a case to sue.
- Ferran Ferguson, another black salesperson, said he was assigned a territory in the Bronx, New York, that required a car. When Ferguson notified the company that the territory would be hard for him to cover because he did not have a car, Ferguson alleges that a vice-president told him he was assigned to the Bronx because "blacks and the Bronx go hand-in-hand."

Douglas thanked the journalist again and sat down.

Ottawa Valley Food Products

*Prepared by Sonya M. Head under
the supervision of Elizabeth M.A. Grasby*

Version: (A) 2001-08-03

At 2:30 on the afternoon of February 13, R.J. Jennings received a hand delivered note from Karen Russell, a highly respected and well-liked administrative assistant. The note explained that all of the executive assistants in the company had vacated their respective posts in support of Mary Gregory, and were gathered in the employees' lounge. Earlier that day, Jennings had told Gregory that her employment would not be continued at the end of her six-week probationary period because she was unable to handle the duties necessary to be his administrative assistant.

The Company

Ottawa Valley Food Products (OVFP) manufactured and distributed a line of low calorie and diet food products to national grocery chains. The company was located in Arnprior, a small town about 65 kilometres southwest of the nation's capital. OVFP employed 100 production workers and 18 management and support staff.

R.J. Jennings

Jennings had worked for OVFP for 31 years beginning as a production line worker at the age of 23. He was well-respected by his contemporaries for his plant management expertise. Administration at OVFP felt that much of the company's success could be attributed to Jennings' dedication to operating the most efficient production process in the Ottawa Valley.

Jennings' high expectations for all employees were surpassed only by his own personal standards. It was common to find him working at his cluttered desk past 8 p.m. and on weekends.

Although Jennings was eligible for early retirement in one year, he had indicated no desire to exercise that option. When approached by the personnel department on the issue of retirement, Jennings had quipped that he was too busy to retire.

Ella Arnold

After 10 years as Jennings' assistant, Ella Arnold had taken early retirement at the beginning of January. Her eyesight had deteriorated and, at 58 years of age, Ella felt she could afford to take life easier. Over the years, Ella and Jennings had become close friends. Ella was willing to work overtime, often without pay, and frequently breaking previous personal commitments. In Jennings' opinion, his long-time assistant had a sixth sense for her job. She knew when things were building up for Jennings and would go out of her way to shield him from distractions to his work. Ella often ran errands for Jennings, even on her lunch hours. When Ella retired, the personnel department replaced her with Mary Gregory.

Mary Gregory

Mary started to work as Jennings' assistant on January 16. She had graduated the previous spring with a bachelor's degree in administrative studies from a well-known Canadian university. For the next few months, Mary had travelled extensively throughout Europe and the far east before returning to her family home in Arnprior to start her job at OVFP. She was 24 years old.

The initial episode in a series of events leading to today's predicament occurred on her first day. About an hour into the morning's work, Jennings called Mary on her interoffice line and asked her to bring him coffee and the morning newspaper on her way back from her break in the staff lounge. This request was a morning routine he had practised for almost 10 years. Mary refused, claiming that she was quite busy. However, Jennings had purposely given Mary a light workload on her first day. Nonetheless, he fetched the coffee and newspaper himself and dismissed the incident as first-day jitters.

The second incident was more disturbing to Jennings. For several months, OVFP had pursued an order from a national chain that did not previously carry OVFP's products. The chain's purchasing agent had requested a meeting with Jennings to discuss production and shipping schedules prior to signing a contract with OVFP.

On the day of the meeting with the purchasing agent, Jennings walked into his office late and found Mary chatting to the agent about her previous weekend's activities. Jennings, surprised to find her in his office and shocked by her chatty attitude toward this important client, bluntly asked Mary to leave the office. Within hearing range of the purchasing agent, Mary not only refused Jennings' request, she elaborated that she had not been drafted into the armed services, finished her anecdotal dissertation to the purchasing agent, and only then left the office, slamming the door behind herself.

Jennings was humiliated and sensed the embarrassment of the agent. When the purchasing agent left, Jennings called Mary into his office and demanded an explanation.

Mary simply repeated her earlier comments:

I wasn't drafted into the army. You're not my drill sergeant. I was having a pleasant conversation with a very friendly client, and you were very rude to ask me to leave like you did. That's all there is to it.

This morning, Mary refused to file the previous day's production reports in a filing cabinet that was inside Jennings' office, far away from her desk. He had called her away from her work, into his office, to ask that she file the reports.

"No bloody way," she snapped and stomped out of his office.

Jennings believed he had worked too long and too hard to achieve his current level of respect, and he was not about to hand over control to a "green" college kid. He was a senior manager at OVFP and he felt that his time was better spent on pressing company problems. Ella Arnold had never refused a request, even on her own time.

THE NOTE

Jennings turned his attention to the note he had been handed by Karen Russell. He read it three times before the message hit home. Either he backed down and reversed his decision to release Mary at the end of her probationary period, or all 10 of OVFP's administrative assistants would travel to Ottawa to publicize their grievances on the Canadian Broadcast Corporation's (CBC) six o'clock newscast. The producer of the evening news had promised to air the women's complaint if it was not resolved by show time.

It was now 2:40 p.m. The women had threatened to leave the lounge for the trip to Ottawa by 3 o'clock. Jennings had less than 20 minutes to take action, if he felt action was necessary.

CTV Newsnet (A)[1]

Prepared by Professors Carol Tattersall and Christina A. Cavanagh

On January 15, 2000, Henry Kowalski, senior vice-president, news, had to move quickly to save the reputation of CTV (Canadian Television) Newsnet. Because of a technical error, a tape of its anchor-person, Avery Haines, making degrading remarks about various minorities, had been aired during a newscast. He had no doubt whatsoever about the integrity of Haines, and that the apparent slurs were part of a private self-deprecating joke made, she believed, off-air. Still, none of these facts made his dilemma easier. It was up to him to address the situation, without delay.

CTV's Position in the Canadian Broadcasting Industry

CTV Inc. was one of Canada's pre-eminent communications companies, with conventional television operations across Canada. Its broadcasting signals reached 99 per cent of English-speaking Canadians and offered a wide range of quality news, sports, information and entertainment programming. CTV Inc. had been in preliminary discussions with BCE (Bell Canada Enterprises), which announced a formal offer to purchase in March 2000.

During the previous four years, the company saw significant growth from its roots in family-run regional broadcasting, such as CFTO in Toronto. In February 1999, CTV Inc. was hoping to complete strategic negotiations that would expand the scale of its on-line operations. It was planning to launch an interactive site in the fall of 2000. At the CTV Inc. annual general meeting, Ivan Fecan, the chief executive officer, announced: "We expect to move into entertainment content production in a meaningful way, in fiscal 2000." While Fecan was clearly excited and optimistic about the direction the company was taking, he also, however, drew attention to the extra interest costs that would be incurred by acquisitions.

CTV's main competitor was Global Television, and at the beginning of the year, both companies were claiming to have won the 1999 Fall ratings war, each interpreting differently the statistics compiled by Nielsen Research. Each of the competing broadcasters would have liked to be able to demonstrate definitively its edge in viewer numbers over the other, knowing the weight that advertisers would give to such ratings.

CTV's Goals and Corporate Philosophy

Fiscal 1999 was the first year of operation for the newly formed CTV Inc., although the brand known as CTV Network, had been very well-known to Canadian audiences and advertisers for the past two decades. The consolidation of CTV and its owned affiliates, along with recent restructuring and innovations, had resulted in the creation of a truly integrated Canadian broadcasting and communications company.

Scope of operations included 25 television stations in Ontario, Saskatchewan, Alberta, British Columbia, Nova Scotia, and New Brunswick. Of these stations, 18 were affiliates of CTV, six were CBC affiliate television stations and one, CIVT, Vancouver, was an independent television station. CTV also owned

ASN, a satellite-to-cable program undertaking and had ownership interests in four specialty cable television services: The Comedy Network; Outdoor Life Network; a headline news channel, CTV Newsnet; and CTV Sportsnet.

CTV Inc. also had a 12 per cent interest in History Television Inc. and held a licence for an additional specialty service, TalkTV, which was scheduled to launch in September 2000. CTV Inc. also had a controlling interest in Sports Specials/Pay-Per-View for digital and DTH.

On March 5, 1999, CTV acquired a 68.46 per cent interest in NetStar Communications Inc. The acquisition of NetStar was held in trust pending regulatory approvals. NetStar owned The Sports Network Inc. (TSN); Le Réseau des Sports (RDS) Inc.; Dome Productions Inc. (one of the largest mobile production facilities in Canada) and, through its 80 per cent owned subsidiary, operated the Discovery Channel. NetStar

also had a 24.95 per cent interest in Viewer's Choice Canada Inc. CTV Inc. also had a 50 per cent interest in Landscape Entertainment Corp., a production venture that would produce worldwide content for film, television and the Internet.

At fiscal year-end 1999, CTV Inc.'s balance sheet showed total assets of $1.1 billion compared with $760 million at the end of the previous year. Revenues for the first quarter 2000 showed a slight decline over the same period the previous year, due mostly to softness in conventional television, which was down four per cent compared with the previous year (see Exhibit 1). Consequently, specialty channels such as CTV Newsnet and The Comedy Network were making significant revenue contributions and it was in this area that CTV Inc. would continue to focus.

Ivan Fecan further remarked that "CTV Inc. is still in the process of becoming the powerful,

	Three Months Ended November 30	
	1999 $ (thousands)	1998 $
Revenue:		
Net airtime	140,695	145,826
Production, distribution and sundry	6,119	5,257
Subscriber	4,776	3,856
Total revenue	151,590	154,939
Expenses:		
Programming and production	80,427	84,270
Selling and administrative	23,863	23,419
Operating and administrative expenses	104,290	107,689
Income before interest, depreciation, amortization, other and income taxes	**47,300**	**47,250**
Interest	7,787	4,520
Depreciation	6,786	6,901
Amortization	3,320	3,264
Income before income taxes	**29,407**	**32,565**
Income taxes	14,332	15,987
Income before the following	**15,075**	**16,578**
Equity in income of investees	(650)	(68)
Minority interest	(290)	(194)
Net income	**14,135**	**16,316**
Weighted average of shares outstanding (000's)	57,873	42,701
Earning per share	$0.24	$0.38

Exhibit 1   Consolidated Statement of Income

integrated broadcasting and communications organization it can and will be. We are leveraging the strengths of every part of the company to create a strong whole." He emphasized the company goal of helping clients to "extend their brands along the entire value chain, from the Internet to local retail," and the need to maintain strong personal relationships and community roots across Canada.

CTV Inc. was clearly moving forward and enthusiastic about further expansion in the future, but it was also determined to continue to demonstrate that social commitment was still a priority. Fecan commended the involvement of individual employees in various fundraising and charitable activities. He also pointed to the contribution of CTV's programming, especially the Signature Series, which "had a significant impact on national awareness of injustice and sexual harassment of children," and stated the intention to do many more projects like them.

The 24-hour news channel, CTV Newsnet, had always observed the company philosophy in its reporting, giving generous broadcast time to social issues, local, national and global. In January 2000, Canadian farmers were voicing their desperation about the crisis in Canadian agriculture, and the impossibility of family-owned farms remaining viable without increased government support. On January 16, a massive benefit concert was planned in Toronto solely to create awareness among urban dwellers on the problems faced by Canadian farmers.

One organizer, Liberal MP (Broadview-Greenwood) Dennis Mills, was quoted in The Toronto Star (January 13) as saying: "if we can get people to make legislators who live in cities—and 80 per cent of Canada's parliamentarians do—more accountable in dealing with farming and agricultural issues, we'll have succeeded."

Canada's public station, CBC (Canadian Broadcasting Corporation), was planning to air a farm crisis program from 10:00 am Sunday, January 16 until 2:00 am Monday, January 17. On the morning of Saturday, January 15, CTV Newsnet in keeping with its social awareness and

community interest policies was about to air the first of a series of its reports on the situation.

HENRY KOWALSKI

Kowalski was a 25-year veteran of television news and had been with the CTV family since 1984. In the first six years of his career, he worked as head of assignment, specials producer, Toronto bureau chief and Vancouver bureau chief. In 1992, he was promoted to chief news editor, where he retooled the newscast and added several innovative features and segments.

His responsibilities included CTV's flagship CTV News with Lloyd Robertson and Sandie Rinaldo, all local newscasts on CTV's owned and operated stations across Canada, Canada AM and the highly acclaimed W5. Under his leadership, CTV News became Canada's most watched newscast, consistently ranking in the Nielsen top twenty.

In January 1997, Kowalski was promoted to senior vice-president and general manager, CTV News. He was responsible for guiding a team towards the successful launch of CTV Newsnet in October 1997 and for the remake of CFTO News, where he increased the audience and cemented it in first place in the competitive Toronto/Hamilton market.

CTV Newsnet's mandate was to become a significant force in Canadian journalism. In the highly competitive and over-serviced Canadian television market, Kowalski knew that a significant effort would be required to build a new service that would take a leadership position. He was no stranger to this type of challenge.

A NEW ANCHOR-PERSON

Early in December 1999, Kowalski signed 33-year-old Haines on a probationary contract to anchor the station's 24-hour cable news channel. Haines had been with the Toronto radio station CFRB for 11 years, having been hired straight from college by Bill Carroll, its news director.

Haines was eager to make the move from radio to television, and Kowalski was impressed with her qualifications: not only had she won several awards in newscasting, but she was well liked and respected by her peers and superiors, and was already a popular radio personality with an enthusiastic following. He felt that she would be a good fit in the fast-paced and demanding milieu of television news and had the ability, ambition and charisma that CTV Newsnet was looking to acquire. He had enjoyed the interview and found Haines relaxed, animated, composed and personable. In all, he was very confident that Haines would quickly adapt and grow into this challenging position.

AN EXCELLENT FIT

Nearly two months had passed, and Kowalski was very pleased with Haines's progress. She had adjusted adeptly to the new medium, and her charisma translated well from voice to visual: she had impressive screen presence. Besides the implicit public approval, Haines seemed already to have gained the support and even affection of all her co-workers. She appeared inherently interested in everyone and everything, and exuded a natural enthusiasm and charm.

It was not only personality, however, that distinguished the new employee, but also her work ethic. Haines gave full commitment to her job; always willing to accept criticism and advice, to apply herself completely to every task, she was also creative and innovative where appropriate. Kowalski felt he had made a good decision and had acquired an employee who would be a great asset to CTV Newsnet.

FLUBBED LINES

On Saturday, January 15, Haines was in the studio taping an introduction to a report on aid for Canadian farmers. For some reason, whether through lack of concentration, or simply because of a slip of the tongue, Haines stammered her way through the opening lines and completely garbled the message. Fortunately this was not a live broadcast, but as a relative newcomer in a very responsible position, Haines felt vulnerable and awkward.

Partly to cover her own embarrassment, but also to ease the tension for the other people in the studio, the anchor person started to make fun of her own ineptness. "I kind of like the stuttering thing," she laughed, "It's like equal opportunity, right? We've got a stuttering newscaster. We've got the black; we've got the Asian; we've got the woman. I could be a lesbian-folk-dancing-black-woman-stutterer." Someone joined in the banter, adding a few other possibilities, and Haines, responded in kind: "In a wheelchair . . . with a gimping rubber leg. Yeah, really. I'd have a successful career, let me tell you." Everyone in the studio knew the statements were very politically incorrect, but the repartee was harmless among those who understood its self-deprecating context, and so typical of the gallows humor among journalists. No one was in the least offended, since Haines herself was a woman of African-Asian heritage. They knew she was poking fun at herself.

Meanwhile, everyone had relaxed, the technicians were ready to roll with a new tape, the original with the flubbed lines having been set aside. Haines went flawlessly through her farm-aid report, and the segment was ready to be aired later in the day.

A TECHNICAL ERROR

It had been a busy Saturday for the technical crew, but despite the re-take, everything was ready to go for the latest broadcast. The control room technician hit play and Haines, composed and pleasant, was on screen–stumbling through her intro to the farm-aid report. "Oh—! Oh—! Wrong tape! Wrong tape!" The cries went up in the studio control room. But things got worse. They realized that not only was the audience seeing Haines, CTV's Newsnet anchor, talking gibberish, they were watching and listening to the appallingly inappropriate exchange that had followed the flawed intro. The tape was rolling and the technical crews were so stunned that before they could react, the short tape had been played in its entirety.

PUBLIC REACTION

The phone lines at CTV's Agincourt studios were flashing instantly with messages from horrified and angry viewers, viewers who had come to trust the integrity and professionalism of CTV. Haines was doing another taped interview when her line-up editor rushed in to tell her about the awful error. Everyone scrambled, as they knew that Haines's comments would be aired by every competitive media source in the Greater Toronto area and could potentially spread beyond. It was essential to apologize on air as soon as possible. Haines was shaken and devastated, more for those she must have horribly offended than for her own sake. She was deeply disturbed that the public, would inevitably, and quite understandably, assume that the bigotry inherent in her remarks represented her real views. She also knew that her position on CTV Newsnet was in jeopardy.

HENRY KOWALSKI'S DILEMMA

Even before Haines's apologies were aired, Kowalski was in the CTV Newsnet studio, quickly trying to get a take on public reaction, and to establish just how this major breach of process could have happened. Regardless of the details or of who was to blame, he was ultimately responsible for managing the brand created by CTV News and now he was faced with the unthinkable—damage control in the wake of a serious error.

Avery Haines had already demonstrated her talent and potential, and clearly was a victim in the fiasco. Nevertheless, Kowalski had to consider the effects of the incident not so much on individuals as on the growing reputation of CTV Newsnet and its ultimate backlash on the parent company, CTV Inc. They could lose major advertisers if the right actions weren't taken. Clearly, this was not going to be a good weekend.

NOTE

1. This case has been written on the basis of published sources only. Consequently, the interpretation and perspectives presented in this case are not necessarily those of CTV Inc. or any of its employees.

2

SEXUAL HARASSMENT

Sexual harassment is problematic for employees, managers, and organizations. The legal definition in the United States identifies two dimensions of sexual harassment. *Quid pro quo* sexual harassment consists of the exchange of work-related benefits or punishments for sexual favors through the use of bribery or threat. *Hostile environment* harassment constitutes unwanted sexual behavior that results in "unreasonably interfering with an individual's work performance or creating an intimidating, hostile, or offensive work environment" (Equal Employment Opportunity Commission [EEOC], 1980, p. 74677). Similarly, in Canada, sexual harassment is legally defined as behavior that may be perceived by the employee as "placing a condition of a sexual nature on employment or on any opportunity for training or promotion" (i.e., quid pro quo harassment) or behavior of a sexual nature that causes offence or humiliation to an employee (i.e., hostile environment harassment). In the United States, sexual harassment is determined by the perception of the victim rather than the intent of the harasser, using the standard of whether a "reasonable woman" would find the incident harassing (Gutek et al., 1999). In Canada, sexual harassment is considered to have occurred if the harasser knew or ought to have known that the behavior was unwanted or if a reasonable observer would consider the behavior to be harassing, taking into consideration the recipient's perspective, including his or her cultural background (see note by Coelho, "Sexual Harassment in the Workplace: Definitions, Cases, and Policy," in this volume).

Researchers have identified three types of sexually harassing experiences: sexual coercion, unwanted sexual attention, and gender harassment (Fitzgerald, Gelfand, & Drasgow, 1995). *Sexual coercion* corresponds to quid pro quo sexual harassment and includes both bribery (e.g., Have you ever felt you were being subtly bribed with some sort of preferential treatment to engage in sexual behavior with a coworker?) and coercion (e.g., Have you ever experienced negative consequences for refusing to engage in sexual activity with a coworker?). *Unwanted sexual attention* and *gender harassment* correspond to hostile environment harassment. Unwanted sexual attention includes a wide range of sexual behavior, both verbal and nonverbal, that is offensive, unwanted, and unreciprocated—for example, repeated requests for dates, sexual comments, or comments about a person's body or attire. Gender harassment refers to a broad range of verbal and nonverbal behaviors that convey insulting, hostile, and degrading attitudes about the person's gender—for example, sexual epithets, slurs or taunts, the display or distribution of pornographic materials, and threatening, intimidating, or hostile acts.

INCIDENCE OF SEXUAL HARASSMENT

Workers report that gender harassment is the most common form of sexual harassment experienced in the workplace. One study indicated that 44% of female university employees reported hearing suggestive stories or offensive jokes in the workplace; 26% reported crudely sexual remarks; 24% reported staring, leering, or ogling; and 22% reported the display, use, or distribution of sexist material or pornography. In the area of unwanted sexual attention, 20% reported experiencing unwelcome seductive behavior, 18% reported unwanted sexual attention, and 11% reported attempts to establish a sexual relationship, despite discouragement. Sexual coercion is less common, but in this study, 11% of female university employees reported unwanted attempts to touch or fondle, 6% reported subtle sexual bribery, and 3% reported subtle threats for sexual noncooperation (Fitzgerald et al., 1988).

Women are far more likely than men to be the victims of sexual harassment, and men are far more likely than women to be the perpetrators (Stockdale, Visio, & Batra, 1999). Most men do *not* engage in the more egregious types of behaviors, such as unwanted touching or sexual coercion. Indeed, a small number of men with a high propensity to harass are responsible for the bulk of coercive sexual harassment experienced by women in the workplace (Pryor, 1987).

Although women are more likely than men to be the victims of sexual harassment, research has documented that men are also sexually harassed at work (Stockdale et al., 1999). The types of behaviors men report to be harassing to them include negative remarks against men (e.g., statements that "men have only one thing on their mind"), lewd comments (e.g., being told offensive or dirty stories or jokes), and enforcement of the male gender role (e.g., a coworker or supervisor saying you were "not man enough") (Waldo, Berdahl, & Fitzgerald, 1998).

A study of 22,372 women and 5,924 men serving in the U.S. Armed Forces found that 37% of men and 76% of women reported being the target of at least one incident of sexually harassing behavior (Stockdale et al., 1999). Compared to only 2% of the women, 53% of the men who provided details about "the most distressing experience" reported that the offender was the same gender. Men's experiences of same-sex sexual harassment seem intended to reinforce norms of hypermasculinity (i.e., a calloused sexual attitude toward women, a conception of violence as manly, and a view of danger as exciting) and were likely to include crude, offensive comments; repeated sexual stories or jokes; and the display of explicitly sexual material.

IMPACT OF SEXUAL HARASSMENT AND COPING STRATEGIES

Employees experiencing sexual or gender harassment suffer stress, lowered morale, and reduced productivity (Fitzgerald, 1993; Gutek, 1985; Schneider, Swan, & Fitzgerald, 1997; U.S. Merit Systems Protection Board, 1981, 1987). One study of 459 women working for a public utility linked experiences of sexual harassment with reduced job satisfaction, reduced life satisfaction, increased mental health distress, and even posttraumatic stress disorder (Fitzgerald, Drasgow, Hulin, Gelfand, & Magley, 1997). Another study of more than 8,500 U.S. federal employees showed that experiencing sexual harassment resulted in higher absenteeism and productivity losses on the job for both men and women (Stockdale, 1998).

Employees who experience sexual harassment can respond in many ways, from ignoring the offense to directly confronting the perpetrator to filing official grievances and lawsuits (Stockdale, 1996). The above-mentioned study of 8,500 federal employees showed that both men and women who confronted their harassers directly experienced worse work outcomes than those who did not use a confrontation strategy (Stockdale, 1998). This finding implies that victims of sexual harassment may experience retaliation for confronting a harasser openly.

MANAGERIAL RESPONSIBILITIES

The high percentages of employees reporting sexually harassing incidents in the workplace should be sobering to managers. As a result of increased absenteeism and reduced productivity, organizations lose the contributions of these employees. In addition, organizations risk financial losses as well as loss of reputation if employees respond to sexual harassment with lawsuits.

Managers who understand sexual and gender harassment dynamics can identify problems and intervene early. Research shows that organizations that take allegations of sexual harassment seriously and impose meaningful sanctions on the perpetrators reduce both the incidence of sexual harassment and the negative consequences resulting from harassment (Fitzgerald et al., 1997).

These findings provide clear direction to managers facing sexual harassment of their employees. Specifically, when managers either receive a complaint of sexual harassment from an employee or observe a sexually harassing incident themselves, they should treat the matter seriously right from the start and offer help. Often, employees cannot control the situation on their own, and if they try confronting the harasser, the situation might simply escalate and become worse (Stockdale, 1998).

If an employee brings a complaint to you, it is important to listen actively and nondefensively. Trivializing the employee's concerns or trying to convince the employee that the incident was not serious simply allows sexual harassment to flourish in your unit. To protect the employee's rights and create a welcoming, professional climate in your workplace, ask the employee what you can do to help and consult with your organization's human resource management department to develop strategies for a solution. If you do not have a human resource manager to turn to, develop a strategy together with your employee for handling the situation in a way that will stop the behavior and ensure full investigation before deciding whether to take any punitive action toward the alleged perpetrator. All reported incidents and actions taken in response should be fully documented and kept on file, in case disciplinary action must be taken.

Prevention is generally preferable to waiting for an employee complaint because employees generally will not complain until the situation has escalated to create serious problems in your unit (Stockdale, 1996). To prevent sexual harassment, you can explicitly state that you expect professional and courteous behavior among employees. You can also be a role model for the professional standards of behavior that you expect. If your organization provides the opportunity, you can send your staff to sexual harassment training, where they will learn the definition of sexual harassment and company policies for handling sexually harassing incidents. Such training is very valuable for its educational content and also because it documents that the company made expectations and consequences clear to employees. Being able to demonstrate that employees knew the rules and consequences clears the way for later disciplinary action that might have to be taken, which can be especially important for handling the small minority of chronic perpetrators who cause the most egregious workplace problems.

In addition, if you observe any form of unprofessional or disrespectful behavior in your group, it is important to intercede and state that courtesy and professionalism is expected at all times. Some members of your group may need additional one-on-one coaching regarding professional workplace norms, and in these cases, you should document any warnings and direction you give to the employee. If, after repeated warnings and discussions, a member of your group does not stop engaging in sexually harassing behavior, you may have to remove the person from your organization.

READING

Sexual Harassment in the Workplace: Definitions, Cases and Policy

This note provides background information on sexual harassment in the workplace. Discussed are what constitutes sexual harassment, the rights of employees under the Human Rights Code, corporate liability in such circumstances, and typical remedies to sexual harassment complaints. In addition, suggestions for designing a sexual harassment policy are presented along with an example of one corporate policy. Finally, a number of significant sexual harassment cases from Canada and their outcomes are presented.

CASES

Rebecca Collier

A team of undergraduate business students consisting of three men and one woman works together on a 48-hour stress examination. The sexual joking that was commonplace and usually considered innocuous among this group, three of whom were friends, escalates until the woman feels a hostile environment has been created. The impact on the students' exam report as well as their relationships is discussed.

Assignment Questions:

1. Trace the key events through the story. To whom would you assign blame for the situation?

2. What could any member of the group have done to prevent the continued escalation of the situation?

3. What action could they take now?

4. As Rebecca Collier, what action would you take?

Ruth Jones (A)

A consultant is trying to sort out her thoughts and feelings after having experienced an appalling incident of sexual harassment by a senior executive in the firm. She must decide what to do now in response to this incident.

Assignment Questions:

1. Should Ruth Jones have handled the incident with Henry differently? Could she have done something to prevent the incident?

2. What should Ruth Jones do in the aftermath of the incident? Should she tell her boss? Should she bring Henry up on charges?

3. What is the firm's responsibility in this situation? If Ruth Jones decides to inform her boss, what is his responsibility?

Telcom

In less than 6 months, a telecommunications company has faced two incidents of alleged violations of the Canadian Human Rights Act. The general manager spent considerable time interviewing employees about the first incident. He then reported his findings, and the Canadian Human Rights Commission confirmed that no discrimination had occurred. Just a few months later, an employee approached her supervisor, alleging sexual harassment by a colleague. The company's general manager must not only deal with the second incident but also wonders whether he needs to draft a human resources policy to outline employee rights and responsibilities under the Canadian Human Rights Act.

Assignment Questions:

1. Analyze the Johnson-Marcado incident and forecast any consequences.

2. What alternatives are available to Mathany with respect to dealing with Johnson and Marcado on Monday morning? What course of action should he pursue?

3. What should be included in a human resources policy to capture the spirit and intent of the Canadian Human Rights Act?

4. What steps would you take to introduce and implement the new human resources policy?

"Most Likely to Sleep With Her Boss . . . and the Winner Is . . . Gail Wilson" (A)

A first-year business student has recently received an award from her classmates, one that was intended as a joke but that had left her feeling embarrassed and angry. Two of her male classmates had created a series of year-end awards to be handed out in fun. She was the recipient of the "Most Likely to Sleep With Her Boss Award." When these awards were given out in a class setting, the student felt uncomfortable and embarrassed but had gone along with it to be a good sport. When she heard that these same "joke" awards were to be given out at the year-end banquet in front of faculty members and the entire student body of the school, she asked one of the creator/presenters to leave her out of the "fun" this time around. To her horror, her classmate did not honor her request, and she was humiliated in front of her teachers and peers in a very public forum.

Assignment Questions:

1. Is Wilson overreacting? Should she be a good sport?

2. Did Bob Schwind and Grant Cooke go too far? Is this a case of sexual harassment?

3. Would it have been different if a male student had been the target of the award?

4. What should be done next? What can Wilson and the teaching team do? What can others do?

5. How can incidents like these be prevented?

REFERENCES

Equal Employment Opportunity Commission (EEOC). (1980). Guidelines on discrimination because of sex. *Federal Register, 45,* 74676–74677.

Fitzgerald, L. F. (1993). Sexual harassment: Violence against women in the workplace. *American Psychologist, 48,* 1070–1076.

Fitzgerald, L. F., Drasgow, F., Hulin, C. L., Gelfand, M. J., & Magley, V. J. (1997). Antecedents and consequences of sexual harassment in organizations: A test of an integrated model. *Journal of Applied Psychology, 82,* 578–589.

Fitzgerald, L. F., Gelfand, M. J., & Drasgow, F. (1995). Measuring sexual harassment: Theoretical and psychometric advances. *Basic and Applied Social Psychology, 17,* 425–445.

Fitzgerald, L. F., Shullman, S. L., Bailey, N., Richards, M., Swecker, J., Gold, Y., et al. (1988). The incidence and dimensions of sexual harassment in academia and the workplace. *Journal of Vocational Behavior, 32,* 152–175.

Gutek, B. A. (1985). *Sex and the workplace.* San Francisco: Jossey-Bass.

Gutek, B. A., O'Connor, M. A., Melançon, R., Stockdale, M. S., Geer, T. M., & Done, R. S. (1999). The utility of the reasonable woman legal standard in hostile environment sexual harassment cases: A multimethod, multistudy examination. *Psychology, Public Policy, and Law, 5,* 596–629.

Pryor, J. B. (1987). Sexual harassment proclivities in men. *Sex Roles, 17,* 269–290.

Schneider, K. T., Swan, S., & Fitzgerald, L. F. (1997). Job-related and psychological effects of sexual harassment in the workplace: Empirical evidence from two organizations. *Journal of Applied Psychology, 82,* 401–415.

Stockdale, M. S. (1996). What we know and what we need to learn about sexual harassment. In M. S. Stockdale (Ed.), *Sexual harassment in the workplace: Perspectives, frontiers, and response strategies* (pp. 3–25). Thousand Oaks, CA: Sage.

Stockdale, M. S. (1998). The direct and moderating influences of sexual-harassment pervasiveness, coping strategies, and gender on work-related outcomes. *Psychology of Women Quarterly, 22,* 521–535.

Stockdale, M. S., Visio, M., & Batra, L. (1999). The sexual harassment of men: Evidence for a broader theory of sexual harassment and sex discrimination. *Psychology, Public Policy, and Law, 5,* 630–664.

U.S. Merit Systems Protection Board. (1981). *Sexual harassment of federal workers: Is it a problem?* Washington, DC: Government Printing Office.

U.S. Merit Systems Protection Board. (1987). *Sexual harassment of federal workers: An update.* Washington, DC: Government Printing Office.

Waldo, C. R., Berdahl, J. L., & Fitzgerald, L. F. (1998). Are men sexually harassed? If so, by whom? *Law and Human Behavior, 22,* 59–79.

SEXUAL HARASSMENT IN THE WORKPLACE: DEFINITIONS, CASES AND POLICY

Prepared by Anjali Coelho
under the supervision of Professor Lyn Purdy

During the 1990s, the highly publicized sexual harassment cases involving Clarence Thomas and Anita Hill, and Bill Clinton and Paula Jones, brought sexual harassment into the public eye. These cases also attracted the attention of corporations, many of whom have since implemented sexual harassment policies, training initiatives and other measures to prevent such occurrences in their workplaces. In today's workplace, employees share details of their personal lives with each other and often have personal relationships with one another outside of work. Hence, it is sometimes difficult to decide what is appropriate conversation/behavior and what is not. A well-written sexual harassment policy and education program can assist with this dilemma.

WHAT IS SEXUAL HARASSMENT?

The *Canada Labour Code* defines sexual harassment as any conduct, comment, gesture or contact of a sexual nature that is likely to cause offense or humiliation to any employee; or that might, on reasonable grounds, be perceived by that employee as placing a condition of a sexual nature on employment or on any opportunity for training or promotion.[1]

Sexual harassment encompasses a wide range of behaviors from sexist remarks to sexual assault. Harassing behavior can include verbally offensive remarks, physical action and gestures, or may simply be visual in nature. Examples of each may include:

Verbally Offensive

- unwelcome jokes, remarks or innuendos;
- sexist remarks about clothing, body, mannerisms or sexual activities;
- sexual invitations, demands or suggestions;
- gender-related verbal abuse, threats or taunting;
- bragging about sexual prowess;
- inquiries or comments about a person's sex life;
- making statements, based on gender, which undermine a person's self-respect or position of responsibility.

Physical Actions and Gestures

- touching someone inappropriately;
- staring or ogling.

Visual

- displaying sexually offensive pictures or other materials.

Flirtation or workplace romance between two consenting adults does not constitute sexual harassment. By definition, sexual harassment is coercive and one-sided; it is unwanted or unwelcome. While more prevalent among women, both men and women are victims of sexual harassment.

THE ONTARIO HUMAN RIGHTS CODE

The Ontario Human Rights Code (the Code) states that every person who is an employee has a right to equal treatment from the employer, or agent of the employer, or by another employee, without discrimination because of sex.[2] The Code covers five areas of interaction: employment; services, goods and facilities; occupancy of accommodation; contracts; and membership in vocational associations such as trade unions.

WHEN IS IT HARASSMENT?

Under the Code, sexual harassment refers to unwanted sexual attention from a person who "knows or ought reasonably to know" that such attention is unwanted. In deciding whether the harasser ought to reasonably know that such comments or actions are unwelcome, two tests are used. First, the harasser's own knowledge of how the behavior is being received is part of the test; the second part takes the point of view of a reasonable third party (i.e., how such behavior might be received). The standard for judging this knowledge has been based on the perspective of a "reasonable person" and has included stereotypical notions of what forms of behavior are, or are not, acceptable. The concept of the "reasonable person" has evolved to take into account the specific perspective of the person who is harassed. This means considering factors (e.g., cultural background, age, etc.) that ought reasonably to be known about the harassed person and about that person's perspective.[3]

Three different types of sexual harassment are listed below. The reward and reprisal scenarios involve an abuse of power in a relationship of trust.

Reward

Implied or expressed promise of reward for complying with a sexually oriented solicitation or advance by a person in a position to confer, grant or deny a benefit or advancement.

Reprisal

Implied or expressed threat of reprisal or actual reprisal for rejecting a sexually oriented solicitation or advance by a person in a position to confer, grant or deny a benefit or advancement.

Poisoned Environment

Sexually oriented remarks or behaviors that create an intimidating, hostile or offensive work environment. A poisoned environment can be created by the comments or actions of any person, regardless of the person's position. The person need not be in a position of power. Furthermore, the comments or conduct need not be directed at a specific person. A person could experience a "poisoned environment" because of membership in the group targeted by unequal treatment or an offensive joke.[4]

More broadly, since sexual harassment refers to unequal treatment based on gender, sexual harassment is sexual discrimination. At times, comments/behavior may not be explicitly sexual but may still constitute harassment if they are related to the person's gender or cause humiliation or offence to the person. For example, someone could indirectly harass a female employee, because of her gender, with the intent of encouraging her to quit her position.

In addition, intent is not necessary to classify behavior/comments as discriminatory. The Human Rights Commission looks at what *result* the treatment had on the recipient. For example, a man may want to compliment an attractive female colleague on her appearance. Even though he may be well-meaning, if it happens frequently or during business meetings, it may set the woman apart as different, and may undermine her credibility in the workplace.

OTHER RIGHTS GUARANTEED UNDER THE CODE

The Code gives individuals the right to enforce their rights under the Code, participate in proceedings and refuse to infringe on another person's rights without reprisal or threat of reprisal for doing so. For example, a person cannot be fired for initiating sexual harassment proceedings against the employer.

As well, a person cannot be discriminated against because of a relationship with a person who is alleged to have been discriminated against (e.g., a colleague who offers to testify in support of a victim of harassment should not be discriminated against or reprised for doing so).

CORPORATE LIABILITY

Employers have a responsibility to ensure that sexual harassment does not occur on their property, in their workplaces or in their facilities. Although harassment is conducted by individuals within a company, the company as a whole may be liable. Under the Code, corporate liability may be found when:

a. the employer's personal action, either directly or indirectly, infringes a protected right, or authorizes or condones the inappropriate behavior; or

b. an employee responsible for the harassment or inappropriate behavior, or who knew of the sexual harassment or inappropriate gender-related behavior or that a poisoned environment existed, but did not attempt to remedy the situation, is part of the "directing mind" of the corporation. Directing mind includes anyone who is in a supervisory/managerial position in an organization.[5]

A number of human rights cases have held the employer responsible when the case involved an executive or managerial-level employee. When employers become aware of inappropriate behavior or comments, they are required to take action right away to remedy the situation. Specifically, if the employer is satisfied that the allegation has been substantiated, then the employer should consider both disciplinary action and preventative steps. Disciplinary measures could range from a verbal warning or a letter of reprimand to termination of employment. Preventative steps may include developing and introducing policy statements and educational initiatives.[6] While individuals who feel they have been harassed may first try to resolve the issue through internal resolution mechanisms, they always have the right to file a claim with the Ontario Human Rights Commission.

It is important for employers to be aware that they may also be liable for incidents that occur outside of work, but that are linked to the employer or the workplace. In fact, a number of incidents of sexual harassment occur at work-related social functions or on business travel.

REMEDIES UNDER THE CODE

Remedies under the code vary depending on the specific case. They might include:

- restoring the complainant to the position that was held before the violation occurred,
- compensation for loss of earnings or job opportunities, or
- damages for mental anguish and humiliation suffered because of the harassment.

In addition, human rights remedies may include requiring changes to an organization's policies, the implementation of training initiatives, the establishment of internal human rights complaint resolution mechanisms, introduction of anti-harassment policies, a written apology, etc.[7]

DESIGNING A POLICY

Under the Canada Labour Code, after consulting with employees, every employer must issue a policy on sexual harassment. The employer must post copies of the policies where they are likely to be seen by employees, and must make every reasonable effort to ensure that no employee is subjected to sexual harassment.

In designing a sexual harassment policy, it is important that the policy include:

- Who is covered, in terms of employees, managers, volunteers, contractors and others;
- What places and situations are covered (e.g., places within the workplace, places off-site, job-related functions such as social functions and travel);
- A definition of harassment;
- What types of harassment are forbidden: some human rights grounds, all human rights grounds and/or other grounds;

- The responsibilities of each of the parties involved: the complainant, the alleged harasser, the manager or other person who receives the complaint, the organization;
- A complaints procedure;
- The consequences to each party when the complaint is valid and when it is not;
- A statement regarding confidentiality;
- The complainant's right to take other action, such as filing a human rights complaint or a grievance under a collective agreement.[8]

For one example, please see Exhibit 1 for The University of Western Ontario's Sexual Harassment Policy.

Although not required, many companies choose to develop policies on "harassment" rather than limit their policies to "sexual harassment." They extend the definition of harassment beyond the grounds identified by the Human Rights Code. For instance, some choose to include the concept of "personal harassment" in their policies. Personal harassment (based on personality clashes or personal dislikes, for instance) is not covered by the Code, but is frequently a subject of action in company policies. Companies hope that by providing guidelines to employees in advance of any incidents, they will be able to avoid problems later on.

SIGNIFICANT SEXUAL HARASSMENT CASES IN CANADA

In Canada, there have been a number of court cases that have set important precedents in the area of sexual harassment. A few of these cases are provided below. Information for these case summaries have been obtained from the Web site www.cdn-hr-reporter.ca.

Sexualized Environment, Position of Trust and Employer Liability: Fariba Mahmoodi Versus University of British Columbia & Donald Dutton (1999)

In this case, the tribunal found that Fariba Mahmoodi was sexually harassed by her professor, Donald Dutton, while she was a student at the University of British Columbia. Two meetings took place at Dutton's home, in a sexualized environment, which included music, candles, wine, dinner, conversation of a personal nature and a present of an audio tape. During the second meeting, Mahmoodi alleged that Dutton kissed and fondled her. She initially gave in to his advances in order to secure his support for her application to graduate school, but later refused additional advances. At the hearing, neither party was found to be credible. Nonetheless, an audio tape that held some conversation between Mahmoodi and Dutton corroborated Mahmoodi's story.

The tribunal found that Dutton controlled a sexualized environment, which failed to acknowledge normal professional boundaries between a professor and a student, and that Mahmoodi did not initiate or welcome the sexualized environment. Dutton also failed to appreciate a professor's position of trust. The tribunal also found the University guilty as it failed to provide Mahmoodi with adequate supervision during the research and writing process for the course she was enrolled in, and that this exacerbated the effect of Dutton's harassment.

The Tribunal found Dutton and the University of British Columbia jointly liable for the harassment. It ordered them to compensate Mahmoodi by reimbursing her for the cost of tuition and books for the directed studies course and by paying her $4,000 for injury to dignity, $5,200 for counseling expenses, $592.01 for expenses related to the audio expert and $3,200 for lost wages and interest on the lost wages and expenses.

Degrading and Rude Behavior Not Necessarily Sexual Harassment: Bailey Versus Anmore (Village) (1992)

In this case, the B.C. Council of Human Rights found that Glennis Bailey was not sexually harassed by her supervisor, Don Brown, when she was employed by the Village of Anmore. Brown did subject Bailey to degrading, rude and puerile behavior and comments, some of which were sexual in their content. Nonetheless,

The UNIVERSITY *of* WESTERN ONTARIO
POLICIES *and* PROCEDURES

1.11 SEXUAL HARASSMENT POLICY AND PROCEDURES

Classification: General   Effective Date: 21MAR91   Supersedes: 26APR84

POLICY

1.00   The University of Western Ontario affirms the right of every member of its constituencies to study and work in an environment free of sexual harassment. The University expects all members of this community to conduct themselves according to standards of professional ethics and behavior appropriate in an institution of higher learning. To this end, this policy applies to all members of the University community.

2.00   In order to develop and maintain an environment free of sexual harassment, it is the policy of the University:

   (a)   to promote a clear understanding and recognition of sexual harassment through the provision of educational and training programs;

   (b)   to hold all persons in positions of authority who make or influence decisions (e.g. supervisors, directors of services and department chairs) accountable for:

      (i)   communicating the tenets of this policy to all who come under their jurisdiction and,

      (ii)   fostering an environment in their area which is free of sexual harassment;

   (c)   to prohibit any act of sexual harassment (subjecting those committing such acts to a range of disciplinary actions);

   (d)   to prohibit reprisal or threats of reprisal against any member of the University community who makes use of this policy or participates in proceedings held under its jurisdiction.

3.00   Notwithstanding this policy, individuals have the right to seek the advice and services of the Ontario Human Rights Commission.

Sexual Harassment

4.00   Sexual harassment is defined as:

   (a)   any sexual solicitation or advance directed at an individual or group by another individual or group of the same or opposite sex who knows (or ought reasonably to know) that this attention is unwanted, or

   (b)   any implied or expressed promise of reward for complying with a sexual solicitation or advance, or

   (c)   any threat of reprisal for refusing to comply with an implied or express sexual solicitation or advance, or

   (d)   repeated behavior, verbal or physical, that, by denigrating an individual or group on the basis of sexual orientation or gender, interferes with the academic or work environment.

5.00   Sexual harassment can be verbal or physical. Examples could include, but are not limited to, behavior such as:

   (a)   demeaning remarks, jokes or other types of verbal abuse of a sexual or sexist nature directed at an individual or group, or

   (b)   the inappropriate and uncalled for comments about an individual's dress or body, or

   (c)   the inappropriate and uncalled for display in the workplace of sexually suggestive objects or pictures, or

   (d)   unnecessary touching, offensive gestures, or

Exhibit 1   The University of Western Ontario's Sexual Harassment Policy   *(Continued)*

(e) compromising invitations, or

(f) demands for sexual favors, or

(g) sexual assault (an offense under the Criminal Code).

Sexual Harassment Office

6.00 Sexual Harassment Officers will be appointed by the President. The appointments will include at least one female and one male. The Officers will report to the President through the Employment Equity Officer who will provide day-to-day support and assistance for the Office.

7.00 The Terms of Reference for these positions shall be:

(a) To increase awareness of the issue of sexual harassment and to provide education to the University community through programs developed to address the needs of all the constituencies;

(b) to be the official contact in receiving allegations of sexual harassment and under certain circumstances to initiate action to protect the complainant(s);

(c) to provide a *confidential advisory service* to any individual or group on complaints of sexual harassment, which may include:

  (i) hearing the concerns of the complainant;

  (ii) assisting the complainant in determining if sexual harassment has occurred; and

  (iii) delineating options for action available to the complainant.

  As appropriate, an Officer may also:

  (iv) investigate the complaint;

  (v) assist in the formulation of a written complaint;

  (vi) advise the respondent and complainant of their rights and responsibilities under University policy and of their option to pursue any other legal avenues that may be available;

  (vii) terminate an investigation; and

  (viii) proceed with a complaint, where warranted, either at the request of a complainant or independently.

(d) to act as a referral to other agencies for other forms of counselling;

(e) to maintain complete statistics on all matters of sexual harassment;

(f) to maintain complete records on all matters of sexual harassment which shall be held in absolute confidence within the Sexual Harassment Office;

(g) to report annually to the University community through the President. The report will contain statistics on matters relating to sexual harassment while maintaining anonymity and confidentiality.

11.02 The Sexual Harassment Officer shall be responsible for carriage of a complaint before the Human Relations Tribunal (or before an External Adjudicator, should one be appointed) and may be represented by legal counsel.

11.03 The complainant and respondent may be accompanied by a colleague from the University community or may be represented by legal counsel.

12.00 The Human Relations Tribunal (and the External Adjudicator, where appropriate) shall report to the President, including its findings and recommendations.

Exhibit 1   The University of Western Ontario's Sexual Harassment Policy   *(Continued)*

13.00   The final decision for the imposition of any sanction or granting of any relief rests with the President who will have due regard for the conditions of employment and academic regulations regarding discipline or termination, as detailed within each agreement between the University and its faculty, staff and students. The President will inform all parties, in confidence, of the decision on the course of action to be taken and the reasons for that decision.

Review

14.00   It will be the responsibility of the President to initiate a review of this policy and its procedures within five years of its adoption, and to report to the Board of Governors, through its Campus and Community Affairs Committee, providing recommendations as may be appropriate.

Exhibit 1   The University of Western Ontario's Sexual Harassment Policy

Source: The University of Western Ontario Policies and Procedures, 2002.

the council ruled that this did not constitute sexual harassment because Brown was equally rude and demeaning in his treatment of male employees.

However, Brown did terminate Bailey's employment, and the Council found that the reason for doing so was the fact that she had filed, or intended to file, a complaint alleging sexual harassment. Her termination thus violated the Code, which prohibits retaliation against any person for filing a complaint.

The Council ordered the Village of Anmore to compensate Glennis Bailey for her full wage loss and to pay her $2,000 as compensation for her humiliation.

Comments Denigrating Sexuality Are Sexual Harassment: Shaw Versus Levac Supply Ltd. (1990)

In this case, the Board of Inquiry found that Carol Shaw was sexually harassed by a co-worker and that her employer was liable for the harassment.

Carol Shaw was harassed over a period of 14 years by a co-worker who constantly criticized her work, denigrated her sexuality and degraded her as a woman. Conduct which denigrates a woman's sexuality or vexatious conduct that is directed at a woman because of her gender also constitutes sexual harassment. Carol Shaw was

subjected to constant negative comments about herself and her performance by a co-worker. Herb Robertson made fun of both the way Shaw walked and her figure by saying "waddle, waddle" when she walked by, or "swish, swish" to imitate the sound of her nylons rubbing against each other. He called her a "fat cow" to another employee and made remarks that indicated his belief that women should be at home looking after their children, as his wife was.

The Board of Inquiry found that Carol Shaw brought Herb Robertson's behavior to the attention of Roger Levac, who was in charge of operations for the company, on a number of occasions over the course of her employment. Levac did nothing effective to stop the behavior, and Shaw left her employment with Levac Supply.

The Board found Herb Robertson, Roger Levac and Levac Supply Ltd. jointly liable for the harassment. It ordered them to pay Shaw $43,273 in compensation for lost wages, as well as $5,000 in general damages.

Sexual Harassment Is Sex Discrimination: Janzen & Govereau Versus Platy Enterprises Ltd. (1989)

In a unanimous decision, the Supreme Court of Canada ruled that sexual harassment is sex discrimination. This overturned a decision of the Manitoba Court of Appeal which found that sexual harassment was not sex discrimination within the meaning the 1974 Manitoba Human Rights Act.

Dianna Janzen and Tracy Govereau were employed as waitresses by Pharos Restaurant in 1982. The Board of Adjudication found that they were sexually harassed by Tommy Grammas, the cook in the restaurant, and that this constituted sex discrimination. The Board also found that Platy Enterprises Ltd., the owners of the restaurant, were liable for the discrimination, and the Board awarded compensation to the two women. On appeal, the Manitoba Court of Queen's Bench upheld the decision of the Board but lowered the amounts of the awards.

The Manitoba Court of Appeal allowed the appeal by Platy Enterprises. Based on the fact that only some, but not all, women were subjected to sexual harassment, the Court reasoned that the discrimination was not because of gender but because of individual characteristics—in this case, the physical attractiveness of the two women.

The Supreme Court ruled that the fact that only some women, but not all women, are the victims of sexual harassment does not mean that the conduct is not sex discrimination. Gender does not need to be the only factor in the discriminatory conduct for it to be sex discrimination; it can be one of many factors. The Court found that the key fact in this case was that only female employees were at risk of being sexually harassed. The women were at a disadvantage because they were women, and no male employee in the situation would have been at the same disadvantage.

The Court found that Platy Enterprises should be held liable for sexual harassment. It also found that the Court of Queen's Bench should not have reduced the awards to the two women, considering the seriousness of the complaints.

NOTES

1. www.info.load-otea.hrdc-drhc.gc.ca/publications/labour_standards/harassment.shmtl, Pamphlet 12 - Sexual Harassment, February 4, 2003.

2. www. ohrc.on.ca, Policy on Sexual Harassment and Inappropriate Gender-Related Comments and Conduct, February 4, 2003.

3. Ibid.

4. Ibid.

5. Ibid.

6. Ibid.

7. Ibid.

8. Ellen E. Mole and Joan A. Bolland, *Best Practices: Employment Policies that Work,* Carswell Publishing, 1998.

REBECCA COLLIER

Prepared by Jennifer Lewis under the supervision of Professor John Haywood-Farmer

Copyright © 2004, Ivey Management Services

Version: (A) 2005-03-09

About noon, one Saturday in late January, Rebecca Collier, an undergraduate commerce student at a Canadian university, was staring out her bedroom window, wondering what to do. She was very tired. Just before 3 a.m. that morning, she had finished a compulsory group strategy project. Although Collier believed the group had done a good job, she was disturbed by many things that had happened between her and her teammates during the project and, as a result, she had not had much sleep. Collier was unsure what she and her three teammates could have done to stop the situation from escalating as far as it had and what action she should take now to let her teammates know how she felt and to avoid similar instances from occurring in the future.

BUSINESS REPORT ASSIGNMENTS

Increasingly, commerce students were required to complete group projects, many of which involved the analysis of a business case and the preparation of recommendations for the management of the organization involved. For the 24-hour strategy project, students were expected to form their own groups of four to six members. Under such conditions, most students chose to work with their friends or other students with whom they had worked successfully in the past.

FORMATION OF THE GROUP

Rebecca Collier, David Rosenbluth and Fred Bly had decided to form a team for the upcoming assignment. The three had been friends for some time and had spent many nights partying together; they had formed a close bond and were more than comfortable together. They had often talked on a range of issues from tough classes and teachers to more delicate matters, such as sex. Although they often joked around in a sexual manner, all three knew the remarks were never intended to harm or make the others feel uncomfortable.

Rebecca Collier

Collier was a very friendly and open individual who highly valued her friendship with Rosenbluth and Bly, often went to them for advice and sometimes joked with them in a sexual context. Her background was in the health sciences; she hoped to pursue a career in the pharmaceutical industry.

David Rosenbluth

Rosenbluth's believed that he had the traits of a "true leader." Rosenbluth often spoke out and

was not afraid to let his voice be heard. He saw himself as being a "people person," who could fit in with any crowd and carry on a conversation with anyone. Rosenbluth's background was in finance; he hoped to pursue a career in investment banking for a major United States firm.

Fred Bly

Bly was extremely friendly, playful and easygoing. He often took a laid-back approach whenever he was in a group. He also tried to make everyone around him feel comfortable, cracking jokes or getting each person involved in one way or another. After three grueling years in the commerce program, Bly still had no idea where his career would take him; he even questioned whether it would be in the business field.

Although Collier, Rosenbluth and Bly had decided that they would work together for the upcoming strategy assignment, they still had to find at least one more student to complete their team. Collier and Bly were enrolled in a marketing course. One day after the Christmas holiday, Collier and Bly had sat in their marketing class beside Viktor Holik, an exchange student from Eastern Europe, who was also taking the strategy course and whom Bly had come to know a little. Holik asked Bly if he knew of any groups for the 24-hour strategy assignment that were looking for additional team members. Bly introduced Holik to Collier and told him that his group was, in fact, looking for an additional member for their team and asked whether he would be interested in joining them. Holik agreed on the spot; he saw Collier and Bly as two very decent and friendly people who often joked and laughed with one another in class.

Viktor Holik

Although Holik was quiet and slightly introverted, when approached by others he was very friendly and easy to get along with. Like Bly, Holik was unsure of what his future would entail—this shared uncertainty had become the common ground upon which the two had built their acquaintance. They often talked and joked about it when they saw each other in class.

BREAKING THE ICE

With only 24 hours to complete the assignment, there would be tremendous time pressure. The day before the project began, Collier, Rosenbluth, Bly and Holik met informally for an hour to get to know each other a bit better and to start discussing how they might tackle the assignment when it was distributed the next day. Although Collier, Rosenbluth and Bly seemed quite comfortable in the group atmosphere, Holik was still somewhat shy. Halfway through the session, Rosenbluth made one of his usual comments to Collier, who responded with a wisecrack of her own. As was not uncommon for these two, both comments had a sexual undertone. Although Holik was a bit shocked at the comments made, Bly reassured him that the three of them "often joke around like that."

THE PROJECT ASSIGNMENT

The 24-hour strategy project began at 8 a.m. Friday and required teams to submit an executive summary by 8 a.m. Saturday. The assignment involved a business case about a company considering a brand extension; students had to analyse the situation and recommend a course of action for the company. Collier and her group met in a reserved room in a local community library. Because she had gone out to a club the night before, Collier was somewhat tired but still in decent form to tackle the assignment. As Collier entered the room, Rosenbluth made a crude comment about Collier's night out and why she looked tired, alluding to whether she had spent the night with another individual she had met at the club. Collier shot back with a comment of her own, stating that she recalled many a time when Rosenbluth had not known where and with whom he had woken up after a night out. Both comments were delivered and

taken in their usual joking manner and in the typical context of their friendship; there was no evidence that either individual had been hurt by the comments directed at them.

The first three hours of work went well. The group analysed the case from a number of angles to improve their understanding of the situation at hand. About that time, the group started to lose focus. Bly, Collier and Rosenbluth cracked a few jokes with their usual sexual context. Although the three were talking only to one another, Holik could clearly hear what was being said. Because of his personality and the fact that Bly was the only one he knew, Holik was timid about joking around with the group. Holik really had no idea of the contours and limits of the group's sexual humor. At one point, Bly tried to involve Holik, who was still working on some analysis, into the conversation. Although Holik felt a bit of pressure to fit in, he subtly turned down the invitation. Soon after, the group regained its composure and resumed working on the case.

At 12:30 p.m., the group decided to take a lunch break and headed to a nearby restaurant for a quick bite. Holik still felt slightly removed from the group, and in an effort to fit in, commented on Collier's great legs. Rosenbluth and Bly greeted his remark was with loud laughter and urged him on. Collier was a bit shocked by the comment, as she only vaguely knew Holik. However, not wanting to make him feel uncomfortable, she tried to go along with the statement. The encouragement of Rosenbluth and Bly brought on two more crude comments before the group entered the restaurant at which point the hilarity died down.

During lunch, Collier started to question the group's respect for her and her feelings. Although she knew that none of the others intended to hurt her and she could handle Rosenbluth's and Bly's comments, with three men talking to her in a degrading manner, she felt belittled. Collier started to question herself: How would other people react if they were in the same situation? She compared her reaction to how her mother, who many considered to be a fairly tough individual, would react. She concluded that her mother would probably say that Collier was being overly sensitive. By comparing herself to her mother, Collier was able to see that her feelings were not consistent with everyone else's. As a result, Collier started to realize that Holik, Rosenbluth and Bly were starting to use poor judgment in realizing the limits of her personality in this academic group setting. To make her situation worse, Collier felt incapable of communicating her feelings to the group for two reasons. First, she knew that Bly and Rosenbluth would question their relationship with her, as they had always joked around in a sexual manner. Second, Collier knew that asking the others to stop would quite possibly jeopardize the group's cohesiveness and thus their prospect of doing well on the strategy project.

After lunch the group returned to their work room. Collier's degree of discomfort continued to rise. More sexual comments continued to surface; some were generic and others were directed specifically at Collier. More importantly, the comments seemed to be becoming more obnoxious. It seemed increasingly clear that no one thought Collier might feel uncomfortable. Although she never clearly indicated that she was upset, Collier started to act increasingly withdrawn and tried actively to stop the comments: "Guys leave me alone. Let's get going on the work." She followed this comment by insisting that the group set a goal of putting their best effort forward with a view to completing what they hoped would be a promising report by 3 a.m. so she could get some much-needed sleep.

After five more hours of work, Rosenbluth got out of his seat and walked over to look at an exhibit Collier was working on. While looking at the computer screen to get an idea of the progress that she had made, he sat down, casually put his arm around Collier, and started massaging her back and neck. Feeling distinctly uncomfortable, Collier stood up; Rosenbluth's arm was now hugging her hips. Because of what had happened earlier in the day, Collier had been unable to concentrate on her work and was seriously lagging behind. Now, Rosenbluth was suggestively touching her! When Rosenbluth discovered Collier's slow progress, he pulled himself away, seemingly frustrated, and turned

to inform the group. Holik, Bly and Rosenbluth, unaware of how Collier had been feeling, raised their voices at the same time. Tension started to build in the group and Collier became increasingly defensive. Before, their comments were intended to be humorous, but each of her teammates' voices now had a much harsher tone. Feeling cornered and vulnerable, Collier remained silent. At about 6:45 p.m., once things had calmed down again, Collier left the room, feeling completely helpless and disoriented as to how the situation had deteriorated to this state. Collier tried to regain her composure in a final effort to complete the project.

When she returned to the group's room at about 7:30, Rosenbluth, Bly and Holik were in the corridor with their coats on. Rosenbluth told Collier that they were going out for dinner and asked if she would care to join them. Collier quietly turned down the invitation. Although Rosenbluth and Bly could both see that Collier was upset, they thought it would be best to leave her alone. They told her they would return at 9:30 to finish the last part of the project.

Collier decided to stay in the building and eat a snack bar while trying to regain her composure. After dissecting the situation repeatedly, she eventually concluded that the best way to get through the final hours of the assignment was to be quiet and contribute to the group as effectively as possible through her written work. She still had an hour left before the others would return. She returned to the group's room and started to work. An early start would not only ensure that she made a positive contribution to the work, but she also believed she would be more productive alone than with the added pressure she felt when with her teammates.

At about 10:10 p.m. Holik, Rosenbluth and Bly returned from dinner. Bly apologized for their late arrival, and the three agreed that they should start working right away. Both Rosenbluth and Bly could see that Collier still seemed uncomfortable around them. Although they concluded that it was best to let the situation settle down, they continued to make occasional sexual comments. Holik, however, apparently did not notice Collier's behaviour. About 12:30 a.m., this lack of judgment finally brought Collier to the edge. Holik had just finished writing up his section of the group's final report and, in an effort to lighten up the atmosphere, he cracked a joke at Collier that he thought fit the group's sense of humor. The joke itself was not unlike jokes he had heard the group of friends say earlier on. After taking a moment to register what Holik had said, Collier stood up and left the room. Although Rosenbluth and Bly both knew Holik's joke would not be well received, neither was able to stop him before the words had left his mouth.

Rosenbluth got up and followed Collier out into the corridor. When he asked her to stop walking away, Collier turned around and told him not move any closer. Rosenbluth saw that tears were starting to build up in Collier's eyes. He suggested that she take a break and return to the room if and when she felt ready.

Collier decided that she would tell the group that she planned to leave at 3 a.m., regardless of the stage of completion of the project. Half an hour passed before Collier returned. Although, upon hearing her decision, Rosenbluth, Holik and Bly pressured her to stay on, Collier refused. The group became frustrated, as they could not complete the project easily without her and believed that she was being a quitter. Feeling pressure from the group as well as trying not to damage their chances of doing well in the assignment, Collier sat back down. However, the pressure she felt at this point prevented her from contributing meaningfully.

The group finished the project at 2:45 a.m., despite the lack of comfort each member felt. When the project was complete, Collier quickly packed her bag and left the room before anyone had a chance to say goodbye. One of the others would hand it in. Although they believed their project was good, each member of the group had been damaged by the experience. Holik felt terrible about how his joke had been received. Bly and Rosenbluth were upset with the state of their friendship with Collier. Collier herself felt very hurt, sullied and uncomfortable.

AFTERMATH

Sitting in her bedroom, Collier did not know what to do next. Numerous questions raced through her mind. Were Holik, Bly and Rosenbluth all equally at fault? Did she share some of the blame? What could she have done to stop the situation before it had gone so far? Granted, Collier would have been able to deal the circumstances differently in a social setting, which is where she usually interacted with Rosenbluth and Bly, but she also felt they should have drawn the line, especially in an academic setting and in the presence of a fourth person none of them really knew. What could she and the others do now to preserve their friendship? Collier was unsure of how to handle the situation in a way that was fair and just and that would prevent this from happening again.

RUTH JONES (A)

Prepared by Professor Mitch Rothstein

Version: (A) 2001-04-05

Ruth Jones, a consultant with Alpha Consulting, was trying to sort out her thoughts and feelings. A few days earlier she had experienced an appalling incident of sexual harassment by a senior executive in the firm. She felt that her trust had been betrayed. She was angry and humiliated. But she also reproached herself for not responding differently, even though, as she kept replaying the events in her mind, she doubted that anything she did would have made a difference in the situation. Most importantly, she had to decide what to do now in response to this incident.

RUTH'S BACKGROUND

Ruth graduated from The University of Western Ontario with an honours degree in Anthropology and a minor in Biology. Both her parents were physicians, and at some point she had also considered becoming a doctor, although she disliked hospitals so much that she did not seriously consider this career option for long. She had also briefly considered a career in law, but after taking one course she realized this was a very poor fit with her interests. By the end of her third undergraduate year, she had developed considerable interest in business and decided that she would get an MBA after her undergraduate degree. Her father had advised her that an undergraduate degree was not as important as a second degree with respect to career choice because an undergraduate education primarily demonstrated your ability to learn or "become educated." Ruth believed that her Anthropology major would not be a problem, therefore, in getting an MBA as long as she had some relevant work experience after her undergraduate degree. After graduation, she planned to return to France, where she had worked the previous summer as an au pair. She had loved France and wanted to go back to live and really learn French. She worked in a medical lab for the summer, and then went to France to attend Domaine Universitaire in Grenoble where she lived for a year and obtained two diplomas in French language and literature. At the end of this year, she moved to England to look for a job.

Initially, Ruth did not have any specific job in mind, but she knew she wanted something that would provide good business experience and enable her to get into the MBA program at The University of Western Ontario. She wanted a job that would stimulate and challenge her intellectually, and involve lots of change. She knew it was important for her to work with people that she liked and respected, and she wanted the opportunity to work as part of a team. Ruth was staying with a cousin in England who coincidentally was working for McKinsey. He suggested to her that she would make a good consultant and encouraged her to look for a job in this area.

Within a short time, Ruth applied for a position at Alpha Consulting. Her interview went very well and she was offered a position as a researcher/analyst. Ruth believed that the job was a perfect fit with her needs and interests at this time in her career. She was delighted to obtain the job offer, in particular because she had beaten out a number of high profile applicants from Oxford. Although she would be the only female consultant in the company, she did not think this was going to be a problem at all. She had interviews with both partners in the firm and they were very professional and collegial. She was very excited at the prospect of working for a small dynamic consulting company and obtaining the type of experience that would contribute significantly to her career goals.

COMPANY BACKGROUND

Alpha Consulting is a "boutique" consulting firm specializing in strategic management. The company was founded in 1986 by two partners, Paul and Michael, who left another consulting firm to go on their own. In addition to Paul and Michael, there was a "senior executive" named Henry, three consultants, and two support staff. Ruth was told that Henry was a "senior executive," but not a partner, due to his involvement in litigation with his previous employer. With the exception of his job title, however, Henry was in other ways regarded as a partner in the firm with respect to his status and power.

Alpha Consulting specialized in advising clients on how to enter new/foreign markets effectively to build a successful business. In this type of boutique consulting firm, the success of the business depended very much on the personal and professional reputations of the three principals, Paul, Michael and Henry. For example, they were able to bring over several clients from their previous firm when they began Alpha. The company was becoming highly successful within its own market niche, particularly in England, France, and Sweden.

EARLY EXPERIENCES

Ruth was thrown head-first into project work as soon as she began the job. There was much to learn, but the smallness of the company and the team orientation facilitated her quick involvement with the company. She quickly became an active team member and felt appreciated by her colleagues. She was excited and happy about her job. Although hired as a researcher/analyst, she quickly became a full consultant when she was assigned to a project in France, since she was the only one in the office who could speak French. Ruth liked and felt very comfortable with everyone in the company with the exception of Henry, the "senior executive," who she had not met during her interviews. There were a lot of rumors and gossip about Henry among the consultants. They told Ruth that Henry was hard to work with and that he was quite formal, even stuffy, and an elitist. He was rumored to be a ladies' man, having been divorced three times. Ruth experienced some of Henry's arrogance shortly after she began her job at Alpha. At the airport, returning from a business trip to Paris, Ruth got up from her chair when boarding was announced. Henry grabbed her arm and pulled her back into her chair, stating that the "plane will wait for us." Ruth presumed that Henry liked to be the last one to board the plane so that people would notice him and think he was important.

As time went on, Ruth got to know Henry a little bit better and understood his role in the company. Ruth found him incredibly bright. He had a number of Masters degrees and a PhD. His primary interest and role in the company was business development and selling projects. He had a valuable network and a talent for convincing clients to hire Alpha Consulting. On the other hand, Ruth found him to be too smooth and

rather manipulative. He did not involve himself in any of the development work or research. Essentially, he would be briefed on the way to a presentation. He often appeared to fall asleep during the presentation made by other members of Alpha but perked up when it was time for him to give his sales pitch. In general, Ruth considered Henry to be quite an eccentric character, and indeed, difficult to work with. But there had been no indication of any unprofessional behavior toward her throughout her first year at Alpha.

After spending over a year based in England and working on assignments in Europe, in addition to her year in France, Ruth was missing Canada. She informed the partners that she was planning to return to Canada for her MBA the following year. The partners did not want her to leave and clearly stated how much she was valued in the company. She attempted to resign but the company had just obtained a few new projects in the United States and they offered these to her since she would be closer to home and it would keep her involved in the company. Ruth decided to continue working for Alpha when she returned to Canada because it would be nearly a year before business school would begin and this opportunity would save her having to look for a new job in Toronto. Also, she wanted to attend the Western Business School, and knew that the MBA program required a minimum of two years' work experience in most cases.

Ruth worked independently out of Toronto and travelled extensively throughout the United States on the projects assigned to her by Alpha. She communicated frequently by phone and fax with either the partners or Henry. One of the projects began with a client meeting in Chicago. Henry flew over from England to attend this meeting as it was standard practice to have one of the partners or Henry, whoever sold the project, to attend important client meetings. Following the meeting, Henry flew back to Europe and Ruth began work on the project, travelling around the northern United States conducting research. A presentation of the interim results was scheduled for a month later at the client's offices in Chicago. Several days before this meeting was to occur, Henry telephoned

Ruth to arrange for a "working dinner" for the evening preceding the meeting. Ruth was somewhat surprised but assumed that one of the partners had convinced Henry to spend more time familiarizing himself with the research on the project. Ruth did not really look forward to meeting with Henry because of the difficulty of working with him, but at least she thought Henry would be more familiar with the project than he usually was which ought to contribute to a more effective presentation to the client. Henry told Ruth that he had booked a table in his "favourite restaurant in North America," but Ruth was not looking forward to this dinner. She knew there was going to be a lot of work to prepare for the presentation and she did not relish the thought of spending an evening with Henry.

THE INCIDENT

Ruth was working in Washington the day before the scheduled meeting in Chicago. Her flight from Washington to Chicago did not arrive until 7:30 p.m. and she had to go directly to Henry's hotel to meet him in time for their working dinner. She left her luggage at the reception desk and met Henry in the hotel bar for a drink before going out to the restaurant for dinner. As Ruth and Henry got into the taxi to leave for the restaurant, Henry told the driver to wait for a minute and turned to Ruth and said that she would not need her briefcase at dinner. He took the briefcase from her before she could reply and went back into the hotel. He returned in a few minutes without the briefcase and they drove to the restaurant. Ruth was concerned that she would not be able to fully brief Henry on the project without her research papers and notes.

On the way to the restaurant, Henry again told Ruth that this was his favourite restaurant in all of the United States and that he had made the reservation from Paris. Apparently, the restaurant owners had told him that the restaurant was closed that night because there was a wine-tasting party in an adjacent private room. However, Henry persisted and because he was travelling all the way from Europe, the owners agreed to serve

him and his guest. Ruth did not quite appreciate the implications of this story until they entered the restaurant and she realized that they were going to be the only two customers there. Ruth began to feel a little strange. Then, when Henry sat her down on a sofa bench and positioned himself right beside her rather than on the opposite side of the table, she definitely began to feel very uncomfortable. Henry proceeded to order a five-course dinner for the two of them, including a different bottle of wine for each course. Ruth noted the outrageous prices on the menu and wine list. She wondered how Henry could justify this on an expense account. She was not very hungry and knew that since she had to be on her toes for the meeting in the morning, she would not be drinking very much. She also was thinking about some additional work she had to do later that evening in preparation for the meeting. However, up until now, she let Henry take control of the situation.

Shortly after the first course arrived, Henry propositioned Ruth. Ruth was completely surprised and, taken somewhat aback, was not sure at first exactly what to do. Initially, she simply ignored him, hoping he would get the message, but she discovered that subtlety was lost on Henry. Henry quickly propositioned her again in a very straightforward manner. Ruth realized she had to be equally straightforward. She was not frightened at all, nor intimidated by Henry in any manner since she had never held him in high esteem. In fact, she and others in the firm had several derogatory nicknames for Henry. Ruth stated in no uncertain terms that she was not interested in Henry's proposition. She tried steering the conversation back to business matters, but Henry was not listening to her and he was not taking "no" for an answer. Throughout dinner, he repeatedly propositioned Ruth, over and over again. At one point, Ruth was keeping count of these propositions but after about 20, each followed by an emphatic "no," she lost count of Henry's repeated suggestions. As the evening wore on and Henry did not give up, his conversation became sillier and sillier to Ruth. He offered to help Ruth set up a Swiss bank account. He insinuated that their relationship would be long-term, although he indicated that the only thing he could foresee coming between them was his children. Ruth thought to herself that Henry was getting crazier and crazier. What possible use could she have for a Swiss bank account, she thought, and Henry's children were only a few years younger than she was, as Henry was 58 at the time.

Throughout the conversation and repeated propositions, Ruth was tense and uncomfortable, but stayed outwardly calm and maintained her professional demeanor while repeatedly telling Henry that she was not interested in his suggestions. Henry ignored everything Ruth told him and began to move closer to Ruth, touching her, putting his arm around her, and attempting to kiss her. Ruth repeatedly told Henry to stop, but Henry continued his advances. Henry was becoming more physically aggressive, and although she was not frightened of the situation, as Henry was relatively small and thin, it was getting out of hand. She remained calm, but pushed Henry back and raised her voice considerably, letting him know that under no circumstances whatsoever, today, or anytime in the future, would she ever consider a relationship of any description with him. Suddenly, Henry seemed to hear her, and immediately moved away and began to sulk. He became very quiet and asked for the bill.

As they waited for the bill, in quiet, Ruth began to think over the situation. Perhaps she had been somewhat naive about Henry's intentions when he told her that she would not need her briefcase during dinner. She reproached herself for consistently giving him the benefit of the doubt and not being suspicious of his out-of-the-ordinary behavior earlier on. Also, although she didn't consider herself a prude in any way, she found the whole situation, being the only customers in the restaurant, the outrageous prices, and Henry's scheme to set all this up, to be rather decadent and pathetic. She was not concerned with what Henry might be thinking, because at last he was quiet and apparently had given up. She wondered if she should have taken action earlier. She had considered leaving the restaurant early on, but had decided to stay because she was alone in a strange neighbourhood in North

Chicago and there was a snowstorm outside, which could have made it difficult to find a taxi. But, perhaps more importantly, she had some practical concerns. She knew she had to work with him the next morning with the client, and she was trying to handle the situation as delicately and diplomatically as possible. She knew that Henry had to be at the meeting tomorrow or the client would be potentially unhappy. She also thought that she did not want to express her real anger at this situation, partially because she was not the type to make a scene, but also because she thought that his eccentric and insecure personality would make him even more difficult to work with, not only the next morning, but in the future. So she continued to grit her teeth and maintain her professionalism in the face of Henry's bizarre and offensive behavior.

Ruth and Henry left the restaurant and hailed a taxi. Ruth was seething with anger and humiliation, while Henry pouted. Once inside the taxi, however, Henry again tried to make advances on Ruth, at one point pinning her against the taxi door. Ruth, again trying to control her anger, told him clearly to stop and that she was not interested in any type of relationship with him. Henry drew back to the other side of the taxi and pouted once again. The taxi had to return to Henry's hotel because Ruth had left her luggage at the reception desk. When Ruth arrived at the hotel, however, she found that her briefcase was not with the rest of her luggage. She asked Henry where he had put her briefcase and he replied, "Oh, it's in my room. I have a wonderful bottle of champagne I brought from France, you must come up and share it with me." Ruth immediately said, no. But Henry, of course, was not listening. He attempted to persuade her to come up to his room over and over. Finally, Ruth told him, "Absolutely nothing would possess me to go to your room. I am leaving, and if you refuse to get my briefcase, just bring it to the meeting tomorrow morning. It contains the presentation material." At this point, the meeting was about seven hours away and Ruth was tired and had reached the end of her string trying to maintain her composure with Henry. She told him that he was acting like a spoiled child and that his behavior was absolutely ridiculous. She then walked away and asked a bellboy to get her a taxi. She realized that she could not do any further work on the presentation at this time of the night and she would have to "wing it" in the morning.

Ruth waited just inside the front door of the hotel while the bellhop tried to find her a taxi as it was very cold that night. Henry disappeared but returned after a few minutes with Ruth's briefcase. Holding onto her briefcase, Henry again tried to get Ruth to come up to his room. Ruth was beyond exasperation and repeatedly said, "No," to Henry's constant suggestions. Still holding onto Ruth's briefcase, Henry suddenly picked up her suitcase as well and ran off out of sight into the hotel. As Ruth's taxi pulled up, she felt tired and sick, angry and humiliated, and simply fed up. She got into the cab and went to her hotel hoping this would be the end to a dreadful evening.

Ruth felt sick all night and was not able to sleep. She went straight to the client meeting the next morning wearing the same clothes as the previous day. Henry arrived with her briefcase containing the presentation and her luggage. She stumbled through the presentation as best she could. The meeting with the client went well and she began to feel a bit better. Throughout the meeting she made no eye contact with Henry, but tried to pretend that nothing was wrong for the sake of the client. She thought that she might find Henry a rather humbled man after the previous evening's incident. However, in the elevator on the way down from the twelfth floor, Henry again propositioned Ruth. Ruth was astounded but at this point she realized that anything she said to Henry was a wasted effort. She walked out of the elevator and out of the office building to look for a taxi. Henry came up from behind her, put his arms around her and kissed her. But finally, she hailed a taxi, closed the door behind her and breathed a sigh of relief as the taxi left Henry standing on the curb.

Ruth had to fly back to Washington immediately to continue the research on the project. Over the next several days she began to reflect on what she had experienced and her thoughts and feelings about her experience were mixed and complex. For example, despite the anger, humiliation and frustration she had felt at the time, she also found herself laughing at the bizarre situation she had gone through. She phoned her sister, with whom she had a close relationship, and together they laughed uncontrollably as Ruth told the story. She also called a colleague in England, with whom she was close, and who also had little respect for Henry, and he expressed serious concerns about the situation. Ruth asked him not to tell anyone at the office, however, until she had some time to think about what she was going to do.

After a few more days, Ruth's feelings began to focus and she realized that she was very angry about what had happened to her and she felt betrayed and violated. She also realized that she was not only angry at Henry, but she reproached herself for not behaving differently at the time. She found herself reliving the incident in her mind over and over, and wondering what she should have done differently at various times. Perhaps she should have expressed her anger more openly at the time, although she thought, "it's really not my nature to make a scene." Perhaps she should have left the restaurant by herself, but at the time there were reasons that she did not want to do this. Was she too passive, she thought, which may have encouraged Henry to continue? She could not help wondering if she was partially to blame, but she knew she had been very straightforward with him, told him exactly how she felt, and in no way gave him any reason to encourage his advances. Nevertheless, she felt disappointed in herself for remaining so calm throughout the situation. Maybe he misinterpreted this attempt to keep things on a professional level. At the same time, she saw Henry as a sad, pathetic character, and in a strange way, felt sorry for him. "Perhaps I was concerned about hurting his fragile feelings," she thought, "and so I did not react more strongly."

Ruth realized that she needed to sort through all these complicated thoughts and feelings about her experience and decide what she was going to do to handle this situation. She thought about simply ignoring it, but knew that this was wrong. Something had to be done because she did not want anyone else to go through a similar experience with Henry, particularly the support staff who could be more victimized by such an incident. She had been faced with inappropriate behavior on two other occasions, both with clients, and although she was uncomfortable at the time, they were relatively easy to handle. Henry's behavior was not only much more intrusive, but in light of his position in the company, also violated a trust that made Ruth especially angry. As a result of her two previous experiences with clients, she had done a lot of thinking about sexual harassment in the workplace and had even spoken to one of the partners about these incidents. Ruth had felt insulted by these experiences. She wondered if the clients were listening to her presentation because she had something interesting to say or because they had something else occupying their minds. She knew she was a friendly person but believed strongly that being friendly did not equate to flirtation and did not have to be misinterpreted. Why should she have to step out of character to do her job? She knew she had to walk a fine line between her friendly, outgoing personality and the need to give a strong impression that she was not interested in anything but a professional relationship. As a result of her experiences, she had an opportunity to think through how she would handle these delicate situations that many women experience in business.

Ruth had to decide what she was going to do in this situation. She knew she had conducted herself professionally at all times with Henry and had in no way encouraged him. Her previous experiences had provided her with a perspective on sexual harassment in the workplace and she knew that Henry's behavior was not only inappropriate and offensive but also against the law. She also recognized that part of her feelings were based on a need for some type of revenge or punishment. She knew there were risks involved in any actions that she might take. She could probably have Henry charged, although this would get very complicated since Henry did not live in North America and she was not entirely sure what the legal situation would involve. She could inform her boss, one of the partners in the firm, although this also involved some risks. She was a "foreigner" working for an English firm and he might think that she was overreacting, or perhaps even take Henry's side, since Ruth was more expendable to the firm than Henry who brought in clients. Although Ruth liked and trusted her boss, this was a different situation and she did not really know what reception this type of news would get. Her parents told her that she might lose her job if she reported it, but she knew she had to do something because Henry could not be allowed to get away with this. He likely would harass somebody else. She had to address her feelings of anger and betrayal, and the bottom line was that her own professionalism was at stake if she failed to do something about this incident.

TELCOM

Prepared by Michael Sartor under the supervision of Professor James A. Erskine

On Friday, February 7, 2003, Tony Mathany, general manager of Telcom, a telecommunications start-up based in Oakville, Ontario was in his office flipping through the *Canadian Human Rights Act* (the Act). Still shaken by an employee's allegation of sexual harassment by another employee, Mathany was unsure whether one of his subordinates had acted in contravention of the Act. Further, if the employee had, in fact, violated the legislation, Mathany wondered whether his company could be held liable for the actions of the employee. Mathany recognized that he needed to investigate the situation further, to develop a course of action to address the employee's complaint and to consider drafting a human resource policy that adhered to the Act.

DEREGULATION OF THE TELECOMMUNICATIONS INDUSTRY

Following efforts in the United States in the early 1980s to dismantle the telecommunications monopoly enjoyed by AT&T, Canada's telecommunications industry began to deregulate. Subsequent to the deregulation of Canada's long-distance telephone industry in the early 1990s, a large number of long-distance telephone companies were incorporated to compete in the provision of long-distance telephone services. However, residential and commercial consumers of local telephone services were still limited to obtaining their local telephone services from their provincial incumbent (i.e., Bell Canada in Ontario). In a series of major telecommunications decisions released in May 1997, the Canadian Radio-television and Telecommunications Commission (CRTC) put an end to the monopoly with respect to local telephone service, effectively opening up most of Canada's $8 billion local telephone service industry to competition. At this point, local and long-distance telephone services were open to full competition.

TELCOM

Telcom was founded to respond to the increased demand for discounted local telephone services among commercial customers in Ontario, as a result of the deregulation of the local telephone service industry. Telcom offered its customers local telephone services, as well as long-distance services, toll-free telephone services and telephone calling cards.

The company employed 35 people in five departments: sales and marketing, regulatory,

information systems, finance and operations (see Exhibit 1).

Telcom sought to be a single-source supplier of a bundle of high quality, reliable and competitively priced telecommunications services and to provide its customers with a "one-bill solution" to their telecommunications needs.

Telcom was targeting small- and medium-sized enterprises that utilized fewer than 100 telephone lines per location and were situated in communities with fewer than 300,000 residents. With more than three million local telephone lines being used by businesses in Ontario, almost 40 per cent of the lines were located in Telcom's target geographic markets. It was estimated that these 1.2 million local telephone lines were being used by 380,000 businesses.

Telcom employed a sales force of independent contractors who developed their own sales networks within communities such as Windsor, London, Hamilton, Oakville, Sudbury, North Bay, Kingston and Ottawa. Telcom provided all of the sales and marketing materials to facilitate sales, and the independent contractors were paid a flat-rate commission for each local telephone service line that they sold. A residual commission, based upon a customer's monthly usage, provided the independent contractor with an incentive to encourage the customer to use additional services (i.e., long-distance services, toll-free services, calling cards, etc.).

Competing with Telcom in the provision of local telephone service to the Ontario market were Ontario's incumbent local exchange carrier (Bell Canada) and five other start-ups. However, the majority of the new entrants decided to concentrate their marketing efforts within the Greater Toronto Area (GTO), providing Telcom with a substantial opportunity to penetrate its target market relatively undisturbed.

TONY MATHANY

Tony Mathany graduated from the law program at Osgoode Hall Law School and passed his Ontario Bar Admission Examinations in 2001.

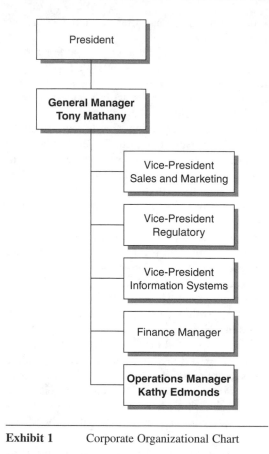

Exhibit 1   Corporate Organizational Chart

THE TELCOM WORK ENVIRONMENT

In terms of valuation, Telcom's principal asset was its customer base. As such, Telcom's success was contingent upon its ability to attract new customers, to facilitate a trouble-free conversion of their telephone service and to provide superior customer service and support following conversion. The smooth and efficient functioning of the operations department was critical to the success of the firm.

After Telcom's sales representatives secured a new customer's signature on Telcom's service contract, the operations department's interaction with the customer commenced. The operations department comprised four teams: the verification team, the conversion team, the moves-adds-changes (MAC) team and the service repair team (see Exhibit 2). Work flowed between members of these teams during their interaction with customers, suppliers and sales representatives during the life cycle of the Telcom customer (see Exhibit 3).

The Verification Team

The verification team was responsible for processing new customer contracts. Once a contract was received from the sales team, the verification team contacted the customer to verify the subscription to Telcom's services. This team effectively provided the customer with a "warm handshake" and welcome to the company, as well as enabling Telcom to confirm that a commission should be paid to the independent contractor who signed the customer to a service contract. A position on the verification team was designed to be an entry-level job since it allowed Telcom to train new employees in the context of a positive customer contact given that few difficulties arose at this stage in the customer life cycle. Three verification representatives reported to the operations manager, Kathy Edmonds.

The Conversion Team

The conversion team ensured a seamless transition from Bell Canada to Telcom. After a customer

During the course of his law school studies, Mathany concentrated on corporate and commercial law, securities regulations, and tax and insolvency law.

Eager to participate in the burgeoning growth of the telecommunications and Internet economy, Mathany bypassed the practice of law and, at the age of 28, he accepted the position of general manager of Telcom. Mathany's prior experience in the telecommunications industry was limited to his summer employment as a door-to-door sales representative for a long-distance telephone company in 1997, while he was still in university. While Mathany had no formal business training, the opportunity to participate in the creation, growth and financing of a telecom start-up promised to be an exhilarating experience.

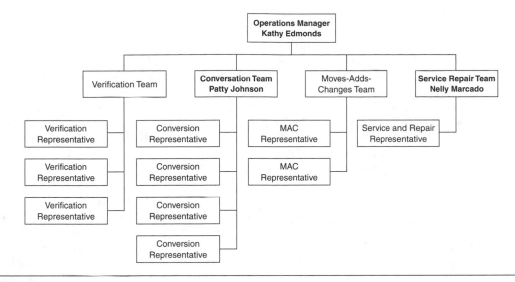

Exhibit 2   Operations Department Organizational Chart

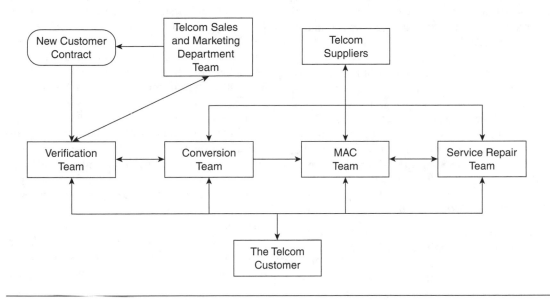

Exhibit 3   Workflow Chart

order was confirmed, the conversion team contacted the customer to make sure the customer's Telcom services had the same configuration as the customer had enjoyed with Bell Canada (i.e., size of the voice mailbox, line rollover, call forwarding numbers, the customer's long-distance calling patterns, such as time of day and destination of calls).

Contact with the customer could last as long as 30 minutes and required more skill than the verification team positions. The conversion team members elicited technical information from customers who were, for the most part, very unfamiliar with the technical configuration of their telephone services. This stage of the customer relationship was most prone to customer cancellation. As such, team members were required to carefully administer this customer contact.

Patty Johnson was the conversion team leader and the most senior member of the five-person conversion team, having worked for Telcom since the company commenced its operations three years earlier.

The Moves-Adds-Changes (MAC) Team

The principal function of the MAC team was to provide ongoing customer service support following conversion to Telcom. The two-person MAC team was responsible for handling routine, but often infrequent, customer inquiries, as well as administering changes to a customer's service configuration. These changes included the addition of new telephone lines or voicemail, moving the customer's telephone service to a new address, as well as changes to a customer's billing information. Both the conversion representatives and service repair representatives were cross-trained on MAC duties to enable them to assist the MAC team during occasional and irregular spikes in customer call volumes (i.e., when a customer invoicing problem impacted the entire customer base).

The Service Repair Team

The service repair team comprised two employees, one of whom, Nelly Marcado, was the service repair team leader. Like Patty Johnson, Marcado had worked at Telcom since its inception. Management regarded the service repair team as the most technically competent and service-oriented members of the operations department. The service repair team was responsible for addressing customers' post-conversion service issues, such as service outages or "static on the lines."

According to operations department employees, a position on the service repair team was the most stressful position within the department. The service repair team routinely dealt with highly agitated and impatient customers, as well as technically sophisticated but poorly service-oriented representatives of Telcom's suppliers, in order to facilitate a resolution to the service issues of Telcom's customers. The volume, nature and complexity of service-related issues could not be forecasted on a daily basis. One service repair team member joked that coming to work each day was akin to being thrown into a barroom brawl.

In order to avoid considerable financial losses associated with losing dissatisfied customers, the service repair team had to be adept at managing customers' intermittent service problems. Team members quickly learned the most effective questions to ask in order to calm the customer and to secure the correct information needed to commence the repair process. Furthermore, it was imperative that team members try to engage the representatives of Telcom's suppliers in a calm, friendly and upbeat manner because the suppliers' representatives became frustrated and defensive if their efforts were not helping Telcom's service repair team to resolve the service issues.

The service repair team was extremely outgoing. Both representatives had positive personalities and enjoyed the opportunity and challenge associated with turning a dissatisfied customer into a loyal customer. Additionally, they had developed a close telephone relationship with their counterparts at Telcom's suppliers. It was not uncommon for the supplier's employees to share their home telephone numbers with Telcom's service repair team in the event that a significant service issue arose outside of normal business hours.

The Operations Department's Call Centre Environment

As a start-up, Telcom's financial resources were very limited. The company secured an advantageous lease rate on a 100-year-old bank building. Mathany's office was situated on the second floor of the building, along with the sales

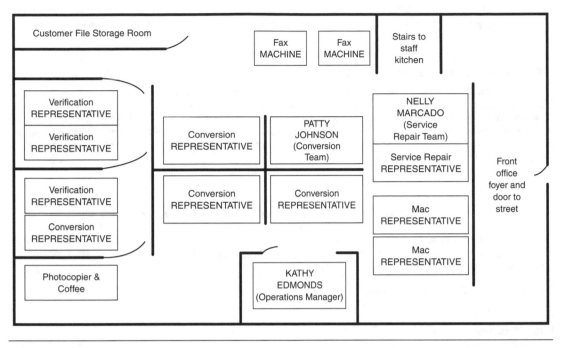

Exhibit 4   Call Centre Layout

and marketing, regulatory, information systems and finance departments.

The first floor of the building was used to house the operations department and was referred to as the "call centre floor." The 2,800 square feet proved to be cramped quarters for the operations department but there was adequate room for each employee to have a computer, a telephone and some workspace. The greatest difficulty with the call centre's configuration was the close proximity between the employees who spent a considerable amount of time on the telephone with customers (see Exhibit 4).

THE INTERVIEW
INCIDENT—SEPTEMBER 2002

In late August 2002, Mathany approved Kathy Edmond's request to hire a verification representative for the operations department, as well as the finance manager's request to hire a telecommunications analyst for the finance department. Telcom placed an employment advertisement in a local newspaper (see Exhibit 5) and requested that the advertisement run in the paper on September 1 and September 12.

Several resumes were received with respect to the telecommunications analyst position, including one from Greg Davidson.

Davidson's cover letter indicated that he had a "strong combination of computer, technical, communication and customer service skills," that he had "worked as a technical support representative . . . providing a wide variety of technical assistance" and that he "was responsible for personal and business computer sales and customer service." Furthermore, under the heading of "communications/customer service," Davidson's resume listed in detail such skills and experiences as "answered telephones, filed and maintained records and handled incoming and outgoing communications." Edmonds felt that he

Telcom is a young and exciting telecommunications company with an exceptional rate of growth situated in Oakville, Ontario.

TELECOMMUNICATIONS ANALYST (#0302)

You have a degree in business and/or accounting and enjoy working with numbers. You are proficient in advance computer applications, specifically spreadsheets and word processing. You are an organized individual and a fast learner who is able to handle multiple projects at the same time. You pay great attention to detail and have a knack for accuracy. Because you will report directly to a Vice-President of the company, you must be able to make timely decisions and produce reports in order to meet deadlines in a fast-paced environment. Experience in the field of telecommunications is a definite asset.

VERIFICATION REPRESENTATIVE (#0303)

You have a minimum of high school education. You have experience working with computers and dealing with business people on the telephone. Your strong communications skills, problem solving abilities and positive attitude will make you successful in our environment. Initiative and the ability to learn quickly are key attributes you posses. Additional languages are a definite asset. You are looking for an entry-level position with opportunity for growth within the company.

Please reference position number and reply to:

Telcom
1280 Explorer Drive
Oakville, Ontario
M6A 3B8

Exhibit 5   September 2002 Employment Advertisement

might be better suited for the verification representative position.

Due to the fact that Davidson did not have a degree in business or accounting, a prerequisite for the position, Davidson was not contacted for the telecommunications analyst position.

On September 3, Telcom received a resume and cover letter from Jason Lambert with respect to the telecommunications analyst position. Lambert seemed to fit the job requirements as his resume indicated that he possessed a bachelor's degree in business administration, with a concentration in finance. Additionally, Lambert indicated proficiency in computer applications such as WordPerfect, Microsoft Word 6.1, Lotus 123 and Excel.

The finance manager contacted Lambert on September 4 to arrange an interview. After the interview on September 5, Lambert was offered the telecommunications analyst position. Lambert accepted the offer and agreed to commence employment on September 10.

On September 5, Edmonds contacted Davidson to arrange for an interview with respect to the verification representative position, despite the fact that he had only applied for the telecommunications analyst position. Davidson accepted the invitation to attend the interview on September 10.

Upon arriving for the interview, Davidson experienced some difficulty gaining entrance to the building since he was in a wheelchair. However, he was able to enter through a side door to the office and made his way to Kathy Edmond's office.

During the interview, Davidson inquired whether the telecommunications analyst position was still open. Edmonds confirmed that the position had already been filled and that Davidson was being interviewed for the verification representative position. Davidson inquired as to how much he would be paid in the verification position. When advised that the standard starting salary for Telcom's verification employees was $9.00 per hour, Davidson indicated that he was making more money at his current job and that he would not be interested in the verification position for this reason. Davidson thanked Edmonds for the interview and left Telcom's office.

Although Telcom had successfully filled the telecommunications analyst position with Lambert on September 5 and Lambert had commenced employment in this position on September 10, the verification position had still not been filled by September 12. Accordingly, Telcom allowed the employment advertisement to run again on September 12. Inadvertently, the entire advertisement was allowed to run again with respect to both positions. Kathy Edmonds had neglected to contact the newspaper to instruct them to remove the portion of the advertisement seeking a telecommunications analyst.

No interviews were conducted in respect of the telecommunications analyst position as a result of the advertisement inadvertently running in the newspaper on September 12, and no further candidates were considered.

On December 18, Telcom received a letter and a Complaint Form from the Canadian Human Rights Commission (the Commission) indicating that Davidson had filed a complaint alleging that he had been discriminated against by the telecommunications company because of a disability (see Exhibits 6 and 7).

Davidson alleged that Telcom told him that the telecommunications analyst position had been filled as of September 10, even though the company ran the employment advertisement again on September 12. Davidson argued that he believed that the September 12 advertisement proved his contention that the telecommunications analyst position was not filled at the time of his interview on September 10 and that he was not offered the position because of his disability.

Mathany conducted an exhaustive internal investigation of the complaint. After interviewing four employees (Edmonds, Edmonds' assistant, Lambert and the finance manager) to review dates, times, the content of verbal exchanges between various parties and all written correspondence related to the matter, Mathany replied to the Commission by providing a detailed timeline of the events related to the recruitment of both the telecommunications analyst and the verification representative. Mathany explained that the September 12 advertisement for the telecommunications analyst position was an oversight and that, in any event, Davidson was not interviewed for the position because he was not qualified. Mathany also confirmed that Davidson was interviewed for the verification position but that he was not interested because he was making more money elsewhere.

The Commission, in turn, confirmed that no further proceedings were warranted, that the investigation was being discontinued and that the file was being closed with respect to the complaint (see Exhibit 8).

Following receipt of the Commission's correspondence, Mathany turned his attention back to the business of running Telcom. He was convinced that his employees had behaved appropriately and that the Commission's correspondence confirmed that no discrimination had occurred. Although he was acutely aware of the importance of complying with human rights legislation, he thought that enough time and effort had been expended on the matter, and he decided that no further action within the company was warranted.

THE CALL CENTRE INCIDENT

On February 7, 2003, at 5:30 p.m., Mathany received a telephone call from Kathy Edmonds. Edmonds indicated that she had received a compliant from Nelly Marcado that Patty Johnson was making inappropriate comments with respect to Marcado's telephone manner with customers and service technicians from Telcom's suppliers.

November 11, 2002

Telcom
1280 Explorer Drive
Oakville, Ontario
M6A 3B8

Dear Mr. Mathany,

The Canadian Human Rights Commission has received a complaint from Greg Davidson alleging that he has been discriminated against by Telcom on the grounds of disability, contrary to section 7 of the *Canadian Human Rights Act*. Enclosed is a copy of the complaint form.

We would appreciate receiving your position with regard to the allegations in the complaint, as well as any supporting documentation, by December 18, 2002. Please bear in mind that the information you provide will be used to decide whether there is sufficient information to submit the matter to the Commission for a decision at this stage, or whether further investigation is required. It is therefore vital that you provide us with a thorough and timely explanation. In the absence of a response, the matter may be referred to the Commission for a decision.

If after reviewing your position with the complainant it is believed that the matter requires further investigation, we will contact you to discuss the next step in the process. Alternatively, if the case is referred to the Commission the investigator's report will be disclosed to you and the complainant, and you will have the opportunity to provide your comments to the Commission for its consideration before a decision is made on the complaint.

This complaint deals with the alleged refusal of employment in that the complainant alleges he was not hired because of his disability.

I would like to draw to your attention section 48 of the *Canadian Human Rights Act* which allows the parties to settle a complaint in the course of investigation. The investigator would be pleased to discuss the possibility of a settlement with you or your representative at any time. I look forward to your cooperation in the investigation of this complaint.

Yours sincerely,

Bob Smith
Complaints and Investigations

Exhibit 6   Excerpts From Correspondence Received From the Canadian Human Rights Commission

More specifically, Marcado alleged that Johnson was teasing her about Marcado's "seductive telephone manner." While Marcado was well-known within Telcom as being extremely adept at calming irate customers and persuading repair technicians from Telcom's suppliers to escalate customers' service repair requests, she was offended and embarrassed by Johnson's comments.

Edmonds went on to explain,

Apparently, this all happened yesterday. I think that Johnson was merely trying to have some fun with Marcado. The problem is that Marcado did

COMPLAINANT:

Greg Davidson

RESPONDENT:

Telcom

DATE OF ALLEGED CONDUCT:

September 12, 2002

ALLEGATION:

Telcom discriminated against me in employment by refusing to employ me on the grounds of disability (paraplegic) in contravention of the *Canadian Human Rights Act.*

PARTICULARS:

- I was involved in a cycling accident where I sustained a spinal cord injury. I am now a quadriplegic and I require the use of a wheelchair. I have been employed for the past three years as a customer service representative for an insurance software company.
- On September 1, 2002, Telcom advertised in the Oakville Observer for the position of telecommunications analyst. Although I do not have a university degree in business, I believe that I have relevant work experience.
- On September 2, 2002, I applied for the telecommunications analyst position because I considered myself qualified, having regard to the other requirements listed.
- On September 5, 2002, I received a telephone message from Telcom. I was invited to attend an interview on September 10, 2002. I did not disclose to the caller that I have a physical disability.
- On September 10, 2002, upon arriving at Telcom's office, I was unable to enter the building through its main entrance because of the steps. However, I did gain access through a side entrance.
- When I met with the respondent's representative, she informed me that the position for which I applied had already been filled. She offered me another position at a rate of pay much lower than that which I earn in my current job. I declined the offer.
- Two days later, on September 12, 2002, Telcom advertised for a telecommunications analyst with the very same job number as the one for which Telcom's representative told me had been filled. I believe that Telcom did not offer either position to me because of my disability.

Exhibit 7   Greg Davidson's Complaint Form

not think that Johnson's comments were humorous at all. In fact, Marcado became really upset when Johnson's banter carried over into the lunchroom in front of several of the other operations department employees. Marcado came into my office a few minutes ago, closed the door and complained that she was being sexually harassed by a colleague. She mentioned that she had called a lawyer friend of hers and the lawyer told her to go and complain to her supervisor immediately. She also said that her lawyer friend told her to consider filing a complaint with the Human Rights Commission. Marcado told me that she simply wants an apology from Johnson. I have just spoken to Johnson about the matter and she said that Marcado would be waiting a long time for any apology from Johnson because Johnson was only kidding and Marcado should know better. I thought that I should speak to you so that we could figure out what to do. I assumed that you probably studied discrimination law so I didn't want to do anything before speaking to you. Do we even have a

January 21, 2003

Telcom
1280 Explorer Drive
Oakville, Ontario
M6A 3B8

Dear Mr. Mathany,

I am writing to inform you of the decision taken by the Canadian Human Rights Commission in the complaint of Greg Davidson against Telcom.

Before rendering its decision, the Commission reviewed the investigator's report and any submissions filed in response to the report. After examining this information, the Commission decided, pursuant to subparagraph 44 (3)(b)(i) of the *Canadian Human Rights Act*, that no further proceedings are warranted because the Commission agrees to the complainant's request to discontinue the investigation of the complaint.

Accordingly, the file on the matter has now been closed.

Yours sincerely,

Nancy Burwell
Secretary to the Commission

Exhibit 8   Excerpts From Correspondence Received From the Canadian Human Rights Commission

human rights policy here? We seem so busy trying to keep up with customer demand that we don't have much time for developing human resources policies. I guess that's another item on our "list of things to do!"

Mathany thanked Edmonds for calling him to apprise him of the day's events. He indicated that he would give the incident some thought and that he would meet with Edmonds on Monday morning to discuss a proposed course of action.

THE CANADIAN HUMAN RIGHTS ACT

As Mathany hung up the telephone, he sunk into his chair and a pit grew in his stomach. He looked over at the copy of the Act, which was still sitting on his bookshelf after he had used it to understand his company's rights and obligations in the context of Greg Davidson's formal complaint last year.

While Davidson's complaint proved to be based upon a mere misunderstanding, Mathany was worried that Marcado might have a legitimate complaint. Marcado had spoken to a lawyer who advised her to file a complaint with the Human Rights Commission. Although Marcado would be satisfied with an apology from Johnson, if Johnson refused, would the harassment continue? How would Marcado respond? It was clear to Mathany that he needed to address the situation at hand and to consider being proactive in developing a formal human resources policy to adhere to the provisions contained in the Act.

DRAFTING THE HUMAN RESOURCES POLICY

As Mathany flipped through the provisions of the Act his eyes began to glaze over. The exercise reminded him of the long days and nights he

The following are some of the sixty-seven sections of legislation comprising the *C.H.R.A.*:

Proscribed grounds of discrimination
3. (1) For all purposes of this Act, race, national or ethnic origin, colour, religion, age, sex, marital status, family status, disability and conviction for which a pardon has been granted are prohibited grounds of discrimination.

Employment
7. It is a discriminatory practice, directly or indirectly,
   (a) to refuse to employ or continue to employ any individual, or
   (b) in the course of employment, to differentiate adversely in relation to an employee, on a prohibited ground of discrimination.

Harassment
14. (1) It is a discriminatory practice,
   (a) In the provision of goods, services, facilities or accommodation customarily available to the general public,
   (b) in the provision of commercial premises or residential accommodation, or
   (c) in matters related to employment, to harass an individual on a prohibited ground of discrimination.

Sexual harassment
(2) Without limiting the generality of subsection (1), sexual harassment shall, for the purposes of that subsection, be deemed to be harassment on a prohibited ground of discrimination.

Exceptions
15. It is not a discriminatory practice if
   (a) any refusal, exclusion, expulsion, suspension, limitation, specification or preference in relation to any employment is established by an employer to be based on a bona fide occupational requirement;

Definitions
25. In this Act . . . "disability" means any previous or existing mental or physical disability and includes disfigurement and previous or existing dependence on alcohol or a drug.

Definition of "discriminatory practice"
39. For the purposes of this Part, a "discriminatory practice" means any practice that is a discriminatory practice within the meaning of sections 5 to 14.

Complaints
40. (1) . . . any individual or group of individuals having reasonable grounds for believing that a person is engaging or has engaged in a discriminatory practice may file with the Commission a complaint in a form acceptable to the Commission.

Designation of investigator
43. (1) The Commission may designate a person . . . to investigate a complaint.

Report
44. (1) An investigator shall, as soon as possible after the conclusion of an investigation, submit to the Commission a report of the findings of the investigation.

Action on receipt of report
(3) On receipt of a report referred to in subsection (1), the Commission:
   (a) may request . . . to appoint a Human Rights Tribunal . . . to inquire into the complaint to which the report relates . . . or,
   (b) shall dismiss the complaint to which the report relates . . .

Exhibit 9   Excerpts from the Canadian Human Rights Act—Chapter H-6   *(Continued)*

Human Rights Tribunal

49. (1) The Commission may . . . request . . . to appoint a Human Rights Tribunal . . . to inquire into the complaint if the Commission is satisfied that . . . an inquiry into the complaint is warranted.

Hearing in public

52. A hearing of a Tribunal shall be public, but a Tribunal may exclude members of the public during the whole or any part of a hearing if it considers that exclusion to be in the public interest.

Complaint dismissed

53. (1) If . . . a Tribunal finds that the complaint . . . is not substantiated, it shall dismiss the complaint.

Order

(2) If . . . a Tribunal finds that the complaint . . . is substantiated, it may . . . make an order against the person found to . . . have engaged in the discriminatory practice and include in that order any of the following terms . . . :

(a) that the person cease the discriminatory practice

(b) that the person make available to the victim of the discriminatory practice, on the first reasonable occasion, such rights, opportunities or privileges as . . . are being or were denied the victim . . . ;

(c) that the person compensate the victim . . . for any or all of the wages that the victim was deprived of and for any expenses incurred by the victim . . . ; and

(d) that the person compensate the victim . . . for any expenses incurred by the victim as a result of the discriminatory practice.

Special compensation

(3) In addition to any order that the Tribunal may make pursuant to subsection (2), if the Tribunal finds that

(a) a person is engaging or has engaged in a discriminatory practice willfully or recklessly, or

(b) the victim of the discriminatory practice has suffered in respect of feelings or self-respect as a result of the practice, the Tribunal may order the person to pay such compensation to the victim, not exceeding five thousand dollars . . .

Offence

60. (1) Every person is guilty of an offence who

(b) obstructs a Tribunal in carrying out its functions under this Part;

Punishment

(2) A person who is guilty of an offence under subsection (1) is liable on summary conviction

(a) if the accused is an employer, an employer association or an employee organization, to a fine not exceeding fifty thousand dollars; or

(b) in any other case, to a fine not exceeding five thousand dollars.

Acts of employees, etc.

65. (1) Subject to subsection (2), any act or omission committed by an officer, a director, an employee or an agent of any person, association or organization in the course of the employment of the officer, director, employee or agent shall, for the purposes of this Act, be deemed to be an act or omission committed by that person, association or organization.

Exculpation

(2) An act or omission shall not, by virtue of subsection (1), be deemed to be an act or omission committed by a person, association or organization if it is established that the person, association or organization did not consent to the commission of the act or omission and exercised all due diligence to prevent the act or omission from being committed and, subsequently, to mitigate or avoid the effect thereof.

Exhibit 9   Excerpts From the Canadian Human Rights Act—Chapter H-6

Source: Canadian Human Rights Act (R.S. 1985, c. H-6).

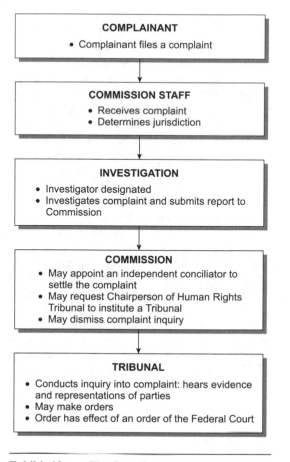

Exhibit 10   The Canadian Human Rights Act
Complaint Process

Source: Shirish Pundit Chotalia, *The 2000 Annotated Canadian Human Rights Act,* Carswell Publishing, 1999.

spent in law school pouring over reams of case law and legislation.

Several questions raced through his mind. What should he do about Marcado and Johnson? Did Johnson's comments constitute sexual harassment? If Johnson had, in fact, sexually harassed Marcado, was Telcom liable and to what extent? What should be included in the policy statement? How technical should he make the statement? Who was the audience for the statement? Once the statement was prepared, how should it be introduced to the staff? Should he simply provide a copy of the Act to each employee? How would he deal with Johnson and Marcado on Monday morning?

Mathany looked at his watch. It was 6:15 p.m. He decided to get started right away and carefully review some of the pertinent parts of the Act while trying to better understand the complaint resolution process (see Exhibits 9 and 10). He had until Monday morning to devise a course of action to address Marcado's complaint and flesh out a policy and associated implementation plan. He turned to page one and began reading:

> The purpose of this Act is to extend the laws in Canada . . . to the principle that every individual should have an equal opportunity with other individuals to make for himself or herself the life that he or she is able and wishes to have . . . without being hindered in or prevented from doing so by discriminatory practices based on race, national or ethnic origin, color, religion, age, sex, marital status, family status, disability or conviction for an offence for which a pardon has been granted. . . .

"MOST LIKELY TO SLEEP WITH HER BOSS . . . AND THE WINNER IS . . . GAIL WILSON" (A)

Prepared by Professor Gerard Seijts

Version: (A) 2002-11-12

INTRODUCTION

Gail Wilson, a first-year student at the Fowler School of Commerce, Mason University, was

getting ready for her year-end banquet. It had been a hectic year for Wilson, with various highs and lows. Most recently, she had fallen victim to what she believed was a deliberate assault on her reputation when two of her classmates presented her with the "Most Likely to Sleep With Her Boss Award" at the end of an organizational behavior class. Though the award was supposed to be satirical, Wilson did not find it remotely funny. She had tried to forget about the incident, knowing that most of her friends thought the award was unfounded and stupid.

Wilson was looking forward to the year-end banquet. Exams were over, and the banquet was the last social function prior to the summer break. It would be a time to relax and have fun. In addition, some of Wilson's classmates had nominated her for the prestigious School Spirit Award, and she thought she had a good chance of winning it.

BACKGROUND

As the school year came to an end, Wilson thought back on it all and was proud. She was proud to be in the commerce program. Wilson had worked hard in all of her courses and felt she had performed quite well, considering the number of talented students in her class. Although she struggled at times with particular subjects, Wilson had persevered and managed to overcome her weaknesses. She realized, in that moment of reflection, how much she had learned. She appreciated and valued more than ever the unique skills the program had taught her. Wilson felt that not only had she learned a tremendous amount from her professors, but also from her peers.

In addition to being committed to the academic program, Wilson had also participated in numerous extracurricular events that were run through the Fowler School of Commerce. For example, she attended the annual Undergraduate Business Games. In addition, she had near-perfect attendance at spirit events, intended to foster a team culture.

Wilson was particularly proud of the status she had recently earned as the joint recipient of the LPC Student Business Award. She was given the award for the development of her graphics business. As the first female recipient in the 15-year history of the national award, Wilson was particularly pleased. To her, the award symbolized that anything is possible if you follow your passion.

However, Wilson's experience in the commerce program was not all a bed of roses. For example, even though she got along with most members of her class, Wilson felt that the class as a whole lacked cohesion. At times, the class seemed too competitive, and as a result, students became impatient with each other. Also, she often heard classmates speaking in a negative fashion about one another. This was particularly evident when the big recruiters came to campus to interview candidates for summer job positions. Students were competing for the good jobs, and a lot of gossiping occurred. Wilson felt that her class did not get along as well as the other two classes of the commerce program did.

Wilson attributed the classroom environment as she saw it to the behavior of several male students. She felt that, at times, their behavior interfered with the class process and subsequent learning, a fact that became more and more evident to Wilson during the final few months of the academic year.

GRANT COOKE

Wilson sat next to Grant Cooke, one of those male students who tended to stir things up, in and out of the classroom, during the final two months of the academic year.

It came to Wilson's attention that Cooke sent out and received links to pornographic Web sites using ICQ messaging. He also made several inappropriate comments about the female students in her class. For example, he was once overheard saying, "Now that's a nice ass!" to one of his female colleagues during a class-break. Wilson explained to Cooke on several occasions that she did not appreciate this behavior, and she asked him to stop showing such disregard for the female students. However, Cooke continued to offer his "commentaries," and Wilson chose to ignore his comments, hoping that if she did not respond to his comments, he would stop.

Wilson was most upset with Cooke one morning when she discovered that, upon returning from the washroom, he had accessed her e-mail account from her PC during her brief absence and had sent an e-mail to a fellow classmate who Wilson especially liked. The e-mail stated:

> Dear Brandon
>   I have been in love with you forever. Please write me back and tell me how you feel about me.
> Love Gail

When Wilson found out that the e-mail message had been sent from her account, she was exasperated! She couldn't believe Cooke would go into her e-mail and send her friend a message like that. She was so embarrassed. Moreover, she felt this action was a violation of her privacy. However, the highlight of these embarrassing situations had yet to come.

THE "MOST LIKELY TO . . . AWARDS"

Two weeks prior to the final exam period, several Most Likely to . . . Awards were given out at the end of an organizational behavior class. This event was scheduled as a means to celebrate the end of the year, a year that had been successful and enjoyable for most students. The awards were intended to be satirical.

Earlier in the year, Cooke had been elected as the social representative for Wilson's class, and the task of organizing and co-ordinating this event fell in his hands. He worked with a classmate, Bob Schwind, to write and present the awards.

It turned out that almost every student in the class received an award. Recipients of awards were asked to come up to the front of the classroom to pick up their certificate, handed out by Cooke and Schwind. The certificates included fake signatures of the dean and the director of the commerce program. Apparently, the signatures were included in an effort to authenticate the award.

While several of these awards were harmless and entertaining (e.g., most likely to become a married couple), others lacked tact or turned out to be an unfortunate choice. Examples of the latter were:

- The Most Likely to Win an Oscar Award was given out to an emotional female student who had difficulties speaking in a public forum.
- The Most Likely to Join Alcoholics Anonymous Award was given to three female students who had had too much to drink at a school get-together. The award turned out to be a slap in the face for one of the recipients, as one of her family members was a recovering alcoholic.
- The Most Likely to Become a Cougar Award was given to Trish Campbell. A cougar refers to a woman aged 35 to 50 who attempts to seduce younger men. Campbell was not pleased with the award and, more importantly, did not understand why it had been given to her. She was irritated, yet not overly upset. She characterized the behavior of Cooke and Schwind as juvenile.

Wilson received the Most Likely to Sleep With her Boss Award. She was embarrassed when the award was called in class. She hesitated to go up and accept the award, but decided to be a good sport. Wilson went up to Cooke and Schwind to receive the certificate, albeit reluctantly.

When the ceremony came to a close, Wilson told Cooke that she did not appreciate the award and that it was given in poor taste. He responded: "I think you took it very well. By accepting it, you showed you know how to take a joke." However, to Wilson, the award was not a joke at all. She was offended and did not see the humor in the award that she had just received.

Several other students were not impressed with the awards presentation. A number of students sent Wilson e-mail messages in which they indicated how badly they felt that she had gone through the ordeal. Others approached her after class. Later in the afternoon, Wilson saw one of the recipients of the Most Likely to Join Alcoholics Anonymous Award crying in the food court. She was talking to Cooke about the award; he seemed to be apologizing. Wilson decided not to get involved.

THE YEAR-END BANQUET

The commerce department's year-end banquet was coming up. The banquet was the last social function prior to the summer break. The banquet provided an evening to celebrate individual and class accomplishments, and all students and instructors typically attended.

The Commerce Students Association social representative, Janice Fanshawe, asked the social representatives of the three classes to come up with ideas for awards to be presented to students at the banquet. Over the years, toasting and roasting students had become a tradition at the banquet. Some of the award ideas that the other two classes compiled seemed rather boring to both Cooke and Schwind. Hence Cooke and Schwind decided to select five Most Likely to . . . Awards to be given out again at the upcoming banquet. The challenge was to choose the five awards that seemed to cause the biggest stir during the class presentation, using input from their class members. Thus, in a sense, the informal award presentation at the end of the organizational behavior class had served as a trial award presentation for the year-end banquet.

Wilson knew that some of the faculty and students who would be present at this banquet would be complete strangers to her. To avoid a repeat of the spectacle that she had encountered in class, she asked Cooke not to repeat her award at the banquet. Wilson felt it was necessary to formally speak to Cooke about the award since he clearly lacked good judgement in these kinds of matters. Cooke responded:

> You are lucky I didn't give out the award I had originally planned. I was going to say, "Most Likely to Be a Secretary . . . Gail Wilson." "Most Likely to Sleep With Her Boss . . . Gail Wilson." And "Most Likely to Sleep With His Secretary . . . Grant Cooke."

He continued: "But, I didn't do it because I knew you'd kill me."

Wilson responded: "You're right, I would have killed you."

Wilson was fairly confident that Cooke would honor her request. She had asked him not to repeat the award, and she hoped that would be the end of it.

3

WORK-LIFE BALANCE

As stated in the introduction to this casebook, one of the major workplace changes in the past three to four decades has been the movement of married women and women with children into the paid labor force (Cohen & Bianchi, 1999). Historically, organizational structures were based on the premise that the most valued workers—specifically, managers, professionals, and skilled craft workers—are heterosexual men whose wives take responsibility for their domestic concerns, including housework and caring for children. Despite the movement of women into the paid workplace, organizational structures have not changed drastically. The highest paid, most desirable positions in many work organizations continue to be arranged in such a way as to make combining work and family life difficult. For instance, work hours do not coincide with school hours, or the work schedule does not allow breaks for children's doctor visits, teacher-parent conferences, or children's extracurricular activities. Many professional and managerial jobs require evening meetings, weekend work, and/or travel, which make it difficult for parents to be present for their children. Old-fashioned work arrangements cause problems for workers with families because "excessive work hours limit time with one's family; the work day either starts too early or ends too late, restricting quality time with the family, and; work schedules often do not mesh with child-care arrangements and other family activities" (Higgins, Duxbury, Lee, & Mills, 1992, p. 35).

As women entered the paid labor force, families could no longer assume that mothers would be present to fulfill children's needs as they arose. Women were the first group to raise the issue of work-life balance to organizational managers, but as younger cohorts of workers enter the labor force, they are asking organizations for a better balance between work and other aspects of life (Smola & Sutton, 2002). Younger workers are more likely to be in dual-career situations, where both adult partners in the family strive to fulfill career aspirations. In addition, younger workers have watched the experiences of their baby boomer parents as corporations jettisoned the notion of employment security in an era of increasing global competition for business. Hence, younger workers know that any devotion they show to the corporation is unlikely to be reciprocated, so that marketability rather than internal promotion has become the reward desired by the most savvy contemporary workers (Arthur & Rousseau, 1996).

WORK-FAMILY CONFLICT

Given the growing prevalence of two-income families, combining work and family has become more difficult, and researchers have identified a variety of forms of work-family conflict resulting from inflexible, old-fashioned organizational structures (Carlson, Kacmar, & Williams, 2000). *Work interference with family* can arise from *time constraints*, as when workers are unable to meet family members' needs because they must spend time away from home and/or conducting work activities. *Strain* resulting from paid work interferes with family when workers are tired, in pain, or emotionally frazzled at the end of the workday and cannot devote the effort and attention needed by their family members. *Behavioral habits* developed in the workplace interfere with family functioning when workers have difficulty modifying behaviors required of them at work. For example, assertiveness, decisiveness, and taking charge are highly valued in a manager but may be less effective for comforting a distraught spouse or child.

Family can also interfere with work. *Family interference with work* can result from *time constraints*, as when a parent must take time off from work to care for a sick child. *Strain* resulting from difficult family situations, such as conflicts in the marital relationship or chronic illness of a family member, may reduce the worker's ability to concentrate on difficult jobs or put forth the level of effort needed to complete work tasks. *Behavioral patterns* developed in the family may be inappropriate in the workplace. For example, deference to elders may be highly appropriate in the family domain but may cause difficulties in relationships between workers who are supervised by managers younger than themselves (Carlson et al., 2000).

Work-family conflicts arising from both work interference with family and family interference with work have negative effects on workers. The results of 50 studies including more than 16,000 workers linked work-family conflict to reduced job and life satisfaction for both women and men (Kossek & Ozeki, 1998). One study of 225 workers showed that the number of children living at home, the amount of stress at work, and the tendency of the individual to experience negative emotions all increased the amount of work-family conflict reported by a worker (Carlson, 1999). In another study of 432 workers, stress and overload at work led to higher levels of work interference with family, resulting in stronger intentions to quit (Boyar, Maertz, Pearson, & Keough, 2003). A third study of 148 professors found that the number of children increased family interference with work while work role stress increased work interference with family, and the resulting job distress led to increased turnover intentions, increased life distress, and an increased prevalence of poor physical health for both men and women (Grandey & Cropanzano, 1999). A study exclusively examining Canadian men showed that men in dual-career families experienced greater work-family conflict than men with a homemaker wife, demonstrating that the change in women's roles has made work-life balance an issue for men as well as women (Higgins & Duxbury, 1992).

WORK-FAMILY ENHANCEMENT

Lest managers decide that workers simply should not have families, it is important to note that research has also shown that workers with satisfying family lives tend to be happier and more effective in the workplace. One study of 122 alumni from a single Canadian university showed that time spent in the parenting role was positively related to organizational commitment, and time spent in community service was positively related to job satisfaction. In the same study, workers reported many benefits of nonwork activities for their work performance, including becoming energized to tackle the challenges of the job, obtaining contacts who are helpful to their work, and developing skills that make them more effective and productive on the job (Kirchmeyer, 1992).

Another study of 790 employees at a U.S. university found that although women experienced emotional depletion at work, which interfered with their ability to care for their families, they experienced emotional enrichment in the family that helped them to cope with their responsibilities at work. In the same study, men experienced emotional enrichment at work, which helped them to better care for their families (Rothbard, 2001). A third study of 177 managerial women found that commitment to the marital and parenting roles was positively associated with interpersonal skills and task-related skills in a 360-degree feedback assessment by the women's employees, peers, and supervisors (Ruderman, Ohlott, Panzer, & King, 2002).

WHY NOT GO BACK TO THE "GOOD OLD DAYS"?

Lest managers decide that women should simply return to the traditional role of wife and homemaker, it is important to develop an understanding of the contemporary social situation. There are at least three reasons that managers cannot simply wish for the "good old days" when fewer women worked for pay. First, single mothers account for about a third of all U.S. and Canadian births. In 2002, only 63.4% of live births in Canada were to married women, and fully 27.5% were to mothers who had never been married (Statistics Canada, 2004). In the United States, 34% of births in 2002 were to unmarried women (U.S. Census Bureau, 2004). Even with child support, which many fathers do not pay (Case, Lin, & McLanahan, 2003), single mothers must develop financial independence to keep themselves and their children out of poverty.

Second, many educated women are no longer satisfied to leave the labor force to devote themselves exclusively to homemaking and child care. Women's career aspirations have risen dramatically in the past three to four decades as structural and legal barriers to their occupational opportunities declined. For example, a study of 270 female college students found that when asked what they would do if forced to choose between marriage and career, 49% indicated they would choose career, and only 38% said they would choose marriage (Novak & Novak, 1996). Clearly, many educated women desire a career as well as children, and they plan the strategies they will use to combine work and family. A 4-year longitudinal study of 207 students participating in a U.S. MBA program showed that women who anticipated having more family responsibilities at a later date showed a preference for jobs providing shorter work hours and greater work flexibility. They did not indicate any desire for less money, less responsibility, or less career advancement than other women, however (Konrad, 2003).

Third, the wages of men with less than a college education have been eroded over time by increased global competition, which resulted in the offshoring of formerly highly paid manufacturing jobs and pressures on corporations to keep payroll costs down (Case et al., 2003). As a result, many contemporary families cannot maintain a middle-class lifestyle with the traditional wife-as-homemaker, husband-as-breadwinner model.

MANAGERIAL RESPONSIBILITIES

Effective managers must understand the need to limit the stress on employees resulting from work-family conflict. Managerial support significantly lessens the negative effects of work-family conflict. For instance, one study of 324 women returning to work after bearing a child showed that supervisor support was one of the most important factors affecting the new mothers' job satisfaction (Holtzman & Glass, 1999). Managers who acknowledge the importance of family to employees and act in a caring manner when employees have family emergencies are valued by employees and reduce the difficulty of balancing work and family responsibilities. When a child is sick or in trouble at school, or an elderly parent requires assistance, employees do not need added stress from a manager who cannot show compassion in these situations.

Organizations can provide a variety of benefits to enhance work-life flexibility, and managers should know their organization's policies. Many organizations offer flexible scheduling, such as flextime, where employees can choose their arrival and departure times from work within certain limits, or a compressed workweek, where employees can work 4 long days instead of 5 regular ones. Increasingly, organizations are offering professional employees the option of job sharing or taking part-time positions during times when family responsibilities are heavy rather than losing these employees altogether (Konrad & Mangel, 2000). With Internet, facsimile, and cellular telephone technology, employers can offer employees flexibility in the place of work, allowing employees in a variety of jobs to work at home one or more days each week (Baruch, 2000).

Although many work-life flexibility benefits exist, not all organizations provide them. The U.S. Bureau of Labor Statistics estimates that only 14% of U.S. workers received assistance for child care from their employers, and only 3% received financial support for child care from their employers in 2004. In that same year, on-site child care was available to 2% of U.S. workers, and employer-sponsored off-site child care was available to 1%. Also in 2004, only 4% of U.S. workers had access to flexible workplace benefits, and only 9% received adoption assistance (U.S. Department of Labor, 2004).

Evidence shows that work-life flexibility benefits have positive effects on employees. Holtzman and Glass's (1999) study of 324 new mothers cited above showed that longer parental leaves, flexible work schedules, and the ability to work at home were all positively related to job satisfaction. Another study showed that providing an on-site child care center was associated with reduced work-family conflict and more positive attitudes toward the organization's benefits package (Kossek & Nichol, 1992). A third study of 745 randomly selected workers in the United States found that employees who had access to work-life flexibility benefits showed significantly greater organizational commitment and significantly lower intentions to quit their jobs (Grover & Crooker, 1995). A summary of 41 separate studies of flextime work schedules showed positive effects on productivity, job satisfaction, and satisfaction with work scheduling, as well as reduced absenteeism, and a summary of 25 studies of compressed workweeks showed positive effects on supervisory performance ratings, job satisfaction, and satisfaction with the work schedule (Baltes, Briggs, Huff, Wright, & Neuman, 1999). A study of 104 telecommuting employees compared to 121 regular employees showed that the telecommuters were more committed to the organization and happier with their supervisors (Igbaria & Guimaraes, 1999).

Offering work-life benefits can also benefit the organization financially. A study of 195 public for-profit firms in the United States showed that among companies employing large numbers of women and professionals, providing more work-life benefits was associated with higher employee productivity, measured as revenues per employee (Konrad & Mangel, 2000). Another study of 527 U.S. firms showed that companies with more extensive work-life programs were perceived as more financially successful (Perry-Smith & Blum, 2000). Given that work-life benefits are associated with positive outcomes for both employees and firms, managers should support the implementation of such benefits if they are not already available in their organizations.

CASES

J. Jerome

A 40-year-old parent of three children is considering a job change. The decision maker must weigh the benefits and challenges of accepting a high-paying, challenging job with a consulting firm, which also involves a move to another city and trying to maintain a "long-distance" marriage. (This case is included only in the instructor's manual.)

Assignment Questions:

1. Complete the questionnaire provided in Exhibit 1 of the case.

Anna Harris

Anna Harris, a highly regarded auditing manager in a large, national accounting firm, wants to return to her job part-time after her pregnancy. Her supervisory partner wants her to come back but is concerned about how clients will respond to a part-time manager looking after their interests.

Assignment Questions:

1. What are the pros and cons of returning Anna Harris to her audit manager position after her pregnancy?

2. What major issues arise if professional firms want to encourage women to raise families and become partners?

3. What actions should Anna Harris and the firm take regarding her part-time appointment and aspirations to become a partner?

REFERENCES

Arthur, M. B., & Rousseau, D. M. (1996). *The boundaryless career.* New York: Oxford University Press.

Baltes, B. B., Briggs, T. E., Huff, J. W., Wright, J. A., & Neuman, G. A. (1999). Flexible and compressed workweek schedules: A meta-analysis of their effects on work-related criteria. *Journal of Applied Psychology, 84,* 496–513.

Baruch, Y. (2000). Teleworking: Benefits and pitfalls as perceived by professionals and managers. *New Techology, Work and Employment, 15,* 34–49.

Boyar, S. L., Maertz, C. P., Jr., Pearson, A. W., & Keough, S. (2003). Work-family conflict: A model of linkages between work and family domain variables and turnover intentions. *Journal of Managerial Issues, 15,* 175–190.

Carlson, D. W. (1999). Personality and role variables as predictors of three forms of work-family conflict. *Journal of Vocational Behavior, 55,* 236–253.

Carlson, D. W., Kacmar, K. M., & Williams, L. J. (2000). Construction and initial validation of a multidimensional measure of work-family conflict. *Journal of Vocational Behavior, 56,* 249–276.

Case, A. C., Lin, I., & McLanahan, S. S. (2003). Explaining trends in child support: Economic, demographic, and policy effects. *Demography, 40,* 171–189.

Cohen, P. N., & Bianchi, S. M. (1999). Marriage, children, and women's employment: What do we know? *Monthly Labor Review, 122*(12), 22–31.

Grandey, A. A., & Cropanzano, R. (1999). The conservation of resources model applied to work-family conflict and strain. *Journal of Vocational Behavior, 54,* 350–370.

Grover, S. L., & Crooker, K. J. (1995). Who appreciates family-responsive human resource policies: The impact of family-friendly policies on the organizational attachment of parents and non-parents. *Personnel Psychology, 48,* 271–288.

Higgins, C. A., & Duxbury, L. E. (1992). Work-family conflict: A comparison of dual-career and traditional-career men. *Journal of Organizational Behavior, 13,* 389–411.

Higgins, C. A., Duxbury, L. E., Lee, C., & Mills, S. (1992). An examination of work-time and work-location flexibility. *Optimum, 23*(2), 29–37.

Holtzman, J., & Glass, J. (1999). Explaining changes in mothers' job satisfaction following child-birth. *Work and Occupations, 26,* 365–404.

Igbaria, M., & Guimaraes, T. (1999). Exploring differences in employee turnover intentions and its determinants among telecommuters and non-telecommuters. *Journal of Management Information Systems, 16,* 147–164.

Kirchmeyer, C. (1992). Nonwork participation and work attitudes: A test of scarcity vs. expansion models of personal resources. *Human Relations, 45,* 775–795.

Konrad, A. M. (2003). Family demands and job attribute preferences: A 4-year longitudinal study of women and men. *Sex Roles, 49,* 35–46.

Konrad, A. M., & Mangel, R. (2000). The impact of work-life programs on firm productivity. *Strategic Management Journal, 21,* 1225–1237.

Kossek, E. E., & Nichol, V. (1992). The effects of on-site child care on employee attitudes and performance. *Personnel Psychology, 45,* 485–509.

Kossek, E. E., & Ozeki, C. (1998). Work-family conflict, policies, and the job-life satisfaction relationship: A review and directions for organizational behavior–human resources research. *Journal of Applied Psychology, 83,* 139–149.

Novak, L. L., & Novak, D. R. (1996). Being female in the eighties and nineties: Conflicts between new opportunities and traditional expectations among white, middle-class, heterosexual college women. *Sex Roles, 35,* 57–77.

Perry-Smith, J. E., & Blum, T. C. (2000). Work-family human resource bundles and perceived organizational performance. *Academy of Management Journal, 43,* 1107–1117.

Rothbard, N. P. (2001). Enriching or depleting? The dynamics of engagement in work and family roles. *Administrative Science Quarterly, 46,* 655–684.

Ruderman, M. N., Ohlott, P. J., Panzer, K., & King, S. N. (2002). Benefits of multiple roles for managerial women. *Academy of Management Journal, 45,* 369–386.

Smola, K. W., & Sutton, C. D. (2002). Generational differences: Revisiting generational work values for the new millennium. *Journal of Organizational Behavior, 23,* 363–382.

Statistics Canada. (2004). *Births, 2002.* CANSIM data tables. Retrieved April 24, 2005, from http://www.statcan.ca/english/freepub/84F0210XIE/2002000/tables.htm

U.S. Census Bureau. (2004). *Statistical abstract of the United States.* Retrieved April 24, 2005, from http://www.census.gov/prod/www/statistical-abstract-04.html

U.S. Department of Labor. (2004). *National compensation survey-benefits.* Retrieved April 25, 2005, from http://www.bls.gov/ncs/ebs/home.htm#data

ANNA HARRIS (A)

Prepared by Dorothy Mikalachki

Version: (A) 2003-06-11

Mark Barron was confronted with a problem that had never come up before in his office. One of his managers, Anna Harris, a highly-regarded auditing and accounting CA in the firm, had just told him that she was pregnant and would be taking maternity leave when her baby was born. The unusual aspect of the problem was that Anna wanted to return to the firm on a part-time basis after her pregnancy, working three days a week. The office had never had a part-time manager, and Mark wondered about the problems this might cause.

THE COMPANY

Mark is a partner working in the audit and accounting group of one of Canada's largest chartered accountancy firms. The firm comprises two major business activities: chartered accountancy and management consulting.

Of the 381 partners in the firm as a whole, nine are women, the first one having been appointed in 1980. The following information on gender statistics of professional staff[1] deals with the Toronto area only. The Toronto area accounts for 40 per cent of the firm's total staff. The figures presented deal only with the chartered accountancy side of the firm.

Hiring

Prior to fiscal 1972, there were very few females hired (none in 1970 and 1971). From 1972 to 1976, women represented about 10 per cent to 15 per cent of the annual intake. From 1977 until 1985, the female complement increased to approximately 35 per cent. In 1985 and 1986, it jumped again to the 40 to 44 per cent range.

Partnership Promotion

Based on the hiring information, one might expect that 10 to 15 per cent of the new Toronto partners since 1982 would be female. (It takes about 10 years to become a partner.) During that period, 48 managers were promoted to the partnership, of which four, or eight per cent of the total, were female.

Manager Promotions

The percentage of new female managers has been approximately the same as the percentage of new females hired five years earlier. (It takes about five years to become a manager.) For example, from 1977 to 1980, 33 per cent of the staff hired were women; five years later, from 1982 to 1985, 30 per cent of the new managers were women.

Manager Retention and Attrition

In 1982, 24 per cent of the new managers were female; four years later, 32 per cent of that 1982 group is female. The same trend holds true for the 1983 and 1984 classes.

Future Female Partners

Based on the fiscal 1977 to 1982 recruiting statistics, which show that approximately 35 per cent of the intake was female, one might expect that a similar percentage of the 1987 to 1992 new partners would be female. However, based on the past promotion of females to partnership and other incidental measurements, it would appear that this percentage will not be reached.

The firm hires fewer women staff outside of Toronto. From Quebec City eastward and Winnipeg westward, only 18 per cent of the managers are women, compared to 30 per cent in the rest of the country.

Mark's office of the firm is located in a medium-sized city in Ontario. There are 20 partners in the office, overseen by a managing partner, with 29 managers reporting to the partners. A manager usually has six staff members reporting to him or her.

There are no female partners in Mark's office. Five of the managers in the office are women, and women constitute about one-third of the CAs on staff.

THE ISSUES

Said Mark:

I didn't want to lose Anna. She is smart, hard-working, and well-liked—she has all of the qualities you need to be a partner. But I was concerned with how our clients would feel having a part-time manager looking after their accounts. Most clients want to talk to their accountants without delay.

Mark's concern with a part-time manager dealing with clients had a personal dimension to it as well. If a client could not get in touch with his or her manager, they often asked for the partner to whom the manager reported. In this case, that would mean asking for Mark, which would involve more business for him to fit into an already busy schedule.

Any partner might well have good reason to be concerned about losing someone with Anna's qualities. According to James Carrothers, a business professor who is also actively involved as a member of the CA profession, the Institute of Chartered Accountants of Ontario is concerned about the decrease in the number and the quality of the students going into CA work. There are, he says, not only fewer people, but fewer well-qualified people in Ontario who are pursuing a CA certificate. Carrothers believes there are a number of reasons for this situation, among them:

1. The differential in salary between university graduates going into a CA firm and those going into a financial group of a business firm.

   The difference in salary is substantial. In 1984, Honours Business Administration graduates from Western averaged $21,300 in salary, while those who went into CA firms averaged $17,600—a difference of almost $4,000 annually.

2. The perceived low pass rate in CA exams and the need to pass qualifying exams in order to write the Uniform Final Exam (UFE). Students may worry about ultimately passing when they see the pass rates from previous years. The provincial pass rates tend to fluctuate. For example, in 1984, Ontario's pass rate declined relative to the other provinces on CA exams. (These exams are marked at the national level.) In 1984, the overall pass rate for Canada increased from 58.5 per cent to 59.3 per cent. Ontario's pass rate decreased from 62.6 per cent to 52.7 per cent.

3. The increase in opportunities now for good university students to apply their skills and knowledge. In the past, CA firms generally attracted the top students. Now, however, these students have a wider range of choices, and may ask themselves, as Carrothers put it, "why they should work in a CA firm to earn less money and run the risk of not passing the UFE."

Carrothers mentioned that at least two of his women students had said they planned to go into CA work because of the flexibility it allowed them as women. They planned to establish themselves in a career, but also to marry and have children. They felt that having a CA would give them the training and professional credentials that would allow them to re-enter the field after time off for child-rearing.

Anna's firm's policies in the area of careers and/or families are set out in the Notes for Professional Staff manual for the firm (see Appendix). However, many of the staff feel that the policies are too general and allow for too much individual interpretation by the partners of the firm. The firm's position is not clear on a number of issues, including part-time work and long-term career prospects for those who do not work full-time while their children are young.

Anna wanted to have children, but she didn't want to jeopardize the career that she had worked very hard at developing. Since high school, she had had the encouragement and support of her father, who felt she should apply her excellent ability in mathematics to pursue a career as a chartered accountant. She received an Honours Business Administration degree from Western, went to work for her current firm, and reached her goal of becoming a CA. Two years later, she was a manager. Her long-term goal is to become a partner in the firm.

Her husband, Eric, is a CA. Both Anna and Eric agreed that they should have their first child before Anna was 30. She explained:

We put off having children until I had established myself and had some credibility at the managerial level. I know there is a lot of opposition to what I want to do from some members of the partnership. It is still definitely a man's world in accounting and business.

Companies are often afraid that women will leave when their husbands are transferred or for maternity, yet out of the 23 people who were hired when I joined the firm, only three are left, and two of us are women. I am the only one of that group left in this office.

It is a waste of manpower not to keep me on. They have spent eight years training me—why lose me? When I leave to have a baby they get six months' notice, which gives them lots of time to plan ahead. When a man leaves, they get four weeks' notice.

Anna knew that by working full-time, with the inevitable overtime in a CA firm, she would not have the amount of time she felt was important to spend with her child.

My priorities are my family, my work, and my leisure time, in that order. I don't think I could not work at all—I think I'd go crazy. Also, I like to have my own money. That way, I have equal say in our decisions.

Many of the other women in the office were interested in how Anna would succeed in her request.

All of the other women are behind me in my asking for a part-time position. I am the guinea pig, and I don't want to jeopardize other women in the office who may want to do this by doing a poor job. I want to have two or three children, so I am looking at four to six years of child-bearing ahead. I know part-time work might hurt my chances of becoming a partner, because I know the type of commitment you have to give to be a partner. If they take me back part-time, I'll just see how it works out. I might consider coming back full-time in a year.

Anna decided that if the firm said "full-time or nothing," she might come back, depending on the partner she had to work with.

Some are easier to work with. I might consider working with someone who is not a workaholic. But if I did have to come back full-time, I would be looking for a job in industry that would be more to my liking. You can find jobs with reasonable workloads and decent pay. I would not like to stop working altogether, as it would be too difficult to come back later on. I would have to become current with all the new laws and would probably have trouble selling myself to an employer.

In summing up her wishes, Anna said:

I have definitely made a mental commitment towards my family and that is definitely jeopardizing my career. Even if I did ignore the family and give my all to the firm, I might not get to be a partner—it's a gamble.

Eric is in agreement with Anna's goals. In addition to his CA, he has an MBA and is the supervisor of planning and analysis in a large multi-media corporation. He felt, as did Anna, that it was important in her profession for her to keep working.

It gives her some alternatives. I would like to see her make partner, although I know that is somewhat jeopardized by having children. I like the idea of her being home with the baby more than 50 per cent of the time—four days out of seven.

Eric felt that Anna would be able to look after most of the household responsibilities since she would only be working part-time. He had grown up in an environment where the mother had the primary responsibilities for the children and the house, and he expected that to continue in his family. He intended to help out with the baby when he came home in the evening.

Anna and Eric both agreed that working part-time was the best solution for them: the baby would have its mother to care for it a reasonable amount of the time, Anna could keep up her expertise in her profession, and the income she earned would be very useful.

Anna and Eric wanted someone to come into their home to look after their child. They knew the cost would be greater, but they felt they could afford it. They estimated it would cost them over $4,000 a year for a sitter, although the maximum deduction under the income tax act is $2,000 for child-care ($2,000 per child to a maximum of $8,000).

Mark was convinced that Anna would not return full-time, and he was equally convinced that he wanted to keep her in the firm. She had good communication skills and got along well with everyone. She also had good teaching skills. This latter quality, Mark thought, might enable her to deal less with clients on her return and do more teaching and training of CA students in the firm.

> She does well at this, and has a pleasing personality. There aren't many who can teach with great proficiency. She has a great talent here.

Not only was Anna a valued employee, but the firm was short-staffed and needed good, experienced people. However, as Professor Carrothers explained, short-staffing is more prevalent at the lower end of the staff hierarchy. CA firms have seen their growth and profitability reduced since the recession in the auditing area, says Carrothers.

> At the managerial level, there are too many people for the number of audit partner slots, so CA firms don't always want to keep all their managers—just the good ones. Specializing helps—for instance, focussing on computer systems or mergers and

acquisitions, or insolvencies. But a CA's strength is usually in auditing, where there is no growth.

When asked about the prospects for a manager who might focus mainly on the teaching and training of CA students, Carrothers replied:

> In CA work, your worth is determined by how much revenue you generate. Teaching doesn't generate revenue.

Some of Carrothers' remarks were echoed by Frank Martin, the Senior Partner of the firm, although he said that there were many paths to partnership, not all of which are revenue-generating ones.

> We are very leering of appointing partners who have only one suit, as they are not adaptable. We have a rare luxury, in that there are many areas in which we can serve clients. For example, employees can move from auditing to management consulting, or to a specialty area, such as mining, sales tax, etcetera. However, the biggest single thing we do is to act as auditors. That is the base of our practice. The largest number of our employees is here.

When asked what qualities he thought a partner should have, he mentioned the following characteristics:

- technical competence
- skill with clients, such as being articulate and persuasive
- adaptability
- administrative skills
- business-getting ability
- initiative and imagination

He added that his acid test is, "Would I really be happy and proud to introduce this person as a partner in the firm? If not, why?"

He agreed that revenue generation is more important than it used to be.

> We are more marketing-oriented now. It is a tough, competitive field where audits are up for grabs all the time. We are a big firm and we have room to accommodate people with different skills. But we have no room for indifference.

In commenting on women in the firm, Martin said, "The women we have are of at least as high a quality as the men." However, he felt that there is still less-than-full acceptance of women by some business people.

I don't think it is a lot, and often it is an initial reaction that is overcome when they deal with the woman. Sometimes the women are treated with more courtesy than the men.

As for women becoming partners, Martin stated that they were appointed on the same basis as the men: on ability.

We have no interest in appointing token women partners. We have no quotas. We are after the best. Men and women are paid the same within a range and the geographical location. In some accounting firms, the first women partners were in personnel, or tax research. Our first woman partner was a client-handling audit manager. Most of our female partners are line people—client-handling professionals.

One of the great debates has always been whether the retention of women in the profession would be as great as men. Our training costs are high, and we lose trained people to industry. A lot of people use firms like us as stepping-stones to something else. I think it is still tougher for women to leave us and get a senior job in industry than it is for men. There aren't many women's appointments at the senior levels announced in the Globe and Mail.

Regarding maternity leave, Martin said:

It is a pain for people working in the auditing practice. It is a personal service business, and the client looks to the partner and manager as their people, available whenever they need them. That is what they pay us for.

The audit area is where it is most difficult to cope with maternity leave. It is harder to substitute here and there are lots of deadlines. It takes about five years to train someone to the manager level. For all practical purposes, it is impossible to hire from outside to fill a manager's position. Accordingly, when someone leaves the firm, whether on two days' or six months' notice, the only possibilities

open to us are to try to have other managers cover off for a period of time or to promote a more junior person to the position. The first option is rather difficult if everyone is already working flat out. The second option is the one we would have to choose in most cases and it sends a ripple right down through the organization, with everyone having to move up one step.

The audit practice may also involve staying late on occasion, for example, when meetings with clients may drag on past normal office hours. A client who is trying to settle all the outstanding audit or reporting problems on financial statements to be presented at a 9:00 a.m. board meeting is not happy to be told that you have to leave to pick up your child at the babysitter's. But we don't have a closed mind on these things, and if we can make it work, we will. Good people are a scarce commodity. We are willing to go the extra mile for them.

Our announced policy is one of flexibility, and we have been willing to try out any arrangement which will accommodate the women in question providing it makes reasonable business sense. However, we have some evidence that different partners are sending out different messages in this respect. One of our challenges will be to eliminate the inconsistency.

Mark Barron felt that the recent technological advances in business would make Anna's part-time position viable. Said Mark:

Over the past five years, the idea of part-time managers has changed. It can be handled in the CA environment today. Anna could manage client accounting from a microcomputer and telephone at home. These could be hooked up to the communication system in the office. However, you still need flexibility with babysitters to handle the uneven demands of CA work.

Mark felt fairly certain that the managing partner would not be enthusiastic about a part-time manager, particularly because of a manager's relationship with his or her clients. Most clients would want their accountant to be readily available, and this would be difficult on Anna's days off. "And," he said:

I don't think Anna could get to be a partner working part-time. It would be difficult for a partner to deal with clients on a part-time basis. I don't think that would work.

The managing partner of the office was not the only partner Mark had to be concerned with, although the final decision would rest with him alone, and he is not obliged to consult with anyone. However, since the firm's CA offices operate as a collegial form of organization, the managing partner would probably want to discuss such an important matter as the part-time employment of managers with his fellow partners in order to have the benefit of their views and to ensure that whatever decisions he might make would have their full support. Mark was not sure how all of the partners felt about this issue.

NOTE

1. The words "professional staff" or "staff" generally indicate those people who have, or are working towards obtaining, a CA degree.

APPENDIX: EXCERPT FROM NOTES FOR PROFESSIONAL STAFF MANUAL

Maternity Leave and Subsequent Work Arrangements

Many of our female professionals are faced with the difficult task of successfully balancing career and family. The firm's position is that we should do everything possible to accommodate our staff in arriving at solutions which are satisfactory not only from their own point of view, but also from that of the firm and its clients.

Maternity Leave

Provincial Employment Standards legislation specifies minimum unpaid leaves of absence which must be granted to employees. In some provinces, professional staff are not covered by the terms of such legislation. Whether or not we are covered, we will always abide by its spirit and grant at least the legally required minimum amount of leave of absence without pay, which is normally 17 weeks (11 weeks before birth and six after). Retention of good staff requires that we approach each situation in as flexible a manner as possible. In some cases staff will need more time off; in others they may wish to return sooner. Whatever the individual needs, staff are encouraged to discuss arrangements with their partner, or if they wish, the Office Director of Personnel or Managing Partner.

Subsequent Work Arrangements

Good professional staff are always in demand. While we want to encourage those with long-term potential to remain with us, preferably on a full-time basis, we recognize that it may be particularly difficult to schedule work and family responsibilities in the early years after childbirth. Staff are encouraged to discuss with their partner or Managing Partner the various options that may be open once they return. The firm will do its best to be as flexible as possible, taking into consideration our commitment to provide our clients with quality service and our other professional staff with proper training and experience.

4

ORGANIZATIONAL DIVERSITY PROGRAMS

Organizations have developed a wide variety of initiatives to both increase the diversity of their members/stakeholders and to serve the needs of their diverse constituencies more effectively. These initiatives focus on customers, suppliers, the community, and employees. Targeted marketing initiatives focus on appealing to various demographic niches to increase sales and brand loyalty among different identity groups (e.g., Brosk, 2005; "Retailers Stocking Up," 2005; Ward, 2005). Supplier programs identify businesses owned by a variety of demographic groups and aim to increase the demographic diversity of suppliers bidding on contracts to the firm (Fine, 2003). Community outreach programs involve providing space, resources, expertise, and even volunteers to a variety of civic groups to increase the organization's visibility and reputation in a variety of cultural communities (Konrad & Linnehan, 1995a). Employee-focused programs involve staffing systems, inclusion, and empowerment. The next sections discuss employee-focused diversity programs in detail.

STAFFING SYSTEMS IN A DIVERSE WORKPLACE

Employee-focused programs aim to welcome a diverse group of employees into the organization to attract, develop, and retain the highest quality talent available in a diverse labor market (Cox & Blake, 1991; Robinson & Dechant, 1997). Staffing systems can be developed to bring a more diverse cohort of new hires into the organization and ensure they receive development and advancement opportunities. Staffing for diversity involves systems for *recruitment, selection, training and development, career progression,* and *retention* (Heneman, Waldeck, & Cushnie, 1996). Explicitly paying attention to diversity in the staffing process is important for reducing the effects of individual biases resulting from stereotypes learned in early childhood and the natural human tendency to prefer similar others. In addition, attention to diversity can help decision makers to identify talented people stuck in dead-end jobs without internal career ladders.

In the area of *recruiting,* organizations can seek feeder pools likely to generate a demographically diverse set of qualified job candidates. If such feeder pools do not exist, they can help build them by supporting training programs in the local schools and/or creating a set of internships for high school and university students (Konrad & Linnehan, 1995a). An excellent example of building a more diverse feeder pool is Innoversity, sponsored by Diversipro, Inc., and supported by the Canadian Broadcasting Corporation (CBC). Innoversity provides a showcase for talented artists and journalists from diverse ethnic groups to pitch their ideas to producers and broadcasters from all over Canada (see the Web site at www.innoversity.com).

In the area of *selection,* organizations can examine selection ratios to determine whether certain demographic groups are more likely to be hired than others. If differences are found, investigation can uncover reasons as well as strategies for enhancing diversity. Organizations can also use a diverse team to interview job candidates and ensure that a structured interview technique is used so that all candidates are asked the same set of questions. A meta-analysis combining the results of 31 U.S. studies found that although Black and Hispanic candidates received lower interview ratings than Whites on average, high-structure interviews showed smaller differences between ethnic groups than low-structure interviews (Huffcutt & Roth, 1998). The reason structured interviewing reduces differences in how groups are judged is because asking the same set of questions to everyone means all candidates have the same opportunities to demonstrate their abilities and qualifications.

In the area of *training and development,* organizations can provide internal leadership development training and ensure that a diverse group is included in the training program. Organizations can also institute high potential programs, which involve identifying people with the ability to rise at least two levels in the hierarchy and connecting them with training, mentoring, and development opportunities to help them move up. Ensuring that each cohort of high-potential employees is diverse builds a strong feeder pool for creating a diverse top-management team in the future (Fine, 2003).

To ensure *career progression* for a diverse workforce, organizations can institute career planning for all employees, where managers meet with each employee individually on an annual basis and discuss career options. Through these meetings, employees participate in developing their own individually tailored career plans and develop an understanding of the skills and accomplishments they will have to develop to achieve their goals. In addition, organizations can ensure that a diverse set of candidates is interviewed for each promotion, and managers should ask questions when this does not occur (Konrad & Linnehan, 1995a).

Two factors that may be the most important to employee *retention* are growth opportunities and fairness. Hence, ensuring that a diverse set of employees receives training and chances for promotion should lead to enhanced retention of all groups. Fairness means ensuring that organizational decisions are made through a rational and transparent process so that ability and achievement are rewarded. In addition, fairness means that employees are treated with dignity and respect and are provided with reasonable explanations for the tough decisions that are made (Colquitt, 2001). Employers can also examine turnover rates by demographic group to see if certain groups are more likely than others to leave the organization. Exit interviews can provide invaluable information regarding why employees are leaving the organization and strategies for improving retention in the future (Fine, 2003; Konrad & Linnehan, 1995a).

Is Staffing for Diversity Fair?

One might question whether paying attention to diversity in the staffing process raises fairness concerns among employees. Indeed, a study of 133 students in a Canadian university showed that 91% believed that a focus on employment equity inevitably results in reverse discrimination against White men (Leck, 2002). Similarly, a study of 349 university students in the United States documented negative views of affirmative action (Kravitz & Platania, 1993).

Interestingly, both studies also showed that the students had a very poor understanding of what employment equity programs in Canada and affirmative action programs in the United States entail. Both studies showed that students equated employment equity or affirmative action with hiring quotas. In fact, private-sector firms are strictly forbidden from using hiring quotas, and quotas are only imposed on U.S. public-sector organizations when a judge determines that a public-sector employer has intentionally engaged in systematic and widespread discrimination (Konrad & Linnehan, 2003).

When people are presented with the actual staffing practices associated with staffing for a diverse workforce, they respond much more positively. One study of line managers in four organizations showed that managers rated most staffing processes that attended to diversity positively, including aggressive recruiting of women and minorities for management, targeting women and minorities to receive management training, and tracking the percentage of women and minorities in jobs that lead to management (Konrad & Linnehan, 1995b). Another study showed that employees in a U.S. organization known for having a strong affirmative action focus, even White male employees, considered their organization to be fair (Parker, Baltes, & Christiansen, 1997).

Why might managers and employees respond positively to diversity-focused staffing processes? One reason is the fact that prior to equal employment, employment equity, and affirmative action initiatives, many employers made personnel decisions in very unsystematic and arbitrary ways. With the advent of mandates that employers demonstrate fairness to a diverse labor force, employers had to rationalize their processes and make them more transparent (Dobbin, Sutton, Meyer, & Scott, 1993). Specifically, employers were required to identify the qualifications needed for effectiveness on the job and to select job candidates on the basis of "bona fide occupational qualifications" only. As a result, opportunities improved for everyone wishing to rise in the organization through merit.

Because people who have a poor understanding of diversity staffing programs also have negative attitudes toward them, providing transparency by explaining the organization's staffing process to employees may improve perceptions of fairness. In addition, Leck (2002) argues that allowing upward communication to process all employee-raised concerns thoroughly helps managers to identify employees' views and adjust practices to deal with any unintended negative results of diversity staffing programs. Leck also recommends employee involvement in developing diversity staffing programs, as well as diversity training to educate employees on issues of stereotyping, prejudice, privilege, and exclusion.

Empowering a Diverse Workforce

For an organization to be truly welcoming to a diverse group, members of all demographic categories must feel both empowered to participate in important organizational decision-making processes and fully included in the organization's information networks and social activities. Because workplace diversity means people have different experiences, perceptions, and values, employee empowerment initiatives focus on developing systems to create true openness to new ideas and viewpoints. Examples of these systems include composing decision-making groups that are diverse in experience and viewpoints, requiring decision-making groups to thoroughly research and discuss ways the majority decision could fail, and training team leaders to create openness to dissent when they facilitate meetings.

Management initiatives are important for developing an empowering decision-making environment in a diverse workplace because people naturally tend to reject new ideas. A large body of literature documents people's consistent resistance to change (Bovey & Hede, 2001; Pardo del Val & Fuentes, 2003). Research shows that opinions originally held by the majority are far more likely to prevail in group discussions than the original opinions of the minority (Meyers, Brashers, & Hanner, 2000). People with minority views in a discussion situation also use different influence strategies than people in the majority. Not surprisingly, people in the majority agree more often with what is being said, while people in the minority disagree more often and make more objections to statements by others (Meyers et al., 2000). Because people like their statements to be validated and supported, individuals who disagree and object may be viewed as unpleasant.

In addition, people whose suggestions are inconsistent with those of the historical majority face skepticism and questioning by the majority (Limon & Boster, 2001). People whose backgrounds and experiences are very different from the historical majority find they must explain their views very explicitly, due to the fact that the majority often does not understand their frames of reference. Hence, disagreeing with the group requires much stamina and preparation, and those who disagree too often risk being labeled as disruptive, unless managers structure the discussion situation in a way that creates space for and rewards constructive disagreement.

INCLUSION IN A DIVERSE WORKPLACE

Social inclusion means members of all demographic have equal opportunities to develop extensive information networks and congenial relationships within the organization. Acknowledging that more introverted personalities may have less desire to socialize with work colleagues, organizations desiring to welcome a variety of members create opportunities for all members to develop cordial relationships with coworkers. Managers can take several steps to establish a positive social environment in their units, including the following:

- Becoming a role model by building a diverse network and showing interest in other cultures
- Encouraging members of the group to reach out to other cultures regularly
- Holding all employees accountable for treating one another with respect
- Creating the expectation that employees will speak up when they see others treated disrespectfully
- Creating social events that are fun for everyone
- Inviting employees' families to workplace social activities on occasion

Management encouragement is especially important for the development of a positive social environment in a diverse workplace because people naturally gravitate toward similar others. A classic finding in social psychology demonstrates that people have a consistent preference to meet and spend time with people who hold values that are similar to their own (Byrne, 1971). People prefer similar others because it is reinforcing to interact with someone who agrees with your views, understands your perspective, and validates your assumptions and conclusions (Riordan, 2000). In the workplace, several research studies document better attitudes toward similar rather than dissimilar coworkers (Chattopadhyay, 1999; Pelled, 1996; Riordan & Shore, 1997), mentors (Ensher & Murphy, 1997; Thomas, 1993), and supervisors (Somech, 2003; Tsui, Porter, & Egan, 2002).

The tendency of people to prefer similar others means that members of the majority group in the organization have many opportunities to build networks and collegial relationships, while members of groups in the numerical minority experience relative social isolation. Research has documented that managers' networks tend to consist of similar others (Brass, 1985; James, 2000; Mehra, Kilduff, & Brass, 1998; Mollica, Gray, & Treviño, 2003). For managers in the numerical minority, having a network that includes both majority and minority members has been linked to career success (Ibarra, 1995). Majority members are needed in the network to provide inside information about the unwritten rules and political alliances that influence organizational decisions. Minority members are needed to provide social support and discuss strategies when individuals face mixed signals from the majority or, worse, exclusion, harassment, or discrimination.

Effectiveness of Diversity Initiatives

More research is needed on the effectiveness of organizational diversity programs. The findings obtained to date are encouraging, however. A study of diversity staffing systems in 138 Philadelphia-area organizations found that formal practices designed to provide management opportunities for women and people of color were associated with having women at a higher management rank and more people of color in management (Konrad & Linnehan, 1995a). Studies of recruiting practices have shown that applicants are attracted to organizations that depict diverse sets of employees in their recruitment materials, such as brochures and Web sites (e.g., Perkins, Thomas, & Taylor, 2000). A study of development and promotion systems showed that these practices were associated with more women in top-management positions in 228 medium- to large-sized firms in Georgia (Goodman, Fields, & Blum, 2003).

Ray Friedman and his colleagues (Friedman, Kane, & Cornfield, 1998; Friedman & Holtom, 2002) have undertaken two extensive studies of corporate employee network groups. Employee network groups are associations of minority or female employees that exist within organizations. Membership in these network groups is voluntary, and the groups generally report to the organization's diversity council, which normally consists of top executives. Many organizations have chartered a wide variety of employee network groups under the banner of workplace diversity. For example, at Microsoft, employees have voluntarily organized the following set of network groups, with the approval of management (for more information on diversity at Microsoft, see the Web site at http://www.microsoft.com/mscorp/citizenship/diversity):

- Arabs at Microsoft
- Attention Deficit Disorder at Microsoft
- Blacks at Microsoft (BAM)
- Brazilians at Microsoft
- Chinese Employees in Microsoft Community
- Dads@Microsoft
- Filipinos at Microsoft
- Friends of Japanese at Microsoft
- Gay, Lesbian, Bisexual, and Transgender Employees at Microsoft
- German Speakers at Microsoft
- Hellenes at Microsoft
- Hispanics Worldwide
- Hong Kong Employees at Microsoft
- Hoppers (for women)
- Huddle (for deaf and hard of hearing)
- Indian Organization
- Koreans Worldwide
- Malaysians at Microsoft
- Military Reservists at Microsoft
- Native American
- Pakistanis at Microsoft
- Persians at Microsoft
- Romanians at Microsoft
- Singaporeans at Microsoft
- Single Parents at Microsoft
- Taiwanese Microsoft Employees
- Thais at Microsoft
- Turks at Microsoft Worldwide
- U.S. Military Veterans at Microsoft
- Visually Impaired Persons at Microsoft (MSVIP)
- Working Parents at Microsoft

The research of Friedman and his colleagues has linked participation in such groups with reduced turnover (Friedman & Holtom, 2002), greater opportunities to receive mentoring, and improved career optimism (Friedman et al., 1998). An additional benefit to the organization is the conduit of information regarding diversity climate when these employee groups bring ideas, concerns, and strategies to the top executives sitting on the organization's diversity council.

Diversity programs may even result in better organizational performance. Wright, Ferris, Hiller, and Kroll (1995) found that the stock price of 34 firms rose after the announcement that they had been awarded an Exemplary Voluntary Effort (EVE) award for affirmative action from the U.S. federal government. Although this finding is intriguing, researchers have more work to do to demonstrate a definitive link between specific diversity practices and firm financial performance.

READING

Diversity: A Quota by Any Other Name?

Underrepresentation of visible minorities in senior positions in Canada's workforce is a serious problem. In 1999, for example, one third of visible minorities in the federal government reported that they had experienced discrimination in their work unit—almost double the average reported for public servants overall. This article argues that this is unacceptable—that the government must create a federal public service that truly reflects and values the contributions of all Canadians.

CASES

Women in Management at London Life (A)

A task force must make recommendations to increase the number of women in the company's management ranks. Various factors help or impede this initiative, including the leadership of the CEO, the attitudes of some of the existing managers, and the attitudes of one senior female manager in the company.

Assignment Questions:

1. What policies can the task force create to move more women into management and, at the same time, ensure the best person is selected for the job?

2. Is there a need for any new policy? Why or why not?

3. What are the main reasons why more women are not in higher level management positions?

4. What is London Life's responsibility to women and men in the company?

The Bank of Montreal—The Task Force on the Advancement of Women in the Bank (A)

A 2-year bank employee is at a decision point in her career. She must assess whether the actions and recommendations of the Task Force on the Advancement of Women in the bank will be successful in managing change. Specifically, she is concerned with the "glass ceiling"—the barriers to the advancement of women—and the process used by the bank to eliminate the barriers.

Assignment Questions:

1. What concerns does Deborah Westman face?

2. How significant is the issue of the "glass ceiling"?

3. Evaluate the Bank of Montreal's change approach. What are the pros and cons of the process used?

4. How successful will the task force be in eliminating the three major barriers to the advancement of women?

5. What should Deborah do?

"Synergy" at City Hall (A)

Inspired by their experiences at an outside conference, a few women managers at city hall join together to form an informal support and information-sharing group (the Synergy Group). They attempt to broaden their base of activities to include a consciousness-raising workshop for senior managers (mostly male), with unforeseen and unsettling results.

Assignment Questions:

1. Using data from the case, what "women in management" issues needed to be addressed?

2. What alternatives does the Synergy Group have?

3. From the points of view of (a) Anna Hewitt, (b) Trudy McNab, and (c) Synergy Group members, what went wrong?

4. What do you think these individuals should do next?

REFERENCES

Bovey, W. H., & Hede, A. (2001). Resistance to organizational change: The role of defense mechanisms. *Journal of Managerial Psychology, 16,* 534–548.

Brass, D. J. (1985). Men's and women's networks: A study of interaction patterns and influence in organizations. *Academy of Management Journal, 28,* 327–343.

Brosk, M. (2005, 22 April). Sears introduces Latina Life line. *Knight Ridder Tribune Business News,* p. 1.

Byrne, D. E. (1971). *The attraction paradigm.* New York: Academic Press.

Chattopadhyay, P. (1999). Beyond direct and symmetrical effects: The influence of demographic dissimilarity on organizational citizenship behaviors. *Academy of Management Journal, 42,* 273–287.

Colquitt, J. A. (2001). On the dimensionality of organizational justice: A construct validation of a measure. *Journal of Applied Psychology, 86,* 386–400.

Cox, T., Jr., & Blake, S. (1991). Managing cultural diversity: Implications for organizational competitiveness. *Academy of Management Executive, 5*(3), 45–56.

Dobbin, F., Sutton, J. R., Meyer, J. W., & Scott, W. R. (1993). Equal employment opportunity law and the construction of internal labor markets. *American Journal of Sociology, 99,* 396–427.

Ensher, E. A., & Murphy, S. E. (1997). Effects of race, gender, perceived similarity, and contact on mentor relationships. *Journal of Vocational Behavior, 50,* 460–481.

Fine, M. G. (2003). Building successful multicultural organizations: Challenges and opportunities. In R. J. Ely, E. G. Foldy, & M. A. Scully (Eds.), *Reader in gender, work, and organization* (pp. 308–318). Malden, MA: Blackwell.

Friedman, R. A., & Holtom, B. (2002). The effects of network groups on minority employee turnover intentions. *Human Resource Management, 41,* 405–421.

Friedman, R. A., Kane, M., & Cornfield, D. B. (1998). Social support and career optimism: Examining the effectiveness of network groups among Black managers. *Human Relations, 51,* 1155–1177.

Goodman, J. S., Fields, D. L., & Blum, T. C. (2003). Cracks in the glass ceiling: In what kinds of organizations do women make it to the top? *Group & Organization Management, 28,* 475–501.

Heneman, R. L., Waldeck, N. E., & Cushnie, M. (1996). Diversity considerations in staffing decision-making. In E. E. Kossek & S. A. Lobel (Eds.), *Managing diversity: Human resource strategies for transforming the workplace* (pp. 74–102). New York: Blackwell.

Huffcutt, A. I., & Roth, P. L. (1998). Racial group differences in employment interview evaluations. *Journal of Applied Psychology, 83,* 179–189.

Ibarra, H. (1995). Race, opportunity, and diversity of social circles in managerial networks. *Academy of Management Journal, 38,* 673–703.

James, E. H. (2000). Race-related differences in promotions and support: Underlying effects of human and social capital. *Organization Science, 11,* 493–508.

Konrad, A. M., & Linnehan, F. (1995a). Formalized HRM structures: Coordinating equal employment opportunity or concealing organizational practices? *Academy of Management Journal, 38,* 787–820.

Konrad, A. M., & Linnehan, F. (1995b). Race and sex differences in line managers' reactions to equal employment opportunity and affirmative action interventions. *Group and Organization Management, 20,* 409–439.

Konrad, A. M., & Linnehan, F. (2003). Affirmative action as a means of increasing workforce diversity. In M. J. Davidson & S. L. Fielden (Eds.), *Individual diversity and psychology in organizations* (pp. 96–111). New York: John Wiley.

Kravitz, D. A., & Platania, J. (1993). Attitudes and beliefs about affirmative action: Effects of target and of respondent sex and ethnicity. *Journal of Applied Psychology, 78,* 928–938.

Leck, J. D. (2002). Making employment equity programs work for women. *Canadian Public Policy, 28,* S85–S100.

Limon, M. S., & Boster, F. J. (2001). The impact of varying argument quality and minority size on influencing the majority and perceptions of the minority. *Communication Quarterly, 49,* 350–365.

Mehra, A., Kilduff, M., & Brass, D. J. (1998). At the margins: A distinctiveness approach to the social identity and social networks of underrepresented groups. *Academy of Management Journal, 41,* 441–452.

Meyers, R. A., Brashers, D. E., & Hanner, J. (2000). Majority-minority influence: Identifying argumentative patterns and predicting argument-outcome links. *Journal of Communication, 50,* 3–30.

Mollica, K. A., Gray, B., & Treviño, L. K. (2003). Racial homophily and its persistence in newcomers' social networks. *Organization Science, 14,* 123–136.

Pardo del Val, M., & Fuentes, C. M. (2003). Resistance to change: A literature review and empirical study. *Management Decision, 41,* 148–155.

Parker, C. P., Baltes, B. B., & Christiansen, N. D. (1997). Support for affirmative action, justice perceptions, and work attitudes: A study of gender and racial-ethnic group differences. *Journal of Applied Psychology, 82,* 376–389.

Pelled, L. H. (1996). Relational demography and perceptions of group conflict and performance: A field investigation. *International Journal of Conflict Management, 7,* 230–246.

Perkins, L. A., Thomas, K. M., & Taylor, G. A. (2000). Advertising and recruitment: Marketing to minorities. *Psychology and Marketing, 17,* 235–255.

Retailers stocking up on diverse employees. (2005, April 18). *Fortune, 151*(8), 50–51.

Riordan, C. M. (2000). Relational demography within groups: Past developments, contradictions, and new directions. *Research in Personnel and Human Resources Management, 19,* 131–173.

Riordan, C. M., & Shore, L. M. (1997). Demographic diversity and employee attitudes: An empirical examination of relational demography within work units. *Journal of Applied Psychology, 82,* 342–358.

Robinson, G., & Dechant, K. (1997). Building a business case for diversity. *Academy of Management Executive, 11*(3), 21–31.

Somech, A. (2003). Relationships of participative leadership with relational demography variables: A multi-level perspective. *Journal of Organizational Behavior, 24,* 1003–1018.

Thomas, D. A. (1993). Racial dynamics in cross-race developmental relationships. *Administrative Science Quarterly, 38,* 169–194.

Tsui, A. S., Porter, L. W., & Egan, T. D. (2002). When both similarities and dissimilarities matter: Extending the concept of relational demography. *Human Relations, 55,* 899–929.

Ward, A. (2005, 19 April). Pepsi takes a lead from down Mexico way: Soft drinks group is introducing taste of home to Hispanic communities in U.S. *Financial Times,* p. 27.

Wright, P., Ferris, S. P., Hiller, J. S., & Kroll, M. (1995). Competitiveness through management of diversity: Effects on stock price valuation. *Academy of Management Journal, 38,* 272–287.

DIVERSITY: A QUOTA BY ANY OTHER NAME?

Prepared by Trevor Wilson

The driving principle must be that what an individual an do on the job must matter more than his or her race or colour.

The Task Force believes the time has come to step up efforts, namely to pursue with determination, for a limited time, a benchmark for the recruitment and advancement of visible minorities.

The above two quotes were taken from the recently released "Embracing Change," a Task Force Report on the Participation of Visible Minorities in the Federal Public Service. These two quotes may seem like an oxymoron. How can you set numeric benchmarks for the representation of visible minorities and still hire the best candidate for the job? This intriguing report, presented to the Treasury Board in March of this year, attempts to tackle the question of under-representation of visible minorities at senior positions within the workforce.

Under-representation of people of colour is not a new issue in Canada. As the task force points out, visible minority representation in Canada is an issue that is "studies rich and results poor." Within the past decade alone, we have had four major reports. These studies rarely hit the mainstream press despite the relevance of their conclusions. Canada's public service does not reflect the diversity of the taxpayers that support it. The facts speak for themselves:

- Visible minorities make up only 5.1 percent of the federal public service compared to a labour availability rate of 10.35 percent in the Canadian workforce
- Out of 2,800 permanent jobs staffed in 1998, only 184 went to people of colour

- Visible minorities still represent only three percent (103) of senior-level positions in the federal public service, a disparity that has barely moved over the past few years
- Visible minorities received less than 20 out of 646 promotions to the federal public-service executive categories in 1998
- Visible minorities are clustered in a few occupational categories and concentrated in four government departments, raising suspicions of tokenism and job ghettoization.

This most recent report speaks to the need for action and results in response to these findings. The primary recommendation of the task force is the setting of a "1 in 5" benchmark for visible minority representation in term appointments, executive feeder groups and executive positions. To some, the idea of numeric benchmarks may seem reminiscent of a quota system, but is it?

The report clearly states that the "Task Force does not seek quotas for visible minorities." At the same time, it calls for specific, measurable results and recommends the creation of "1 in 5 representation benchmarks." What's the difference?

A quota is an externally imposed, inflexible number usually mandated by a court or legal tribunal like the Human Rights Commission. A goal, target or benchmark, on the other hand, is generally seen as an internally determined and flexible objective. While quotas have never officially been a part of the Canadian employment equity scene, they have been used at least twice. In 1987, Canadian International Railway was forced to increase the representation of women after it lost its legal battle against Action Travail des Femmes, and in 1997, Health Canada was forced to hire racial minorities at double the rate of labour-market availability when it lost its case against the National Capital Alliance on Race Relations. It is interesting to note that both organizations seemed to have little difficulty reaching their quotas. Nevertheless, quotas continue to be avoided as a means of dealing with under-representation both here and in the United States.

One of the most compelling arguments against quotas is not just that they garner backlash reactions from those perceived to be excluded, but that they are actually harmful to those whom they are meant to help. Shelby Steele examines the issue of tokenism in his book, *The Content of Our Character.* He puts forth an interesting theory called "implied inferiority." This applies to minorities who obtain positions because of their skin colour, not their competence. Steele suggests that those who appear to benefit from quotas stand a good chance of being negatively and personally affected by implied inferiority because it inevitably leads to feelings of self-doubt and reduced motivation. According to Steele, qualified minorities may then harbour as much doubt about their own competency as they actually face. The task force report points out that its concept of benchmarks is not the same as the concept of quotas because its benchmarks have flexibility in at least two ways. First, because government departments have three- and five-year horizons to reach the prescribed annual rate of performance. Second, departments can devise strategies that are adapted to their particular situation. In their words, "departments can determine where and how they can best make faster progress." For most critics of quotas, these will not be totally convincing arguments.

The key to the report is in the following quote: "Changing the culture and changing the numbers can and must move in concert." As the task force points out, benchmarks, quotas, goals or targets have no sustainability unless they are set in the context of real organizational change. For example, last November the federal government issued a major employee survey to evaluate the health of its workplace culture. One-third of visible minorities reported experiencing discrimination in their work unit—almost double the average reported for public servants overall. While the federal government hired approximately 200 visible minorities into permanent jobs in 1998, during that same period, because of issues like discrimination, over 860 visible minorities left the government. At this rate of attrition it would be almost impossible to meet a 1 in 5 representation benchmark. Since the formation of the visible Minority task force, the federal government has also established a task force to create an inclusive work environment. Its mandate is to create a new culture within the federal public service that "cultivates diversity— where everyone is valued and works to their maximum potential." While this task force has not yet tabled its report, it would seem beneficial that these two commissions work in concert to create a federal public service that truly reflects and values the contributions of all Canadians.

WOMEN IN MANAGEMENT AT LONDON LIFE (A)

Prepared by Gavin Hood under the supervision of Jeffrey Gandz

Version: (A) 2001-07-24

In September 1981, a management task force was established to discuss the managerial development and promotion of women at London Life. Specifically, the task force was responsible for reviewing policies, procedures and attitudes affecting the development of women into supervisory and management positions. They had just one month to recommend to the senior management operating committee what action, if any, London Life should take to address the current under-representation of females in management positions.

LONDON LIFE INSURANCE COMPANY

London Life was founded as an insurance company in 1874 to serve a small number of London clients and, by 1981, had the fourth largest assets of all Canadian insurance companies and was one of the largest mortgage lenders in Canada. The company served Canadians at all income levels with life insurance, health coverage, pension and other financial products through more than 100 regional offices. Operating statistics are summarized in Exhibit 1. The company had a sales force of 2,089 employees, the largest insurance sales force in the country, supported by an administrative staff of 2,535, over 1,000 of whom worked at the head office in London, Ontario.

In 1977, Brascan Ltd., a Canadian holding company, acquired a significant stake in London Life. Earl Orser was brought in from Brascan and appointed as chief operating office, and subsequently as president and chief executive officer. His evaluation of the organization led him to restructure management and focus the company strategy on marketing and investments. No layoffs occurred during the restructuring, but the previously highly paternalistic company atmosphere was transformed to a performance orientation in which employees were expected to make a productive contribution to the company's operations.

The new management philosophy was based on improving service, increasing employee productivity and reducing costs. In addition to structural reorganization, head office renovations, state-of-the-art office planning and new computer technology aimed at making the company's operations more efficient were begun in 1981. It was clear at that time that the future organization would be flatter, with fewer levels of management, and that there would be a gradual reduction in total number of staff as more and more computer technology was introduced. (Exhibit 2 outlines the projected number of management openings at head office and in the sales divisions.)

WOMEN IN MANAGEMENT AT LONDON LIFE

When Earl Orser joined London Life he raised the issue of the relatively few women in

	1977	1978	1979	1980	1981
Premium Income					
Individual	284	286	299	332	396
Group	159	172	152	299	260
Total	443	458	451	631	656
Total Assets	2926	3223	3513	3860	4318
R.O.A. %	8.23	8.56	8.92	9.16	9.57
Net Income					
Total	n/a	29	35	53	46
Shareholder	n/a	10	12	23	23
R.O.E. %	n/a	9.6	11.1	18.6	16.2
Employees					
Sales	2112	2154	2071	2084	2089
Admin	2480	2490	2478	2421	2535

Exhibit 1   Operating Summary ($ millions)

	1983	*1984*	*1985*	*1986*	*1987*
Projected employee growth	22	12	10	4	4
Projected retirements	0	2	6	4	5
Projected terminations	0	0	0	0	0
Projected openings	22	14	16	8	9
General Sales Division					
Projected employee growth	6	5	6	7	7
Projected retirements	4	4	3	4	4
Projected terminations	2	2	2	2	2
Projected openings	12	11	11	13	13
District Sales Division					
Projected employee growth	8	7	8	7	8
Projected retirements	9	9	10	10	11
Projected terminations	19	24	25	29	28
Projected openings	36	40	43	46	47
Group Sales Division					
Projected employee growth	5	4	4	5	0
Projected retirements	1	1	1	0	0
Projected openings	6	5	5	5	0
Corporate projected openings	76	70	75	72	69

Exhibit 2   Projected Management Openings, Head Office

	Male	*Female*
Total Corporate Management	98% (595)	2% (14)
Head Office Management	95% (231)	5% (11)
Individual Sales Division Management	99%	1% (2)
Group Sales Division Management	98%	2% (1)

Exhibit 3   Female Management Representation by Division

management at a strategic planning meeting. In 1981, females held 14 of 595 management and senior technical positions at London Life despite the fact that 73 per cent of the head office staff were female (Exhibit 3). At the next level below this (supervisory and specialist), females represented 47 per cent of the population.

In 1981, the Ontario Provincial Government was strongly urging employers to create equal working opportunities for women. There were various initiatives taken including the establishment of the Ontario Women's Directorate, the creation of a ministerial portfolio responsible for women's issues, and active consideration of various legislative initiatives including employment equity and pay equity in the public and private sectors.

At that time, many insurance companies—which were very large employers of women, primarily in administrative and clerical roles—were addressing the concerns of women. Of the "Big Eight" life insurers which dominated the industry, the Prudential, Metropolitan, ManuLife, Mutual Life, and Sun Life all had women board members. While London Life had no women on its board, London Life's female distribution and management representation were about average for the industry.

Orser's view was that London Life could be missing an opportunity to improve its performance because it was not developing the managerial potential of female employees, many of whom had extensive experience in the insurance industry and had a high level of commitment to London Life. This view was apparently shared by some other managers and executives in the company, although not many considered the issue to be a high priority. He encouraged the human resources department to hire an experienced consultant, Fran Kennedy, and to develop a strategy and action plan to address this issue.

In response to Orser's expressed concerns, the human resources department held a series of three meetings, in which a total of thirty women, representing positions ranging from clerical to the management level, discussed women's opportunities, the attitudes in the company toward promoting women into managerial positions, and women's level of aspirations. Two of the generalizations drawn from these sessions were that: (a) women were not aware of the opportunities that existed in their departments or, for that matter, in other departments, and (b) women did not receive the necessary support from their spouses to pursue managerial opportunities. Most married women reported that they assumed sole responsibility for household management and were in no position to take on the longer and more irregular hours, and travel, required of management personnel. In fact, it was quite difficult to assess the attitudinal environment because most women had simply never considered the possibility of moving into management.

Following these sessions, the director of human resources recommended a program to encourage more career-oriented women inside and outside of London Life to become aware of, to get interested in, and to prepare themselves through effective career planning for managerial and higher specialist career opportunities throughout London Life. Excerpts from the memo are outlined below:

By learning to assess their personal/career needs realistically and to acknowledge their strengths and limitations, more women should gradually qualify and be appointed to managerial and higher specialist positions over the next three years.

Developing the potential of employees is good business. This program would affirm better utilization and efficiency of our human resources and payroll dollars as more women progress to higher responsibilities. Such equal career opportunities could attract more qualified, career-oriented women to the company legitimately outside the current restraints of our present job posting program, whenever necessary. Both the morale and quality of work life should be enhanced. Lastly, such action should lessen the potential attractiveness of third party pressures/intervention, whether they be from government (federal, provincial, municipal) or unions.

We have very few women in higher level positions. This is a current and historical fact. With a few encouraging exceptions, the past five years have seen minimal senior appointments of women for finance, marketing (home office), investments, actuarial, group and administration, while many men have been promoted internally and appointed from outside. There are five women compared to 138 men in positions at or above manager level at home office today.

There is a need to take "affirmative action" to correct past career inequities to make sure every employee has the chance to reach his or her full potential, based on performance and personal responsibilities for one's own career growth.

We would like to see more women qualify and be selected for such future opportunities. Both Premier Davis and Labor Minister Elgie are also encouraging voluntary affirmative action programs for 1981. As we know, this movement is not a fad, but a major social force with growing impact on business.

Subsequent to the submission of the memo, twelve managers holding the following positions were appointed to a task force to study the situation, assisted by the external consultant, Fran Kennedy:

- Human Resources Consultant
- Program Coordinator, Employee Relations
- Vice-President, Investments
- Director, Human Resources
- Manager, Group Regional Office Services
- Manager, Individual Product Design, Marketing
- Vice-President, Group Insurance
- Operations Improvement Consultant
- Manager, Underwriting Operations
- Manager, Group Underwriting
- Manager, Administrative Services

Their mandate was to recommend to the operating committee the particular steps that should be present in a development program and to suggest changes to company policies which discriminated against women. The task force scope for making recommendations was unlimited.

HUMAN RESOURCE POLICIES AT LONDON LIFE

London Life had many policies and procedures which the task force realized had some impact on the progression and status of women within the company.

Salaries

Salaries were determined by market wages, job complexity, and individual performance. Benchmark internal salaries were compared annually with those at other local companies and large national employers by a management committee and the senior job evaluation staff. Internal job comparisons based on know-how, problem solving, accountability and working conditions, determined relative salary ranges. Immediate supervisors reviewed employee achievements and development to determine their salary within the defined range. Employees transferred for development received salaries corresponding to their performance and the salary range for the new job.

Maternity Leave

Eighteen weeks of maternity leave were available to women at London Life. During this maternity leave, Unemployment Insurance covered 60 per cent of salary up to a maximum of approximately $20,000 over 15 weeks. A woman's position was not posted unless she resigned before going on leave, declared that she was not returning from the leave, or did not return to work at the end of the leave.

Flexible Hours

With management consent, employees could select start and stop times for their job within ranges which were deemed acceptable to the function of the departments in which they worked. In practice, people could elect a working day which was somewhere between the hours of 7.30 a.m. to 6.00 p.m.

Promotion

Promotion to supervisory and managerial positions depended on training and technical knowledge, attendance, ability to work with others, and self-development. Progress was reviewed annually by an employee's immediate supervisor. Positions up to first line supervision were posted at London Life. Management, senior technical positions and task force opportunities were not posted and were filled by candidates nominated by their senior managers. The job posting system is outlined in Exhibit 4.

ELIGIBILITY

All employees except for those employed on a temporary basis may apply for any posted position. You should, however, assure yourself that you have at least the minimum qualifications required for the position in which you are interested. The selection process gives consideration to education and experience, length of service, job performance, attendance and supervisor's comment on your recent performance appraisals as indicators of potential for advancement. Other factors could also play a key role, depending, of course, on the type of opening, e.g. ability to communicate verbally and/or in writing, diplomacy, telephone courtesy, ability to work with minimum supervision, etc.

POSTING PROCEDURES

Vacancies from the S02 position level up to and including division supervisor will normally be posted. Positions posted remain open for at least three days while qualified applicants are considered. Since new postings are made regularly, it's a good idea to read the job postings daily on the bulletin board in your department or the staff lounge. The information posted includes job title, department, division, position level, a brief description of the job and any special qualifications, as well as the number of vacancies that exist. If a job appeals to you, you should post for it immediately.

Jobs on which no selection is made are normally posted a second time. The word REPOSTED will be printed on the second posting description. Only applicants who did not apply on the first posting are eligible to apply for the reposted position.

A record of all past job posting descriptions for each department is maintained in Employment Services for your perusal.

If you are interested in the regional office positions, contact Employment Services for further information.

WHAT TO DO NEXT

If you see a position that appears particularly well suited to you, pick up an application either in your department, the lounge or Employment Services. Fill it out and send it to Employment Services. You should feel free to talk with your supervisor or section head about your interest in the position. However, should you wish your posting application to be kept confidential, this will be done.

Attach a resume if available. This will be kept on file by employment services and included on future applications until such time as you wish to revise it.

When you post for the first time, a member of the Employment Services staff will contact you as soon as possible to discuss your work experience, qualifications and interests and try to answer any questions you may have. An interview with the supervisor in the department where the vacancy exists will then be arranged in Employment Services. At that time, the requirements of the position will be explained and other points discussed, including an appropriate flexible hours schedule.

Should you take sick after the posting or are away because of any illness or maternity leave at the time a posting of interest arises, **it is your responsibility** to get in touch with Employment Services. Arrangements can then be made, if feasible, for an appropriate interview by the area involved either personally or by telephone.

If you should post on a job and know that you will be absent shortly thereafter, please bring your posting application directly to Employment Services. This will ensure that the appropriate interviews are conducted before you leave.

NOTIFICATION

After all candidates have been interviewed, you will be notified of the result of your application.

Exhibit 4   Excerpts From the Job Posting Guidelines   *(Continued)*

If you are successful, your transfer date will be determined after consultation with your present and prospective departments. The transfer should normally take place within two weeks from the day you are selected. If your application was not selected, you are free to consult your present supervisor and/or Employment Services concerning your career plans.

ADMINISTRATIVE GUIDELINES

If you are successful in receiving a new job posting, you would normally not be expected to apply again for a new position for at least six months.

Exceptions to the job posting principle will occur whenever:

1. personnel become available for transfer as a result of reorganization, reduction in the work load or the introduction of a systems change. In situations of this kind, the normal job posting policy may not apply, as those employees made available for transfer should receive first priority.

2. the reduction of a unit's staff complement occurs as the result of a resignation, posting, etc. and it is desirable to fill that vacancy from within the unit **without** restoring the complement to its original strength.

3. the employee is following an approved career progression within the unit and the staff complement is not to be increased, e.g., progressing from a grade 1 to a grade 2 clerk.

4. when a position is reevaluated, the person occupying it assumes the new level without the need for a posting.

5. a new job is created in the unit that can be filled by means of present staff, without requiring an increase in that unit's staff complement.

6. the employee's job has been phased out due to reorganization, redundancy or systems change and, therefore, no replacement is required.

7. temporary jobs, positions of a project nature and unique back-up training situations occur. The Company reserves the right to transfer or hire personnel throughout its operation without using the job posting system.

8. jobs require specialized qualifications and/or experience not available within the Company.

9. jobs are normally held in reserve for employees returning from maternity leave or extended illness.

Exhibit 4   Excerpts From the Job Posting Guidelines

Personal Development

London Life offered nine different life insurance courses and reimbursed 100 per cent of tuition and 50 per cent of text book costs for external self-improvement courses. Funding for external courses was subject to approval by the human resources department and the employee's manager. It was extremely rare for individuals in non-managerial positions to request or take such courses.

WOMEN AT LONDON LIFE

Before the introduction of job posting and an extensive compensation review in the early 1970s, female high school graduates were essentially hired to be clerks. Because there was no maternity leave policy before 1970, pregnant women had to leave the company and reapply for their old jobs if they wanted to return.

Diane Haas, a member of the task force established to look at this issue and one of the very few women who had risen to the middle management level in the company, gave other members of the task force with less experience at London Life a brief history of what it was like for women in the company in the fifties and sixties:

When I started working here, women earned approximately one half of what the men earned and women's raises were typically one-third of what the men's were. So there was definitely pay discrimination in those days.

Women tended to be longer term employees. They trained most of the males who were hired, in anticipation that within two years, those same men, better or worse, would become their bosses. I remember challenging my boss about this in the mid-1960s and basically what he said to me was: "Hey lady, you're a second salary. He has to support a family. Tough luck!"

In the early 1970s, there were some major corporate changes made with regard to measurable things, pay equity and job evaluation based on the job, not the incumbent. In 1973, London Life completely changed their salary positioning. We used to be one of the worst payers in the city. Now we are good, around the median.

The interesting thing is that I wasn't aware of the changes taking place. There was no announcement, the changes were evolutionary rather than revolutionary. What hasn't changed are the soft factors. Most men don't recognize that there are talented women around who want to get ahead.

I believe that a lot of long term female employees have said to themselves, "Hey, getting ahead here is a lost cause. I'm not going to fight the system; I'm going to come in, work my 9–5 and then go home." It was really uncomfortable to be one of the scrappers. You were fighting an uphill battle against discrimination. Most women didn't even think about promotion. It was just too frustrating.

The task force coordinator, a member of the employee relations department, added her own views:

There is a lot of subtle discrimination at London Life. Most male managers don't realize that they are preventing women from being promoted. As entry level employees, men tend to promote the fact that they are career-oriented. When they ask to take self-improvement courses, they get management approval, because the courses develop their ability to meet future responsibilities.

Women, on the other hand, are limiting their horizons to becoming supervisors. That's perceived as their ceiling, and we don't have many examples to contradict the perception. If women don't tell their managers that they aspire to a higher position, their requests for the same courses will be turned down, because the development isn't necessary for their current job. Therefore, men get the posted jobs, because they are better qualified.

The human resources manager on the task force pointed out that the recent hiring history and practices of the company made it difficult but not impossible to address the issue of moving more women into management:

From the early 1970s to the 1980s, all of our recruiting has been at entry level positions. We are hiring at the clerical level, not university graduates, male or female. I would also agree that we aren't encouraging women to excel. There is very little cross fertilization and we aren't encouraging women to take extra courses, to take a chance. I think that opportunities exist and women aren't taking advantage of them, but I also think that because they aren't considering themselves as potential candidates, they aren't coming forward.

Diane Haas, who had spent most of her career in operations as a clerk, a senior clerk, a section supervisor and then a division supervisor, related her experience of some men's attitudes to her progression into management:

Men in this company, with some exceptions, don't think they have to be concerned about women as competition. There is the odd woman like myself starting to progress, but as much as anything my progress has been based on tenure and experience. In most men's minds, I am a credible person, not necessarily a female. Men accept that there will always be the odd female who will bubble up, but there's certainly no concern on their part about having to be as good as the women.

The new director of human resources really rattled my own cage about three years ago. He told me to get moving and start to chase opportunities that were there.

Three or four months after I moved to human resources, I was promoted to a manager. The immediate talk was, "She got the job because she was a woman." Subsequently, I got a position as a more senior manager in marketing. There were 22 applicants for that job. The manager who selected me told me that he thought I was the best candidate but an awful lot of the other 21 people indicated to him that they felt he had made the decision based on the fact that I was a woman.

A senior manager of Property and Investments talked about his views on the promotion of women:

There are issues associated with promoting women that have nothing to do with competence.

To start with, I don't think that society has accepted the concept of role reversal. If a woman is not a single career person, there is a whole set of associated problems. Not very many married women will uproot their spouse from his career. The concept still is that the male partner's career should be fostered. This is a real problem, because one of the conditions of contest in my organization is that you have to be mobile. I believe very strongly that the qualitative judgement needed to become an investments manager is only going to be achieved by working in three or four different market places. The dynamics that influence value in each area, in each region of our country are very different. Without experiencing all of them, you are not a fully seasoned mortgage lender.

It's also my observation, without a lot of experience, that women don't focus on their career in the same way as men do. There is not the expectation in most women that they will work for 40 years. The path they are setting out at the age of 23 or 24 is not a 40-year path. It's until they get married, until they have children, until a lot of things happen. That's not a universal statement, because if a man or a woman were to approach something with a single-minded purpose, I think either one is going to achieve it. Not many men approach their career in that manner, but I think fewer women do, because they have these other uncertainties as to which direction they are going.

So it's my recent experience—and I guess it's not unique to me—that women have a harder time progressing even though they understand the conditions of contest for getting ahead. They are less willing to give up friends and a social environment

outside of work. It's also a very rare exception where, when there is overtime to be done, the woman will stay and the husbands are home at four o'clock to pick up the children.

Another reality is that most women have gaps in their career. Women do get pregnant, and if a woman is going to have two to three children, the gaps in her career are more than an irritant. From a philosophical point of view, it's fine, but if you have a key person who disappears for five months every two to three years, it's going to be difficult to build around. We have become a lean organization and we don't have three or four layers of competent people who can step into the gap. We plan and make sure that we have someone to pick up the pieces, but the person who has to fill in is already fully employed, so it stresses the whole organization when you do it.

The biggest danger I caution, is that you can't force increased female representation in management faster than natural growth will allow it to happen. I wouldn't like to see a United States quota program. If it was mandated that I had to hire a female manager from the outside, presumably I could, but I don't do that with men, because I believe very strongly in training our own managers for reasons of consistency of ideas and focus. Quality control is very important in investments. Loan losses can be significant if you don't know what you are doing and it's an area where there is a wide divergence of thought. I don't think equal representation objectives for management should ever transcend the fundamental objectives of the business.

Diane Haas expressed her own concerns about quotas which specified the percentage of various levels of management which had to be filled by women:

I don't agree with the classic affirmative action program, that says you must have 20 per cent of women in management, for two reasons: first, from a corporate perspective, it's quite conceivable that you will get people who are not qualified in those positions because you are striving to achieve quotas; second, I think it's grossly unfair to put people in positions that they have trouble coping with. There are still days when I scare the living daylights out of myself doing what I'm doing, thinking, is this for real or am I a fake? So I can imagine what someone who is not qualified would feel in the job.

I'll be darned if I want to see women in management who are not good, who are not qualified and who cannot handle it. I think if that happens, the reflection of non-performance is on all the women in management, not just the ones who are failing. Right now, we are like giraffes in the forest. We are a very visible small minority and we are being watched. Therefore, it's crucial that we do well. I don't want to see someone, a non-performer, promoted simply because of their sex. At the same time, we have to get commitment from a predominantly male management to start encouraging women to develop.

THE TASK

As the meeting ended, the task force coordinator summed up the task:

We have only three or four meetings left to complete our recommendations, so we have to start developing our plan. Where should we start? What do we need to do to tackle this issue?

THE BANK OF MONTREAL—THE TASK FORCE ON THE ADVANCEMENT OF WOMEN IN THE BANK (A)

Prepared by Pamela Tebbutt under the supervision of Professor Bernard Portis

Version: (A) 2002-04-29

It was Monday afternoon, January 13, 1992. Deborah Westman had just completed her training through the Bank of Montreal's (BMO) Management Development Program (MDP) and had received an offer to join the Personal and Commercial Financial Services Group (PCFS) as a Commercial Account Manager. With MDP behind her, Deborah was considered management potential—but was she really? Deborah had become familiar with the "glass ceiling"— women's ability to see senior management ranks but not reach them. She did not want to work in a "boys' club," yet she knew that very few mid-market Commercial Account Managers were female.[1] Her decision to accept the offer instead of assuming a more "traditional" head office role would depend on her belief that change could happen—that the BMO's recently established Task Force on the Advancement of Women in the Bank would be a success.

THE BANK OF MONTREAL

The Bank of Montreal, established in Montreal in 1817, is Canada's oldest chartered bank. The BMO offers personal, commercial, corporate, government and international financial services and operates across Canada and in selected centres throughout the world. United States operations are primarily carried out through a wholly owned subsidiary, Harris Bankcorp Inc. The BMO also owns 75 per cent of Nesbitt, Thomson Inc., a fully integrated Canadian investment dealer. Through Nesbitt, Thomson, the Bank offers underwriting, brokerage, advisory and investment services. Finally, specialized portfolio management services are offered through Bank of Montreal Investment Limited.

In terms of average asset base,[2] the BMO is the third largest chartered bank after the Royal Bank and the Canadian Imperial Bank of Commerce.

However, based on the results of the fiscal year ended October 31, 1991, the BMO was the fastest growing of the large Canadian banks, with loan growth of 9.2 per cent to $55.1 billion and asset growth of 13 per cent to $87.4 billion. Achieving its targeted return on common equity of 15 per cent in 1991, the BMO's profitability ranked third behind the Bank of Nova Scotia and the Royal Bank.

Two principal mandates dominated the BMO's operations in 1991. First was the challenge to maximize efficiencies and bring the expense/revenue ratio in line with the industry average of 59.4 per cent. During 1991, rationalization and the elimination of excess overhead contributed to an improvement in the expense/revenue ratio from 67.1 per cent at fiscal year end 1990 to 61.6 per cent at fiscal year end 1991. Second, the BMO strived to enhance its competitive position in 1991 by refocusing on the delivery of superior customer service at both the retail and commercial banking levels. To achieve this goal, customer service training courses were developed and offered to front-line employees. Expenditures were also made to rebuild the public image of the Bank through branch renovations, enhancements and a new advertising campaign that capitalized on the slogan "We're paying attention." For these reasons, Deborah identified the BMO as one of the more progressive Canadian banks to work for; the BMO was out to improve its image to all stakeholders, including the employees.

THE GLASS CEILING

The glass ceiling is an invisible barrier through which women can aspire to the more senior ranks of management, but cannot reach them. It is not exclusive to the BMO, or the Canadian banking industry. However, females accounted for 75 per cent of the Bank's employees in 1990, while only 13 per cent of senior management and six per cent of executives were women. In Deborah's opinion, this was a modest improvement since the first three female executives were

appointed by the Bank in 1982. Over the past six years, the number of senior managers at the Bank has grown by 33 per cent, while the number of female senior managers has grown by a mere one per cent per year. These statistics provided a strong argument that the glass ceiling exists.

THE TASK FORCE ON THE ADVANCEMENT OF WOMEN IN THE BANK OF MONTREAL

In response to the glass ceiling, Tony Comper, President and Chief Operating Officer, established a Task Force on the Advancement of Women in the Bank, in December 1990. Mr. Comper commented on the goals of the Task Force:

> It may well mean setting a numerical goal. But numerical targets will only be a means to our real goal. That is, to create an environment where women will meet no barriers to advancement, where there will be continuous advancement toward true equality, where both women and men can progress and enjoy rewarding careers.

Mr. Comper appointed Marnie Kinsley, Vice-President, to head the Task Force. Ms. Kinsley, a chartered accountant, joined the Bank in 1985. She had held senior positions in Corporate Audit and the Securities Service Centre in Toronto, Ontario. Ms. Kinsley reported directly to Tony Comper and was responsible for four full-time Task Force members and 11 part-time members (refer to Exhibit 1). The members represented several banking groups, geographic regions, and the gender composition of the Bank (75 per cent female and 25 per cent male). Also involved in the process was a Steering Committee, responsible for directing the activities of the Task Force, and a Consultative Group, both of which were chaired by Tony Comper. The Consultative Group, formed to provide feedback on decisions and directions of the Task Force, offered a unique perspective as it was comprised of the female executives of the Bank. As a result, the Task Force was able to benefit from the experiences of these women and use them as role models for

---

President and Chief Operating Officer

Tony Comper

Vice-President and Task Force Leader

Marnie Kinsley

Full-Time Task Force Members

Maureen Bell, Administration
Brian Bieniara, Research
Mary Lou Hukezalie, Human Resources
Terri Mabey, Communications

Part-Time Task Force Members

Judith Bonaparte, Deborah Casey, Donald Dixon, Moyna Laing, Danielle Malka,
Ian Mole, Eleanor Morrison, Kathy Pack, Carl Rehel, Karen Rubin, Pamela Rueda

Consultative Group

Beverly Blucher, Yvonne Bos, Loretta Hennessey, Catherine Irwin, Kim MacNeil, Penny Chard,
Deanna Rosenswig, Carol Snider, Penny Somerville, Harriet Stairs, Peggy Sum, Catharina Van Berkel,
Pamela Ward, Jane Weatherbie, Linda Fitzsimmons (Harris Bankcorp), Maribeth Rahe (Harris Bankcorp),
Kristine Vikmanis (Nesbitt, Thomson)

Steering Committee

Ronald Call, Tony Comper, Deanna Rosenswig, Penny Somerville, Harriet Stairs,
Robert Tetley, Jane Weatherbie

Exhibit 1   The Task Force Participants

success. Through an effective internal and external communication strategy, the Task Force had become highly visible to the employees and the media. This visibility spurred both criticism and support.

Deborah had the opportunity to meet Marnie Kinsley following a presentation by the Task Force. Ms. Kinsley had been very open with Deborah in discussing her beliefs on the issue of employment equity. She spoke of her own personal experience with the glass ceiling, as she had accepted the position as Task Force Leader amid criticism from men and women that it was a "token" role. Ms. Kinsley responded to the criticism with confidence that she had the talent and skills necessary to make change happen. This was her opportunity to become a visible change agent within the Bank. She was committed to

succeed as, both in the Bank's and the public's eyes, her credibility was at stake.

The Task Force became the topic of conversation among Deborah and her co-workers on many occasions. A number of her female peers argued that real change was unlikely and that *forced* change would foster increased tokenism and rivalry between the sexes. Certain of her male colleagues did not agree that there was an equality problem; others were concerned about reverse discrimination.

During her discussion with Deborah, Ms. Kinsley described her own view of resistance as the "clay layer." Between the progressive, "blue sky" views of Matthew Barrett, Chairman and Chief Executive Officer, and Tony Comper, and the change-oriented, "grass roots" view of the more junior employees, there is the seemingly "immoveable" middle management. She attributed this resistance to change to issues such as fear of personal loss, insecurity and outright denial that a problem existed. This "clay layer" presented a substantial challenge to Ms. Kinsley, as the success of the Task Force demanded the support of all management.

The Task Force had three primary objectives: identify the barriers to advancement; recommend changes to remove the barriers; and recommend goals and methods of measurement. Advancement had been defined by the Task Force to include promotion, job enrichment and the ability to balance work and family life. Aside from the earlier statistics given on representation of females in the BMO's management ranks, the Task Force's study of work force trends identified four factors that supported the need for change.

- Women have become significant participants in the workforce. In 1951, 25 per cent of women were in the Ontario workforce. By 1990, the number reached 60 per cent.
- The province's employers are facing a "demographic crunch" due to the aging population and the declining birth rate. Specifically, Ontario workforce growth slowed from 2.8 per cent during 1956–1961 to 1.7 per cent during 1986–1991.
- Employers are facing a change in workforce values as employees are expressing concern for quality of work life and outside commitments, such as family and the community.
- With the convergence of the above, the BMO must become "an employer of choice" in order to attract and maintain a committed, satisfied human capital base.

Furthermore, proponents of the Task Force believed that the time for change was now. The BMO had undergone a dramatic shift in leadership style from the top-down approach of William Mulholland, a former Wall Street investment banker, to the teamwork-oriented, visionary styles of Matthew Barrett and Tony Comper. Matthew Barrett, considered an "icon of the caring, socially aware manager of the 1990s,"[3] had announced to his employees his desire to "breathe new life into the Bank." The Chairman and his executive team

had developed a comprehensive strategic plan for the Bank, and through a series of videos and personal visits he had taken this plan to every BMO employee. As part of the strategic plan, both Matthew Barrett and Tony Comper vowed to shatter the glass ceiling.

INITIATING CHANGE

Marnie Kinsley believed that the change process should begin with a full understanding of how employees felt about the glass ceiling and the types of barriers that women were facing in the Bank. While the issue was the Advancement of Women, the Task Force wanted the opinions of both men and women. As a first step, the Task Force met with several banking groups through employee focus sessions, open forums, presentations and interviews with executives. Marnie Kinsley, herself, did over 100 presentations across Canada. These sessions served to enhance the Task Force's understanding of the employees' concerns and the employees' awareness that change was forthcoming.

The Task Force then studied the data from the BMO's Human Resource Information System (HRIS) to develop a complete view of the Bank's employee base. The HRIS was also used to track the progress of certain key employee groups and, specifically, males versus females. The Task Force also examined the Bank's human resource policies in order to identify areas in which policies were outdated and/or lacking. Furthermore, various organizations in the financial services and other industries were visited in order to enhance the Task Force's understanding of different approaches to dealing with the glass ceiling.

From their discussions with employees, the members of the Task Force discovered a set of "conventional beliefs" among employees regarding "why women don't get promoted." The five beliefs were: women are either too young or too old; women are less committed to their work because they leave to have children; women are not as highly educated as their male peers; women don't have the right stuff to compete with men; and, time will take care of the advancement of women to senior jobs at the Bank.

The Task Force decided that a more in-depth study of the employees' concerns could be achieved through a survey. With the assistance of the consulting firm, William M. Mercer Limited (Mercer), a comprehensive 19-page survey was developed and distributed to more than 15,000 employees, or approximately 55 per cent of the Bank's staff. The survey was strictly confidential, and the questions were divided into four sections: "Your Experience at the Bank"; "Your Personal Views"; "Background Information"; and one open-ended question entitled "Your Comments." The survey was sent out in June 1991, and a 62 per cent response rate was received.

Mercer was retained to tabulate and analyze the survey responses and present the findings to the Bank. The survey revealed that women and men perceive the opportunities for women to advance differently. For example, at all management levels, at least 74 per cent of men in the Bank believe that women have the same opportunities as men to get ahead. A maximum of 33 per cent of female management share the same optimism.

Mercer also concluded that the Bank's employees saw three major barriers to the advancement of women. First, women suffer from a set of outdated assumptions and conclusions, or "conventional beliefs," held by both men and women. Second, women have not received adequate access to information regarding career opportunities and have not been encouraged by their supervisors to seek opportunities to realize their potential. Third, when employees have responded to commitments outside of the Bank (family, education or community), their commitment to their career has been questioned. As a result, their ability to advance has been limited. The following comment, written in the survey by one of the Bank's female senior managers, reflects the type of outdated assumptions that prevailed.

> Once a woman reaches middle management, she is told she has done very well—after all, look how far you have come in the Bank. For men, however, the sky is the limit and if they aspire to be a senior vice president, more power to them! If a woman aspires to be a senior vice president, everyone snickers and wonders who she thinks she is!

The Task Force believed that the only way to "test" the conventional beliefs was through a study of the HRIS system. The data substantiated the following:

- The average age of women at the BMO (at all management and non-management levels) combined is one year younger than the average of men. Therefore, women are neither too young nor too old.
- On average, a woman's service record is one year shorter than a man's, and longer at all levels except senior management. Despite the birth of children, women are as committed to their careers as men.
- At the non-management and junior management levels, the primary feeder groups into more senior management positions, the number of females with university and college degrees outnumber the number of males with degrees by a factor of 2.64 times. Therefore, women do have the necessary education to succeed.
- At all management ranks, the percentage of females achieving the top two performance levels exceeds the percentage of males achieving these levels by seven to 14 per cent. Therefore, women can compete on performance.
- With the current pace of change, only 22 per cent of BMO senior management and 18 per cent of executives will be female by the year 2000. Therefore, time alone will not eliminate the glass ceiling.

DEBORAH WESTMAN

Deborah Westman had been employed by the BMO for two years. She had joined the Commercial Banking Officer Program (CBO), a fast-track program designed to bring university graduates into the Bank. As a CBO, Deborah was responsible for analyzing the financial and operational riskiness of the BMO's corporate clients. The CBO Program was a feeder into the Bank and, more specifically, the MDP Program. Deborah was promoted into the MDP Program after 12 months as a CBO. She went on to complete her MDP training during the following year, focusing on tasks such as commercial account management and credit analysis. Because the purpose of the MDP Program was to bring young, highly educated professionals into the Bank, it consisted of solely temporary positions. As her training was complete, Deborah was required to leave the MDP Program and assume a permanent position.

Career paths beyond MDP depended on the skills and interests of the individual as well as the demands of the Bank. Since Commercial Banking had become a strategic focus of the Bank, there were Commercial Account Management positions open. However, other opportunities that Deborah faced included senior analyst positions within Corporate Banking and the Treasury Group. Deborah believed that the salary and responsibility levels offered by these positions would be very similar to Commercial Account Management. In any case, Deborah would be required to interview for these positions, as would any MDP graduate.

Deborah had been recognized by her supervisors as a strong performer. Her progress, in terms of promotions and pay increases, was indicative of that performance. Despite the competitive nature of the MDP Program, Deborah was admired by her fellow CBO/MDP peers for her degree of commitment to her job and her personal development. She had an undergraduate business degree. Despite the long hours she spent at the Bank, her personal time was used to study for part-time MBA courses.

While extremely motivated by her career progress, Deborah had two personal commitments to satisfy over the next few years. She wanted to complete her MBA and, after two years of part-time study, she felt that she would receive more from the program if she studied the final year on a full-time basis. Her motivation for doing the MBA was twofold: she enjoyed the challenge and she had been told in an initial interview at the Bank that an MBA was a requirement for "vice-president potential." For these reasons, she knew that she would be requesting an eight-month unpaid leave of absence to complete her studies. From the experience of one of her colleagues, she knew that a leave of absence was something that the BMO closely scrutinized.

Deborah was turning 30 this year and celebrating her fourth wedding anniversary. She and her husband had agreed that at age 30 they would begin thinking about a family. Deborah wanted children, but did not want to begin a family until she had completed her MBA and was well-established in her career. Her husband was more eager. Deborah did not want their plans to upset her career. She was frustrated by the notion that having children was a joint responsibility, and yet her husband's career in the investment brokerage business would likely continue unaffected.

Deborah recalled the information released by the Task Force. She had read about the survey results and, specifically, about the employees' perceptions regarding the third barrier to the advancement of women. She was concerned that her request for an unpaid leave of absence to complete her MBA and her eventual desire for maternity/child care leave would tarnish her managers' perceptions of her commitment to her job. Deborah recalled her early experiences as a CBO. She felt that it was odd that four of the six supervisors that had moved in or out of the Program over the course of her stay were females that had just returned from maternity leave. These women had left Account Management positions to go on their maternity leaves. Deborah realized that these women may have requested a career change from Account Management to a head office/supervisory role; however, she wondered whether there were other forces at play.

Deborah was concerned that she would feel relatively isolated in the predominantly male Commercial Banking environment. She recalled the comment of one of her peers:

> Women tend to get excluded from "going to lunch groups," "going for coffee" groups and "drinks and dinner in the evenings and weekends" groups. These tend to be organized by men who feel comfortable with each other. When these groups get

together, business is discussed, so women automatically miss out on useful and, at times, important information.

At the same time, the challenge of Commercial Account Management attracted her, particularly now that the executive management had targeted the commercial segment as a key area for future growth. Deborah also knew that she had the talent and skills that would allow her to do well in either a head office or Commercial Banking "line" role.

THE RECOMMENDATIONS OF THE TASK FORCE

The Task Force took eight months to fully comprehend and develop recommendations from their findings. This effort involved extensive interaction with Mr. Comper, and several executives and senior managers of various banking groups. Two full months were then spent negotiating and further refining the recommendations, with the assistance of several executives, managers, Mr. Comper and the Steering Committee. Among the parties' considerations were the potential effect on the employees, the ease of implementation and the cost. The approval of the Bank's Board of Directors was also sought and received during a presentation by Marnie Kinsley in November 1991. This process gave rise to a final set of action plans that focused on four major strategies: *get the facts out; help all employees get ahead; reduce the stress; and make it official.* These plans are detailed below.

Get the Facts Out

The emphasis was to bridge the gap between the employees' perceptions, as revealed by the surveys, and the reality of women's abilities, career interests and degree of commitment. The Task Force recommended that all of their significant findings be communicated to the employees by way of a comprehensive 24-page "Report to Employees." Results were made public via press conferences with Tony Comper and Marnie Kinsley.

The Task Force recommended the implementation of one-day training sessions to focus on the attitudes and behaviours that contribute to the glass ceiling. The intention was to build consensus that the barriers were real and that change must occur. The sessions were to begin at the executive level, as early as February 1992.

Help all Employees Get Ahead

Improving the employees' access to information on career paths, job opportunities and career-enhancing activities was expected to benefit both genders. The Task Force recommended the implementation of a manager-training program to focus on the "coaching" and teamwork-oriented styles of leadership. The courses had been developed by the Bank's Human Resources Group and sessions were to begin in January 1992.

Access to job information was to be expanded with a pilot job vacancy notification system. The pilot was to be implemented by May 1992, and subsequently used to model a Bank-wide system for all employees at all levels.

The designation of certain management personnel as job information counsellors was recommended to increase the employees' access to career development opportunities. Individuals were to be assigned to counsellors other than their supervisors, thereby allowing them to discuss their suitability for particular jobs in complete confidence. The coaching skills developed in the manager-training sessions were expected to enhance the managers' abilities to deal with employees on a personal level. The program was to be operational by April 1992.

An Executive Advisor program was also recommended to provide senior management, male and female, with the opportunity to share ideas with executives in an informal setting. The objective of the program was to promote the level of networking among women and men in different banking groups, and ultimately to eliminate the tendency for a "boys' club." An Executive Advisor pilot was to be operational by April 1992.

The Task Force also recommended the implementation of cross-training exchanges for all employees as a means of career development. For satisfied employees not desiring increased responsibility through promotions, these activities were expected to enhance their interest in, and personal reward from, their jobs.

Finally, the Task Force recommended an increase in the participation rate of women in the Bank's commercial credit training program, CBO Program (to 50 per cent) and MDP Program (to 50 per cent). These initiatives, which were scheduled to begin immediately, were established to ensure the constant flow of talented, high-potential female candidates into the Bank's management streams.

Reduce the Stress

The focus of this strategy was to revise and/or implement policies that formally support women and men in balancing their multiple commitments to their job, family, education and communities. One of the objectives of this strategy was to revise policies in order to eliminate any discriminatory attitudes towards maternity leaves, child-care days and absences for educational purposes.

Specifically, the Task Force recommended the development of human resources policies that support flexible work arrangements such as compressed work weeks, job-sharing, part-time management positions, telecommuting (working at home via the computer) and opportunities for women to phase in their return to work following maternity leave. As an example, "People Care Days" were recommended to allow short-term leaves for employees to meet their multiple commitments. Secondly, a revision of the unpaid leave of absence policy was recommended in order to facilitate leaves for family, educational and other reasons. A "how-to" booklet on possible flexible work arrangements was to be distributed to all employees.

The Task Force also studied the concept of offering in-house daycare programs. On the basis of costs and accessibility, the study concluded that offering a daycare referral service would be a more effective means of assisting employees in finding suitable child-care providers in their own communities. This service was concurrently introduced with the report of the Task Force.

Make It Official

Lastly, and possibly most importantly, the Task Force recommended that all managers be accountable for ongoing change towards workplace equality in all job categories at all levels. The Task Force recommended that all managers be responsible for setting goals and devising action plans for the hiring, development and promotion of women. These goals, or "flexible targets," were to focus all management's efforts on eliminating barriers with true equality being the ultimate measure of success. The goal setting and planning process was scheduled to become a part of the annual business planning process, commencing in fiscal 1992.

Finally, the Task Force recommended that the rate of women's advancement in key managerial and specialty roles, including Commercial Account Management and Credit, should be monitored on a quarterly basis. Furthermore, the whole Bank's systematic progress in advancing women was to be measured quarterly, with a report published annually to outline the progress to all employees. The reports were to include a survey and analysis of how employees were responding to the changes. The first annual report was to be published in November 1992.

PERSONAL DECISIONS

Deborah sat staring at her copy of the "Report to Employees." Immediately, she identified personal gains with the proposed revisions to the leave of absence and maternity/child care policies. But if outdated attitudes and false conclusions were also roots of the glass ceiling, were attitudes likely to change? Were the actions employed and recommendations put forth by the Task Force sufficient to change attitudes and, as a result, smash the glass ceiling? Were the recommendations regarding goal setting, monitoring and hiring likely to cause charges of reverse discrimination? With the leadership styles of Matthew Barrett and Tony Comper and the focused strategic plan of the Bank, Deborah believed that there were opportunities for a challenging and rewarding career at the BMO. Was she wrong in feeling that she could take advantage of a heightened awareness of women? Was she wrong in believing that the barriers would be removed?

NOTES

1. Mid-market was a term that referred to commercial accounts with sales between $5 million and $500 million.

2. Average asset base is a typical measure used to evaluate the size of a bank. Average assets is defined as beginning-of-the-year assets plus end-of-year assets, divided by two.

3. *The Financial Post,* January 6, 1992.

"SYNERGY" AT CITY HALL (A)

Prepared by E.D. Jackie Watson

Version: (A) 2002-03-05

Anna Hewitt, Equal Opportunity (EO) Director for the City of Graniton, was worried. She had just seen the "trial run" of the workshop being prepared for City Hall senior management in March 1989. Planned and organized by an informal group of women managers (the "Synergy Group") and two outside consultants, the workshop was intended to make the EO Senior Managers[1] aware of issues affecting women in management at City Hall.

"We can't allow that presentation to be given," Anna had said, on her way out the door to her next meeting. "And I can't act as the lone spokesperson on behalf of City Hall women once again. I thought you were taking the initiative, this time . . . I am disappointed!"

The following day, seated at her office desk, Anna thoughtfully considered the activities of the Synergy Group—past, present, and future. "Where do we go from here?" she wondered. "Are our goals and methods completely off-base? What's happening to the Synergy Group process? What kinds of results *should* we expect? . . . and will we ever become the dynamic force for change at City Hall that I envision?"

CITY GOVERNMENT

Graniton was a bustling Canadian metropolis with a population of 600,000 in 1989. The city was governed by elected officials—a mayor and a city council composed of 13 councillors representing the city's 13 wards. The departments, agencies, and boards dealing directly with municipal responsibilities such as public transit, police protection, social services, fire protection, public works, taxes, public health, and zoning and development control, reported regularly to City Council through standing committees (see Exhibit 1).

City Hall controlled an annual budget of almost one billion dollars. Graniton's 5,800 employees worked in various locations throughout the city—area health offices, community recreation centres, parks and playgrounds, fire stations, local permit and inspection offices, and the new City Hall building. City government dealt with urgent issues daily—insufficient housing, poverty, racial tension, and crime, to name a few. Graniton's Equal Opportunity Director expressed her view of the most pressing municipal problems as follows:

CITY HALL
|
EXECUTIVE COMMITTEE
|

STANDING COMMITTEE	*CIVIC DEPARTMENT*	*HEAD*
City Services Committee	City Property Department	Commissioner
	Fire Department	Fire Chief
	Public Works Department	Commissioner
Land Use Committee	Planning & Development Department	Commissioner
Board of Health	Public Health Department	Medical Officer of Health
Neighbourhoods Committee	Housing Department	Commissioner
	Parks & Recreation Department	Commissioner

Departments Responsible to the Executive Committee

CIVIC DEPARTMENT	*HEAD*
Audit Department	City Auditor
City Clerk's Department	City Clerk
Finance Department	Commissioner
Legal Department	City Solicitor
Management Services Department	Executive Director
Office of Labour Relations	Director
Purchasing & Supply Department	Commissioner

Exhibit 1   Relationships Among Committees of Council and Civic Departments

As in all large Canadian municipalities, the face of Graniton City is changing every day. Police, transit, and all city services must change and develop so we can serve the full population. The race relations issue is important for the City and the Mayor right now; and the poverty of women is a disgrace. Our public officials are saying how wonderful it is that for the first time we've got four food banks operating—is that our solution? And the housing problem . . . the cost of housing here is phenomenal, and it's not going to get any better. We have just erected a multi-million dollar City Hall, and we have people with no place to sleep—where's the logic in that?

MANAGEMENT SERVICES

One arm of civic government was the Management Services Department (see Exhibit 2 for an organization chart), described as "one of a number of City Departments providing a range of valuable administrative functions and services enabling the Corporation to operate smoothly and effectively." Management Services assisted other City departments in formulating strategic plans and solving problems; it administered policies and programs affecting City Hall employees—equal opportunity, personnel services, and occupational health and safety; and its computer division developed, coordinated, and maintained the use of computer software and equipment in all City departments.

Talking about the difficulties they encountered in achieving their individual work objectives under the banner of Management Services, several staff members mentioned the need to "change the mentality of the corporation" from "13 little fiefdoms, each operating like an individual

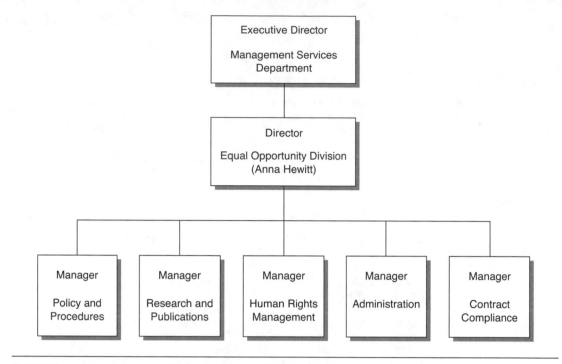

Exhibit 2   Organization of Equal Opportunity Division, 1989

company within the organization," to one collaborative, unified team. They also worried that the corporation had "no clearly defined overall vision, no five-year plan"; and one manager reported, "It's scary when operating budgets are prepared year by year, with no five- or 10-year projections."

Part of the difficulty in achieving a unified approach appeared to lie in the deeply entrenched corporate culture which supported the male-dominated "fiefdoms," and in individual differences between "two sets of commissioners[2]—the long-term old-timers and the new ones, much younger," each type operating with different management and leadership styles and priorities.

One manager hoped for a change in focus of the efforts of the Management Services Executive Director:

> It is my dream that he would be really concerned with the conditions within our workplace, and the extent to which his staff experts in Management Services could contribute to a real advancement of internal conditions. Externally, the City supports

major initiatives like "Plan for Progress" and "Environmental Horizons 2001"—future-directed efforts to create a better urban environment. As part of that movement, we could make a profound statement about the role which the infrastructure, the people who provide the services, can play in contributing to these future visions.

> I wish his main concern would be the creation of a truly safe, equitable, flexible, future-directed civic corporation. That's where we in our unit direct our efforts; and we really need him to help us do that. Otherwise, the health and well-being of our people will continue to be sacrificed. Was it really a good pyramid if 90,000 slaves dies constructing it? Was that a good vision, to build it anyway, regardless of the human cost?

EQUAL OPPORTUNITY

The history of Equal Opportunity initiatives at Graniton City Hall on behalf of women, people with disabilities, native peoples, and racial and ethnic minorities began in the mid-1970s with Council's establishment of a Mayor's Task Force on the Status of Women in Graniton. After completing a wide-ranging report on issues such as child-care programs and job evaluations, the Task Force was disbanded, with a part-time Affirmative Action Administrator being retained to help implement its recommendations.

A full-time EO Coordinator, Anna Hewitt, was appointed in 1980. Anna came to the City from a government post, where she had spearheaded the development of an Affirmative Action program within a large federal ministry. Anna recalled:

> I've always had a strong interest in women's issues. I was brought up by a single parent in an all-female family, and I am a single parent myself. I never experienced any "negatives" in the exciting life my mother, aunt, grandmother and I led together, so I've never had any hang-ups about lacking a father figure; Mother was Father, and she was great! She taught us we could do anything we wanted—there was *nothing* we couldn't do!

> And most of the other women I've dealt with in my career are competent professionals, stimulating individuals. I've had some very good business relationships with men, but I like to be around women, and I like to work with women.

One of Anna Hewitt's first projects was the publication of a comprehensive "Equal Opportunity Overview" containing a number of recommendations directed toward the achievement, over the next five years, of a more equitable representation and fuller utilization of women and men at all levels and in all categories of the organization, as well as a full recognition of their contribution to the work of the City of Graniton.

Subsequent "milestones" included a comprehensive job evaluation study; the establishment of Goals and Timetables (a reporting system to increase the numbers of minorities, women, native and disabled people hired); the inauguration of an annual Institute on Women in the Workplace; support for the appointment by City Council of the first woman Commissioner; the introduction of a Contract Compliance policy;

and many other initiatives. An EO specialist remarked:

> We've been training our managers for years now on what Equal Opportunity means and what their responsibilities are—the Human Rights Code and how that affects good management practice. We're most concerned with changing the *behaviour* of our managers; changes in attitudes will follow! And already we are seeing some changes in behaviour, some increased awareness. There's still lots of work to do, many barriers; but there has been some progress made.

Concurrent with these changes and her increasing responsibilities, Anna recruited and developed a well-qualified staff. The value and scope of EO operations were formally recognized with the creation in 1984 of an Equal Opportunity Division, headed by Director Anna Hewitt. Although responsibilities for different EO functions were shared among all staff within her Division, Anna herself was perceived as the standard bearer for women's equality throughout the Corporation. Her name had become synonymous with "women's issues," although her actual concerns were much broader. Anna said:

> I work 24 hours a day on issues of equal opportunity for all. In this kind of job, personal goals are work goals. You're implementing your own values and beliefs, so you can't separate who you are from what you do. But it's always been a concern of mine that people depend too much on me personally, in this organization. They think *I'm* the program, the *program* isn't the program. I'd like to detach myself somewhat—not be seen as the "issue," myself—but that's not happening.

> My vision for this organization is that any woman should be able to be whatever she wants in this workplace. Women should be allowed to work here without harassment, with dignity, and be allowed to move through this organization the same way as anybody else—get promoted and get paid equally. To do this, we have to put women back on the agenda—and I think they're not on the agenda, right now. At a meeting yesterday, the Chairperson said, "The Province is looking for eight senior businessmen . . . ," and I interjected, " . . . or women!" It's that kind of thing. I would like women to be included automatically.

WOMEN IN MANAGEMENT AT CITY HALL

Approximately 2,100 of the 5,800 City employees were female. Marked variations in gender composition were observed from one department to another. For example, there was a striking difference between Recreation (approximately 50 per cent men and 50 per cent women) and Parks (of approximately 250 full-time employees, only seven were women).

A smaller number of female City employees were represented in management ranks (see Table 1 below). All department heads had been male until 1989, when a woman was appointed City Clerk in spite of strong opposition from some quarters to a female occupying that important post.

The comments of individual women managers about advancing in management gave some indication of their perceived areas of difficulty:

One of our most urgent issues at City Hall occurs as women are trying to move into positions of power. The problem is lack of support from colleagues and peers, from support staff, and inadequate structural support. You need all of those. We do have a good Equal Opportunity program, which ensures that women candidates will at least be put forward along with minority candidates and disabled. There's a reporting system, "Goals and Timetables," that says each department has to report back how many minority and disabled employees are hired. But there's still a lot of resistance—and people like Anna have to be pushing EO all the time, while people on the other side are working hard to try to find a way around it.

Table 1   Men and Women in City Hall Management, 1989

Level	Men	Women	Total
Department Head	12	1	13
Deputy Department Head	27	2	29
Executive Director	38	5	43
Director	78	13	91
Manager	131	76	207

In Graniton City Hall, I see a few women getting into senior positions. There's a filtering-up effect. But they haven't gotten there easily. They have arrived there by playing the game as it is played now, in this organization's culture. And being culturally in tune with the organization functions best!

*****

When I expressed my interest in being considered for a higher position, most of my colleagues, many of whom were female, expressed disbelief: "Why would you want to become a manager?" I applied for three or four management positions in a row, and got none. The last one . . . I had been working in that same area for years, and I was the most senior person in the group, and was well-qualified for that position, in my view. But instead of making an internal appointment that time, they chose an outside candidate for the first time! So I said, "Screw you," and left the Department.

After every rejection, I went back and asked why. This was a debilitating experience, because they wouldn't say, "It's because you're a woman"— they pointed out my flaws, different ones with each rejection. (I have since gone back to my original manager and discussed my perception of this selection process as discriminatory, and he now sees my point of view.)

*****

The other side of the coin—you've got to have women who believe they have the *right* to aspire to the office, and that they are as good as a male candidate. We've a long way to go before we stop judging *ourselves* on the basis of gender! There are a lot of women who enter the corporation who believe that you shouldn't push yourself—and part of the culture here says it's unseemly for women to promote themselves.

Historically, City Hall women in management tended to avoid seeking support from one another. ("We often tend not to make connections for ourselves—we stay so isolated. I've never figured out why . . .") However, by the late 1980s, at least two informal women's groups had emerged. One was a group of four senior women who met regularly for dinner "to plan strategies and to support each other. We discuss how to operate politically, how to make it in the system. We share information about what is happening."

Another group was composed of seven upper-middle managers who had come together during a 1988 conference, and continued to meet afterwards for mutual support and information-sharing. Anna Hewitt was perceived as the "active ingredient" in the formation of both groups. The ultimate goal of each was improving the climate at City Hall for the advancement of women in management ranks: "We're fighting the glass ceiling, and we're fighting our own culture."

Many individual women managers felt discriminated against in their progress toward higher positions in the Corporation, but in difficult-to-define subtle ways. Several mentioned the problems associated with an undervalued management style:

> Women are perceived differently than men, as managers. There's a general discomfort with our management style. We're not accorded credibility, not given recognition for our strengths, which include people skills. In some jobs, non-traditional management skills are essential. The ability to manage by consensus, through coordination, convincing through influence, not autocratically "ordering," ought to be valued more. The range of acceptable behaviour is very narrow. Where one woman might be perceived as successful by her staff because of her participative style, she could be perceived by her superiors as too easily swayed. Another woman with an authoritarian style could be perceived by senior management as too aggressive. The range gets narrower and narrower as you get nearer the top.

*****

Many women managers tend to be peacemakers, wanting things to go smoothly. Even when you're giving bad news, you do it in such a way as not to demean the person. It's a feminine trait, caring for people, nurturing them. You don't want to be a mother hen, but you need to recognize that people don't leave all their personal problems behind when they come to work. Yet my male boss says, when two of my people aren't getting along, "*Fire* one!"

One opinion, frequently expressed, was that women exhibited superior expertise in certain aspects of City Hall administration. Often cited was most women's ability to handle the many details supporting the systems which create a healthy workplace.

> Women come in as administrators, see the details, and try to pick them all up. I feel I do that all the time. Men have never attended to these details. But I can't say: "You don't pay any attention to what needs to be done here. Can't you see that people are tired, and putting in too much overtime, and are working with antiquated equipment, and don't have enough telephones, and don't have adequate space?" And these things become exhausting . . . but *they* have what they need, why worry about us?

Women managers agreed that personnel policies and practices were often a problem for women who aspired to senior positions. In conversation with the Director of another department, one woman remarked on the fact that many of the recent appointments in his department had been white Anglo-Saxon males. The Director responded that the selection process he had used was fair and above-board. The female manager replied "Yes, except that the perceptions people bring to that process are so subconsciously biased that the result tends to be predetermined." She continued:

> This intelligent man looked at me and said, "Then you're not talking about instances of individual discrimination, you're talking about something that's systemic." I said, "Bingo! You got it!" He shook his head in disbelief—there just couldn't be anything that wide-ranging and insidious in this organization . . .

Another time, we had an experience where we were doing a selection process for a manager's position. I encouraged two or three women whose professional reputations I knew to be above-average, to apply; but when the applications came over from Personnel, the women applicants had already been screened out of the short list. Just a quick look at all the applications told me that the women I had spoken to were more qualified on paper than four of the men on the list. I was furious! If the names had been removed from those applications before Personnel screened them, I have no doubt the women would have been among the top choices.

Another senior manager stated that equality in tangible terms of higher compensation was her objective: "My personal goals include getting equal pay with the men at City Hall. I'm $10,000 lower now; and when the next increase comes in, my salary will be even lower than comparable positions held by males!"

According to many women managers, instances of feeling left out, even personally rejected, in workplace interactions with their male colleagues, were common occurrences.

Your voice never gets *heard* in the way they hear each other. They seem to unite together against your opinion, as if they've all agreed to ignore your suggestions. I've had the experience many times of being in a meeting and feeling that I've just articulated something significant, well thought out . . . and it's as if my voice didn't register on the air. Nobody turns their eyes or acknowledges that I've spoken. That's just plain rude. I'm no shrinking violet; but what about other women who have difficulty speaking out? It's so easy to feel intimidated and discounted. This is definitely a *gender* issue. A man is not treated this way.

And why do the senior men keep throwing up road blocks, resisting our efforts? We spent months preparing and advertising an award-winning special course for women; and at the last minute, the men's negative reactions stopped our progress. They suddenly and belatedly became so critical— why have a program just for women? Why a university program? Why hold it in the workplace? And they *often* refuse to give legitimacy to programs we propose, that we expect them to support.

"Critical incidents" were experienced by women managers, which illustrated the type of discrimination and rejection most difficult to confront and deal with. "Vera" described such an incident:

We have a serious space problem, so I agreed to give one of my unit's offices to someone from another section, temporarily. This was the only "extra" space we had, and we need it back now. I

requested this person be moved out, and offered to find a space for him somewhere else; but my boss broke his promise to me, and said this person couldn't be moved.

I gave logical arguments, and proposed an alternative plan to my boss; but when I continued to be stonewalled, I very strongly *insisted* this person *had* to get out! My boss's response was, "Do you eat your young, too?" I was thus identified as a vicious female, which made me feel self-conscious and abused . . . and very, very angry.

"Barbara" mentioned another incident, and touched on the possibility of serious side-effects resulting from the insensitive behaviour of one male manager:

I was meeting with a male colleague in his office, together with another woman from my department. He interrupted what I was saying to bellow over our heads at his secretary in the outer office, "Betty! Hold my calls!" And we had scheduled a half-hour meeting, but when another male manager appeared at the door after 15 minutes or so, my colleague said, "I'll have to kick you out now, ladies."

We tolerated that behaviour as we would tolerate bad behaviour from a child. Maybe he would have acted the same way with men in the room . . . but it was really insensitive behaviour; and if we were two men, I think he would have said, "OK, guys, I have to go to another meeting now." And as much as you might say he's just a jerk and nobody listens to him anyway, there is a part of you in the pit of your stomach that feels badly. And the cumulative effect can be actual illness . . . like my stomach ulcer . . .

One woman manager expressed her heartfelt gratitude at her good fortune in finding a helpful male mentor when she entered the Corporation. Early in her career, she took the initiative of asking for a meeting with her Director, to ask about the long-term plans for the Department. From that time on, the Director took an active interest in her progress; and he took a "significant risk" to promote her the first time, into what had traditionally been a "man's job."

The female manager progressed through the management levels to eventually report directly to that Director, where "he spent time teaching me the ropes. He put me in situations where I had to sink or swim, letting me deal with situations on my own. An old-style manager wouldn't have let me learn that way; but this man would watch my performance without comment, then give me feedback quietly afterwards . . . unfortunately, I have no mentor in the senior position I hold now."

A SIGNIFICANT CONFERENCE

In January 1988, a landmark conference was held at Toronto's Harbour Castle Hotel. Entitled "The New Workplace Synergy," the conference drew nearly 1,000 men and women together to discuss how to work more effectively and productively within gender-integrated teams. Organizers offered a half-dozen free registrations to any organization making a donation to start-up costs. Graniton City Hall was one such organization. EO Director, Anna Hewitt, obtained the funding from Council, indicating that she would disregard the suggestion to choose a male/female mix, and send female delegates only. Anna invited the following managers to attend with her:

Linda Peterson (Manager, Employees' Health Services Division, Management Services Department), "because of her enthusiasm, energy and the fresh perspective she brings to this workplace. A revitalizing energy, that some of the people who've been around here for a long time need."

Suzanne Best (Manager, Housing Development Division, Housing Department), "because she works in a role at Housing that has left her alone for a long time. She needs to be brought in so she can work with a community of other women."

Mavis Decker (Director, Finance and Administration), "because she has done some excellent work for the organization in providing equal opportunities for minorities and other target groups. She's tough and resilient, and I feel it would be beneficial for her to meet with some other exceptional women, to focus that energy."

Lois Wilde (Director, Parks Division, Parks and Recreation Department), "because of her management

ability and her personal style. She will pull us back on track when we wander. She's steady, a rational-logical thinker—we need her."

Two other City Hall women, Dianne Smith (Consultant, Personnel Services Division, Management Services Department) and Cheryl Cranston (Consultant, Community Health Section, Department of Public Health) were invited speakers at the Conference. Dianne made a presentation describing the City's innovative "New Horizons" program, and she and Cheryl joined the City group for a team discussion during the final session of the three-day event.

Although the attendees from City Hall said they had no particular expectations of the conference in advance, most were delighted with the content and the participative process used throughout. Suzanne Best remarked:

> The conference was an apocryphal experience for some of us. For me personally, because I had let my feminism lie dormant for a few years, it reawakened a lot of my feelings of anger around the issues raised. For some of the other women, it was a time when they started to think of things that had affected them, in a new way; and they started to perceive that there might be an alternate world view by which their experiences could be more comfortably explained. And no matter what our individual views, it was helpful for all of us to make contact with each other.

> The concepts being discussed weren't new to me. Learning how to do something to help men and women work together more effectively was an important goal; but in the small groups I was part of, the men were learning far more than the women, and some were fighting very hard not to learn anything! But generally speaking, I don't think we learn all that much from the sessions at conferences. It's the contacts that are most important; and somehow, the experience should be brought back to your workplace.

CITY HALL'S "SYNERGY GROUP"

The eight women from Graniton City Hall decided to continue to meet after the conference for an indefinite period of time. Their first "Synergy Group" meeting was held the following month, with subsequent luncheon meetings scheduled every four to six weeks. Meetings were often held in the private dining room of a nearby professional association where a warm, congenial atmosphere prevailed.

Some members attended more regularly than others who had "incredibly busy" work schedules. Other women managers were invited to attend from time to time. These tended to be women perceived to be dynamic and enthusiastic feminists, who would make a positive contribution to group discussions and activities. Also, most were known to be in positions where they were isolated, where the kind of support the Synergy Group could give would be welcome. The value of the Group's support and information-sharing functions is illustrated by the following comments:

> I personally am finding the Synergy Group extremely valuable as a support network. It's like a microwave oven—if you don't have it, you get along without it, but . . . I was aware of feeling isolated, but I don't think I understood how isolated I was feeling. Then that group sort of happened, and all of a sudden, I felt very connected.

*****

> These women are movers and shakers, and I need to get their perceptions through those kinds of eyes. And I want to get to know them better as people— they are such an interesting group. Also, I am learning more about the politics at City Hall, beyond just the organization chart. But the support element is the most valuable asset of this group, for me.

ACTION PLANS

From the first luncheon meeting, some Synergy Group members advocated moving beyond the support and information functions, to taking action on behalf of City Hall women in management. One woman remarked, "The City sent us to that Synergy Conference, so we have some kind of a responsibility to feed back impressions

to the Corporation, or do something in return." Another said, "We can provide a valuable service by bringing the 'lessons' of the Conference back to our workplace."

The first step was the preparation of a draft mission statement for the Group, presented by Mavis Decker at the June meeting:

THAT THE BEHAVIOURAL STANDARDS OF THE CITY'S CORPORATE CULTURE BE REDEFINED IN ORDER TO RECOGNIZE WOMEN'S CONTRIBUTIONS AND VALUE SYSTEMS.

In the free-wheeling discussions which followed, some action-oriented strategies to achieve this goal were suggested:

- Make women's needs validated and known throughout City Hall (e.g., training programs for women);
- Learn from other organizations;
- Hold breakfast awareness sessions for men managers;
- Invite men managers to attend the next Synergy Conference and on-going workshops;
- Hold a day-long session for City Hall men and women (invitation only) at which videos from the Synergy Conference would be screened, followed by case studies—a consciousness-raising session;
- Create a women's "pod" within each department;
- Second some men managers to meet with us;
- Second women from departments not already represented to meet with us.

Discussions about various ways of presenting the women's perspective to City Hall managers continued throughout the balance of the year. Suzanne Best recalled:

> It soon became quite clear to us that most of the mechanisms we were discussing fell within the purview of the Training and Development section; so one of our problems became how to achieve sufficient credibility to exert influence over the Training and Development program. We considered presenting something to the department heads ourselves. Anna suggested the EO Senior Managers as the appropriate forum.

I remember discussing in some detail the riskiness of the proposition, and the difficulty of designing a saleable presentation. Most of us knew little about Training and Development, so we agreed to use a consultant. The consultant of our choice was not available, however, and we agreed to try out the ones actually retained.

Two consultants were contacted by a Synergy sub-group (three members who agreed to serve as organizers), and were commissioned to design a workshop, " . . . subject to our review and approval. We spent a lot of time with them, told them who we were, what we were trying to do. They claimed they had done a lot of this type of workshop; and so away they went to develop their plan."

The Equal Opportunities Director sent out a letter of invitation to the senior managers group to attend a meeting in March 1989, to be held in a City Hall board room (see Exhibit 3). All invitees indicated they would attend. Anna planned to send another memo in February, indicating that a few women in the organization had attended the Synergy Conference and were talking about the possibility of doing some training involving men and women in the organization; and their first step would be to conduct a workshop at the senior managers' March meeting.

THE "DRESS REHEARSAL"

In planning for the workshop, members of the Group often talked about how difficult some of the issues would be to effectively present to the EO Senior Managers; but Anna always seemed confident that an appropriate presentation could be designed. After the consultants completed their workshop design, the workshop sub-group suggested that the training materials be tested on members of the larger Synergy group, prior to the actual presentation to the senior managers.

MEMORANDUM

TO: E.O. Senior Managers

FROM: Anna Hewitt, Director

DATE: January 10, 1989

SUBJECT: 1989 Workshops

Happy New Year! To help with "Goals and Timetables" implementation and to ensure you are kept up to date on issues we will run a series of workshops for you in 1989. We also intend to send invitations to the Administrative Advisory Council because the issues covered should be of interest to members of the Council who are not already EO Senior Managers.

Please book March 14, 1989, from 9:30 a.m. to 12:00 for the first workshop. This promises to be an exceptional meeting! More information and content will follow shortly.

Looking forward to a productive year.

Anna

Anna Hewitt
Director
Equal Opportunity Division
Management Services Department

Exhibit 3   Anna Hewitt's Memo to Employment Equity Senior Managers

Table 2   Workshop Agenda for the "Dress Rehearsal"

2:00	Introduction (total group)
2:10	Measuring management skills (individual questionnaire)
2:20	Video: Women in Management
2:40	Discussion of video (total group)
2:55	Small group discussion (complete forms by consensus)
3:30	Warm-up: Discussion of findings (total group)
4:00	Close

Because they had committed to sponsor an unfamiliar type of training process, they felt they needed to learn more about it in advance.

The "dress rehearsal" was held in a training room. Synergy Group members were seated three or four to a table, with a copy of the workshop agenda (Table 2), structured exercises, and other printed materials at each place. Group members were to role play various EO Senior Managers, so that the type of feedback expected could be fielded by the consultants. A sub-group member explained:

> Those EO Senior Managers don't get to sit on the EO Committee because they're feminists—far from it, in most instances—but because they're Directors of Administration representing their Departments. They will be unsympathetic, perhaps downright hostile, during the workshop.

Anna Hewitt sat close to the door, arms folded, portraying one of the most "difficult" managers. Her recollections of the workshop were as negative as the role she was playing:

> The two consultants started out with a joke about Anna Hewitt—a nasty one, a put-down. It seemed to me that they were making Anna the brunt of their comments in order to get her established as *outside* of the Group, so that the Group would be seen as a unit separate from the EO function. I said nothing. I just sat with my arms folded, as would the Manager I was portraying. Then they described their five goals for the three-hour session, and

began their presentation by having everyone fill out a form—a duplicate of the exercise that the Heads were going to work on. Seemed like "school." I remained silent.

The newly appointed Manager of Training and Development for Graniton City Hall, Trudy McNab, was present throughout the session. Trudy had been invited by the organizing subgroup to meet the Synergy members, and to contribute her ideas and expertise in critiquing the workshop content.

The session proceeded according to the planned agenda. Inwardly, all of the attendees were experiencing some discomfort with the content and process: "We were beginning to see that the workshop probably would not achieve our goals, and that senior people were unlikely to want to risk their own credibility by being associated with it." Anna observed:

> Trudy asked a few pointed questions, but the leaders paid little attention. Unaware of her position, they ignored her as if she wasn't there. Or gave a real flip answer. I kept wondering how this workshop would be received by the City's Senior Managers.

> Time was running out for the completion of the scheduled agenda when someone asked, "Who of our Group will actually be attending the workshop?" I had assumed that *all* members of the Synergy Group would be present; but instead, they said that they'd be too uncomfortable being there—"Maybe Anna should carry it on her own!"

> I was stunned, shocked, hurt. I listened to the discussion for several minutes, then expressed my feelings: "No way! I won't do it any more. We share common issues; you are all supportive; so I stand up to be counted . . . but when I look behind me, you guys are scattered to the four winds, and I'm standing out there all by myself. *Not this time.* I have to leave now, for another meeting. When you've decided what you want to do, let me know. I can change the March agenda if you decide not to do the workshop."

After the EO Director's departure, Trudy McNab spoke quietly but firmly to the workshop leaders: "I cannot allow this to continue, for several reasons." She gave the consultants some direct feedback about the quality of their presentation, emphasizing that such a workshop was not appropriate for managers in the City Hall environment—"I can foresee it creating more problems than it would solve—it might endanger all progress to date."

THE FOLLOWING DAY

The next day, various members of the Group tried to sort out what had gone wrong. Anna's unwillingness to be the sole representative at the meeting seemed to indicate that the presentation as designed would not work, and that Anna was uncomfortable with it, too. Whether a more effective presentation could, in fact, be designed so that the Group members could feel comfortable with it in what they perceived as a hostile environment (i.e., the EO Senior Managers meeting) was a subject that would have to be explored further—but it was clear that this particular approach would not be used.

Some of the Synergy Group women concluded that the consultants had not done their homework well enough—they had failed to read the Group and the City culture accurately. Others said that the professionals came poorly prepared, and did not handle conflict well. But most of all, they felt the "blame" somehow could be attached to the extreme difficulty of dealing with gender-related issues in the workplace:

> We've all been daunted by the difficulty of actually coming to grips with this question of values and the softer issues, the subconscious things that go on. We're now fully aware of the difficulty of trying to convey some of the texture and the quality of the situations we face daily.

The Manager of Training and Development, Trudy McNab, was thinking about the reasons behind her intervention, and was reaching some conclusions about her involvement in the Synergy Group's activities:

I attended yesterday's session because I heard the Synergy Group was now prepared to take its involvement beyond the support they were giving each other. They were prepared to take the issue of integration of male-female styles and the acknowledgement of women's styles into the Corporation, presenting their concerns to the senior group. They were also planning to offer courses to groups of men and women in the future. And although their motivation is admirable, the process by which that was thought out and planned—the connections and the analysis—wasn't really all that sound.

They were proposing to use a considerable number of training dollars to hire outside consultants to put together a workshop which would sensitize the senior managers and help them to see the issues. But knowing what I do about the EO senior managers . . . there's a bit of support, but mostly apathy or hostility to "the new workplace synergy." I had a vision of this group of women being damaged by the way the whole process would be received.

Because of the way the consultants were going to facilitate the process, the EO senior managers were not going to take it well—they wouldn't understand it. They're all very bright administrators, but as for being conscious and aware of these issues, they're not sophisticated at all. I had this dreadful vision of what they would do—especially when, on concrete issues, they tried to corner a speaker with aggressive questions about "What are you trying to get at?" It wouldn't be clear.

That's what I was thinking about when I attended the walk-through session yesterday. It was worse than I had anticipated. A major portion of what the consultants were proposing, I'd never recommend. They got through most of it, then ran out of time. From an instructional design perspective, it was way off. Each individual woman had no idea what part she was supposed to play in the dress rehearsal—the consultants did not make it clear. Technically, even the film they were using was wrong . . . I thought, we're going to set ourselves back about a thousand years. I could imagine all the senior managers asking, "Why did you haul us in for this garbage?" Finally, I stood up and said, "I can't support this."

And now I'm feeling responsible. Here's a group that has been meeting for a long time, and I just came in out of the blue and dashed their plans. And I realize by pulling the pin on that project, I also need to offer them something. So I'll offer to operate as a consultant for the Group. And I will stay with them—I feel I owe that to them. And if they as a group decide that they still want to do that workshop another time in the future, I won't stop them . . . although I can't associate Training with that design. But I want to support them in any way I can.

QUESTIONS ABOUT WORKPLACE SYNERGY

Seated at her office desk, Equal Opportunity Director, Anna Hewitt, was considering the activities of the Synergy Group—past, present, and future. "After such a promising beginning,

what went wrong?" she wondered. "And where should the Group go from here? How can we, as responsible women managers, become a dynamic force for change at City Hall?"

NOTES

1. The group responsible for the day-to-day implementation of Equal Opportunity policies and systems at Graniton City Hall. Membership consisted of 18 Directors of Administration representing every City department, each appointed by his/her Commissioner.

2. Commissioners: the title used as a blanket term for all senior department heads (Fire Chief, MOH, City Auditor, City Clerk, City Solicitor, Executive Director).

5

CROSS-CULTURAL DIVERSITY

The globalization of business has greatly increased the frequency and importance of cross-cultural interaction for business managers. The dynamics of value clashes, ethnocentrism, sexism, racism, and miscommunication create challenges that managers must surmount to carry out business effectively. Each of these issues is discussed in the next sections.

CULTURALLY DETERMINED BELIEFS AND VALUES

Studying the survey responses of tens of thousands of employees in a large multinational company, Hofstede (1980) identified four major dimensions of national culture. These dimensions are *individualism/collectivism, uncertainty avoidance, power distance,* and *masculinity/femininity,* each of which is discussed below.

Hofstede (1980) defined *individualism/collectivism* as the extent to which people view themselves as individuals or members of a group. Other authors have confirmed that individualism/collectivism is a fundamental dimension of culture that distinguishes societies from one another (Kluckhohn & Strodtbeck, 1961; Triandis, 1994). Individualists believe they are responsible for caring for themselves and their nuclear family and that others are similarly responsible for themselves. Collectivists owe considerably more loyalty to the extended family or the group, and group members have an ultimate obligation to help and care for each other.

Uncertainty avoidance is associated with the tendency of individuals to avoid taking risks. Ambiguity is uncomfortable, and deviating from norms is less tolerated in societies where uncertainty avoidance is high.

Power distance is the extent to which hierarchy and inequality are accepted in a society. In societies where power distance is high, those lower in the hierarchy are expected to comply with orders from those in authority. At the same time, they have the right to expect those in authority to look after, protect, and provide for them.

Finally, *masculinity/femininity* refers to core values around dominance and nurturance. In masculine societies, people value assertiveness, achievement, and acquisition of material wealth. In feminine societies, people place more value on interpersonal harmony, high-quality relationships, and caring for others.

Management researchers have identified links between cultural values and workplace behavior. For example, in India, where power distance is high relative to North America, employees frustrated American managers by their reluctance to embrace empowerment. From the perspective of the Indian employees, the American managers appeared extremely inefficient, and the Indian employees wondered why they were taking so much time to discuss simple decisions with everyone, when just telling everyone what to do and letting them get on with it would be so much more efficient (Lane, DiStefano, & Maznevski, 2000, p. 38). A survey research study comparing Canadians and Indians confirmed that Indian employees reported less autonomy on the job (Aycan, Kanungo, & Sinha, 1999).

Other important dimensions of culture concern beliefs about the nature of human beings and the nature of time (Kluckhohn & Strodtbeck, 1961). Christians tend to have a negative view of human nature, stemming from the story of original sin in the Bible, while the Muslim and Shinto faiths view humans as essentially good (Lane et al., 2000). A view that humans are more evil than good affects managerial control systems based on an underlying suspicion of people. This negative view may explain why electronic productivity and theft monitoring systems are so popular in North American organizations (Lane et al., 2000).

Time tends to be viewed as a commodity in North America, something valuable that must be well used and not "wasted." As a result, North Americans structure their lives around a rigid schedule designed to maximize productivity and value fulfillment. This view is not shared as stringently around the world, where people may be more relaxed about schedules (Lane et al., 2000). In addition, North Americans tend to be extremely present oriented. In other societies, it is important to take the time to build relationships to generate the trust needed to conduct business. North Americans can make the mistake of trying to rush business deals to have something to show in the short term, which can alienate members of other less present-oriented cultures (Lane et al., 2000).

CULTURAL MISUNDERSTANDINGS AND ETHNOCENTRISM

Culturally determined differences in values, beliefs, and assumptions cause at least two types of problems for conducting business across cultures. First, people can easily misunderstand each other. Using the same words or gestures, members of different cultures can mean very different things. For example, in one culture, nodding in agreement or saying "yes" may mean willingness to comply with the other person's views, while in another culture, nodding in agreement or saying "yes" may mean understanding but not necessarily compliance. The two parties to such a conversation can easily walk away with very different views of what has been decided and what will happen next. As a result, people's expectations for each other's behavior are not fulfilled, and disappointment with the other party can lead to conflict, attempts at control, or dissolution of the relationship.

Treacherous as miscommunications can be, the problem of ethnocentrism can be even worse for the effective conduct of business. Ethnocentrism is the natural human tendency to view one's own culture and values as the best or most appropriate (Triandis, 1994). Inability to see the value in different goals and methods can cause inflexibility in dealings with members of other cultures. Diversity research shows that deep-level value differences exacerbate negative experiences in work groups over time (Harrison, Price, & Bell, 1998; Harrison, Price, Gavin, & Florey, 2002).

INEQUALITY, SEXISM, AND RACISM ACROSS CULTURES

Members of all human societies appear to have their prejudices about some other group or groups. Sidanius and Pratto (1999) argue that all non-hunter-gatherer societies are organized as group-based social hierarchies, where certain demographic groups are accorded greater status and power than others. Furthermore, they argue that age and gender are two factors showing universal status differences, with older people and men being accorded higher status in human societies. In addition, they observe that all societies have an additional set of status distinctions beyond age and gender. These status distinctions vary between cultures and include such factors as nationality, ethnicity, religion, race, and class. The differences between societies mean that certain religious and ethnic groups are accorded low status in some societies while being accorded high status in others.

Sidanius and Pratto (1999) conducted research in a variety of settings and found that members of high-status social groups in any given society have more favorable attitudes toward inequality than members of low-status groups. In other words, high-status groups tend to believe that their status and power in society is natural and proper, which Sidanius and Pratto call "social dominance orientation." Low-status groups, on the other hand, are more likely to believe that their low status is due to injustice. Importantly, individuals differ in their level of social dominance orientation, such that some members of low-status groups are unconscious of disadvantage, and some members of high-status groups consider group-based societal inequality to be unjust.

THE LEGACY OF COLONIALISM

In addition, the history of colonialism has influenced how demographic groups view each other and themselves. At the height of the colonial age, Europe's colonies covered almost 85% of the globe (Prasad, 1997). As such, it is difficult to overstate the influence of European colonialism on human consciousness as well as intergroup relations.

The idea that one society should be able to "colonize" another is based on an inherent belief in the superiority of the colonizer. The view that the White race and European culture were superior was essential for the conquerors to be able to feel that the coercion of other human societies for the purpose of extracting their wealth was just (Prasad, 1997).

The relationship created between colonizer and colonized was more complex than simply superior to inferior, however. The colonized group was also viewed as "a highly desirable object for Western possession" (Prasad, 1997, p. 290). Stories of the "haunting beauty of the East" or the "vast unspoiled expanses of Africa" reflected the attraction of the colonies for the colonizers.

The decolonization of the 20th century gave autonomy to the formerly colonized societies but left them to deal with the results of decades of plundering and oppression. Under colonization, it was not in the interests of the European colonizers to build the infrastructures in their colonies beyond the minimum needed for the extraction of natural resources. Nor was it in their interests to educate the population beyond the level needed to provide the colonizers with a source of cheap labor. Furthermore, attitudes of inferiority and superiority became ingrained in literature, media portrayals, and human psyches (Prasad, 1997).

In part, negative views of formerly colonized peoples remain due to the dynamics of status characteristics. Ridgeway's (1997) *status characteristics theory* suggests that historical inequalities between demographic groups linger in people's consciousnesses due to the material consequences of differential access to education and other resources for achievement. Specifically, Ridgeway argues that because certain groups have not had the education and resources needed to excel on various tasks, people's experiences tell them that members of those groups are less capable. As a result of these experiences, when a new member of a historically disadvantaged group enters a task arena, members of the advantaged group begin the interaction with the assumption that the low-status group member will be incompetent.

This assumption of incompetence affects how the low-status group member is treated. Given that the person is expected to be incompetent, others are less likely to assign complex or difficult tasks to that person, with the result that the person has little opportunity to demonstrate higher level capabilities. In addition, the low-status person is given less speaking time in the group (why waste the group's time with incompetent ideas?) and is more likely to be interrupted by other group members. As such, the person has less opportunity to demonstrate the value of his or her ideas.

As the result of being provided few opportunities to demonstrate competence, the low-status person in the group usually does perform less well than the others, thereby reinforcing their original expectations (Ridgeway, 1997; Ridgeway, Johnson, & Diekema, 1994). Such cycles of negative self-fulfilling prophecies are difficult to break unless one is cognizant of the dynamics of status characteristics and takes steps to intervene.

Managerial Implications

Lane et al. (2000) argue that effective cross-cultural management requires adaptability, cross-cultural expertise, and interpersonal skills. Adaptability is needed to break out of the assumptions of one's home culture to see the value of other cultural perspectives. Cross-cultural expertise is valuable for understanding the specific cultural context in which one is working. Such expertise helps to promote effective communication and avoid cultural blunders. Interpersonal skills are needed because building relationships across cultures requires establishing rapport with dissimilar others who may not share one's views and values. Ability to listen to others and make them feel acknowledged, understood, and valued is critical to bridging the cross-cultural divide.

In addition, understanding the dynamics of prejudice and discrimination can also be important to effectiveness in a cross-cultural situation. Given the critical importance of expectations for performance, ensuring that all parties are provided ample speaking time and opportunities to undertake important and challenging tasks is valuable for eliminating the effects of stereotypes.

Finally, managers in a cross-cultural situation should be prepared to face inequalities in the society they are visiting. It is very important to avoid judging others on the basis of ethnocentrism, which makes it difficult to know what to do when members of other cultures make statements that seem intolerant or bigoted. Cultural relativism, or a stance that "it is their culture, so it is OK for them," is an inappropriate stance, however, when low-status members of that society are calling for change themselves. Handling inequalities in culturally appropriate ways requires consulting local experts. The most effective global diversity initiatives involve substantial participation by local representatives in goal setting, strategizing, and implementation.

CASES

Ellen Moore (A): Living and Working in Bahrain

A female expatriate manager working for a large multinational financial institution must contend with gender discrimination. She had been offered a promotion to one or two positions of which she could choose. When she makes her decision and informs her boss, he tells her she cannot have the one she chose because it would mean periodic travel into an Arab culture that, he believes, would not be possible for a woman.

Assignment Questions:

1. What would you advise Ellen to do and why? What should be her objectives? Are these objectives and actions consistent with what you would do if you were in her situation?

2. Why is Ellen successful as a manager?

3. Did the general manager make the right decision?

4. What are the responsibilities of male colleagues (seniors, subordinates, and peers) toward female managers?

5. What, if anything, in the case differed from your expectations?

Ellen Moore (A): Living and Working in Korea

Ellen Moore, a systems consultant, was sent to Korea to manage a project involving a team of North American and Korean consultants representing a joint venture between a major Korean conglomerate and a significant North American information technology company. The Americans were to be involved for the first 7 months in order to transfer expertise and knowledge to the South Koreans who had little experience in this area. Ellen's superior had played an integral part in securing the contract in Korea due to his depth of knowledge on the subject. He chose Ellen to be the key North American project manager because she had significant project management skills and impressive international experience. Upon Ellen's arrival, she discovered that the Korean consultants were far less skilled than she had expected. In addition, Ellen had understood that she and the Korean manager were to be comanagers, but immediately tensions arose regarding who was giving direction to the team and the scope of the project. Tensions escalated until it was clear that the project was behind schedule and the Koreans were not taking direction from Ellen. The Koreans insisted that Ellen was the problem. Ellen's superior disagreed; he and Ellen must decide how to proceed. The challenge is to balance strategic goals with individual action.

Assignment Questions:

1. What are the problems and why do they exist?

2. What alternatives exist at this point?

3. In Andrew's position, what would you do?

4. What changes would you recommend making for future projects?

Julie Dempster (A)

A Black Canadian woman is hired as vice president of marketing and brand position-ing for an Amsterdam-based computer software company. Shortly after joining the firm, she encounters a number of cross-cultural and equality issues. She must decide whether to renew her contract with the company.

Assignment Questions:

1. Put yourself in Dempster's shoes. How should she proceed at the meeting tomorrow? What should she focus on?

2. How is Nederberg likely to react to the issues Dempster raises?

3. Prepare for the meeting as if you were Dempster.

The European Experience (A)

A group of international business majors from a large Boston-area university traveled to Spain, France, and Germany for a yearlong period of study and work. Some of the students described their initial impressions and reactions to living and studying in another country and functioning in another language. Topics discussed include adapting to life in Europe (including language, pace of life, personal space, smoking, local food, sexual norms, per-sonal appearance, and government and bureaucracy), being away from family and friends during the holiday seasons, academics (including differences in learning and teaching styles), and language. The objective of the case is to help undergraduate students who will be living, studying, and working in another country to prepare for their experience.

Assignment Questions:

1. What are the issues that create problems for the students, and what is your reaction to their experiences?

2. How would you have handled these situations? What advice would you give to the students?

Being Different: Exchange Student Experiences

This case is about African American, Latin American, and Asian undergraduate, inter-national business majors from a Boston-area university who traveled to Spain, France, and Germany for a yearlong period of study and work. Presented are their experiences being minority students in Europe. The experiences range from annoying stares to aggressive propositions from men.

Assignment Questions:

1. What are the episodes of prejudice happening to the students?

2. What would you have done if you had been in Felicia's situation?

3. What advice would you give the students about personal security in metropolitan areas?

4. What should Professor Rhodes do? What should the universities do?

The Changing Face of Europe: A Note on Immigration and Societal Attitudes

This note discusses the impact of immigration on attitudes and government policy in Western Europe's three largest countries—Spain, France, and Germany. It also examines how the histories and political structures of these countries have influenced immigration policy and the integration of immigrant populations. Finally, it predicts the impact that immigration policy will have on employment and productivity in what some observers have dubbed "Fortress Europe."

REFERENCES

Aycan, Z., Kanungo, R. N., & Sinha, J. B. P. (1999). Organizational culture and human resource management practices: The model of culture fit. *Journal of Cross-Cultural Psychology, 30,* 501–526.

Harrison, D. A., Price, K. H., & Bell, M. P. (1998). Beyond relational demography: Time and the effects of surface- and deep-level diversity on work group cohesion. *Academy of Management Journal, 41,* 96–107.

Harrison, D. A., Price, K. H., Gavin, J. H., & Florey, A. T. (2002). Time, teams, and task performance: Changing effects of surface- and deep-level diversity on group functioning. *Academy of Management Journal, 45,* 1029–1045.

Hofstede, G. (1980). *Culture's consequences.* Beverly Hills, CA: Sage.

Kluckhohn, F. R., & Strodtbeck, F. L. (1961). *Variations in value orientations.* New York: Row, Peterson & Co.

Lane, H. W., DiStefano, J. J., & Maznevski, M. L. (2000). *International management behavior: Text, readings and cases* (4th ed.). Oxford, UK: Blackwell.

Prasad, A. (1997). The colonizing consciousness and representations of the other: A postcolonial critique of the discourse of oil. In P. Prasad, A. J. Mills, M. Elmes, & A. Prasad (Eds.), *Managing the organizational melting pot: Dilemmas of workplace diversity* (pp. 285–311). Thousand Oaks, CA: Sage.

Ridgeway, C. L. (1997). Interaction and the conservation of gender inequality: Considering employment. *American Sociological Review, 62,* 218–235.

Ridgeway, C. L., Johnson, C., & Diekema, D. (1994). External status, legitimacy, and compliance in male and female groups. *Social Forces, 72,* 1051–1077.

Sidanius, J., & Pratto, F. (1999). *Social dominance: An intergroup theory of social hierarchy and oppression.* New York: Cambridge University Press.

Triandis, H. C. (1994). *Culture and social behavior.* New York: McGraw-Hill.

ELLEN MOORE (A): LIVING AND WORKING IN BAHRAIN

*Prepared by Gail Ellement and Martha Maznevski
under the supervision of Professor Henry W. Lane*

          Version: (A) 2003-07-15

The general manager had offered me a choice of two positions in the Operations area. I had considered the matter carefully, and was about to meet with him to tell him I would accept the accounts control position. The job was much more challenging than the customer services post, but I knew I could learn the systems and procedures quickly and I would have a great opportunity to contribute to the success of the operations area.

It was November 1989, and Ellen Moore was just completing her second year as an expatriate manager at the offices of a large American financial institution in Manama, Bahrain. After graduating with an MBA from a leading business school, Ellen had joined her husband, who was working as an expatriate manager at an offshore bank in Bahrain. Being highly qualified and capable, she had easily found a demanding position and had worked on increasingly complex projects since she had begun at the company. She was looking forward to the challenges of the Accounts Control position.

ELLEN MOORE

Ellen graduated as the top female from her high school when she was 16, and immediately began working full time for the main branch of one of the largest banks in the country. By the end of four years, she had become a corporate accounts officer and managed over 20 large accounts.

I remember I was always making everything into a game, a challenge. One of my first jobs was filing checks. I started having a competition with the woman at the adjacent desk who had been filing for

years, except she didn't know I was competing with her. When she realized it, we both started competing in earnest. Before long, people used to come over just to watch us fly through these stacks of checks. When I moved to the next job, I used to see how fast I could add up columns of numbers while handling phone conversations. I always had to do something to keep myself challenged.

While working full time at the bank, Ellen achieved a Fellowship in the Institute of Bankers after completing demanding courses and exams. She went on to work in banking and insurance with one of her former corporate clients from the bank. When she was subsequently promoted to manage their financial reporting department, she was both the first female and the youngest person the company had ever had in that position.

Since she had begun working full time, Ellen had been taking courses towards a bachelor's degree at night in one of the city's universities. In 1983 she decided to stop working for two years to complete her bachelor's degree. After she graduated with a major in accounting and minors in marketing and management, she entered the MBA program.

I decided to go straight into the MBA program for several reasons. First, I wanted to update myself. I had taken my undergraduate courses over 10 years and wanted to obtain knowledge on contemporary views. Second, I wanted to tie some pieces together—my night school degree left my ideas somewhat fragmented. Third, I wasn't impressed with the interviews I had after I finished the Bachelor's degree, and fourth I was out of work anyway. Finally, my father had already told everyone that I had my MBA, and I decided I really couldn't disappoint him.

Just after Ellen had begun the two-year MBA program, her husband was offered a position with an affiliate of his bank, posted in Bahrain beginning the next spring. They sat down and examined potential opportunities that would be available for Ellen once she completed her MBA. They discovered that women could work and assume positions of responsibility in Bahrain, and decided they could both benefit from the move. Her husband moved to Bahrain in March, while Ellen remained to complete her masters. Ellen followed, with MBA in hand, 18 months later.

BAHRAIN

Bahrain is an archipelago of 33 islands located in the Persian Gulf (see Exhibit 1). The main island, Bahrain, comprises 85 per cent of the almost 700 square kilometres of the country and is the location of the capital city, Manama. Several of the islands are joined by causeways, and in 1987 the 25-kilometre King Fahad Causeway linked the principal island to the mainland of Saudi Arabia, marking the end of island isolation for the country. In 1971, Bahrain gained full independence from Britain, ending a relationship that had lasted for almost a century. Of the population of over 400,000 people, about one-third were foreigners.

Bahrain has had a prosperous history. Historically, it has been sought after by many countries for its lush vegetation, fresh water, and pearls. Many traditional crafts and industries were still practiced, including pottery, basketmaking, fabric-weaving, pearl-diving, dhow (fishing boat) building, and fishing. Bahrain was the pearl capital of the world for many centuries.

Fortunately, just as the pearl industry collapsed with the advent of cultured pearls from Japan, Bahrain struck its first oil.

Since the 1930s, the oil industry had been the largest contributor to Bahrain's Gross National Product. The country was the first in the Persian Gulf to have an oil industry, established with a discovery in 1932. Production at that time was 9,600 barrels a day. Eventually, crude output had

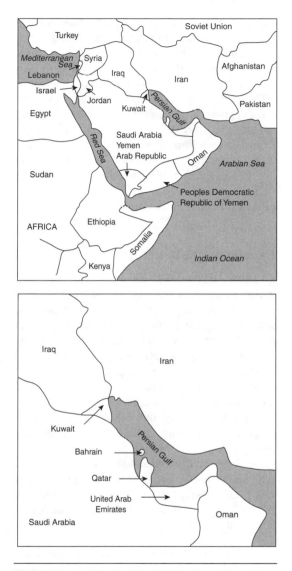

Exhibit 1   Maps of the Middle East

reached over 40,000 barrels a day. Bahrain's oil products included crude oil, natural gas, methanol, ammonia, and refined products like gasoline, jet fuels, kerosene, and asphalts.

The Bahraini government had been aware for several years that the oil reserves were being seriously depleted. It was determined to diversify the country's economy away from a dependence on one resource. Industries established since 1971 included aluminum processing, shipbuilding, iron and steel processing, and furniture and door manufacturing. Offshore banking began in 1975. Since Bahraini nationals did not have the expertise to develop these industries alone, expatriates from around the world, particularly from Western Europe and North America, were invited to conduct business in Bahrain. By the late 1980s, the country was a major business and financial centre, housing many Middle East branch offices of international firms.

Expatriates in Bahrain

Since Bahrain was an attractive base from which to conduct business, it was a temporary home to many expatriates. Housing compounds, schools, services, shopping and leisure activities all catered to many international cultures. Expatriates lived under residence permits, gained only on the basis of recruitment for a specialist position which could not be filled by a qualified and available Bahraini citizen.

To Ellen, one of the most interesting roles of expatriate managers was that of teacher. The Arab nations had been industrialized for little more than two decades, and had suddenly found themselves needing to compete in a global market. Ellen believed that one of her main reasons for working in Bahrain was to train its nationals eventually to take over her job.

Usually the teaching part was very interesting. When I first arrived in the office, I was amazed to see many staff members with microcomputers on their desks, yet they did not know the first thing about operating the equipment. When I inquired about the availability of computer courses, I was informed by a British expatriate manager that "as these were personal computers, any person should be able to use them, and as such, courses aren't necessary." It was clear to me that courses were very necessary when the computer knowledge of most employees consisted of little more than knowing where the on/off switch was located on a microcomputer.

Although it was outside of office policy, I held "Ellen's Introduction to Computers" after office hours, just to get people comfortable with the machines and to teach them a few basics.

Sometimes the amount of energy you had to put into the teaching was frustrating in that results were not immediately evident. I often worked jointly with one of the Bahraini managers who really didn't know how to develop projects and prepare reports. Although I wasn't responsible for him, I spent a great deal of time with him, helping him improve his work. Initially there was resistance on his part, because he was not prepared to subordinate himself to an expatriate, let alone a woman. But eventually he came around and we achieved some great results working together.

The range of cultures represented in Bahrain was vast. Expatriate managers interacted not only with Arabic nationals, but also with managers from other parts of the world, and with workers from developing countries who provided a large part of the unskilled labor force.

The inequality among nationalities was one issue I found very difficult to deal with during my stay in Bahrain. The third world immigrants were considered to be the lowest level possible in the pecking order, just slightly lower than nationals from countries outside the Gulf. Gulf Arabs, being of Bedouin origin, maintained a suspicious attitude towards "citified" Arabs. Europeans and North Americans were regarded much more highly. These inequalities had a major impact on daily life, including the availability of jobs and what relations would develop or not develop between supervisors and subordinates. Although I was well acquainted with the racial problems in North America, I haven't seen anything compared to the situation in Bahrain. It wasn't unusual for someone to be exploited and discarded, as any expendable and easily replaceable resource would be, because of their nationality.

Although many expatriates and their families spent their time in Bahrain immersed in their own cultural compounds, social groups, and activities, Ellen believed that her interaction with the various cultures was one of the most valuable elements of her international experience.

Managing in Bahrain

Several aspects of the Middle Eastern culture had tremendous impact on the way business was managed, even in Western firms located in Bahrain. It seemed to Ellen, for example, that "truth" to a Bahraini employee was subject to an Arab interpretation, which was formed over hundreds of years of cultural evolution. What Western managers considered to be "proof" of an argument or "factual" evidence could be flatly denied by a Bahraini: if something was not believed, it did not exist. As well, it seemed that the concept of "time" differed between Middle Eastern and Western cultures. Schedules and deadlines, while sacred to Western managers, commanded little respect from Bahraini employees. The two areas that had the most impact on Ellen's managing in a company in Bahrain were the Islamic religion and the traditional attitude towards women.

Islam[1]

Most Bahrainis are practicing Muslims. According to the Muslim faith, the universe was created by Allah who prescribed a code of life called Islam and the Qur'an is the literal, unchanged Word of Allah preserved exactly as transcribed by Muhammad. Muhammad's own acts as a prophet form the basis for Islamic law, and are second in authority only to the Qur'an. The five Pillars of Islam are belief, prayer, fasting, almsgiving and pilgrimage. Muslims pray five times a day. During Ramadan, the ninth month of the Islamic calendar, Muslims must fast from food, drink, smoking and sexual activity from dawn until dusk, in order to master the urges which sustain and procreate life. All Muslims are obliged to give a certain proportion of their wealth in alms for charitable purposes; the Qur'an stresses that the poor have a just claim on the wealth of the prosperous. Finally, if possible, all Muslims should make a pilgrimage to Mecca during their lives, in a spirit of total sacrifice of personal comforts, acquisition of wealth and other matters of worldly significance.

Certainly the Muslim religion had a tremendous impact on my daily working life. The first time I walked into the women's washroom at work I noticed a tap about three inches off the floor over a drain. I found this rather puzzling; I wondered if it was for the cleaning crew. When a woman came in, I asked her about the tap, and she explained that before going to the prayer room, everyone had to wash all uncovered parts of their bodies. The tap was for washing their feet and legs.

One time I was looking for one of my employees, Mohammed, who had a report due to me that afternoon. I searched for him at his desk and other likely spots throughout the office, but to no avail, he just wasn't around. I had had difficulties with Mohammed's work before, when he would submit documents long after deadlines, and I was certain he was attempting to slack off once again. I bumped into one of Mohammed's friends, and asked if he knew Mohammed's whereabouts. When he informed me that Mohammed was in the prayer room, I wasn't sure how to respond. I didn't know if this prayer room activity was very personal and if I could ask questions, such as the length of time one generally spends in prayer. But I needed to know how long Mohammed would be away from his desk. Throwing caution to the wind, I asked the employee how long Mohammed was likely to be in prayers and he told me it usually takes about 10 minutes. It wasn't that I felt I didn't have the right to know where my employee was or how long he would be away, I just wasn't certain my authority as a manager allowed me the right to ask questions about such a personal activity as praying.

During Ramadan, the hours of business are shortened by law. It is absolutely illegal for any Muslim to work past 2:00 in the afternoon, unless special permits are obtained from the Ministry of Labor. Unfortunately, business coming in to an American firm does not stop at two, and a majority of the non-Muslim workers are required to take up the slack.

Unlike religion in Western civilization, Islam permeates every function of human endeavour. There does not exist a separation of church, state and judiciary. Indeed, in purist circles, the question does not arise. The hybrid systems existing in certain Arab countries are considered aberrations created by Western colonial influences. Accordingly, to function successfully, the expatriate must understand and learn to accept a very different structuring of a society.

Women in Bahrain

Bahrain tended to be more progressive than many Middle Eastern countries in its attitude towards women. Although traditions were strong, Bahraini women had some freedom. For example, all women could work outside the home, although the hours they could work were restricted both by convention and by the labor laws. They could only work if their husbands, fathers, or brothers permitted them, and could not take potential employment away from men. Work outside the home was to be conducted in addition to, not instead of, duties performed inside the home, such as child-rearing and cooking. Most women who worked held secretarial or clerical positions; very few worked in management.

Bahraini women were permitted to wear a variety of outfits, from the conservative full length black robe with head scarf which covers the head and hair, to below-the-knee skirts and dresses without head covering.

Arabic women who sincerely want change and more decision-making power over their own lives face an almost impossible task, as the male influence is perpetuated not only by men, but also by women who are afraid to alter views they understand and with which they have been brought up all their lives. I once asked a female co-worker the reason why one of the women in the office, who had previously been "uncovered," was now sporting a scarf over her head. The response was that this woman had just been married, and although her husband did not request that she become "covered," she personally did not feel as though she was a married woman without the head scarf. So she simply asked her husband to demand that she wear a scarf on her head. It was a really interesting situation; some of the more liberal Bahraini women were very upset that she had asked her husband to make this demand. They saw it as negating many of the progressive steps the women's movement had made in recent years.

Although Bahrainis had been exposed to Western cultures for the two decades of industrial expansion, they were still uncomfortable with Western notions of gender equality and less traditional roles for women.

One day a taxi driver leaned back against his seat and, while keeping one eye on the road ahead, turned to ask me, "How many sons do you have?" I replied that I didn't have any children. His heartfelt response of "I'm so sorry" and the way he shook his head in sympathy were something my North American upbringing didn't prepare me for. My taxi driver's response typifies the attitude projected towards women, whether they are expatriates from Europe or North America, or are Bahrainis. Women are meant to have children, preferably sons. Although Bahrain is progressive in many ways, attitudes on the role of women in society run long and deep, and it is quite unlikely these sentiments will alter in the near, or even distant, future.

Another time I was greeted with gales of laughter when I revealed to the women in the office that my husband performed most of the culinary chores in our household. They assumed I was telling a joke, and when I insisted that he really did most of the cooking, they sat in silent disbelief. Finally, one woman spoke up and informed the group that she didn't think her husband even knew where the kitchen was in their house, let alone would ever be caught touching a cooking utensil. The group nodded in agreement. Although these women have successful business careers—as clerks, but in the workforce nonetheless—they believe women should perform all household tasks without the assistance of their husbands. The discovery that this belief holds true in Bahrain is not remarkable, as I know many North American and European businesswomen who believe the same to be true. What is pertinent is these women allow themselves to be completely dominated by the men in their lives.

The one concept I faced daily but never accepted was that my husband was regarded as the sole decision maker in our household. He and I view our marriage as a partnership in which we participate equally in all decisions. But when the maintenance manager for our housing compound came by, repairs were completed efficiently only if I preceded my request with "my husband wants the following to be completed." It's a phrase I hated to use as it went against every rational thought I possess, but I frequently had to resort to it.

These attitudes also affected how Ellen was treated as a manager by Bahraini managers:

One manager, I'll call him Fahad, believed that women were only capable of fulfilling secretarial and coffee serving functions. One day I was sitting at my desk, concentrating on some documents. I didn't notice Fahad having a discussion with another male manager nearby. When I looked up from my papers, Fahad noticed me and immediately began talking in French to the other manager. Although my French was a bit rusty, my comprehension was still quite serviceable. I waited for a few moments and then broke into their discussion in French. Fahad was completely dismayed. Over the next few years, Fahad and I worked together on several projects. At first, he was pompous and wouldn't listen to anything I presented. It was a difficult situation, but I was determined to remain above his negative comments. I ignored his obvious prejudice towards me, remained outwardly calm when he disregarded my ideas, and proceeded to prove myself with my work. It took a lot of effort and patience but, in time, Fahad and I not only worked out our differences, but worked as a successful team on a number of major projects. Although this situation had a happy ending, I really would have preferred to have directed all that energy and effort towards more productive issues.

Bahraini nationals were not the only ones who perpetuated the traditional roles of women in society. Many of the expatriates, particularly those from Commonwealth countries, tended to view their role as "the colonial charged with the responsibility to look after the developing country." This was reflected in an official publication for new expatriates that stated: "Wives of overseas employees are normally sponsored by their husbands' employers, and their Residence Permits are processed at the same time . . ."[2] However, wives were not permitted to work unless they could obtain a work permit for themselves.

The first question I was often asked at business receptions was "What company is your husband with?" When I replied that I worked as well, I received the glazed over look as they assumed I occupied myself with coffee mornings, beach, tennis and other leisure activities as did the majority of expatriate wives.

Social gatherings were always risky. At typical business and social receptions the men served themselves first, after which the women selected their food. Then women and men positioned themselves on opposite sides of the room. The women discussed "feminine" topics, such as babies and recipes, while the men discussed the fall (or rise) of the dollar and the big deal of the day. At one Bahraini business gathering, I hesitated in choosing sides: should I conform and remain with the women? But most of these women did not work outside their homes, and, consequently, they spoke and understood very little English. I joined the men. Contrary to what I expected, I was given a gracious welcome.

However, on another occasion I was bored with the female conversation, so I ventured over to the forbidden male side to join a group of bankers discussing correspondent banking courses. When I entered the discussion, a British bank general manager turned his nose up at me. He motioned towards the other side of the room, and told me I should join the women. He implied that their discussion was obviously over my head. I quickly informed him that although I personally had found the banking courses difficult to complete while holding a full time banking position, I not only managed to complete the program and obtain my Fellowship, but at the time was the youngest employee of my bank ever to be awarded the diploma. The man did a quick turnabout, was thoroughly embarrassed, and apologized profusely. Although it was nice to turn the tables on the man, I was more than a little frustrated with the feeling that I almost had to wear my resume on my sleeve to get any form of respect from the men, whether European, North American, or Arab.

A small percentage of Bahraini women had completed university degrees in North America and Europe. While residing in these Western cultures, they were permitted to function as did their

Western counterparts. For example, they could visit or phone friends when they wished without first obtaining permission. After completing their education, many of these women were qualified for management positions; however, upon returning to Bahrain they were required to resume their traditional female roles.

> The notion of pink MBA diplomas for women and blue for men is very real. Although any MBA graduate in North America, male or female, is generally considered to have attained a certain level of business sense, I had to constantly "prove" myself to some individuals who appeared to believe that women attended a special segregated section of the university with appropriately tailored courses.

Ellen discovered that, despite being a woman, she was accepted by Bahrainis as a manager as a result of her Western nationality, her education, and her management position in the company.

> Many of my male Arabic peers accepted me as they would any expatriate manager. For example, when a male employee returned from a holiday, he would typically visit each department, calling upon the other male employees with a greeting and a handshake. Although he might greet a female coworker, he would never shake her hand. However, because of my management position in the company and my status as a Western expatriate, male staff members gave me the same enthusiastic greeting and handshake normally reserved for their male counterparts.

Ellen also found herself facilitating Bahraini women's positions in the workplace.

> As I was the only female in a senior management position in our office, I was often asked by the female employees to speak to their male superiors about problems and issues they experienced in their departments. I also had to provide a role model for the women because there were no female Bahraini managers. Some of them came to me not just to discuss career issues but to discuss life issues. There was just no one else in a similar position for them to talk to. On the other hand, male managers would ask me to discuss sensitive issues, such as hygiene, with their female staff members.

The government of Bahrain introduced legislation that restricted the amount of overtime hours women could work. Although the move was being praised by the (female) director of social development as recognition of the contribution women were making to Bahraini industry, Ellen saw it as further discriminatory treatment restricting the choices of women in Bahrain. Her published letter to the editor of the Gulf Daily News read:

> . . . How the discriminatory treatment of women in this regulation can be seen as recognition of the immense contribution women make to the Bahrain workforce is beyond comprehension. Discrimination of any portion of the population in the labor legislation does not recognize anything but the obvious prejudice. If the working women in Bahrain want to receive acknowledgement of their indispensable impact on the Bahrain economy, it should be through an increase in the number of management positions available to qualified women, not through regulations limiting the hours they work. All this regulation means is that women are still regarded as second class citizens who need the strong arm tactics of the government to help them settle disputes over working hours. Government officials could really show appreciation to the working women in Bahrain by making sure that companies hire and promote based on skill rather than gender. But there is little likelihood of that occurring.

The letter was signed with a pseudonym, but the day it was published one of Ellen's female employees showed her the letter and claimed "if I didn't know better, Ellen, I'd think you wrote this letter."

CAREER DECISIONS

When Ellen first arrived in Bahrain, she had great expectations that she would work somewhere where she could make a difference. She received several offers for positions and turned down, among others, a university and a high profile brokerage house. She decided to take a position as a special projects coordinator at a large American financial institution.

In fact, the records will show I was actually hired as a "financial analyst," but this title was given solely because at that time, the government had decided that expatriate women shouldn't be allowed to take potential positions away from Bahraini nationals. The expertise required as a Financial Analyst enabled the company to obtain a work permit for me as I had the required experience and academic credentials, although I performed few duties as an analyst.

In her special projects role, Ellen learned a great deal about international finance. She conducted efficiency studies on various operating departments. She used her systems expertise to investigate and improve the company's microcomputer usage, and developed a payroll program which was subsequently integrated into the company's international systems. She was a member of the strategic review committee, and produced a report outlining the long-term goals for the Middle East market, which she then presented to the senior vice-president of Europe, Middle East and Africa.

After one year, Ellen was rewarded for her achievements by a promotion to manager of business planning and development, a position which reported directly to the vice-president and general manager. She designed the role herself, and was able to be creative and quite influential in the company. During her year in this role, she was involved in a diverse range of activities. She managed the quality assurance department, coordinated a product launch, developed and managed a senior management information system, was an active participant in all senior management meetings, and launched an employee newsletter.

At the end of her second year in Bahrain, Ellen was informed that two positions in operations would soon be available, and the general manager, a European expatriate, asked if she would be interested in joining the area. She had previously only worked in staff positions, and quickly decided to accept the challenge and learning experience of a line post. Both positions were in senior management, and both had responsibility for approximately 30 employees.

The first position was for manager of accounts control, which covered the credit, collection and authorization departments. The manager's role was to ensure that appropriate information was used to authorize spending by clients, to compile results of client payment, and to inform management of non-payment issues. The manager also supervised in-house staff and representatives in other Gulf countries for the collection of withheld payments.

The second post was manager of customer services, new accounts, and establishment services. The manager's role was to ensure that new clients were worthy and that international quality standards were met in all customer service activity. The manager also worked with two other departments: with marketing to ensure that budgets were met, and with sales to manage relationships with the many affiliate outlets of the service.

After speaking with the two current managers and considering the options carefully, Ellen decided that she would prefer working in the accounts control area. The job was more oriented to financial information, the manager had more influence on operations at the company, and she would have the opportunity to travel to other countries to supervise staff. Although she was not familiar with the systems and procedures, she knew she could learn them quickly. Ellen went into her meeting with the general manager excited about the new challenges.

Ellen Meets With the General Manager

Ellen told the general manager she had decided to take the accounts control position, and outlined her reasons. Then she waited for his affirmation and for the details of when she would begin.

"I'm afraid I've reconsidered the offer," the general manager announced.

> Although I know you would probably do a terrific job in the accounts control position, I can't offer it to you. It involves periodic travel into Saudi Arabia, and women are not allowed to travel there alone.

He went on to tell Ellen how she would be subject to discriminatory practices, would not be able to gain the respect of the company's Saudi

Arabian clients, and would experience difficulty travelling there.

Ellen was astonished. She quickly pointed out to him that many businesswomen were representatives of American firms in Saudi Arabia. She described one woman she knew of who was the sole representative of a large American bank in the Eastern Province of Saudi Arabia who frequently travelled there alone. She explained that other women's experiences in Saudi Arabia showed professional men there treated professional women as neither male nor female, but as businesspeople. Besides, she continued, there were no other candidates in the company for either position. She reminded the general manager of the pride the company took in its quality standards and how senior management salaries were in part determined by assuring quality in their departments. Although the company was an equal opportunity employer in its home country, the United States, she believed the spirit of the policy should extend to all international offices.

The general manager informed her that his decision reflected his desire to address the interests of both herself and the company. He was worried, he said, that Ellen would have trouble obtaining entry visas to allow her to conduct business in Saudi Arabia, and that the customers would not accept her. Also, if there were ever any hostile outbreaks, he believed she would be in danger, and he could not have lived with that possibility.

Ellen stated that as a woman, she believed she was at lower risk of danger than her Western male counterparts since in the event of hostility, the Saudi Arabians would most likely secure her safety. There was much greater probability that a male representative of the firm would be held as a hostage.

The general manager was adamant. Regardless of her wishes, the company needed Ellen in the customer service position. New Accounts had only recently been added to the department, and the bottom line responsibility was thus doubled from what it had been in the past. The general manager said he wanted someone he could trust and depend upon to handle the pressure of new accounts, which had a high international profile.

Ellen was offered the customer service position, then dismissed from the meeting. In frustration, she began to consider her options.

Take the Customer Services Position

The general manager obviously expected her to take the position. It would mean increased responsibility and challenge. Except for a position in high school where she managed a force of 60 student police, Ellen had not yet supervised more than four employees at any time in her professional career. On the other hand, it went against her values to accept the post since it had been offered as a result of gender roles when all consideration should have been placed on competence.

She knew she had the abilities and qualifications for the position. She viewed the entire situation as yet another example of how the business community in Bahrain had difficulty accepting and acknowledging the contributions of women to international management, and didn't want to abandon her values by accepting the position.

Fight Back

There were two approaches which would permit Ellen to take the matter further. She could go to the general manager's superior, the senior vice-president of Europe, Middle East and Africa. She had had several dealings with him, and had once presented a report to him with which he was very impressed. But she wasn't sure she could count on his sympathy regarding her travelling to Saudi Arabia as his knowledge of the region was limited, and he generally relied on local management's decisions on such issues. She could consider filing a grievance against the company. There were provisions in Bahraini Labor Law that would have permitted this option in her case. However, she understood that the Labor Tribunals, unlike those held in Western countries, did not try cases based on precedents or rules of evidence. In other words, the judge would apply a hodgepodge of his own subjective criteria to reach a decision.

*Stay in the Business
Planning and Development Job*

Although the general manager had not mentioned it as an option, Ellen could request that she remain in her current position. It would mean not giving in to the general manager's prejudices. Since she had been considering the two operations positions, though, she had been looking forward to moving on to something new.

Leave the Company

Ellen knew she was qualified for many positions in the financial centre of Bahrain and could likely obtain work with another company. She was not sure, though, whether leaving her present company under these circumstances would jeopardize her chances of finding work elsewhere. Furthermore, to obtain a post at a new company would require a letter of permission from her current employer, who, as her sponsor in Bahrain, had to sanction her move to a new employer who would become her new sponsor. She was not sure that she would be able to make those arrangements considering the situation.

I always tell my employees: "If you wake up one morning and discover you don't like your job, come to see me immediately. If the problem is with the tasks of the job, I'll see if I can modify your tasks. If the problem is with the department or you want a change, I'll assist you in getting another position in the company. If the problem is with the company, then I'll help you write your resume." I have stated this credo to all my employees in every post I've held. Generally, they don't believe that their manager would actually assist with resume writing, but when the opportunity arises, and it has, and I do come through as promised, the impact on the remaining employees is priceless. Employees will provide much more effort towards a cause that is supported by someone looking out for their personal welfare.

Ellen's superior did not have the same attitude towards his employees. As she considered her options, Ellen realized that no move could be made without a compromise either in her career or her values. Which choice was she most willing to make?

Notes

1. *Resident in Bahrain,* Volume 1, 1987, Gulf Daily News, pp. 61–63.
2. *Resident in Bahrain,* Volume 1, 1987, Gulf Daily News, p. 57.

Ellen Moore (A): Living and Working in Korea

*Prepared by Chantell Nicholls and Gail Ellement
under the supervision of Professor Harry Lane*

Version: (A) 2000-01-10

Ellen Moore, a Systems Consulting Group (SCG) consultant, was increasingly concerned as she heard Andrew's voice grow louder through the paper-thin walls of the office next to her. Andrew Kilpatrick, the senior consultant on a joint North American and Korean consulting project for a government agency in Seoul, South Korea, was meeting with Mr. Song, the senior Korean project director, to discuss several issues including the abilities of the Korean consultants. After four months on this Korean project, Ellen's evaluation of the assigned consultants suggested that they did not have the experience, background, or knowledge to complete the project within the allocated time. Additional resources would be required:

> I remember thinking, "I can't believe they are shouting at each other." I was trying to understand how their meeting had reached such a state. Andrew raised his voice and I could hear him saying, "I don't think you understand at all." Then, he shouted, "Ellen is not the problem!"

WSI IN KOREA

In 1990, Joint Venture Inc. (JVI) was formed as a joint venture between a Korean company, Korean Conglomerate Inc. (KCI), and a North American company, Western Systems Inc. (WSI) (Exhibit 1). WSI, a significant information technology company with offices world wide employing over 50,000 employees, included the Systems Consulting Group (SCG). KCI, one of the largest Korean "chaebols" (industrial groups), consisted of over 40 companies, with sales in excess of US$3.5 billion. The joint venture, in its eighth year, was managed by two Regional Directors—Mr. Cho, a Korean from KCI, and Robert Brown, an American from WSI.

The team working on Ellen's project was led by Mr. Park and consisted of approximately 40 Korean consultants further divided into teams working on different areas of the project. The Systems Implementation (SI) team consisted of five Korean consultants, one translator, and three North American SCG consultants: Andrew Kilpatrick, Ellen Moore, and Scott Adams, (see Exhibit 2).

This consulting project was estimated to be one of the largest undertaken in South Korea to date. Implementation of the recommended systems into over 100 local offices was expected to take seven to ten years. The SCG consultants would be involved for the first seven months, to assist the Korean consultants with the system design and in creating recommendations for system implementation, an area in which the

Korean consultants admitted they had limited expertise.

Andrew Kilpatrick became involved because of his experience with a similar systems implementation project in North America. Andrew had been a management consultant for nearly 13 years. He had a broad and successful background in organizational development, information technology, and productivity improvement, and he was an early and successful practitioner of business process reengineering. Although Andrew had little international consulting experience, he was adept at change management and was viewed by both peers and clients as a flexible and effective consultant.

The degree of SCG's involvement had not been anticipated. Initially, Andrew had been asked by SCG's parent company, WSI, to assist JVI with the proposal development. Andrew and his SCG managers viewed his assistance as a favor to WSI since SCG did not have plans to develop business in Korea. Andrew's work on the proposal in North America led to a request for his involvement in Korea to gather additional information for the proposal:

> When I arrived in Korea, I requested interviews with members of the prospective client's management team to obtain more information about their business environment. The Korean team at JVI was very reluctant to set up these meetings. However, I generally meet with client management prior to preparing a proposal. I also knew it would be difficult to obtain a good understanding of their business environment from a translated document. The material provided to me had been translated into English and was difficult to understand. The Korean and English languages are so different that conveying abstract concepts is very difficult.

> I convinced the Koreans at JVI that these meetings would help demonstrate our expertise. The meetings did not turn out exactly as planned. We met with the same management team at three different locations where we asked the same set of questions three times and got the same answers three times. We did not obtain the information normally

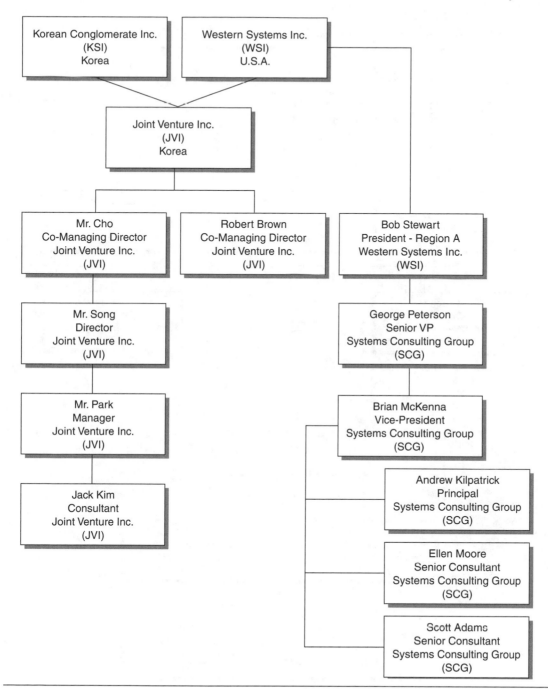

Exhibit 1   Organizational Structure—Functional View

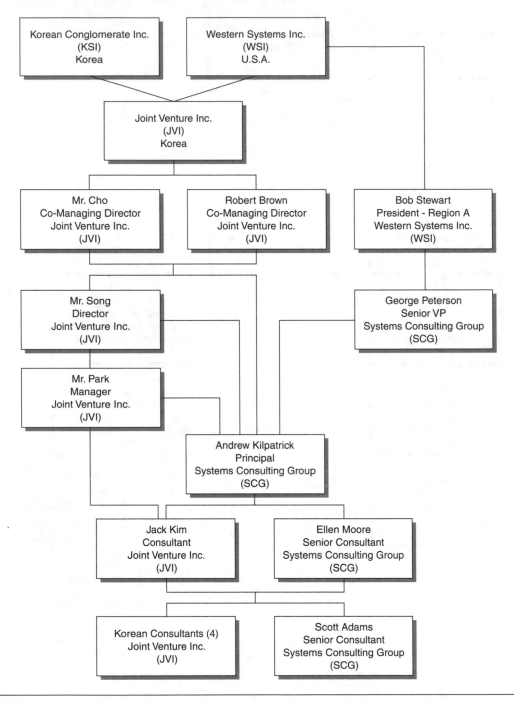

Exhibit 2 Organizational Structure—SI Project Team

provided at these fact-gathering meetings. However, they were tremendously impressed by our line of questioning because it reflected a deep interest and understanding of their business. They also were very impressed with my background. As a result, we were successful in convincing the government agency that we had a deep understanding of the nature and complexity of the agency's work and strong capabilities in systems development and implementation—key cornerstones of their project. The client wanted us to handle the project and wanted me to lead it.

JVI had not expected to get the contract, because its competitor for this work was a long-time supplier to the client. As a result, winning the government contract had important competitive and strategic implications for JVI. Essentially, JVI had dislodged an incumbent supplier to the client, one who had lobbied very heavily for this prominent contract. By winning the bid, JVI became the largest system implementer in Korea and received tremendous coverage in the public press.

The project was to begin in June 1995. However, the Korean project team convened in early May in order to prepare the team members. Although JVI requested Andrew to join the project on a full-time basis, he already had significant commitments to projects in North America. There was a great deal of discussion back and forth between WSI in North America, and JVI and the client in Korea. Eventually it was agreed that Andrew would manage the SI work on a part-time basis from North America, and he would send a qualified project management representative on a full-time basis. That person was Ellen Moore.

At that time, Andrew received immediate feedback from the American consultants with WSI in Korea that it would be impossible to send a woman to work in Korea. Andrew insisted that the Korean consultants be asked if they would accept a woman in the position. They responded that a woman would be acceptable if she were qualified. Andrew also requested that the client be consulted on this issue. He was again told that a woman would be acceptable if she were qualified. Andrew knew that Ellen had the skills required to manage the project:

I chose Ellen because I was very impressed with her capability, creativity, and project management skills, and I knew she had worked successfully in Bahrain, a culture where one would have to be attuned to very different cultural rules from those prevalent in North America. Ellen lacked experience with government agencies, but I felt that I could provide the required expertise in this area.

ELLEN MOORE

After graduating as the top female student from her high school, Ellen worked in the banking industry, achieving the position of corporate accounts officer responsible for over 20 major accounts and earning a Fellowship in the Institute of Bankers. Ellen went on to work for a former corporate client in banking and insurance, where she became the first female and youngest person to manage their financial reporting department. During this time, Ellen took university courses towards a Bachelor Degree at night. In 1983, she decided to stop working for two years, and completed her degree on a full-time basis. She graduated with a major in accounting and minors in marketing and management and decided to continue her studies for an MBA.

Two years later, armed with an MBA from a leading business school, Ellen Moore joined her husband in Manama, Bahrain, where she accepted a position as an expatriate manager for a large American financial institution.[1] Starting as a Special Projects Coordinator, within one year Ellen was promoted to Manager of Business Planning and Development, a challenging position that she was able to design herself. In this role, she managed the Quality Assurance department, coordinated a product launch, developed a senior management information system, and participated actively in all senior management decisions. Ellen's position required her to interact daily with managers and staff from a wide range of cultures, including Arab nationals.

In March 1995, Ellen joined WSI working for SCG. After the highly successful completion of two projects with SCG in North America, Ellen was approached for the Korea project:

> I had never worked in Korea or East Asia before. My only experience in Asia had been a one-week trip to Hong Kong for job interviews. I had limited knowledge of Korea and received no formal training from my company. I was provided a 20-page document on Korea. However, the information was quite basic and not entirely accurate.

After arriving in Korea, Ellen immediately began to familiarize herself with the language and proper business etiquette. She found that English was rarely spoken other than in some hotels and restaurants which catered to Western clientele. As a result, Ellen took advantage of every opportunity to teach herself the language basics:

> When Andrew and I were in the car on the way back to our hotel in the evening, we would be stuck in traffic for hours. I would use the time to learn how to read the Korean store signs. I had copied the Hangul symbols which form the Korean language onto a small piece of paper, and I kept this with me at all times. So, while sitting back in the car, exhausted at the end of each day, I would go over the symbols and read the signs.

The third SCG consultant on the project, Scott Adams, arrived as planned three months after Ellen's start date. Upon graduation, Scott had begun his consulting career working on several international engagements (including Mexico, Puerto Rico, and Venezuela), and he enjoyed the challenges of working with different cultures. He felt that with international consulting projects the technical aspects of consulting came easy. What he really enjoyed was the challenge of communicating in a different language and determining how to modify Western management techniques to fit into the local business culture. Scott first met Ellen at a systems consulting seminar, unaware at the time that their paths would cross again. A few months later, he was asked to consider the Korea assignment. Scott had never travelled or worked in Asia, but he believed that the assignment would present a challenging opportunity which would advance his career.

Scott was scheduled to start work on the project in August 1995. Prior to arriving in Seoul, Scott prepared himself by frequently discussing the work being conducted with Ellen. Ellen also provided him with information on the culture and business etiquette aspects of the work:

> It was very fortunate for me that Ellen had arrived first in Korea. Ellen tried to learn as much as she could about the Korean language, the culture, mannerisms, and the business etiquette. She was able to interpret many of the subtleties and to prepare me for both business and social situations, right down to how to exchange a business card appropriately with a Korean, how to read behavior, and what to wear.

About Korea[2]

Korea is a 600-mile-long peninsula stretching southward into the waters of the western Pacific, away from Manchuria and Siberia to the north on the Asian mainland. Facing eastward across the Sea of Japan, known to Koreans as the East Sea, Korea lies 120 miles from Japan. The Republic of Korea, or South Korea, consists of approximately 38,000 square miles, comparable in size to Virginia or Portugal. According to the 1990 census, the South Korean population is about 43 million, with almost 10 million residing in the capital city, Seoul.

Korea has an ancient heritage spanning 5,000 years. The most recent great historical era, the Yi Dynasty or Choson Dynasty, enlisted tremendous changes in which progress in science, technology, and the arts were achieved. Although Confucianism had been influential for centuries in Korea, it was during this time that Confucian principles permeated the culture as a code of morals and as a guide for ethical behavior. Confucian thought was designated as the state religion in 1392 and came to underpin education, civil administration, and daily conduct. During this time, Korean rulers began to avoid foreign contact and the monarchy was referred to as the "Hermit Kingdom" by outsiders. Lasting over 500 years and including 27 rulers, the Yi Dynasty came to a close at the end of the 19th century. Today, in Korea's modern era, the nation is quickly modernizing and traditional Confucian values mix with Western lifestyle habits and business methods.

Although many Korean people, particularly in Seoul, have become quite Westernized, they often follow traditional customs. Confucianism dictates strict rules of social behavior and etiquette. The basic values of the Confucian culture are: (1) complete loyalty to a hierarchical structure of authority, whether based in the family, the company, or the nation; (2) duty to parents, expressed through loyalty, love, and gratitude; and (3) strict rules of conduct, involving complete obedience and respectful behavior within superiors-subordinate relationships, such as parents-children, old-young, male-female, and teacher-student. These values affect both social and work environments substantially.

MANAGING IN KOREA

Business etiquette in Korea was extremely important. Ellen found that everyday activities, such as exchanging business cards or replenishing a colleague's drink at dinner, involved formal rituals. For example, Ellen learned it was important to provide and to receive business cards in an appropriate manner, which included carefully examining a business card when received and commenting on it. If one just accepted the card without reading it, this behavior would be considered very rude. In addition, Ellen also found it important to know how to address a Korean by name. If a Korean's name was Y.H. Kim, non-Koreans would generally address him as either Y.H. or as Mr. Kim. Koreans would likely call him by his full name or by his title and name, such as Manager Kim. A limited number of Koreans, generally those who had lived overseas, took on Western names, such as Jack Kim.

WORK TEAMS

Teams were an integral part of the work environment in Korea. Ellen noted that the Korean consultants organized some special team building activities to bring together the Korean and North American team members:

> On one occasion, the Korean consulting team invited the Western consultants to a baseball game on a Saturday afternoon followed by a trip to the Olympic Park for a tour after the game, and dinner at a Korean restaurant that evening. An event of this nature is unusual and was very special. On another occasion, the Korean consultants gave up a day off with their families and spent it with the Western consultants. We toured a Korean palace and the palace grounds, and we were then invited to Park's home for dinner. It was very unusual that we, as Western folks, were invited to his home, and it was a very gracious event.

Ellen also found team-building activities took place on a regular basis, and that these events were normally conducted outside of the work environment. For example, lunch with the team was an important daily team event which everyone was expected to attend:

> You just couldn't work at your desk every day for lunch. It was important for everyone to attend lunch together in order to share in this social activity, as one of the means for team bonding.

Additionally, the male team members would go out together for food, drink, and song after work. Scott found these drinking activities to be an important part of his interaction with both the team and the client:

> Unless you had a medical reason, you would be expected to drink with the team members, sometimes to excess. A popular drink, soju, which is similar to vodka, would be poured into a small glass. Our glasses were never empty, as someone would always ensure that an empty glass was quickly filled. For example, if my glass was empty, I learned that I should pass it to the person on my

right and fill it for him as a gesture of friendship. He would quickly drink the contents of the glass, pass the glass back to me, and fill it for me to quickly drink. You simply had to do it. I recall one night when I really did not want to drink as I had a headache. We were sitting at dinner, and Mr. Song handed me his glass and filled it. I said to him "I really can't drink tonight. I have a terrible headache." He looked at me and said "Mr. Scott, I have Aspirin in my briefcase." I had about three or four small drinks that night.

Ellen found she was included in many of the team-building dinners, and soon after she arrived in Seoul, she was invited to a team dinner, which included client team members. Ellen was informed that although women were not normally invited to these social events, an exception was made since she was a senior team member.

During the dinner, there were many toasts and drinking challenges. During one such challenge, the senior client representative prepared a drink that consisted of one highball glass filled with beer and one shot glass filled to the top with whiskey. He dropped the whiskey glass into the beer glass and passed the drink to the man on his left. This team member quickly drank the cocktail in one swoop, and held the glass over his head, clicking the glasses to show both were empty. Everyone cheered and applauded. This man then mixed the same drink, and passed the glass to the man on his left, who also drank the cocktail in one swallow. It was clear this challenge was going around the table and would eventually get to me.

I don't generally drink beer and never drink whiskey. But it was clear, even without my translator present to assist my understanding, that this activity was an integral part of the team building for the project. As the man on my right mixed the drink for me, he whispered that he would help me. He poured the beer to the halfway point in the highball glass, filled the shot glass to the top with whiskey, and dropped the shotglass in the beer. Unfortunately, I could see that the beer didn't cover the top of the shot glass, which would likely move too quickly if not covered. I announced "One moment, please, we are having technical difficulties." And to the amazement of all in attendance,

I asked the man on my right to pour more beer in the glass. When I drank the concoction in one swallow, everyone cheered, and the senior client representative stood up and shouted, "You are now Korean. You are now Korean."

The norms for team management were also considerably different from the North American style of management. Ellen was quite surprised to find that the concept of saving face did not mean avoiding negative feedback or sharing failures:

It is important in Korea to ensure that team members do not lose face. However, when leading a team, it appeared just as important for a manager to demonstrate leadership. If a team member provided work that did not meet the stated requirements, a leader was expected to express disappointment in the individual's efforts in front of all team members. A strong leader was considered to be someone who engaged in this type of public demonstration when required.

In North America, a team leader often compliments and rewards team members for work done well. In Korea, leaders expressed disappointment in substandard work, or said nothing for work completed in a satisfactory manner. A leader was considered weak if he or she continuously provided compliments for work completed as required.

Hierarchy

The Koreans' respect for position and status was another element of the Korean culture that both Ellen and Scott found to have a significant influence over how the project was structured and how people behaved. The emphasis placed on hierarchy had an important impact upon the relationship between consultant and client that was quite different from their experience in North America. As a result, the North Americans' understanding of the role of a consultant differed vastly from their Korean counterparts.

Specifically, the North American consultants were familiar with "managing client expectations." This activity involved informing the client of the best means to achieve their goals and included frequent communication with the client. Generally, the client's customer was also interviewed in order to understand how the client's system could better integrate with their customer's requirements. Ellen recalled, however, that the procedures were necessarily different in Korea:

> The client team members did not permit our team members to go to their offices unannounced. We had to book appointments ahead of time to obtain permission to see them. In part, this situation was a result of the formalities we needed to observe due to their rank in society, but I believe it was also because they wanted to be prepared for the topics we wanted to discuss.

The Korean consultants refused to interview the customers, because they did not want to disturb them. Furthermore, the client team members frequently came into the project office and asked the Korean consultants to work on activities not scheduled for that week or which were beyond the project scope. The Korean consultants accepted the work without question. Ellen and Scott found themselves powerless to stop this activity.

Shortly after arriving, Scott had a very confrontational meeting with one of the Korean consultants concerning this issue:

> I had been in Korea for about a week, and I was still suffering from jet lag. I was alone with one of the Korean consultants, and we were talking about how organizational processes should be flow-charted. He was saying the client understands the process in a particular manner, so we should show it in that way. I responded that, from a technical standpoint, it was not correct. I explained that as a consultant, we couldn't simply do what the client requests if it is incorrect. We must provide value by showing why a different method may be taken by educating the client of the options and the reasons for selecting a specific method. There are times when you have to tell the client something different than he believes. That's what we're paid for. He said, "No, no, you don't understand. They're paying our fee." At that point I raised my voice: "You don't know what you are talking about. I have much more experience than you." Afterwards,

I realized that it was wrong to shout at him. I pulled him aside and apologized. He said, "Well, I know you were tired." I replied that it was no excuse, and I should not have shouted. After that, we managed to get along just fine.

The behavior of subordinates and superiors also reflected the Korean's respect for status and position. Scott observed that it was very unusual for a subordinate to leave the office for the day unless his superior had already left:

> I remember one day, a Saturday, when one of the young Korean consultants who had been ill for some time, was still at his desk. I made a comment: "Why don't you go home, Mr. Choi?" Although he was not working for me, I knew his work on the other team was done. He said, "I can't go home because several other team members have taken the day off. I have to stay." I repeated my observation that his work was done. He replied: "If I do not stay, I will be fired. My boss is still here, I have to stay." He would stay and work until his boss left, until late in the evening if necessary.

Furthermore, Scott found that the Korean consultants tended not to ask questions. Even when Scott asked the Korean consultants if they understood his instructions or explanation, they generally responded affirmatively which made it difficult to confirm their understanding. He was advised that responding in a positive manner demonstrated respect for teachers or superiors. Asking a question would be viewed as inferring that the teacher or superior had not done a good job of explaining the material. As a result, achieving a coaching role was difficult for the North American consultants even though passing on their knowledge of SI to the Korean consultants was considered an important part of their function on this project.

WOMEN IN KOREA

Historically, Confucian values have dictated a strict code of behavior between men and women and husband and wife in Korea. Traditionally, there has been a clear delineation in the respective responsibilities of men and women. The male preserve can be defined as that which is public, whereas women are expected to cater to the private, personal world of the home. These values have lingered into the 1990s, with Korean public life very much dominated by men.

Nevertheless, compared to the Yi dynasty era, the position of women in society has changed considerably. There is now virtual equality in access to education for men and women, and a few women have embarked on political careers. As in many other areas of the world, the business world has until recently been accessible only to men. However, this is changing as Korean women are beginning to seek equality in the workplace. Young Korean men and women now often participate together in social activities such as evenings out and hikes, something that was extremely rare even 10 years ago.

Dual income families are becoming more common in South Korea, particularly in Seoul, although women generally hold lower-paid, more menial positions. Furthermore, working women often retain their traditional household responsibilities, while men are expected to join their male colleagues for late night drinking and eating events which exclude women. When guests visit a Korean home, the men traditionally sit and eat together separately from the women, who are expected to eat together while preparing the food.

Although the younger generation are breaking from such traditions, Scott felt that the gender differences were quite apparent in the work place. He commented:

> The business population was primarily male. Generally, the only women we saw were young women who were clerks, wearing uniforms. I suspected that these women were in the workforce for only a few years, until they were married and left to have a family. We did have a few professional Korean women working with us. However, because we are a professional services firm, I believe it may have been more progressive than the typical Korean company.

THE SYSTEMS IMPLEMENTATION TEAM

Upon her arrival in Korea, Ellen dove into her work confident that the Korean consultants she would be working with had the skills necessary to complete the job in the time frame allocated. The project work was divided up among several work groups, each having distinct deliverables and due dates. The deliverables for the SI team were required as a major input to the other work groups on the project (see Exhibit 3). As a result, delays with deliverables would impact the effectiveness of the entire project:

> JVI told us they had assigned experienced management consultants to work on the project. Given their stated skill level, Andrew's resource plan had him making periodic visits to Korea; I would be on the project on a full time basis starting in May, and Scott would join the team about three to four months after the project start. We were informed that five Korean consultants were assigned. We believed that we had the resources needed to complete the project by December.

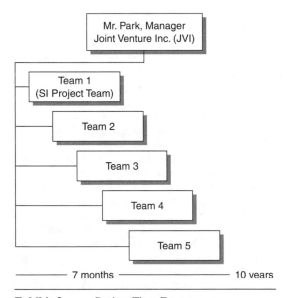

Exhibit 3   Project Time Frame

JACK KIM

J.T. Kim, whose Western name was Jack, was the lead Korean consultant reporting to Mr. Park. Jack had recently achieved a Ph.D. in computer systems from a reputable American university and he spoke English fluently. When Andrew initially discussed the organizational structure of the SI team with Mr. Park and Jack, it was agreed that Jack and Ellen would be co-managers of the SI project.

Three weeks after her arrival, Jack informed Ellen, much to her surprise, that he had never worked on a systems implementation project. Additionally, Ellen soon learned that Jack had never worked on a consulting project:

> Apparently, Jack had been made the lead consultant of SI upon completing his Ph.D. in the United States. I believe Jack was told he was going to be the sole project manager for SI on a daily basis. However, I was informed I was going to be the co-project manager with Jack. It was confusing, particularly for Jack, when I took on coaching and leading the team. We had a lot of controversy—not in the form of fights or heated discussions, but we had definite issues during the first few weeks because we were clearly stepping upon each other's territory.

Given Jack's position as the lead Korean consultant, it was quite difficult for Ellen to redirect team members' activities. The Korean team members always followed Jack's instructions. Scott recalled:

> There were frequent meetings with the team to discuss the work to be completed. Often, following these meetings the Korean consultants would meet alone with Jack, and it appeared that he would instruct them to carry out different work. On one occasion, when both Andrew and Ellen were travelling away from the office, Andrew prepared specific instructions for the team to follow outlined in a memo.

> Andrew sent the memo to me so I could hand the memo to Jack directly, thereby ensuring he did

receive these instructions. Upon his return, Andrew found the team had not followed his instructions. We were provided with the following line of reasoning: you told us to do A, B and C, but you did not mention D. And, we did D. They had followed Jack's instructions. We had a very difficult time convincing them to carry out work as we requested, even though we had been brought onto the project to provide our expertise.

In July, a trip was planned for the Korean client team and some of the Korean consulting team to visit other project sites in North America. The trip would permit the Koreans to find out more about the capabilities of WSI and to discuss issues with other clients involved with similar projects. Jack was sent on the trip, leaving Ellen in charge of the SI project team in Korea. While Jack was away on the North American trip, Ellen had her first opportunity to work with and to lead the Korean consultants on a daily basis. She was very pleased that she was able to coach them directly, without interference, and advise them on how to best carry out the required work. Ellen felt that everyone worked together in a very positive manner, in complete alignment. When Jack returned, he saw that Ellen was leading the team and that they were accepting Ellen's directions. Ellen recalled the tensions that arose as a result:

> On the first day he returned, Jack instructed someone to do some work for him, and the person responded, "I cannot because I am doing something for Ellen." Jack did not say anything, but he looked very angry. He could not understand why anyone on the team would refuse his orders.

THE MARKETING RESEARCH PROJECT

A few days after Jack returned from the North American trip, the project team realized they did not have sufficient information about their client's customer. Jack decided a market research study should be conducted to determine the market requirements. However, this type of study, which is generally a large undertaking on a project, was not within the scope of the contracted work. Ellen found out about the proposed market research project at a meeting held on a Saturday, which involved everyone from the entire project—about 40 people. The only person not at the meeting was Mr. Park. Jack was presenting the current work plans for SI, and he continued to describe a market research study:

> I thought to myself, "What market research study is he talking about?" I asked him to put aside his presentation of the proposed study until he and I had an opportunity to discuss the plans. I did not want to interrupt his presentation or disagree with him publicly, but I felt I had no choice.

DINNER WITH JACK

Two hours following the presentation, Ellen's translator, Susan Lim, informed her that there was a dinner planned for that evening and Jack wanted everyone on the SI team to attend. Ellen was surprised that Jack would want her present at the dinner. However, Susan insisted that Jack specifically said Ellen must be there. They went to a small Korean restaurant, where everyone talked about a variety of subjects in English and Korean, with Susan translating for Ellen as needed. After about one hour, Jack began a speech to the team, speaking solely in Korean. Ellen thought it was unusual for him to speak Korean when she was present, as everyone at the dinner also spoke English:

> Through the limited translations I received, I understood he was humbling himself to the team, saying, "I am very disappointed in my performance. I have clearly not been the project leader needed for this team." The team members were responding "No, no, don't say that." While Jack was talking to the team, he was consuming large quantities of beer. The pitchers were coming and coming. He was quite clearly becoming intoxicated. All at once, Susan stopped translating. I asked her what was wrong. She whispered that she would tell me later. Five minutes went by and I turned to her and spoke emphatically, "Susan, what

is going on? I want to know now." She realized I was getting angry. She told me, "Jack asked me to stop translating. Please don't say anything, I will lose my job."

> I waited a couple of minutes before speaking, then I interrupted Jack's speech. I said, "Susan is having difficulty hearing you and isn't able to translate for me. I guess it is too noisy in this restaurant. Would it be possible for you to speak in English?" Jack did not say anything for about 30 seconds and then he started speaking in English. His first words were, "Ellen, I would like to apologize. I didn't realize you couldn't understand what I was saying."

Another thirty minutes of his speech and drinking continued. The Korean team members appeared to be consoling Jack, by saying: "Jack, we do respect you and the work you have done for our team. You have done your best." While they were talking, Jack leaned back, and appeared to pass out. Ellen turned to Susan and asked if they should help him to a taxi. Susan insisted it would not be appropriate. During the next hour, Jack appeared to be passed out or sleeping. Finally, one of the team members left to go home. Ellen asked Susan, "Is it important for me to stay, or is it important for me to go?" She said Ellen should go.

When Ellen returned to her hotel, it was approximately 11 p.m. on Saturday night. She felt the situation had reached a point where it was necessary to request assistance from senior management in North America. Andrew was on a wilderness camping vacation in the United States with his family, and could not be reached. Ellen decided to call the North American project sponsor, the Senior Vice President, George Peterson:

> I called George that Saturday night at his house and said: "We have a problem. They're trying to change the scope of the project. We don't have the available time, and we don't have the resources. It is impossible to do a market research study in conjunction with all the contracted work to be completed with the same limited resources. The proposed plan is to use our project team to handle

this additional work. Our team is already falling behind the schedule, but due to their inexperience they don't realize it yet." George said he would find Andrew and send him to Korea to further assess the situation.

THE MEETING WITH THE DIRECTOR

When Andrew arrived in August, he conducted a very quick assessment of the situation. The project was a month behind schedule. It appeared to Andrew that the SI team had made limited progress since his previous visit:

> It was clear to me that the Korean team members weren't taking direction from Ellen. Ellen was a seasoned consultant and knew what to do. However, Jack was giving direction to the team which was leading them down different paths. Jack was requesting that the team work on tasks which were not required for the project deliverables, and he was not appropriately managing the client's expectations.

Andrew held several discussions with Mr. Park concerning these issues. Mr. Park insisted the problem was Ellen. He argued that Ellen was not effective, she did not assign work properly, and she did not give credible instructions to the team. However, Andrew believed the Korean consultants' lack of experience was the main problem.

> Initially, we were told the Korean team consisted of experienced consultants, although they had not completed any SI projects. I felt we could work around it. I had previously taught consultants to do SI. We were also told that one of the Korean consultants had taught SI. This consultant was actually the most junior person on the team. She had researched SI by reading some texts and had given a presentation on her understanding of SI to a group of consultants.

Meanwhile, Andrew solicited advice from the WSI Co-Managing Director, Robert Brown, who had over ten years experience working in Korea. Robert suggested that Andrew approach Mr. Park's superior, Mr. Song, directly. He further directed Andrew to present his case to the Joint Venture committee if an agreement was not reached with Mr. Song. Andrew had discussed the issues with George Peterson and Robert Brown, and they agreed that there was no reason for Ellen to leave the project:

> However, Robert's message to me was that I had been too compliant with the Koreans. It was very important for the project to be completed on time, and that I would be the one held accountable for any delays. Addressing issues before the Joint Venture committee was the accepted dispute resolution process at JVI when an internal conflict could not be resolved. However, in most cases, the last thing a manager wants is to be defending his position before the Joint Venture committee. Mr. Song was in line to move into senior executive management. Taking the problem to the Joint Venture committee would be a way to force the issue with him.

Andrew attempted to come to a resolution with Mr. Park once again, but he refused to compromise. Andrew then tried to contact Mr. Song and was told he was out of the office. Coincidentally, Mr. Song visited the project site to see Mr. Park just as Ellen and Andrew were completing a meeting. Ellen recalls Mr. Song's arrival:

> Mr. Song walked into the project office expecting to find Mr. Park. However, Mr. Park was out visiting another project that morning. Mr. Song looked around the project office for a senior manager, and he saw Andrew. Mr. Song approached Andrew and asked if Mr. Park was in the office. Andrew responded that he was not. Mr. Song proceeded to comment that he understood there were some concerns about the project work, and suggested that perhaps, sometime, they could talk about it. Andrew replied that they needed to talk about it immediately.

Andrew met with Mr. Song in Mr. Park's office, a makeshift set of thin walls that enclosed a small office area in one corner of the large open project office. Ellen was working in an area just outside the office when she heard Andrew's voice rise. She heard him shout, "Well, I don't think you're listening to what I am saying." Ellen was surprised to hear Andrew shouting. She knew Andrew was very sensitive to what should and should not be done in the Korean environment:

> Andrew's behavior seemed so confrontational. I believed this behavior was unacceptable in Korea. For a while, I heard a lot of murmuring, after which I heard Andrew speak adamantly, "No, I'm very serious. It doesn't matter what has been agreed and what has not been agreed because most of our agreements were based on inaccurate information. We can start from scratch." Mr. Song insisted that I was the problem.

NOTES

1. For an account of Ellen's experience in Bahrain, see Ellen Moore (A): Living and Working in Bahrain, 9A90C019, and Ellen Moore (B), 9A90C020; Ivey Publishing, Ivey Management Services, c/o Richard Ivey School of Business, University of Western Ontario, London, Ontario, Canada, N6A 3K7.

2. Some of the information in the "About Korea" and "Women in Korea" sections was obtained from "Fodor's Korea," 1993, Fodor's Travel Publications, Inc.: NY; and Chris Taylor, "Seoul-city guide," 1993, Lonely Planet Publications: Colorcraft Ltd., Hong Kong.

JULIE DEMPSTER (A)

Prepared by Rachel Knight under the supervision of Professor Christine Pearson

Version: (A) 2003-03-24

In August 2002, Julie Dempster reflected on her experiences as vice-president of marketing and brand positioning at Overflow, an Amsterdam-based provider of content management solutions. Since she signed her contract a year ago, she had been trying to negotiate an equity stake in the company. Dempster had arranged a meeting for the following day with Overflow's chief executive officer (CEO) to revisit this issue. Although Dempster was responsible for many positive changes at Overflow, she often disagreed with the decisions made by the company's directors and frequently butted heads with the CEO. Her contract was up for renewal in a week's time and she wondered whether staying at Overflow was the best decision for her, regardless of how the next day's meeting played out.

JULIE DEMPSTER

A 34-year-old native of Ontario, Dempster aspired to run an international company, preferably in the media and entertainment sector. Working towards this goal, she earned both a bachelor's degree (1992) and a master's degree (1996) in journalism from Carleton University, and completed two media-related management fellowships in the United States. In the past, Dempster had worked as a correspondent in Africa for various media firms, as a consultant for the Canadian government and the Canadian Advisory Council on the Status of Women as a journalist for WETV (an Ottawa-based global TV network), as a Web developer for the Tribune Company (one of the largest media companies in the United States) and as a marketing specialist for the *New York Times*.

Dempster left the *New York Times* because she had grown tired of being constrained by the rigid and hierarchical structure there. She decided to move to Europe in December of 1999 to focus on broadband and interactive television developments. She chose Amsterdam for a number of reasons. It was an information technology (IT) hub with a multicultural and cosmopolitan environment that appealed to her. Also, she felt she would be able to function there as an English-speaking professional, despite the fact that Dutch was the official language.

Once there, she was hired by Von Trapp & Partners (Von Trapp), a company that focused on conduction pan-European digital media research and strategy development for media and entertainment companies. She wanted to use this position as a means to learn about both industry trends and the European landscape. After 18 months with Von Trapp and despite promises, Dempster still had not received an equity stake, and she decided to move on.

OVERFLOW

In July 2001, Dempster agreed to a two-month consulting contract with Overflow. She accepted it because the position paid a very high salary (by Dutch standards) and she saw it as an opportunity to learn about the role that technology plays in furthering business objectives. Additionally, Overflow's management had agreed to her request for a three-day workweek, giving her time to complete renovations on her apartment.

Overflow was officially founded in January of 2000 and had rapidly become a leader in the field of content management in Benelux (Belgium, the Netherlands and Luxembourg). The company's success was attributable to its innovative technology that enabled information to be distributed in various formats to devices such as personal digital assistants (PDAs), personal computers (PCs), Web browsers, mobile browsers and digital TVs. The technology served to reduce "content chaos," thereby helping companies to lower costs and improve efficiencies.

Overflow was divided into three divisions: software development, sales and eServices. Each was managed by one of the company's three founding members and self-appointed directors: the CEO, chief technical officer (CTO) and chief communications officer (CCO). At the time, the company had 30 Dutch employees, only three of whom were women. As a black Canadian woman, Dempster stood out.

As she began her consultancy, Dempster quickly learned that the formal hierarchy was virtually meaningless. Employees of all levels seemed comfortable sharing their thoughts and complaints at will. At Overflow, from Dempster's perspective, company culture dictated that everyone's opinion was heard regardless of whether the employee was qualified to speak on the subject, or whether management was remotely interested in what the person had to say.

The environment at Overflow was much less professional and much less interactive than what Dempster had been accustomed to, so when her short contract expired, she expressed her plans to move on. The company's CEO, Johannes Nederberg, was extremely disappointed by the news and convinced Dempster that she could play a key role in managing the company if she stayed. It would be her job to put the company on the map, and position it among global competitors in the content management industry. Excited by the prospects, Dempster signed the full-time contract with Overflow as vice-president of marketing and brand positioning in September 2001. She was told that equity was not available to new hires at this time but if she proved herself, she would be offered it in the future.

When Dempster signed on, Nederberg was 28 years old. She found him extremely bright and ambitious, with exemplary sales abilities, despite his lack of formal education beyond high school. Nederberg was clearly the leader among the three directors. The CTO, Klaas Driehuizen, was also young and very bright, and was credited for developing Overflow's software. Driehuizen was not known for his communication skills, but was extremely hard-working. The CCO, Jens Dekker, was very easygoing and friendly, but did not have any management skills. Dempster's position fell under the jurisdiction of the CCO, but she reported informally to the CEO. It was clear to Dempster that he was the best resource the company had, and he was insistent on being involved in her activities.

Overflow did not have a formal value statement but performance was considered "key." It was clear that non-performers had no future at the company. In fact, employees who were not seen as living up to a particular standard were fired.

SETTLING IN

In order to accommodate Dempster's needs, Nederberg announced that Overflow would adopt English as its official language. (Prior to this, the company's official language had been Dutch, due to its focus on the Dutch market and its Dutch employees.) To ensure her comfort at Overflow, Dempster was provided with a nice, roomy workspace in the location of her choice. From these accommodations, she began developing relationships with Overflow's most important clients. These relationships were vital to Dempster's success and Overflow's future because the clients played a key role in marketing Overflow's technological solutions.

Dempster's mandate was to develop Overflow's image through a mixture of marketing, public relations (PR), corporate communications and client relations. This entailed developing and implementing Overflow's core strategy, managing all marketing activities, managing the distribution of news releases, cultivating relationships with journalists, making sure the senior executives received coverage in the mainstream media, drafting all key marketing collateral, keeping staff up-to-date on business and communicating frequently with clients.

Overflow's employees were respectful and friendly towards Dempster, but she found them generally less professional than her North Americans colleagues. For example, Dempster overheard the Nederberg's secretary telling a client that the CEO couldn't come to the phone because he was "on the toilet." As a result, Dempster drafted a set of standard phone responses for secretaries to use.

On another occasion, a co-worker confronted her aggressively, stating that he "refused to change from Dutch operations just because she was an English-speaker." Dempster reported the incident to Nederberg but refused to identify the co-worker in question. The CEO became very angry. A few days later, Nederberg explained to all employees that "the company's official language was now English in order to compete in the international game." Shortly after this announcement, Dempster requested and received permission to take a Dutch language course, which was paid for by Overflow.

THE FINANCE PARTY

In early November 2001, Overflow obtained a new round of financing from two private investors. The financing was secured despite the dot-com burst and was viewed as a great success. In order to celebrate, the CEO planned a large party that would include current and prospective clients, suppliers, supporters and the media.

When Dempster arrived at the party, she was shocked to find that the wait staff (all young, attractive women) were sporting tiny, revealing T-shirts emblazoned with the Overflow logo across the chest. Dempster was furious that she hadn't been consulted about a decision that would affect that brand image of the company. She wondered if she'd been deliberately left out of the loop. Dempster confronted Nederberg immediately and a heated exchange ensued just as the party was beginning. Nederberg stormed away. Dempster left the party as soon as the scantily clad waitresses began drinking and dancing provocatively with some of the male guests.

When Dempster returned to work on Monday, she was surprised to find the CEO acting as if nothing had occurred. She approached Nederberg and apologized for losing her temper but expressed her disappointment at not being involved in the planning for the party. She explained that she felt the T-shirts and the waitresses' behavior were inappropriate and unprofessional, and she conveyed her desire to be involved in future decisions about how the company would market itself. In response, Nederberg became angry and accused Dempster of embarrassing him in front of his family and friends. In his view, Dempster had over-reacted, and she needed to become more sensitive to European practices. Nederberg claimed that most of the people at the party were men and that men enjoyed parties with young women as entertainers. Because neither Dempster nor Nederberg could understand the other's point of view, they agreed to disagree on the issue and move on.

About a month after the incident, Dempster received her first performance review. Nederberg indicated that management was very happy with her work and felt lucky to have her on board. The company, as a whole, was impressed that one person could make such a difference to an organization: Overflow had become more organized and more professional as a result of Dempster's presence. Nederberg told Dempster that one area she needed to improve was her cultural sensitivity, citing the finance party. Dempster took this as an opportunity to defend her actions surrounding the finance party again. The conversation escalated into another unresolved argument. For months after, Nederberg continued to make snide comments about Dempster's response to the women at the finance party.

THE DUTCH MEETING

In March 2002, Dempster arranged a meeting between Overflow and one of their key technical partners. The meeting was intended for the two sales forces to discuss strategic moves in sales and marketing, for which Dempster would ultimately be responsible. The CEO, CTO, CCO, director of business development and three sales reps were there to represent Overflow. A dozen visitors represented the partner company. Counter to plan, the one-and-a-half hour meeting took place entirely in Dutch, leaving Dempster unable to understand what was being discussed. Even the written materials provided by the other company were entirely in Dutch, despite the fact that they knew that Dempster did not speak the language. She felt out of place. Most of all, she was disappointed and hurt that none of her co-workers stood up for her by speaking English.

That evening, Dempster contemplated leaving Overflow. First, she considered what she was gaining from working there. She had developed insights into the future direction of technologies for digital media and entertainment, learned a lot about venture capitalism and due diligence, and strengthened her skills in strategic communications. Furthermore, she felt proud of the significant organizational change she had inspired within the company. She was certain that staying at Overflow would provide her with many more challenges and character-building experiences. But she felt isolated and different from everybody there, and that made her wish for more. Dempster contacted a professional recruiter that evening. She would stay at Overflow until something else materialized.

SOME NEW DEVELOPMENTS

Five months later, Dempster had yet to find another job that she wanted because the digital media industry was in the midst of significant restructuring and downsizing. However, some positive opportunities had improved her situation at Overflow. Initially, Dempster was invited to attend meetings involving the company directors. Ironically, this change had been precipitated by a sarcastic comment by Nederberg about the "T-shirt" party. Fed up by one more comment, Dempster had given notice, but Nederberg refused to take it. Rather, he vowed that things would change. She agreed to stay and was granted more management involvement.

Also, Dempster was excited that Overflow's rapid growth was outpacing the company's human resources. They would have the opportunity to create new positions and hire new employees. Dempster knew she could play a key role in hiring the right kind of people to shape Overflow's future.

Finally, Overflow had been nominated to receive a prestigious award recognizing the company as "the most promising startup in the Netherlands." Dempster had conducted a presentation for a panel of judges, explaining why Overflow deserved the award, but the recipient had not yet been named. The award was highly coveted. It would attract large-scale venture capitalists, and it would bring recognition to the winner's management team.

SOME LINGERING ISSUES

Despite these positive developments, Dempster felt unsettled about certain issues. She was concerned with the way management treated some employees. If employees weren't producing, they were let go, often without any chance to improve.

Dempster was concerned also about the way management treated small-sized customers. Little was done to appease them. Nederberg's justification was that the small customers were unimportant and the focus should be placed on "the big fish." Dempster was concerned that this attitude would affect other employees and, ultimately, spill over to the larger customers, as well.

Perhaps the most unsettling issue was Dempster's accidental discovery that other employees did have equity stakes in Overflow. Christian Hoogendam, who had been hired at the same time as Dempster, had a 0.5 per cent stake in the company as a part of his contract. Dempster estimated that this could be worth nearly $1 million. Although he had an excellent reputation as an IT specialist, Hoogendam had yet to prove himself at Overflow. Other equity allocations seemed somewhat random but all recipients were Dutch.

So, with the contract renewal meeting tomorrow, Dempster sat down to evaluate the pros and cons of staying with Overflow. Certainly, her concerns about financial equity should be voiced. She had bargaining power, after all. But, she was concerned about how Nederberg might react. As she reflected on her experiences at Overflow, with or without an offer of equity, Dempster wondered whether it was time for her to move on.

THE EUROPEAN EXPERIENCE (A)

Prepared by David Wesley under the supervision of Professor Henry W. Lane

Copyright © 2002, Northeastern University, College of Business Administration   Version: (A) 2002-06-27

In September 1999, a group of international business majors from a large Boston-area university travelled to Spain, France and Germany for a yearlong period of study and work. A few weeks after arriving in Europe, they began discussing their experience in an asynchronous online meeting over the Internet. This case reflects parts of the discussion in which some of the students described their initial impressions.

GETTING SETTLED

"Coming to France was one of the scariest moments of my whole life," recalled Andrea.

Being told is one thing, but doing it yourself, is another. Tiny details like sheets, laundry, the bus, and even different keyboards. Things you never think about in Boston are big challenges here. Plus, I had never before been out of the United States, so customs and the long flight were all new to me.

The minute I stepped foot in the airport, I never felt more alone in my life! The first day was terrible. I was tired and had to get to the school, sign a lease, go grocery shopping and do it all in French! After 15 hours of sleep, things were much brighter, but the first weekend by myself was awful. I didn't know anyone, and there's only so much time you can spend by yourself. I was missing home, and began having thoughts of "What have I done?"

When Mario left the airport, the narrow streets and small cars made an immediate impression, as he compared them with the relatively wide boulevards and expressways of the United States. When he arrived at the building where he was to stay, he couldn't help but notice how small the elevator was. He observed,

> I doubt any of the elevators I have been on in Spain would pass U.S. laws. A recent experience in my building comes to mind. An elderly woman was being returned to her apartment. Her sons had to place the wheelchair sideways and lift up the foot rests, so they could squeeze her feet in. Then she had to ride up to her floor by herself! Among the many differences here, it is clear to me that the Spanish are different in the amount of space they need.

Jim arrived in Madrid after missing his connection in New York. Fortunately he met another classmate who had also just arrived and the two began their first undertaking—looking for a place to live.

> After dropping my bags off at the hostel and taking a quick shower, we sped off in search of an apartment. We picked up the *Segundamano* and began dialing, but no luck. We decided to ask a woman walking past us if she knew of any *pisos* available for rent. She then took us to a restaurant to meet her husband. They decided that we looked clean enough to show the apartment directly above the restaurant, and what an apartment! It had three rooms, art and a big kitchen and living area. Then we returned downstairs and wrote up a contract on a napkin and had beers for about two hours with our new *dueños*. Needless to say these wonderful people have treated us like their own sons.

Don echoed Jim's sentiment.

> The owners really take care of us. They make sure that we have everything we could possibly need. That was my first realization that business was done a little differently around here. Money doesn't seem to be the first priority. I think they were actually surprised when we gave them the rent on the first of the month!

When John landed at the airport, he and Mike got into a "junk" cab and had to push it out of the airport. On John's first day, he looked at one

apartment, but was not interested in spending more time than necessary on his search.

> I don't get all worried about little things like where to live. I came here on a Monday, looked at one apartment that I didn't like, then went to Ibiza to party for six days. When I came back I ran into this English girl from school who had a room free and I took it on the spot.

Katie, however, was less fortunate, and found her first days in Madrid to be somewhat bewildering.

> I arrived. I was alone without the comfort of friends or family. I already began feeling homesick. I thought to myself, "Time to call home, tell them I arrived in one piece." Ok! How do you use these phones? I don't understand the operator. Frustration! I'm hungry—what does the menu say? Do you guys know what kind of food this is? How much money? How many pesetas to a dollar? Questions, questions, questions!

She soon met three other American women and they began looking for an apartment to share.

> It wasn't an easy task, at least for us. Some of the other girls started the research before I arrived, so they were a few steps ahead of me. We made a million phone calls. Finally we saw a few places together and eventually decided on one.

For Angela, finding an apartment was the most difficult thing she encountered during her first few weeks.

> The first day that I arrived, I bought a mobile phone (because it is a basic necessity here), went to the school and got a list of apartments for rent. I began calling people on my mobile phone, but I was not used to communicating with native speakers. I got by, but it took three long and hard days of calling people to find a decent apartment. But I am glad that I was forced to start speaking and I got over my fear of making mistakes really quickly!

ADJUSTING TO LIFE IN EUROPE

Language

Mary, who was studying in Germany, also found speaking on the phone to be a challenge.

She related the difficulties she encountered when she tried to arrange an internship interview.

> I had to call a man at BMW. It was not the best conversation, but I tried my best to converse with him. I tend to get really flustered when I am speaking on the phone in German. As soon as I cannot understand a few words, I begin to panic. So that is what I did—panic. I was trying to ask him how he spelled the street name where I should go, and I used the informal form and conjugated the verb incorrectly. When he stopped what he was saying, I became so flustered that I actually asked again in the same way as the first time. Well, it may have been my imagination, but he sounded very brisk and then just spelled it out in English.

Claudia, who was a native of an Eastern European country, enjoyed returning to a country that had a culture similar to her own. Nevertheless, language was a barrier and she became frustrated when some Germans would speak to her in English because she could not respond fluently in German.

> It seems to me that they try to show that their English is better than my German and that they are better at learning foreign languages. I never bother to explain to them that English is also my second language, and that I have learned it as well as, if not better, than they have. Still, only a few people do this to me, so I don't pay that much attention to it. There are just as many who are supportive and help me correct my mistakes.

On her first day in France, Andrea was exhausted by her efforts to speak French for the whole day. She was relieved when she encountered a tour guide who had been on a student exchange in the United States and was glad to speak with her in English.

Dana's first day was also her most difficult. "No one understood me," she recalled. "I couldn't even make a simple phone call to my parents." She continued,

> I found some Mexican friends who helped me to settle in on that awkward first day. To get by, I would just stick with the people who had been at the school for one month. They made things much easier. Then, as I got to know the students and

faculty, I began to feel more comfortable with the French. However, language is still the most difficult thing because it takes a lot of mental energy to be able to communicate.

Although all of the exchange students in Spain had a reasonable level of Spanish proficiency before arriving, many had to adjust to living in a non-English environment. Eric was surprised at "how fast the people speak."

> I realize that we speak fast in English, but I soon realized that they speak Spanish just as fast, if not faster.

> When I am talking to someone from the United States and I see a Spanish student who I know, the person will say "hi" and start up a conversation. I have to jump into Spanish, because if I cannot, I get strange looks. I have to learn to be able to jump from Spanish to English and back again without any problems.

Mike found that living with a family helped ease his adjustment.

> I think the tough part about going abroad is learning to speak the language. I've been here over a month and I feel myself getting more comfortable with the language each day. One thing that has helped facilitate this is living with a family. In the house, I speak Spanish only, unless I speak English with other Americans.

Mario agreed, adding,

> I recommend that everyone stay with a family, at least to start. It makes your transition much easier, especially if you have never lived abroad and you are not quite familiar with the culture.

Although Jim found Spanish to be a "stumbling block," his transition was made easier by spending time with his English-speaking friends.

> It is easy to escape and just hang out with our friends from the United States. I think it is natural to do so, since English is the language we speak best. But I also believe that most of us are doing a great job of meeting new people and practising our Spanish. Most of the students go to the parties

every Thursday, and most of us go out to other parties on weekends. It is not just a Spanish university where people who do not speak Spanish are singled out. There are people from many different countries whose level of Spanish is about the same as ours. I really had anticipated more difficulty in adjusting to being here. It all just takes an open mind and a little patience. In reality, things are pretty similar to home.

Although language was perhaps the most obvious adjustment for most of the exchange students, it was only one of the many challenges that had to be overcome. Rebecca, for example, believed that "culture is just as important as language" as she found herself trying new foods and making new friends. She soon found out that going on exchange was very different than travelling. Reflecting on her situation, she noted, "The biggest challenge for me is to accept the fact that this place had to be called home for a while."

Pace of Life

In Spain, one of the more obvious differences was the slower pace of life, something that Angela found to be particularly annoying. "People move very slowly here, especially on the sidewalks, and I am always in a rush to get nowhere, so I get aggravated."

Katie agreed.

They do things that we're not used to, like walking slowly. They seem oblivious to the people around them. I'll be honest and say that my patience grows very thin at times. I keep telling myself that it is an adjustment.

"Every night before dinner it seems like all of Madrid goes out for a walk," recalled Eric. "If you're in a rush, too bad, because you're not going anywhere fast!"

Personal Space

Not only did it seem as though everyone went out for walks, but they also seemed to have a very different level of comfort with regard to personal space. Eric noted how Spaniards "bump

into each other all the time without excusing themselves. If they did that in the States," he observed, "there would be a lot of fights." In France, Andrea found that the students spoke "really close to your face," which required some getting used to.

In France and Spain it was also common to greet people with kisses. At the beginning, this created some confusion. Andrea had become used to it, but wondered "Who do you kiss, how many times, and when you leave also, or only upon greeting?"

Smoking

In addition to the slow pace, many of the American students were annoyed by the amount of smoking. This was the first thing that Jim noticed as he stepped off the plane. "I could tell I wasn't in my own country as soon as I arrived at the terminal and into a cloud of smoke," he recalled.

Katie, who did not enjoy smelling "like an ashtray" all the time, found it difficult to get used to. Of all the differences he encountered, Mario found that smoking had the strongest impression on him.

I am slowly getting over it, but it has been hard to walk into the school cafeteria and see a cloud of smoke. It is nothing like what people describe in the United States. In the United States, most restaurants, bars, and other establishments where smoking is permitted, ventilation systems are common.

Local Cuisine

Tara found it difficult to adjust to the food, both in restaurants and markets. "I really don't like Spanish food," she conceded.

What's on the menu is what you get, and that's that! If you try and change or substitute anything, they usually get upset or confused. I was a vegetarian for a few years, but it is quite difficult to live on the minimal vegetarian options they have here, so I have decided to experiment. When I go to the market, I usually get this sensation like I am going to pass out. It's not because of the whole animal body parts blatantly displayed (although that is quite disgusting), but the aroma makes me ill. What I wouldn't give for just one day at a Super Stop and Shop.

Katie, on the other hand, preferred Spanish markets to U.S. supermarkets.

We go to the markets in the neighborhood to buy our groceries, as opposed to the supermarket back home. And you tend to become friendly with the man behind the meat counter or the woman picking out your fruit. It's a very comfortable atmosphere.

Sexual Norms

Germany had very different levels of public acceptance concerning the open display of sexual themes. Meena, who was originally from India, noticed this as soon as she arrived.

I was coming down the escalator in the Frankfurt airport, and the first thing that I saw was a sex and lingerie shop. That is far from the norms of more conservative countries like India. I see a lot more public displays of affection, and people don't stop or even look twice. I definitely have to say that for the first few weeks, my head was always whipping around in amazement.

Another thing that comes to mind was a conversation that I had with two students from Ireland. They said they did not understand why we are always shocked to see nudity in commercials, shows and posters, yet we Americans subject our kids to the most horrific massacre scenes in our American movies. I guess it's just a matter of where you were brought up and what you are used to. The important thing is to try your best to have an open mind about other cultures. I learned that when I came to the United States from India. To me, those are very different cultures too.

When Mary went on an "integration weekend" in Germany, she was surprised to discover that the games they were asked to play were almost all sexual in some way. In one game, participants were asked to exchange clothes with someone of the opposite sex.

Many of the Europeans were so open about it and did not mind standing naked in a farmer's field. But it caused some apprehension for me and for another American. Needless to say, we stuck to our American ways and did not exchange all of our clothing.

Andrea, who had a similar experience in France, felt that the games for her integration weekend were "a little lame." She reflected on her experience.

These ridiculous games involved, in some fashion or other, a sexual undertone. I personally thought it was a little lame, but I tried to remember that it was planned for first year students. I'm now in my fourth year, have lived on my own, paid my own bills and held two jobs. But these were kids in their first year. I probably acted just as stupid three years ago.

Personal Appearance

Mary was also puzzled by the attitude of a female professor at the college.

She told us that we must do our best to keep up our appearance for an interview, even down to the finest detail of your nails, because it is very difficult for women to hold important positions in the business world and we must work extra hard. But I would be very surprised if that were really true. I guess I am just used to America, where women have the same chances as men and can move up the ladder at the same speed.

France and Spain were much more formal in dress and appearance. In addition, Europeans were, on average, more health conscious and slim. When Andrea decided to go out in her usual American style clothing, namely running pants, a T-shirt and sneakers, she noticed the strange looks she received from many of the French pedestrians. "These clothes are completely normal in the States, but the looks I was getting! Most everyone here goes out in trousers and blouses, or suits."

Government and Bureaucracy

For some, dealing with government bureaucracy represented a significant challenge. To

Rebecca this became apparent after she tried to renew her visa. The government office responsible for issuing renewals opened at 9:30 a.m. Rebecca planned to arrive at 7:30 in order to get in line and allow for sufficient time to process her application—she thought!

> When I arrived, there were already over 200 people in line waiting to renew their visas. I waited in line for four hours. The joke was that it's easier to get into heaven than it is to get a number for your visa. When I went on Friday morning, there were people who had been sleeping in the street since 9:00 the day before.

THE HOLIDAY SEASON

For most of the exchange students, spending the holidays in Europe was exciting, even though, for some, it would be the first time away from family. Although they would "miss Mom's cooking," the students were looking forward to sharing American traditions with their new European friends.

In Spain, the students special-ordered two large turkeys to share among them, although logistics was going to be a major hurdle. Jim explained,

> We will need to think about having 30 people coming over to our house for a big meal. We don't even have an oven or a microwave! Last time I counted, we had only 11 plates, seven forks and five chairs—hmmm. And besides, everyone has class the next day. What time is the football game on? Oh, 2:00 a.m. I *might* be awake.

> Still, we should have a great time. The turkey might be overcooked, the stuffing a bit dry, and maybe someone will have to sit on the floor, but all in all, the feeling will be the same. I think we have a pretty nice family here in Spain.

In France, where there were only two exchange students from Boston, it was more difficult to recreate an American Thanksgiving. Still, Andrea viewed it as an opportunity to share her culture with her new European friends and as an

opportunity to correct some misconceptions. In anticipation of the event, Andrea commented,

> Everyone who is coming will be a first-timer. But after learning so much about everyone else's culture, it's exciting to be able to share some of my own. It was funny when I told a French student about Thanksgiving, he said, "Oh, is that the day when you watch football and drink beer?" "No, that is the Super Bowl," I replied. He insisted that, while he understood what the Super Bowl was, Thanksgiving was another day for these activities. Then he added that he thought America was a great country! It seems that he missed the true spirit of the holiday.

When Thanksgiving finally arrived, the event exceeded everyone's expectations. Some of the students brought homemade pies and other traditional American foods. Jim invited his landlords, who appeared to enjoy the event. Rebecca went so far as to claim that, for her, it had been "the best Thanksgiving holiday."

Despite their efforts to reproduce an American holiday experience, being away from family was difficult for some. As the Christmas decorations began to go up around Madrid, Angela anticipated her homesickness.

> Seeing all of the Christmas decorations is very hard, but I don't think that the idea of spending Christmas without my family will actually set in until around that time. I will miss my family, but I am excited to experience a European Christmas. After all, I may never get the chance to do this again!

Tara was glad to have her American friends near her. They would sit together and talk about their families and tell stories about previous holiday seasons. She commented,

> Lots of times it brings back memories that we had forgotten, and it really helps to know we are all in the same boat. I know I have the rest of my life to be at home, so I am going to enjoy this chance to spend the holidays in Europe.

Andrea, who was Protestant, found it difficult to spend Christmas in a Catholic country, where the traditions were so different. She reflected on the differences,

> In America, we have become too intent on being politically correct and inclusive. I hardly noticed the Happy Holidays signs in Boston, as opposed to Merry Christmas. Here in France, where the country is 85 per cent Catholic (although only a fraction actually practise), I think it would be really tough to be a Jewish student. I've found it hard enough as a Lutheran.

ACADEMIA

When the students arrived in Spain on the first of October, they were placed into student "families." These were groups of students organized as social units. A local student was given responsibility for arranging social events for the "family" as a way to help facilitate the integration of the exchange students. Nevertheless, Katie's first few days were "scary."

> Spanish was everywhere. Students from Germany, France, England, Sweden and Denmark were all speaking Spanish, except me! I found it to be an intimidating atmosphere.

Some were surprised to discover that the campus was much smaller than their home university. Many of the first impressions of the Spanish university were positive however, particularly with regard to the faculty and staff. Angela noted,

> The faculty values our input and comments and look way beyond mistakes that we might make while speaking.

Rebecca was ecstatic when one of the staff members arranged "*Intercambios*" with Spanish students.[1]

> One of my *Intercambios* is from the South of Spain. When we met at a wine and cheese luncheon, I was spit on about three times in a half hour, and the hardest thing was not to wipe my face in front of him. But he turned out to be the sweetest guy in the world and even treated me to a *bocadillo* (snack) and a movie. We spent an entire day in *Retiro* park and the night in *Sol* (a funky area of Madrid where people go out on the weekends), and we spoke eight straight hours of Spanish. We almost forgot to speak English! That's how I am learning the language here—*Intercambios*.

Before leaving the United States, the exchange students were advised that all instruction would be in Spanish. Therefore, some were surprised to find out that most of the Spanish students spoke English and that class assignments were frequently in English. Some courses, however, were exclusively in Spanish, and the exchange students found it necessary to spend long hours reading and translating class assignments.

John was concerned about the attitude some students seemed to have toward Americans.

> It is a very cliquey school, and it seems as though there are many students here that feel that it is their school and that we are just visitors, or to be more precise—intruders!

> It seems to me that the idea here is to integrate and make contacts all over the world, but many students are content to live with their preconceived notions of Americans as world police and so they stick to themselves. Granted, there are many Americans who act like idiots and perpetuate these perceptions, but it still gets frustrating sometimes. The funny thing is this, these same people seem to be obsessed with our products and pop culture.

Some of the exchange students felt like they had returned to high school again, with class bells and all. Tara noted,

> I have noticed a certain aura of immaturity in the students. I don't quite understand it, but they just seem extremely young. Maybe it has something to do with the fact that we've been out in the working world for a couple of years now and the great majority of us are living completely on our own, while the students here are still supported by their parents.

Respect for Faculty

Jim expected the Spanish students to have the "highest respect" for faculty. Instead, he was dismayed that professors had to repeatedly tell the students to "shut up" during class. Mike commented,

> It has the feeling of a high school. The reason I say this is that the classes are small, with the same students all day and the students talk during class.

For Katie, many of the students seemed to be disinterested in class.

> They will talk right over the teacher while they're in the middle of a lecture. You just don't do that! We personally find it very rude, but it seems normal and doesn't appear to bother the professors. It's very easy to be slack here because there isn't any consistent work.

In France, Dana had the opposite experience. To her, classes appeared very formal and the faculty demanded the attention of each student. She recalled an awkward situation she had encountered.

> Everybody in my class was taking notes as the professor was talking. But I was used to our standard, that as long as you are not talking while the professor is talking there is no problem. So I am listening with my notebook closed, when suddenly the professor stops to ask me if I was planning to take notes. I thought to myself, *"What!"* I just told the professor, "Non, j'ecoute," which means "No, I am listening." It was so embarrassing. In all the years that I have been at university, never has a professor stopped a class to ask me to take notes, especially if I seemed to be paying attention.

Dana found the French school, with its formalities, to be more like a boarding school than a college, especially since most of the students appeared to be younger than at home. She also found the French professors to be far more formal than she had been accustomed to in Boston. "One day I was walking down the hall with a French student," she recalled,

> One of the faculty members said "Bonjour," and I replied "Salut." The faculty member looked at me reproachfully and the French student started

laughing. I asked what it was that I had said, and he proceeded to explain that you should not say "Salut" to an older person, because it is too informal and considered impolite. Believe me that ever since that incident, I always try to say "Bonjour." However, when "Salut" slips out every now and then, I wish I could turn into an ostrich!

> Whenever I do something like that, which appears to be silly, I just laugh at myself, learn from it and move on. Everything just takes time, and some days are easier than others. If it is one of those days when I am not in a good mood and everything seems to be going wrong, I just lock myself in my room and meditate a bit so I don't get discouraged.

Teaching Style and Quality

While Dana found that the lecture style of teaching required some adjustment, she believed that the quality of teaching in France was good. Still, she expressed some misgivings.

> At this college, if you don't pass the exams the first time, you get a second chance! The only bad thing is that, most of the time, the finals are 100 per cent of the grade. Therefore it is hard to measure your progress along the way. It is all or nothing.

Andrea found the class projects in France to be "pointless." "They mostly fall into one of three categories," she explained,

> Either we have already had it, or it is not applicable to our major at all, or it's applicable only to the French system, and will be useful only if I work in France. It gets frustrating at times, but the value of the out-of-the-classroom learning definitely more than cancels it out. It's a good experience overall.

Germany was much like France. While Mary lauded the ability of her professors, she was concerned that they often expected the students to understand the material without providing in-depth explanations. She continued,

> Another thing I have noticed is that the teachers are always correct here, at least in the students' eyes. Many students don't even question the teachers if they disagree, which is very different. I often

find myself becoming frustrated because I don't understand what they are talking about or what they mean.

Meena was critical of the lecture style. She complained that "there is no room for disagreement and there is very little interaction in class."

There are some classes here that are cancelled frequently, and although they may not be good classes, it doesn't help if we never had them. I'd have to say that I would be retaining more knowledge if the teaching were in the style we are used to in Boston. I don't feel as though I am gaining significant value. Although this may be one of the more harsh comments about this project, it's definitely one of the largest differences in my international experience so far.

Despite the drawbacks, Claudia added that the "professors have been very nice to us and have been kind to organize different outside-of-school activities. They have invited us to their houses for dinner or gone on trips with us."

In Spain, Jim found that the teaching was not so different. "While classes are definitely different," he observed, "they are not quite as different as I expected them to be."

I anticipated exclusively lecture, with our grade based solely on the final exam, and to some extent this is true. But it seems as though things are changing around here. Teachers are bringing real world news into the classroom, and students can participate, ask questions and state their opinions. There are presentations, company analyses and other ways to earn points.

Mario, on the other hand, was more critical.

The professors *expect* students to go out on Thursday nights and skip class on Friday morning, and will often repeat the same material the following class if the attendance is very low. At home, a professor would refuse to repeat class information during office hours, let alone during class.

Karen agreed,

Every class is with the same group of students and the work is much easier. In some aspects this is frustrating; however, it is also a welcome break from the high-paced teaching styles. I think one of the biggest downfalls of the teaching style here is the fact that most of us have to return to normal classes in Boston.

In Don's view, the classes were "close to worthless."

The professors teach directly out of the book. They use transparencies that are copied from pages directly out of the book. They fail to share any of their own personal experience. The students fail to question the methods being taught. Basically, they believe that what the book says is the only way of looking at things. In presentations, the students analyse companies but have no insight or recommendations of their own.

While Mike agreed with Don, he still found value in the experience. He noted,

The experience of being here, seeing the differences, seeing different cultures and learning a different language completely made up for the fact that we are learning less in the classroom.

Rebecca found her classes to be more interesting, particularly international marketing, for which she had to prepare a presentation on TelePizza, Spain's leading Pizza chain. She extolled the opportunity to study in an international atmosphere with other exchange students from across Europe and North America. "I absolutely think that that is one of the best things about being here."

Katie also had to prepare a presentation. She reflected on the experience: "Getting up in front of people to do a presentation is hard enough, let alone doing it in another language. It was an obstacle to overcome."

After the first two months, some students started to become anxious about final exams. Angela was particularly worried that, since many of the classes were in Spanish and there were no graded assignments by which she could gauge her progress, she felt that she was missing "everything." Still, "each day it gets a little easier," she said. Tara seconded that view, adding,

> It's tough because we don't have much homework, no tests or quizzes, very little expectation to show up to class and virtually no grades before the final exam. It's very easy to slack off. Needless to say, finals week is going to be lethal!

NOTE

1. Intercambios were Spanish students who wanted to converse in English with foreign students, while at the same time allowing the foreign students an opportunity to practise Spanish and immerse themselves in the local culture.

BEING DIFFERENT: EXCHANGE STUDENT EXPERIENCES

Prepared by David Wesley under the supervision of Professor Henry W. Lane

Returning to his office after teaching his Monday morning class, Professor Rhodes logged on to an Internet discussion group that he was facilitating for students who were on exchange in Europe. By this time, the students had been living in Europe for only about a month where they attended classes at well-known universities. Once they completed a semester of studies, the students were expected to work for locally based companies for an additional four to six months. Classes were taught in the language of the host country, and students were expected to have sufficient foreign language skills to study and work in the local setting.

Professor Rhodes always enjoyed reading their postings about the joys and heartaches of adapting to a new country, language and culture. Most students were somewhat naïve when they left the United States, but a year later they returned with language fluency and a more cosmopolitan attitude.

The new topic that Rhodes found on the discussion board that morning, "Race and Discrimination," surprised him. This was the first time the issue had been raised in the two years since he began facilitating these online discussions. He wondered if possibly it was because, this year, more minority students were on exchange or perhaps because students just did not discuss it in previous years.

INITIAL EXPERIENCES: CURIOSITY AND SUSPICION

Paul (Asian, Spain)—Well . . . after one month of being in Spain, I feel pretty good. I have learned so much already about cultural differences and language differences between regions and have improved my speaking and listening skills.

People are really nice here, but from what I have seen so far, they do tend to stick to their own "kind." Maybe it's wrong of me to say this because I have been here for only one month, but I feel as though I don't belong here sometimes. There are some places that I go and people just stare at me and they don't stop. Some have a look of disgust and some look with curiosity. It gets to me, but I'm learning to shake it off. People here say I'm being paranoid, but I know it's not that because I have had to deal with this my whole life. I know when people are joking and when people are being rude about things like race. This bothers me, but not enough to make me want to go home. I love it here and I can't wait to see more. Regardless of some feelings of racism, which don't arise very often, this place is amazing.

Mei (Asian, Germany)—I feel the same way about the stares. It's a little awkward. Sharon and I are both Asian, and we live in a very small town in Germany where almost everyone knows each other. Going into the town centre, we definitely get the hardest stares that we've ever gotten in our lives. It's a bit different, but not harmful in any way. I wonder what they're thinking sometimes. We usually just laugh it off though. But when I'm in a bad mood, it gets annoying really fast!

Robin (African-American, Spain)—I don't like the stares Felicia and I get when walking down the street or even at school. I guess the Spaniards are not used to seeing black Americans. To me, it seems the only people of color you see on the streets are selling bootleg CDs, or they are the prostitutes you see on every corner of Gran Via.

While we were struggling to get into our own building (the front door is hard to open and we had a lot of groceries), this lady came and started asking who we were and what we wanted. We told her we were going to our *piso* (apartment) and she acted like she didn't believe us. Then she proceeded to start talking about us to her neighbors. I'm sure not all Spaniards are like this, but so far I have run into a lot of this kind.

But not to complain about everything, Madrid is a beautiful city and despite all the complaining, I am glad that I have this opportunity to experience it. Our motto is, "What doesn't kill you makes you stronger."

BEYOND CURIOSITY

Latin American students in Spain also had posted comments expressing concerns about racism. Their Spanish was different and set them apart. They also thought there was a negative stereotype of Latin Americans, which came from people linking an increase in gang and drug-related murders to an increase of Latin American immigrants. The students hoped that this discussion would help their American colleagues realize they were not being paranoid.

Professor Rhodes responded with some supportive comments, but he was not worried since no one sounded like they were in any danger. However, his surprise turned to concern when the topic surfaced again a few weeks later.

Felicia (African-American, Spain)—Yesterday afternoon after class, I was walking up the stairs in my apartment building. We live on the fifth floor. On the second floor, I saw a man knocking at a door, so of course I said *buenos días*. He muttered something to me, (all this is in Spanish, but for those who don't speak Spanish, I'll tell it in English). So I said, "What?" and he muttered it again. I just continued going up the stairs, and he said something again. So as not to be rude, I stopped and told him that I did not speak Spanish. He asked me if I spoke Portuguese. I said no, that I spoke English. Then in English he said, "Wait, wait!" and he was trying to tell me something else in broken English as I continued up the stairs.

He started following me and he was trying to speak English, but I still couldn't understand this man. I finally told him in Spanish, "I still don't understand what you are saying, talk to me in Spanish." He asked me if I lived in the building, and I told him, "No, I'm going to see an *amigo*." I don't know if he believed me, since I did have keys in my hand. I tried to get away from him because he was getting assertive and he was right in my face. He kept following me, so I stopped and asked him where he was going. He pointed up and said he was going with me. I asked, "For what?" and he said in a very explicit and crude way that he was going to have sex with me. I couldn't believe what this man had said to me. And then it dawned on me; he thought I was a prostitute.

I then realized what he was muttering when I first came up the stairs. He was asking me if

I was a *puta.*[1] I decided that I was not going to my apartment if he was following me. I just walked around him and left my building. There's a plaza just outside and I went and sat down. I was still in shock. I don't think I've ever been treated like that in my life. It took me a few minutes to comprehend what had just happened.

Like my friend Shante, I've had the experience of old men grabbing at me or muttering at me in a club, but for a man to just tell me he's following me to my apartment because he feels like it. It's not just what this man said; it was also how he said it. He just had this unassuming manner, like it was his right. And when I told him "no," he actually acted surprised. Plus he was blowing smoke in my face all the time. He didn't even say *buenos días* back to me! Basically, to him, I was nothing.

So that made me think, Robin made an entry about an old woman interrogating us while we were trying to open our front door, asking us what we were doing. She really watched us walk all the way up to our apartment, struggling the whole time with all our groceries. Did she think we were prostitutes also? Every time we see someone in our building, although they are cordial, we always get "the look," a confused expression about what we are doing in this building, *their* building. Do they think we are prostitutes? We thought it was because we were black, but maybe it's more than that.

Why does being a young, black female in Madrid mean you are a prostitute? That whole experience disgusted me. That man made me feel dirty, and I'm upset with myself for giving someone the power to make me feel so bad about myself when none of this was my fault. Every single time this whole "mistaken identity" thing has happened, I haven't been dressed in anything that could be considered provocative.

I went back to my building about 10 minutes later, after the shock had worn off, and I was very angry. I don't know whether it was fortunate or unfortunate that he was no longer there because I really wanted to use all the colorful phrases I've learned since being here. But I figured, unfortunately, this might happen again, and I'm better

prepared now. I will get a chance to use those phrases—eventually.

Shante (African-American, Spain)—Sure you can get over people staring at you all the time and never knowing whether they think you are a prostitute or not, but when you have old nasty men grumbling in your face all the time, when you're walking down the street in normal clothes with your backpack or bag of groceries, it's scary, insulting and potentially dangerous. Thank God nothing has happened and people don't appear violent here. At first you don't expect it, but now that I understand the language a little bit better, I realize that some people who start muttering in my direction aren't asking me for directions! And that happens at least once, usually a couple times a week.

Belinda (African-American, France)—I realize it is very difficult to shrug off. But it is even harder if you take it personally. Hopefully, as everyone's language skills improve, we will all be able to better defend ourselves. I am really sorry to hear that you are having such a difficult time with people's opinions, stereotypes or whatever it is that is making them act so rudely.

Epilogue

Seven months later, Felicia and Robin were on a bus tour to Mátalascañas, a little beach town in Andalucía, where they planned to spend the long weekend. Soon after boarding the bus, they realized they were among their "mortal enemies," a term they used to refer to older Spaniards, who always seemed suspicious of them and, at times, made their lives a living hell in Madrid. As they began the long ride, they prepared themselves for a torturous journey. Instead, both students came away with newfound understanding. Felicia explained,

> A lot of my bad experiences in Spain have been with older people. But on this trip I learned that not all old Spaniards are bad. In fact, most of them were nice—after they realized we weren't on the

trip to pick up some old sugar daddies. At first we kept to ourselves, due to the "what are they doing here" looks we got when we first boarded the bus. During the trip we were told that we were missed when we did not join in a couple of the excursions. And we were even invited to sit with some of them during the party hours.

As usual we stuck out, but we've become good at dealing with it. One thing I know that I have learned in Spain is to be comfortable in my own skin. I always thought I was, because that was how I was raised, but being in Spain has definitely reinforced it.

NOTE

1. Translated: prostitute, literally "slut."

THE CHANGING FACE OF EUROPE:
A NOTE ON IMMIGRATION AND SOCIETAL ATTITUDES

*Prepared by David Wesley under
the supervision of Professor Henry W. Lane*

By the end of the 20th century, many Europeans may have imagined that they were being invaded by immigrants from Africa, Asia and Latin America. These newcomers were people who looked different, spoke different languages and practised different religions and customs. According to a widely held belief, immigrants were responsible for soaring crime rates, and they threatened to "jeopardize [Europe's] common values."[1]

Historically, the European and American models of immigration mirrored those of ancient Greece and Rome respectively. Under the Greek model, foreigners were excluded from the rights of citizenship, except those "under perpetual exile from their own country, or [those who] came with their whole family to trade there."[2] Under such exclusion, few foreigners could become Greek citizens, and most were treated as second class members of society. In contrast, Rome welcomed foreigners from all known corners of the world. They were given the same rights as native-born Romans, and many achieved high social status. Among them are counted some of Rome's most famous poets and philosophers, such as Virgil, Cato, Horace and Cicero. Writes Edward Gibbon,

> The narrow policy of preserving, without any foreign mixture, the pure blood of the ancient citizens, had checked the fortune, and hastened the ruin, of Athens and Sparta. The aspiring genius of Rome sacrificed vanity to ambition, and deemed it more prudent, as well as honorable, to adopt virtue and merit for her own wheresoever they were found, among slaves or strangers, enemies or barbarians.[3]

Therefore, while the number of citizens of Athens gradually declined to only 21,000, the number of Roman citizens multiplied from less than 100,000 in the sixth century BC to approximately seven million in 47 AD.[4]

In 2002, Europe, like ancient Greece, faced a crisis of demographics. Its population was rapidly ageing, while birthrates continued to test new lows. If current trends were to continue, by 2050, Europe's population will have declined, while America's will have doubled. According to an *Economist* special report on demographics,

If the rising fertility rate among native-born Americans persists, it will mean that the growth is steady—there will be no sudden addition of a huge pool of poor, as occurred with German unification—and a bit more balanced ethnically than was previously assumed. The most important aspect, though, can be summed up in one word: youth. While Europe's population will, on average, be ageing, America's will stay much younger.[5]

Driving this divergence in population was immigration (see Exhibit 1 for a comparison of selected countries). In 2002, approximately half of all children in America were of Latin American origin, and Hispanic Americans had a birth rate of three children per woman, higher than in most developing countries. That translated into a younger society. Thus, by 2050, the median age in the United States was expected to be 37 years, while Europe's would be almost 53.[6] In countries like France, where the retirement age was 55 or less, retirees would come to outnumber workers.

	Annual Inflows	Foreigners		Annual Inflows	Foreigners
Australia			**Germany**		
New Zealand	22.2	7.5	Poland	10.9	3.8
United Kingdom	10.4	27.4	Fed. Rep. of Yugoslavia	10.2	9.8
China	7.3	2.8	Turkey	8.0	28.6
South Africa	6.0	1.4	Italy	5.9	8.3
Philippines	3.9	2.4	Russian Federation	4.7	2.3
Belgium			**United States**		
France	14.6	11.5	Mexico	19.9	21.7
Netherlands	12.3	9.1	China	5.6	2.7
Morocco	8.5	14.7	India	5.5	2.3
Germany	6.3	3.7	Philippines	5.2	4.6
United States	5.6	1.4	Dominican Republic	3.1	1.8
Canada			**Netherlands**		
China	11.3	4.6	Morocco	6.5	20.0
India	8.8	4.7	Turkey	6.3	16.9
Philippines	4.7	3.7	Germany	5.8	7.9
Hong KongChina	4.6	4.8	United Kingdom	5.8	5.8
Pakistan	4.6	—	United States	4.0	1.9
Denmark			**France**		
Somalia	8.6	4.1	Algeria	14.3	16.4
Former Yugoslavia	7.1	13.5	Morocco	13.8	16.9
Iraq	6.3	3.4	Turkey	5.8	5.2
Germany	5.5	4.8	China	4.9	0.3
Norway	5.3	4.8	Tunisia	4.6	6.3
Finland			**Sweden**		
Former USSR	29.8	23.6	Iraq	15.1	4.5
Sweden	9.6	9.3	Finland	8.4	18.4
Estonia	8.1	12.0	Former Yugoslavia	5.4	6.1
Somalia	4.3	6.5	Norway	4.6	5.6
Iraq	3.2	3.0	Iran	4.1	4.8

Exhibit 1   Top Five Nationalities of Immigrants in Selected Host Countries (1998)

Source: Organisation for Economic Cooperation and Development.

This note will consider the impact of immigration on attitudes and government policy in Western Europe's three largest countries, Spain, France and Germany. It will also examine how the histories and political structures of these countries have influenced immigration policy and the integration of immigrant populations.

SPAIN

As early as 750 BC, Greece established colonies along Spain's Mediterranean coast. The next 1,000 years saw the establishment of Phoenician and Roman colonies, the latter of which developed an intricate road system connecting all corners of the Iberian Peninsula with the rest of Europe.[7]

In the fifth century, marauding vandals of Germanic origin, known as Visigoths, sacked Rome and eventually settled in Spain where they converted to Roman Catholicism and became important allies of the Romans. At this time, Spain's population was mainly Roman (six million), while others, such as the Visigoths, made up only 200,000 of its inhabitants.[8]

By the eighth century, the Visigoth kingdom was rife with dissention, much of which was blamed on Jews, who were either compelled to convert to Christianity or forced into slavery. Their liberation came at the hands of Muslim invaders (mainly Arab and Syrian) between 711 AD and 713 AD, after Islam had already spread across much of the Middle East, North Africa and parts of Europe. The surviving Spanish monarchy was exiled to the rugged north regions of the peninsula. With the invasion of Spain, a spirit of toleration abounded, in which "Jews and Christians of the Turkish Empire enjoy[ed] the liberty of conscience that was granted by the Arabian caliphs."[9]

Under Muslim rule, Spain prospered to become one of the great centres of learning. Rivaling Baghdad in splendor, the imperial city of Cordoba became the greatest and most advanced in Europe. Historian Jawaharlal Nehru described the condition of the city as it stood at the end of the first millennium.

This was a great city of a million inhabitants, a garden city 10 miles in length, with 24 miles of suburbs. There are said to have been 60,000 palaces and 700 public baths . . . There were many libraries, the chief of these, the Imperial Library of the Emir, containing 400,000 books. The University of Cordoba was famous all over Europe and even in western Asia. Free elementary schools for the poor abounded.[10]

When civil war erupted between the country's Muslim rulers in the 11th century, it took a severe toll on the country's defences. Taking advantage of the situation, the Spanish monarchy in exile began to retake captured territory. After securing Cordoba in 1236, Spain's Christian kings continued to advance on the Muslims, eventually expelling the last remnants of Muslim resistance in 1492.[11] Spain would not come into direct conflict with its Muslim neighbors again until the invasion and colonization of Morocco in the 19th century.

As soon as it had dealt this final blow to its Muslim occupiers, the Spanish monarchy turned its attention to the Jewish population, the largest in Europe. With the demise of Muslim Spain, Jews were no longer permitted freedom of religion. Instead, they were forced to convert to Catholicism or face exile. In 1492, some 170,000 Jews were expelled from Spain, while the remainder became converts to Christianity, known as *conversos*. Many of the latter came under suspicion of the Spanish Inquisition, which exercised authority over members of the Catholic Church. As a result, "several thousand *conversos* were condemned and burned for Judaizing practices," while their property and other assets were appropriated by the crown and added to the general treasury.[12]

Spain's Muslim inhabitants faced a similar fate as their Jewish counterparts.

Though many Muslims chose conversion, the problem became virtually insoluble. There were never enough Arab-speaking priests or money for education to make outward conversion a religious reality. The *Moriscos* (Muslim converts) remained an alien community, suspicious of and suspect to the "old" Christians.[13]

Nevertheless, Spain's rich Muslim heritage continued to play an important role in the country's art, architecture, music and language. To this day, many commonly used Spanish words have Arabic etymologies, such as *Ojalá* (Oh Allah)[14] and *Jarra* (Jar). For all that, the purging of religious minorities from Spain's ethnic landscape produced a relatively homogeneous white Catholic society.

In the 1920s, French and Spanish forces combined to overthrow Morocco's Arabic government and subsequently split that country into French and Spanish protectorates. Despite the repression of the Franco dictatorship, Spanish Moroccans enjoyed many more freedoms than their French African neighbors.

Though the Spanish had fewer resources than the French, their subsequent regime was in some respects more liberal and less subject to racial discrimination. The language of instruction in the schools was Arabic rather than Spanish, and Moroccan students were encouraged to go to Egypt for a Muslim education.[15]

Both the French and the Spanish relinquished control over the region in 1956.

Until the 1970s, Spain's only attempt at democratic government had been a short-lived experiment in the early 1930s. Civil war ensued when a secular constitution met stiff opposition from Royalists and the Roman Catholic Church.[16] In 1936, General Francisco Franco successfully launched an attack on Spain's Republican government from his base in Spanish Morocco. For nearly four decades, the Franco regime banned political parties, trade unions and private associations. He also showed support for the Fascist regimes of Hitler and Mussolini, though he shrewdly avoided any direct confrontation with the Allies.

In the late 1960s and early 1970s, Spain had the second fastest growing economy in the world after Japan. With the death of Franco in 1975, his successor, King Juan Carlos, re-established democracy and decriminalized political parties and private associations.

The economic boom of the late Franco period facilitated democracy by rendering authoritarian institutions anachronistic. It also afforded Spaniards the opportunity to travel abroad and experience firsthand the freedoms enjoyed by people elsewhere. The boom also undermined the traditional influence of the Catholic Church, which itself ceased to support the Franco regime by the late 1960s, and lessened the tendencies toward political extremism.[17]

In the post-Franco years, Spaniards liked to boast of their tolerance towards minorities. Yet most minorities had been assimilated, expelled or killed during five centuries of totalitarian rule and few remained to enjoy claims of Spanish forbearance. That changed in the 1990s as economic refugees began arriving from North Africa and Latin America. Despite the increase in immigration, Spain continued to have one of the lowest levels of immigration in the developed world (see Exhibit 2).

Because of its proximity to Africa, Spain was a particularly suitable transit point for illegal migrants destined to other European countries. (Statistics on foreign nationals in Spain are provided in Exhibit 3.) At the Strait of Gibraltar, the crossing was less than nine miles. Yet, thousands died attempting to reach Spain in poorly constructed rafts, which sometimes resulted in disturbing images of dead refugees washing up on Spanish shores. To "protect" itself from the threat of immigration, Spain began to install a monitoring system of radar and night vision units along its coastal border with Morocco.[18]

A Test of Tolerance[19]

The increase in the number of immigrants in Spain severely tested Spanish claims of tolerance. In fact, by the end of the 1990s, race-related violence and discrimination were at least as bad as other European countries. The number of racist organizations, such as neo-Nazis and skinheads, quadrupled between 1995 and 2002, claiming some 10,000 members.

The most serious racist violence in Southern Europe occurred in February 2000 in El Ejido on Spain's southern coast.

			Total Population (%)				"Total Labor Force (%)"	
	1988	1998	1988	1998	1988	1998	1988	1998
France	3,714	3,597	6.8	6.3	1,557	1,587	6.4	6.1
Germany	4,489	7,320	7.3	8.9	1,911	2,522	7.0	9.1
Ireland	82	111	2.4	3.0	35	48	2.7	3.2
Italy	645	1,250	1.1	2.1	285	332	1.3	1.7
Spain	360	720	0.9	1.8	58	191	0.4	1.2
United Kingdom	1,821	2,207	3.2	3.8	871	1,039	3.4	3.9
Australia	3,965	4,394	22.9	23.4	2,182	2,294	25.7	24.8
Canada	4,343	4,971	16.1	17.4	2,681	2,839	18.5	19.2
United States	19,767	26,300	7.9	9.8	11,565	16,100	9.4	11.7

Exhibit 2   Foreign or Foreign-Born Population and Labor Force in Selected OECD Countries (000s)

Source: Organisation for Economic Cooperation and Development.

	Total	"% Increase From 2000"
Morocco	234,937	17.6
Ecuador	84,699	174.3
United Kingdom	80,183	8.4
Germany	62,506	3.2
Colombia	48,710	97.2
France	44,798	5.9
Portugal	42,634	1.5
China	36,143	26.0
Italy	35,647	15.5
Peru	33,758	21.0
Dominican Republic	29,314	10.7
Romania	24,856	126.3
Former USSR	22,230	85.8
Cuba	21,467	12.0
Argentina	20,412	22.9
Netherlands	17,488	4.6
Algeria	15,240	10.1
Philippines	14,716	11.8
Rest of countries	239,322	—
Total	**1,109,060**	**23.8**

Exhibit 3   Foreign Nationals in Spain: 2001

Source: Instituto Nacional de Estadística.

According to reports, hundreds of immigrants in El Ejido came under repeated attack between 5–8 February when Spanish nationals, armed with sticks, knives, stones, iron bars or baseball bats, and cans of petrol, entered the vicinity in vans or trucks, threatened, insulted, stoned and pursued Moroccans, burned their homes and destroyed or looted their possessions. Instead of intervening to prevent the extensive criminal damage that took place in the area, action by police officers appears to have consisted in getting immigrants away from their homes—sometimes by firing rubber bullets, using tear gas, or physically attacking the Moroccans—and in forming a barrier between the immigrants, on the outside, and the invading rioters on the inside, thereby actually favoring the arson attacks.[20]

Justification for such attacks usually amounted to a perceived increase in crime and insecurity associated with immigrants. For example, 40 per cent of incarcerated criminals were of foreign origin, and many were implicated in prostitution and drug rings. The attitude of one Barcelona resident reflected widespread opinion.[21] He noted,

It is becoming hard for people to maintain their goodwill towards immigrants. It is undeniably them robbing people, tourists and Catalonians alike, and throwing their garbage anywhere it suits them.[22]

Although the Spanish constitution of 1978 expressly provided foreigners with the same rights as Spanish citizens in all matters except participation in public affairs, a new law enacted in 2000 set out to limit those rights. Under the Foreigners Law, only documented immigrants were entitled to protection under the law. Moreover, in the same year, the constitutional court ruled that skin color or foreign appearance could be used by police officers as criteria for carrying out identity checks.[23]

In most cases, those detained by police were undocumented foreigners. Many were sent to detention centres as they awaited deportation. According to human rights organizations, because of their vulnerability and their inability to file complaints, many deportees, including children, have been raped or tortured by police and guards in such centres. "Undocumented women immigrants have been particularly vulnerable to torture in the form of rape or sexual assault while in custody."[24]

Criminal gangs frequently transported female immigrants into Western Europe with offers of legitimate work as nannies, housekeepers or laborers. Upon arrival they were sold to brothels and forced to become chattel prostitutes. In Spain, the problem had become so visible that women immigrants were often mistaken for sex workers.

In many cases, the precarious legal situation of undocumented immigrants prevented them from pressing charges. Thus, government officials, such as police and guards, often acted with impunity. According to Amnesty International,

> Impunity casts a dark shadow across this landscape of human rights abuse: victims, or alleged victims of ill-treatment who are immediately served with counter-complaints, victims unable to even contemplate the bringing of complaints, through fear, lack of adequate legal aid or the apathy and bias of the judicial authorities. Police officers with criminal records, or against whom disciplinary proceedings are still pending, have not only been allowed to continue to work as public officials in situations which demand respect for human rights and sensitivity to racial discrimination, but have been roundly supported by the political authorities.[25]

Other forms of assault have also become increasingly commonplace.[26] Men of African descent are particularly targeted by police and racist gangs. In one incident, an American citizen was severally beaten by police because of his African racial origin. Rodney Mack, a cousin of the famous trumpeter Wynton Marsalis, was in Spain as the principle trumpet player for *Orquesta Sinfónica de Barcelona y Nacional de Cataluña.*

> [On January 15, 2002, he was] attacked by four police officers who mistook him for a car thief, who had been described as a black man of about the same height. Rodney Mack had just finished a rehearsal when he was approached in an underground garage in central Barcelona by plainclothes officers wearing jeans and leather jackets. The men grabbed his arms and threw him to the ground, pressing his face onto the concrete. He said he was beaten on the back and legs and there was an attempt to cram an object into his mouth. He thought he was being mugged and shouted to them to take his wallet. The Spanish police reportedly admitted there had been a "misunderstanding" and that, owing to "the color of his skin and his height," the officers had believed him to be a car thief who had been operating in the garage.[27]

Police charged Mack with resisting arrest, even though he believed he was being assaulted by thieves. Meanwhile, the undercover officers involved in the attack remained on duty. Mack's wounds were so severe that he had to cancel appearances at Carnegie Hall in New York the following month, and he spent several months recovering from his injuries.

FRANCE

France distinguished itself from other European nations by its republican values borne of the French Revolution. According to the First Article of the "Declaration of the Rights of Man and of the Citizen" ratified by the National Assembly in 1789, and reaffirmed in 1958, "Men are born and remain free and equal in rights. Social distinctions may be based only on considerations of the common good."[28] Based on that defining principle, the entire social structure was designed to eliminate ethnic, linguistic and religious differences. Moreover, foreigners enjoyed many of the same rights as citizens, regardless of their legal status.

Demographic Transformations

France had always been an important destination for artists, students and other elitist segments of the population. By the late 19th century, however, immigrant demographics underwent a radical transformation as France began to import labor to fuel the industrial revolution and stem a decline in the population brought about by the lowest birth rate in Europe. Working class laborers and their families began to pour in from Spain, Poland, Russia, Italy, the Ukraine and elsewhere. The program was further intensified following the First World War as a way to replace the labor capacity of some 1.4 million war casualties.[29] France continued to import labor until the mid-1970s, when a continent-wide ban eliminated the practice.

Even though France, much like America, had been built on immigration, it was never considered to be a country of immigrants. The reason was simple. For most of its history, French immigration was characterized by an influx of white Christians who easily blended into the local population. The school system, in particular, became an instrument of integration, requiring all children to learn French and the cultural values of The Republic. Within one generation, immigrants were no longer identifiable by their ethnic heritage, but had become French in every sense of the word.

The Republican ideal of cultural and linguistic assimilation began to be tested in the 1960s and 1970s during the height of the Cold War. A new front for the struggle of ideologies was developing in North Africa, Asia and the Middle East. French colonies, such as Vietnam and Cambodia, became Cold War battlegrounds, while leaders of various independence movements embraced communism as a way to rally public support and to solicit military and economic

Nationality	Total	"% of All Resident Aliens"
1. Portugal	649,714	18.1
2. Algeria	614,207	17.1
3. Morocco	572,652	15.9
4. Italy	252,759	7.0
5. Africa (other)	239,947	6.7
6. Southeast Asia	226,956	6.3
7. Spain	216,047	6.0
8. Tunisia	206,336	5.7
9. Turkey	197,712	5.5
Other	420,272	11.7
Total	**3,596,602**	**100.0**

Exhibit 4   Foreign Nationals in France 1990

Source: INSEE (National Institute of Statistics).

aid from the Soviet Union. These wars devastated local populations with millions of dead, wounded and homeless. Moreover, the tyranny of colonialism was, in many cases, replaced by the tyranny of local warlords. Africa, in particular has seen a continuous succession of civil wars as tribal factions battled for control.

Against this backdrop, France became an important destination for its former colonial subjects as they sought to escape a seemly endless cycle of poverty and violence (see Exhibit 4).

According to a 1999 national census, France had 4.3 million immigrants (7.4 per cent of the total population). Net annualized immigration stood at 60,000 in 2001, an increase of 10,000 over the previous year. Full-time workers accounted for the largest number of immigrants, followed by refugees and relatives of immigrants granted residency under the country's family reunification program, known as *regroupement familial.*

Race and Racism

In some respects, France was ill-equipped to deal with the ethnic transformation of its immigrant population. For example, Muslim girls were sometimes excluded from the education system for wearing identifiable religious symbols (headscarves) prohibited by law. A secular education system that had been created to assimilate foreigners and break down ethnic differences suddenly became an instrument of exclusion and segregation.[30]

Illegal immigration, which stood at more than 200,000, was blamed by many for a perceived increase in crime across most of the country, particularly in French cities where pick pocketing had become commonplace. The link between crime and immigration often centred on low-cost housing in poor Parisian suburbs. In one Paris suburb, where unemployment was around 50 per cent, police have been "unable to prevent second or third generation French citizens of North African descent from terrorizing neighbors."[31]

Despite the perception that immigration was partially to blame for higher crime rates, socioeconomic status, more than ethnicity, seemed to define the propensity to commit serious offenses. While research conducted in the late 1990s demonstrated an overrepresentation of foreigners among criminal suspects and convicts, many of the offences were immigration related. Excluding these, the differences in crime rates between foreigners and native French were much smaller than what was commonly assumed to be the case.[32]

Responding to public concerns about crime, the French cabinet approved an anti-crime bill aimed at "beggars and prostitutes."[33] The bill did little to address violent crime, which increased four-fold between 1994 and 2002.[34] Nor did it address a wave of hate crimes directed against visible minorities, such as the October 2002 shooting of several teenagers believed to be of North African descent and, in the same month, the burning to death of a 17-year-old North African girl outside her home near Paris.[35]

A less dramatic but more pervasive problem was the systematic discrimination exhibited toward foreigners, notwithstanding legal protections. For instance, employers used code words in job advertisements, such as BBR (Bleu, Blanc, Rouge—the colors of the French flag) and 001, which told employment agencies that only ethnic Europeans should apply. Immigrants have also been excluded from housing in some areas on account of visible racial or religious differences.[36]

The growing resentment toward foreigners of African and Middle Eastern descent was reflected by the fortunes of the neo-Fascist National Front Party, whose leader, Jean-Marie Le Pen, was the second most popular presidential candidate in the 2002 election, garnering nearly 20 per cent of the vote.[37] In his campaign, Le Pen announced that his first priority as president would be to "defend poor white families menaced by North African immigrants."[38] He also promised to reverse 150 years of Republican law by placing illegal immigrants in "transit camps" and deporting any immigrant convicted of a crime, including permanent residents.[39] The popularity of Le Pen's sentiment was reflected in the book "The Rage and the Pride," "an extremist tirade against Muslims" that spent several weeks on France's bestseller list.[40] Yet, most French were appalled by Le Pen's strong showing in the French election, and not a single National Front candidate won a seat in the French parliament.[41]

Le Pen's hatred of Africans may have started with his involvement in the Algerian war of independence. In 1957, as an officer in the French army, Le Pen was involved in suppressing a rebellion by Algerians opposed to colonial rule.[42] Years later, several prisoners of war accused Le Pen of torture that included "beatings, kickings, floggings with whips and chains, submersions and electric shocks."[43] At the same time, white French settlers formed a paramilitary organization known as the Secret Army Organization, which, with the tacit approval of the French military, engaged in terrorism against the local population. By the time Algeria finally secured its independence in 1962, "some 10,000 French troops and officers and possibly as many as 250,000 Muslims had lost their lives in the fighting; scores of villages had been destroyed, and two million peasants had been moved to new sites."[44]

In the decades that followed, Algerians represented a large portion of France's immigrant population. Le Pen and his followers continued to view these and other Muslim immigrants as enemies of France. "Despite their French citizenship," Le Pen explained, "these Muslims feel an affiliation with another entity. They naturally become suspect in the eyes of those who one day will be compelled to confront them."[45]

In unlikely solidarity with France's neo-Fascists, the country's Jewish leaders blamed North African Muslims for a series of attacks against synagogues and other Jewish assets. However, the French Interior Minister played down any connection between the attacks and Muslims after police failed to find evidence that could implicate Islamic groups.[46] Nevertheless, tension between Muslims and Jews continued to escalate as a consequence of the Israeli occupation of Palestine.

Many French of European ancestry showed little sympathy for the plight of immigrants. In a March 2000 poll of French citizens, 60 per cent believed that there were "too many people of foreign origin in France, 63 per cent said there were too many Arabs and 38 per cent said there were too many blacks,"[47] even though immigrants as a percentage of the total population remained constant between 1975, when Italians, Portuguese and Spaniards represented the largest number of immigrants, and 1999, when North Africans dominated immigration.[48]

Nevertheless, discrimination more often suggested social rather than racial differences. Thus, successful professionals encountered less discrimination than poor immigrants who found it difficult to integrate. Accordingly, Asians, who tended to be more financially independent and well educated, experienced significantly less discrimination than North Africans, who were often unskilled, uneducated and underemployed.[49]

GERMANY

Germany possessed a diverse and breathtaking landscape, from the coastal plains of the north, through the Rhine Valley spotted with medieval castles, to the majestic Bavarian Alps. Cultural festivities revolved around the country's world-renowned beer and wine industry. As home to some of the world's most advanced and innovative companies, Germany's reputation for scientific and engineering achievement was well deserved.

Yet, for all its achievements, Germany had a dark history of racism and ethnic intolerance. As early as the late 19th century, German eugenicists distorted the evolutionary theory of Charles Darwin by asserting that "a struggle for survival was taking place between a productive German-Aryan race and parasitic Semites."[50] As this view began to disseminate among the populous, the National Socialist regime of Adolf Hitler capitalized on it by blaming minorities for the country's economic woes. What began with the vandalism of Jewish assets soon escalated to personal assaults and finally resulted in the systematic and ignominious enslavement and extermination of millions of Jews, Gypsies and other minorities.

Although most Germans repudiated the ideas that gave rise to the horrors of the Holocaust, the underlying sentiment remained entrenched in some elements of the German population, as manifested in the type of extremist violence described in Dietmar Schirmer's *Identity and Intolerance:*

> A mob of extremists firebombs a shelter for asylum seekers in the German town of Rostock. A crowd of bystanders applaud. The police stand idly by. The police in the town of Mölln receive an anonymous call saying, "There's a house burning in Mühlenstrasse. Heil Hitler!" The arson attack leaves nine Turkish immigrants injured and three women dead . . . At a bar in Oberhof, Thuringia, Duncan Kennedy of the American bobsled team, which is using the local training facilities, is injured by skinheads when he attempts to defend his African-American teammate, Robert Pipkins, against a crowd of 15.[51]

Hate crimes of this nature were more of a problem in the formerly communist eastern *Länder* (states), despite having the lowest foreign population in the country (two per cent). A report of the European Commission against Racism and

Intolerance (ECRI) expressed concern about the apparent proliferation of racist Internet sites that provided an outlet for xenophobic propaganda.[52] The ECRI also noted that while acts of violence were perpetrated by a small number of extremists, "a much greater number of people sympathize with some of the racist, xenophobic, and anti-Semitic ideas that are part of the ideology of these groups; as such these acts may be viewed as an extreme manifestation of a broader climate of racism, anti-Semitism and intolerance."[53] The extent of the problem was highlighted in a July 2002 poll in which 78 per cent of respondents sought curbs on immigration, 59 per cent wanted restrictions placed on the right to seek asylum, and 52 per cent thought that Germany already had too many immigrants.[54]

Despite the anti-immigrant feeling, Germany needed more immigrants. As it entered the 21st century, Germany faced a crisis of demographics. Declining birth rates in particular placed increasing strain on the social welfare system, as fewer working-aged Germans were available to support the country's aging population. Immigration offered the only hope for continued economic prosperity and growth.

At the turn of the century, Germany's population stood at 82.2 million. To maintain that level, Germany would have to admit 310,000 immigrants a year. On the surface, Germany appeared to be meeting this level with more than 300,000 arrivals per year. However, more than a third of these arrivals were ethnic Germans who had been repatriated under the 1949 Basic Law, which provided citizenship to Eastern Europeans of German descent. Those numbers were expected to decline to near zero by 2010, at which point the overall population would also begin to decline.[55]

While recognizing the need to increase immigration, the political establishment was loath to ignore the concerns of the electorate. Therefore, when the government approved legislation that would, for the first time, allow some residents of non-German descent to obtain citizenship, it fell well short of the radical changes that would be needed meet Germany's future labor requirements. For instance, restrictions continued to limit the number of foreigners that could qualify and left many lifetime residents without citizenship. Although limited provisions for *jus soli,* or citizenship by place of birth, were included for the first time, the immigration reform bill of 1999 continued to favor those born of German parents and particularly those with German fathers. According to the reformed law,

> Children of foreign nationals can acquire German citizenship upon being born in Germany [after] 1 January 2000 and therefore [the changes] do not apply to children born prior to this date. The new law does however grant a segment of this latter group special entitlement to naturalization. Children who are born in Germany prior to 1 January 2000 can also acquire German citizenship upon application when they are under 10 years of age on 1 January 2000 and have their lawful place of abode in Germany. The respective child's legal guardians must submit a corresponding application by 31 December 2000.[56]

Germany liked to boast that, at nine percent, the number of immigrants surpassed France and several other European countries. Yet that number included large numbers of non-Germans who have known no other country, including second- and third-generation descendents of migrant workers from Turkey and elsewhere (see Exhibit 5). In France, they would have been granted citizenship and classified as French rather than "foreigners."

The lack of permanent status for many of Germany's foreigners prevented their integration into German society. Children of immigrants were often placed in special schools and denied access to an academic education in traditional grammar schools. Their visibility also made them targets for discriminatory hiring, and many had a difficult time obtaining housing in white German neighborhoods.[57]

CONCLUSION

According to a United Nations estimate, France alone will need 1.7 million immigrants a year to

Nationality	Total	"% of All Resident Aliens"
1. Turkey	2,110,223	28.8
2. Yugoslavia	719,474	9.8
3. Italy	612,048	8.4
4. Greece	363,514	5.0
5. Poland	283,604	3.9
6. Croatia	208,909	2.9
7. Bosnia-Herzegovina	190,119	2.6
8. Austria	185,159	2.5
9. Portugal	132,578	1.8
10. Spain	131,121	1.8

Exhibit 5   "Foreigners" in Germany: The 10 Largest Nationality Groups 1998

Source: www.german-info.org.

maintain its population base and to support its retirees.[58] Even so, on average, fewer than one million immigrants arrive on European shores each year.

In some European countries, the population has already begun to decline. Italy, for example, is shrinking despite the arrival of 70,000 new immigrants a year. All the same, the Italian government has put new restrictions on immigration. Notes Professor Andrew Geddes of the University of Liverpool, "The Italian government and a broad swathe of Italian public opinion appears to see immigration as a poisoned chalice rather than a magic bullet."[59]

By severely limiting legal immigration, Europe had to contend with the arrival of large numbers of illegals. As such, they were denied the right to work, to social services, to education, etc., and many have had to resort to stealing in order to survive.[60] This has created an image in Europe that immigrants are habitually thieves and criminals.

By contrast, in Canada, where immigration as a percentage of population is an order of magnitude larger than European levels, most citizens believe that immigration has a positive effect on their communities and that immigration provides the country with a stronger culture.[61] Likewise, a 2001 Gallup poll in the United States found that most Americans favor increasing the number of immigrants.[62]

Canada has had a long history of immigration. At beginning of the 20th century, approximately 25 per cent of the population was foreign-born. By the end of the century, that number had declined to about 15 per cent. Despite the decline, Toronto, Canada's largest city, boasted a foreign-born population of nearly 50 per cent, a large number of whom were skilled professionals arriving from every corner of the world.[63] A few European countries have tried to copy Canada's example, by which large numbers of immigrants enter the country by passing a point system that rewards education, language skills and work experience. However, when Germany tried to attract skilled workers, it did so only halfheartedly. For example, whereas Canada offered citizenship to immigrants who resided more than three years in the country, Germany's immigrants perpetually remained on work permits. Under the so called "green card" system, losing one's job could result in loss of residency and even deportation. More importantly, immigrants had to have high-paying job offers prior to arriving in Germany. The result: Canada admitted nearly a quarter of a million immigrants in 2000, while Germany admitted fewer than 20,000 under its new green card system.[64]

At a summit convened by Spain in June 2002, the European Union agreed to jointly increase border controls, to expedite deportations, and to "adopt measures" against originating countries that fail to co-operate on migration, thereby reflecting the growing intolerance of the electorate. Despite the obvious need to increase immigration, Europe's continued refusal to welcome foreigners assured that matters of crime and racism would worsen in the coming years. Observed BBC World Affairs correspondent Paul Reynolds,

Fortress Europe is willing to lower the drawbridge for the few but keep it firmly up for the many . . . All this is driven by recent electoral trends which show that people across Europe are reacting against others they regard as strangers in their midst. And yet those strangers might have been born and bred in the same [European] town.[65]

NOTES

1. "Analysis: Who Gains from Immigration?," *BBC News,* June 17, 2002.

2. R.M. Hutchins, The Great Ideas Vol. 1, Great Books of the Western World, Encyclopedia Britannica, 1989.

3. E. Gibbon, "A History of the Decline and Fall of the Roman Empire," *Britannica Great Books,* Encyclopedia Britannica, 1989 (1776).

4. F. Tenney, "Roman Census Statistics from 508 to 225 B.C.," *American Journal of Philology 51,* 1930.

5. "A Tale of Two Bellies," *The Economist,* August 22, 2002.

6. "Demography and the West," *The Economist,* August 22, 2002.

7. E. Gibbon, "A History of the Decline and Fall of the Roman Empire," *Britannica Great Books,* Encyclopedia Britannica, 1989 (1776).

8. "Spain, history of," *Britannica 2002 Deluxe Edition,* December 3, 2002.

9. E. Gibbon, "A History of the Decline and Fall of the Roman Empire," *Britannica Great Books,* Encyclopedia Britannica, 1989 (1776).

10. J. Nehru, *Glimpses of World History,* J. Day Co., New York, 1960.

11. "Cordoba," *Britannica 2002 Deluxe Edition,* December 3, 2002.

12. "Spain, history of," *Britannica 2002 Deluxe Edition,* December 3, 2002.

13. Ibid.

14. From the Arabic ua xa Alah or inshallah, this is translated "Oh Allah," or "God willing."

15. "Morocco, history of," *Britannica 2002 Deluxe Edition,* December 3, 2002.

16. The Spanish Civil War pitted conservative Catholics and land owners (known as Nationalists) against a coalition of democrats, moderate socialists, communists, secular labor and the educated middle class (collectively known as Republicans). Lacking co-ordination and unified objectives, the Republicans were eventually defeated by the more disciplined Nationalist forces, whose leader, General Francisco Franco, secured important military aid from Nazi Germany and fascist Italy, both of which were eager to test newly developed weapons systems. The Republicans received less effective support from the Soviet Union. Shortly after the Second World War, the Franco dictatorship was ostracized as a relic of fascism, but international relations normalized during the Cold War when Franco was praised for his stalwart opposition to communism.

17. O. Encarnación, "Spain After Franco: Lessons in Democratization," *World Policy Journal,* Winter 2001/2002.

18. "Spain unveils coastal spy system," *BBC News,* August 14, 2002.

19. The section "A Test of Tolerance" is primarily drawn from the findings of an Amnesty International report titled "Spain: Race-related torture and ill-treatment" (April 2002), which contains nearly 100 pages of documented cases of torture, rape and violence against immigrants.

20. "Spain: Race-related torture and ill-treatment," Amnesty International April 2002 AI Index: EUR 41/001/2002.

21. In a May 2002 poll, 60 per cent of Spaniards linked increased crime to immigration, and nearly 70 per cent believed that Spain was becoming less tolerant of foreigners. Source: BBCi (news.bbc.co.uk) *Europe and Immigration,* December 5, 2002.

22. "Immigration to Spain," *Barcelona Business,* November 2000.

23. Everyone, including Spanish citizens, over the age of 14 was required to carry identity documents at all times and failing to do so could result in detention.

24. "Spain: Race-related torture and ill-treatment," Amnesty International April 2002 AI Index: EUR 41/001/2002.

25. Ibid.

26. According to Amnesty International, "Nineteen people, all in Cataluña, were arrested for racist crimes in 1996. In 1997, there were 24 (13 in Cataluña, six in Madrid and five in Melilla). In 1998, the figure rose to 31 (17 in Cataluña, four in Andalucía, four in Aragón, three in Valencia, two in Madrid and one in Rioja). In 1999, the number almost tripled. Out of 89 suspects for racist crimes 50 were from Cataluña, 14 in Navarra, nine in Valencia, six in Andalucía, five in Canarias, two in Extremadura, two in Madrid and one in Murcia. In 2000, 112 people were arrested and the figures for Andalucía and Cataluña are reversed (54 in Andalucía, 13 in Cataluña, 12 in Madrid, 12 in Valencia, 10 in Castilla-La Mancha, nine in Murcia and two in Aragón and Castilla-León)." Spain: Race-related torture and ill-treatment, Amnesty International April 2002 AI Index: EUR 41/001/2002.

Author's note: The numbers reported by Amnesty may also reflect a greater awareness by law enforcement officials of crimes motivated by race. If so, some earlier incidents may not have been reported.

27. "Spain: Race-related torture and ill-treatment," Amnesty International April 2002 AI Index: EUR 41/001/2002.

28. "Declaration of the Rights of Man and of the Citizen," *Britannica 2002 Deluxe Edition,* December 17, 2002

29. D. Schnapper, et al., "French Immigration and Integration Policy," *EFFNATIS Working Paper 30,* Ecole des Hautes Etudes en Sciences Sociales, Paris, January 2000.

30. Ibid.

31. "France: Le Pen," *Migration News,* May 2002.

32. P. Tournier, "Nationality, Crime, and Criminal Justice in France," *Crime and Justice,* Vol. 21 (1997), p. 523.

33. "France Anti-crime Bill Aimed at Cleaning French Streets of Beggars and Prostitutes," *The Associated Press,* October 24, 2002.

34. "There were 400,000 violent crimes in 2001, up from 100,000 in 1994. France: Le Pen," *Migration News,* May 2002.

35. "A Crime-Weary France Plans a Crackdown," *The New York Times,* October 24, 2002.

36. D. Schnapper, et al., "French Immigration and Integration Policy," *EFFNATIS Working Paper 30,* Ecole des Hautes Etudes en Sciences Sociales, Paris, January 2000.

37. "During his campaign, Le Pen proposed limiting immigration by Muslims and non-whites. A Question of Colour, A Matter of Faith," *The Economist,* November 16, 2002.

38. "France: Le Pen," *Migration News,* May 2002.

39. Ibid.

40. "A Question of Colour, A Matter of Faith," *The Economist,* November 16, 2002.

41. "French Election Results a Further Blow to Socialists in Europe," *The Salt Lake Tribune,* June 17, 2002.

42. "In 1955, at the age of 28, Le Pen became the youngest elected member of the French parliament. The following year he enlisted as a paratrooper. Serving under General Massu's 10th division, he participated in the Suez campaign and the Algerian war. Le Pen Ultimate," *Ha'aretz News,* April 22, 2002.

43. "Le Pen Ultimate," *Ha'aretz News,* April 22, 2002.

44. "Algeria, history of," *Britannica 2002 Deluxe Edition,* November 25, 2002.

45. "Le Pen Ultimate," *Ha'aretz News,* April 22, 2002.

46. "French Jews accuse North Africans," *BBC News,* October 16, 2000.

47. Ibid.

48. J. Boëldieu, and C. Borrel, "La proportion d'immigrés est stable depuis 25 ans," *INSEE Première,* November 2000.

49. D. Schnapper, et al., "French Immigration and Integration Policy," *EFFNATIS Working Paper 30,* Ecole des Hautes Etudes en Sciences Sociales, Paris, January 2000.

50. Ottmar Beta [Ottomar Bettziech]: Darwin, Deutschland und die Juden oder Juda-Jesuitismus, Berlin 1875.

51. N. Finzsch, & D. Schirmer, "Identity and Intolerance," *Cambridge University Press,* London, 2002.

52. "Second Report on Germany," European Commission against Racism and Intolerance, December 2000.

53. Ibid.

54. "Germany: Immigration Policy," *Migration News,* August 2000.

55. Ibid.

56. "Germany's new citizenship law," *www .germanembassyottawa.org/cala/citizen,* November 26, 2002.

57. "Second Report on Germany, European Commission against Racism and Intolerance," December 2000.

58. "A New Balance," *The Economist,* September 12, 2002.

59. "Europe's ageing workforce," *BBC News,* June 20, 2002.

60. "Spain: Race-related torture and ill-treatment," Amnesty International April 2002 AI Index: EUR 41/001/2002.

61. "Canadians Welcoming Again: Poll," *The National Post,* May 14, 2002.

62. "Americans View Immigration Positively," *www.ilw.com,* July 2001.

63. Over 100 countries have each supplied more than 1,000 immigrants to the Toronto region, *www.city.toronto.on.ca.*

64. "Germany Tackles Skills Shortage," *BBC News,* August 1, 2000.

65. "Fortress Europe Raises the Drawbridge," *BBC News,* June 18, 2002.

6

ENTREPRENEURSHIP

W omen are increasingly interested in entrepreneurship, and in the Western world, new businesses are equally likely to be started by women as by men. In Canada, women own one third of small- to medium-sized businesses and now start half of all new businesses (Status of Women Canada, 2004). Similarly, in most regions of the European Union, 25% to 35% of business owners are female, and women are starting new businesses at an increasing rate (Centre for Enterprise and Economic Development Research [CEEDR], 2005). In the United States, 10.6 million firms are owned at least 50% by women, nearly half (48%) of all privately held firms are at least 50% owned by women, and between 1997 and 2004, the estimated growth rate in the number of women-owned firms was nearly twice that of all firms (17% vs. 9%) (Center for Women's Business Research, 2005).

Ethnic minorities are also increasingly interested in entrepreneurship. Minorities' share of the total U.S. population grew from 21% in 1982 to 32% in 2002. During the same time period, the percentage of businesses owned by minorities in the United States grew from 6.8% in 1982 to 15.1% (Lowrey, 2005), and one in five women-owned firms in the United States are owned by women of color (Center for Women's Business Research, 2004). In the European Union, roughly 13 million of the 380 million residents are members of ethnic minority groups (3% to 4%). Although data are not available for all member states, in at least two European nations, ethnic minorities are more likely than the population as a whole to start new businesses (Europa, 2005).

The businesses founded by women and ethnic minorities sometimes tap market niches ignored or underserved by traditional organizations. Diverse entrepreneurs also develop new organizational structures that meet the needs of their identity groups more effectively and efficiently than traditional organizations do. Managers can learn the challenges faced by entrepreneurs from these examples. Also, these examples provide ideas regarding ways to better embrace diversity in both entrepreneurial firms and the traditional corporate sector.

CASES

Marie Bohm and The Aspect Group

Marie Bohm is a highly successful communications entrepreneur. When Marie founded her firm, The Aspect Group, she wanted to develop a very different organizational culture than that found at the typical communications firm. Her network-structured organization strives to combine work-life balance and concern for organizational members with top-quality service to customers. To grow, Marie is considering creating a partnership with another firm. Two opportunities have presented themselves. One, a small entrepreneurial firm in London, Ontario, is similar to Marie's own organization. The other, a boutique firm in Toronto, is highly prestigious and would offer an immediate credibility boost. Marie wonders, however, whether the Toronto firm will value her commitment to work-life balance. Marie must decide which partnership will be best for her business goals as well as her life goals.

Assignment Questions:

1. What features of The Aspect Group's organizational design contribute to the firm's effectiveness? What features need to be changed to promote success?

2. As The Aspect Group grows, will the organizational design need to change? In what ways?

3. Which partnering option should Marie take to grow The Aspect Group and why?

The Purchasing Co-Op

One of the founders of a small business owner's purchasing cooperative organized 4 months earlier was reflecting on its successful performance. The members of the co-op were willing to share responsibilities in the management of the co-op's primary activities of obtaining price quotes, invoicing members, and making delivery arrangements. The members were currently considering the possibility of extending the types of materials purchased collaboratively to services such as photocopying and printing of brochures and business cards. She wondered how best to promote the growth of the purchasing co-op and therefore needed to create an action and implementation plan, considering membership size, types of products and services purchased, qualitative and quantitative benefits of co-op involvement, vendor management, and allocation of resources.

Assignment Questions:

1. As Margaret Warren, what would you do to promote the growth of the purchasing co-op?

2. How would your action plan change if the purchasing co-op involved organizations with combined purchase in the million-dollar range?

Rubenesque

As Rubenesque, a consignment store specializing in women's plus-size fashions, celebrates its third anniversary, the part owner examines the performance of the business to date. While the business has grown and become profitable, the store is still not achieving its potential. Although it already subscribes to an online coupon service, Rubenesque is in the process of developing its own Web site as a means of reaching a greater client base. As the Internet continues to grow and become a valuable information resource, the owner feels it is necessary for Rubenesque to establish its own Internet presence, but she wonders to what extent she should use the online community. What concepts should be incorporated into the company's Web site? Would there be an opportunity to develop customer loyalty? And finally, Rubenesque has always tried to present a certain image to its customers, and the Web site must be an extension of that image.

Assignment Questions:

1. Should Shawnda Walker develop an online community as part of the Rubenesque Web site? Why or why not?

2. What information does Shawnda Walker need to make this decision? How can she get that information?

3. What are the strengths and weaknesses of the Rubenesque business model? What suggestions do you have for Shawnda Walker as she works to grow the business?

Growth, Strategy and Slotting at No Pudge! Foods, Inc.

The health and fitness trend that started in the 1980s and became a staple of American lifestyle in the 1990s created numerous opportunities for new firms to introduce niche products. The founder of No Pudge! Brownies worked with a consultant to develop a fat-free brownie mix. She then designed a lean organization where production, distribution, and Internet orders were all outsourced. Immediately she is faced with her "Achilles heel," the slotting fees required by supermarkets to obtain shelf space. After 2 years of negotiating with supermarkets, an important grocery chain finally agrees to carry her product without any slotting fees. By 1997, sales totaled a meager $250,000. Aggressive lobbying with the National Food Distributors Association and a multipronged strategy for dealing with slotting eventually pushed sales above the $2 million mark. No Pudge! is at a major decision point. New growth opportunities, such as muffin mix and fast-food distribution of premade brownies, are abundant. Slotting continues to be a source of frustration for the firm, and No Pudge! is now on the radar screen as a possible acquisition target by major food purveyors.

Assignment Questions:

1. Describe the target market for No Pudge!

2. What is slotting? How does it work? Is slotting unethical?

3. How has Lindsay Frucci maneuvered her way around slotting? Are there other ways around slotting? Will she be able to avoid slotting as the firm continues to grow?

4. Describe the "virtual" structure of the firm, and assess advantages and disadvantages of this design.

5. What are Frucci's strategic options for the future?

6. How would you describe No Pudge!'s competitive strategy? Would the firm perform better in a different niche?

English Center for Newcomers

An English major at Baruch College, New York, is considering opening an English language center that would offer a variety of English as a second language and/or English courses targeted mainly at foreigners coming to New York. She has already done some research and identified a few potential market segments, some aspects of the strategies used by the competition, and elements in the U.S. immigration policy that might threaten her project. She needs to decide if her business idea is feasible. If she decides to go ahead with her project, she has to develop a strategy and a detailed implementation plan before she can open her school.

Assignment Questions:

1. What are the key success factors for each of the customer segments? What impact will these have on the decisions Ronaldson has to make?

2. What problems and/or opportunities exist within the competitive environment?

3. Could political, social, and economic factors affect Ronaldson's business proposal?

4. Evaluate the alternatives available to Ronaldson. Develop the most viable strategy.

5. Should Ronaldson proceed with her business idea? Why? If so, how should it be implemented?

REFERENCES

Centre for Enterprise and Economic Development Research (CEEDR) Middlesex University Business School, UK. (2005, July). *Young Entrepreneurs, Women Entrepreneurs, Co-Entrepreneurs and Ethnic Minority Entrepreneurs in the European Union and Central and Eastern Europe: Final report to the European Commission.* Retrieved from http://europa.eu.int/comm/enterprise/entrepreneurship/craft/craft-studies/entrepreneurs-young-women-minorities.htm

Center for Women's Business Research. (2004). *Businesses owned by women of color in the United States, 2004: A fact sheet.* Retrieved from http://www.nfwbo.org/index.asp

Center for Women's Business Research. (2005). *Top facts about women-owned businesses.* Retrieved April 30, 2005, from http://www.nfwbo.org/index.asp

Europa. (2005). *Ethnic minority entrepreneurs.* Retrieved April 30, 2005, from http://europa.eu.int/comm/enterprise/entrepreneurship/craft/craft-minorities/minorities.htm

Lowrey, Y. (2005, February). *Dynamics of minority-owned employer establishments, 1997–2001* (Small Business Research Summary, No. 251). Washington, DC: U.S. Small Business Administration. Retrieved from http://www.sba.gov/

Status of Women Canada. (2004, 19 March). *Women and economic equality.* Retrieved from http://www.swc-cfc.gc.ca/pubs/b5_factsheets/b5_factsheets_3_e.html

MARIE BOHM AND THE ASPECT GROUP

Prepared by Professor Alison Konrad

 Version: (A) 2005-05-10

Summarizing one of the key values that guided her business, Marie Bohm said, "Gloria Steinem said 'the personal is political.' Well, in my view, the personal is *business, too.*" Bringing her personal values to her business, Bohm founded The Aspect Group with the goal of developing a humane work environment and supporting the work-life flexibility needs of all organizational members. Now, however, she faced a decision that was testing those values against the profitability imperative. In growing her business, she was faced with two opportunities. She could partner with another small local firm in London, Ontario,[1] or she could forge a link with a high-profile Toronto firm. The latter option offered a considerably greater boost in terms of visibility and credibility; however, Bohm was concerned that the demands of such a venture might dilute the work-life flexibility qualities she valued.

THE INDUSTRY ENVIRONMENT

The Aspect Group was a small, entrepreneurial company in the field of brand management, and included professionals in the fields of communications, art, web design and management. The Canadian advertising industry was a mix of large agencies and a set of smaller "boutique" firms. Cossette Communication Group of Quebec City, MDC Partners of Toronto and Maritz Canada of Missisauga, Ontario, ranked as the top three marketing communications services companies in Canada.[2]

Globalization was driving many Canadian firms to focus on size, resulting in consolidation within the industry. At the same time, a number of talented professionals had left the large agencies in order to establish creative boutique shops.

Examples included such names as Rethink, CKK, Republik and Toronto-based Zig, each of which had roughly nine to 30 staffers each.[3] While large agencies derived sustainable profitability and growth by winning new assignments from an established client list constituted of the corporate giants,[4] smaller clients found they sometimes fared better with a boutique firm for whom they were the large fish. J.J. Johnston, general manager for Corus Radio in Toronto, explained why he switched his account to a boutique firm, "When you are dealing with a larger agency, quite often you are at the bottom of the barrel. Agencies allocate their time appropriately. We are not a Molson account or a Future Shop, so we would rather have more of a boutique that could give us the attention."[5]

The boutique route attracted talented designers who preferred to work without the hierarchy and bureaucracy of the agency environment. Many of these shops emphasized their ability to provide highly creative campaigns. Chris Staples, a partner at Rethink, said,

> There are a lot of agencies that talk about how strategic they are, and they criticize agencies like ours by saying, "They are just creative, they are a creative boutique." Well, you can't separate the two things . . . Most agencies spend more time coming up with the strategy than they do coming up with the idea, the concept. It's the reason Canadian advertising is so terrible, because all of the interesting edges get rubbed off in this grueling process that just wears advertising and turns it into this bland dust.[6]

Another value for many creative professionals was freedom and autonomy. Zig creative director Elspeth Lynn explained, "I guess that's the beauty of having your own shop and not having to report to New York—you are able to make your own decisions.[7]

MARIE BOHM: CAREER HISTORY AND WORK EXPERIENCES

Marie Bohm earned her BA in arts and communications from The University of Western Ontario in 1985, and earned an Associate of the College of Art (AOCA) in design from the Ontario College of Art in 1989. She had been self-employed since art college, spending much of her earlier career freelancing and working with a number of different companies on contract. For a short time, she had been a regular employee of a small design house. Her first job with a large design company started as a one-year freelance contract, which generated enough work to be full-time. Then, she was offered an employee position, and as she had just married, she took the position because the security and benefits seemed attractive.

When Bohm became pregnant a few months later, she retained the job but found she was very tired all the time. She got her work done and didn't miss any deadlines, but didn't have a lot of energy. After four months with the company, she received her first performance review, where she received a rating of average. It seemed odd that she had moved from being a stellar freelancer to being only an average employee. At seven months pregnant, she was fired. Bohm was not certain why that happened, because she wasn't missing deadlines, so it seemed to come from out of the blue. Since then, she learned that the firm has a reputation for being a real sweatshop, "Their view is drive them hard, work them hard, 60 hours a week. It is important to stay late and eat pizza with everyone else to look like you were working a lot." Bohm believes that maybe she was fired despite her performance because she didn't put in that "face time."

After her daughter, Lisa, was born, Bohm stayed home as a full-time mother. After a year, she needed to bring money into the household, and the idea of some adult stimulation was attractive; so, Bohm upgraded her computer and started doing freelance work again. Arranging things at home and finding a babysitter was hard. It was emotionally difficult to be separated from Lisa and to have to worry about the quality of care Lisa was receiving; however, on the positive side, work provided a break from caregiving, which according to Bohm, "is the most rewarding—and the toughest—job there is."

In the early 1990s, the recession hit, but according to Bohm, that can be good for freelancing because companies don't want employees on payroll during those times. Also, combined with parenting and running the household, part-time work was more than enough:

> Financial self-sufficiency is very important, but I didn't want to lose the first five years of Lisa's life. Early childhood doesn't last, you have to enjoy it while it's there and also provide the child with the close relationship she needs during that time. Money will come later, money is always there, but it was important to me to start my child's life in the best possible way.

Of course, there was unrelenting financial stress, so Bohm would regularly look for positions and go on interviews to see if there was something out there that would pay enough to make it worthwhile (so that all the money wasn't going to the babysitter) and that would provide the flexibility to allow her to spend enough time with her daughter. At one organization, the interviewer asked her, "So, you're a mom. Are you going to be OK with working 60-hour workweeks? Are you going to be OK going home to dinner with your family and then coming back to work afterwards?" Bohm doesn't remember what she said in response, and the interview was just another nail in the coffin of the idea of trying to work for a firm and raise a family.

THE FOUNDING OF THE ASPECT GROUP

Bohm realized there was a ceiling of how large you can grow as a freelancer and how large of projects you can take on as one person. In 1995,

Bohm was hired for a two-year contract with Visual Arts Western, and Lisa started kindergarten. Bohm was working full-time, and Lisa was in school. At the same time, Bohm kept up her freelance work, because the Visual Arts Western contract wasn't going to last forever, and also she wanted to retain her independence. Her supervisor, Madeline Lennon at Visual Arts Western, was also amazing, very flexible and willing to work with Bohm's schedule, which provided a very positive environment. However, working all day, freelancing at night, and maintaining a home and family kept Bohm on a cycle of exhaustion.

In the meantime, the freelance jobs started to get bigger. When the time came to renew the Visual Arts Western contract in 1997, Bohm decided not to renew, because the freelance work was sufficient to create a natural transition at that point. The work was becoming larger, too much for one person.

The first major contract that turned Bohm from a lone freelancer into a business manager, who coordinated a team of people, came from Axiom Technologies. Axiom Technologies, an industrial automation company, was run by Phil Jacques, who Bohm termed as, "a great guy who put his values into his business," and Bohm learned a lot by watching him. The first project required a team of two people, and Bohm brought in Terry Wallace to share the project. Wallace's specialty was technology and building, while Bohm's was project management and design.

The head of Axiom recommended Bohm to other industrial companies, which generated a stream of business. A landmark project for Bohm was the 2000 launching of the Visual Plant software product for the company EMT. Prior to this project, Bohm had done all the different pieces, but had never before co-ordinated a whole product launch of this magnitude. She had to figure out how to organize the project, and decided to pull together a team of all home-based people who were high-quality experts in their fields rather than start an office-based company. Bohm chose her team members carefully, and it worked well. The two-year launch was very successful,

with Bohm assuming the responsibilities of keeping EMT on track, keeping all the team members on track and managing the project. Bohm found the work exciting, and realized she had developed a model that could potentially be successful for a stream of projects of considerably greater size and scope than would be possible for any of the individuals involved if they were working alone.

ORGANIZATIONAL DESIGN, VALUES AND CULTURE

The Aspect Group was organized very much along the lines of the EMT project. As president, Bohm took responsibility for business development. For each project she brought in, Bohm served as project manager and formed a team consisting of all home-based entrepreneurs. Her supplier network consisted of three primary people, with five or six others covering specialties on an as-required basis. The specific demands of the project, as well as personnel availability, determined who was assigned to what project. Web design and development specialist, Lynne Dionne, explained the project management process:

> Marie takes the input from the client, puts them in a document, and creates a timeline and a budget for each person. I'll give her input on the time and tell her if it's doable or not. She covers all the details; there's not a lot she'll miss. She's good at getting all the information needed up front. Marie is also very good at managing client expectations and directing them in the way that is best for them and won't add a lot to their budget. She's got a good sense of what people need, even if they don't know. She's good at communicating professional knowledge to the client in a persuasive way.

Describing The Aspect Group, Bohm focused on quality and flexibility:

> The business model is very organic. We have very high expectations for the level of talent and ability, and we are very professionally demanding of high-quality standards. We do

smaller, high-profile projects. We have a high-end hourly rate, comparable to agency rates, but we have a higher profit margin. What we save in overhead is pure profit.

In selecting project partners, Bohm screened for the highest quality talent and expected a high level of professionalism and reliability. Art director Dan Floyd agreed that The Aspect Group selected only top-quality professionals into the team:

A key success factor is bringing in the right people; not just anybody. We need people who know how to move just as fast as we do. We attempted to hire kids out of school but they walk away. Reality hits them, and they have failed for one reason or another. After giving it a shot, we realized that we don't have clients that allow for entry-level positions. What takes young people two weeks in school, we need students to be able to do in two hours.

Bohm also sought people with a positive attitude and good interpersonal skills:

In a smaller environment, excellent communication is even more important, and there need to be strong links within the team. We must be above average in how we communicate with each other. We don't have time for negativity and politics.

She gave very direct feedback to those team members whose behavior reduced the productivity of others on the team, and if they were unable or unwilling to change, she wouldn't work with them again. A particularly painful example concerned moving one of the core people out of the business:

The chemistry just isn't right. I had a meeting with him where he started off with half a dozen little jibes that were hurtful to me. For example, I recently got a dog, and his comment was, "Now here's someone who will take Bohm's attention away from the business." I just don't have the energy to deal with that.

The Aspect Group was able to attract the highest caliber of people due to the high-level work Bohm brought in. Writer Vicki Sanderson explained:

My first project with Bohm was very creative, and not the kind of thing one would often get to do from a home office. I do corporate annual reports, supplements for magazines, newspaper articles, on my own, but this work is really creative. The first project was a brochure for a new company promoting a manufacturing software system. The client wanted something different, new, fresh.

Web designer Lynne Dionne concurred:

The work I do with Marie is really different from the other work I do. Her projects make my work more interesting; and she brings in different types of organizations than I would normally have a chance to work with. Primarily what pulled me in to join The Aspect Group was that the work was intriguing.

Providing a humane workplace with flexibility for work-life balance, as opposed to the sweatshop mentality of the agencies, is a key value Bohm brought to The Aspect Group. She gave the example of a time when one Aspect Group member's grandmother was very ill, and her inability to complete her part of a project delayed a presentation to a client. Bohm decided to change the date of the presentation to accommodate her group member's needs. She said, "I wasn't happy about it, but that decision upheld the values of balance and humanity."

The members of The Aspect Group expressed how Bohm's focus on balance affected the work. Dan Floyd explained, "Marie plans everything well so there is breathing space. If she wants to take time off, she'll take it off because she wants to be with her daughter." Vicki Sanderson commented:

At The Aspect Group, there is no embarrassment about saying, "I can't have that done by Tuesday afternoon because I have to take my kid to the doctor," or "I'm going on my child's field trip that day." With other clients, you'd say things like, "I have meetings all day," or "I'm having my appendix out." Being open about valuing your family life could hurt your reputation with others, and it's very liberating just to be able to be straight about what's going on. On the flip side—I might have to say that I can't have that done on Friday afternoon, but I can do a few hours on Saturday morning.

Lynne Dionne concurred:

> Marie has strong values and she is essentially the organization. She's committed to her clients; wants to give them the best quality work and service possible. There is a lot of accountability within the group; high expectations that quality will be met. But not pressure. I never feel any pressure at all. Marie takes the pressure off because she deals with the clients. She takes a lot of pressure, but she doesn't put it on me. For me, meeting high standards and timelines is natural to me. I share those values: commitment, trust, loyalty, relationships. You earn that too. You earn trust, confidence in clients. It shows when they keep coming back.

The organic, home-based design created a number of business advantages for The Aspect Group as well. Bohm explained:

> Agency hours are typically $300 to $500, but each hour combines multiple talents, including design, writing and management. Each talent gets about $100/hour. Also, we can bill a little less than agencies do. We have no IT department because each person maintains their own home computer. We have no leasehold monthlies. Physical presence as an agency is a completely different ballgame, but I don't see it as adding value for the client. I meet the clients at their offices, which saves them time and means I don't need to maintain a slick office with a fancy conference room. Most agencies, even boutique ones, have an office front in the business plan. It is not in my business plan. If we had an office, we would lose the ability of people to work at home and combine work and family and we would also lose the profits. So the work-family value and the profit motive work together to create a positive synergy.

LEADERSHIP STYLE AND DECISION-MAKING

Internet technology allows for quick sharing of information, including text and pictures across geographically dispersed locations and greatly reduces the need for communications specialists to meet in person in order to make design decisions. The Aspect Group's home-based structure took advantage of the reduced need for people to be co-located in a central office. Writer Vicki Sanderson liked the lack of an office:

> It is almost an advantage that we're not in the same physical building. What will happen is we agree on a concept. Then I draft some copy, send it to Bohm. We talk about it by phone for 10 to 30 minutes. After that, we hang up the phone, and I go back to do what I do best, I focus on the job of writing. Later that day or the next day, we can check in. That's different from feeling there's somebody down the hall waiting for me to come out of the office and plop that great copy down on their desk. It's a feeling of psychological freedom. We have deadlines but there is a psychological advantage to feeling that the deadline is not right on top of my shoulder. Working at home gives me a lot more freedom to work more creatively. I feel less stress, and I think I perform better.

Of course, face-to-face communication is sometimes the most efficient way to process a lot of information in order to make a complex decision, and when needed, members of The Aspect Group would meet. According to Lynne Dionne, there was a collaborative side to creative work that was missing when working from home:

> One thing I've envisioned an environment kind of like a doctor's office; we'd all rent the same space but have separate businesses. There would be a photographer, a writer, graphic designers, and a couple of lead people who pull everything together. The benefit to this structure would be an environment where you can sit and collaborate together. I miss times with my corporate team where we'd whiteboard 10 ideas, brainstorming and collaborating. It's really fun to do it together with a larger group of people, and I miss that."

On the other hand, Dionne agreed that working from home meant people had the ability to walk away from a project when energy levels dropped or the ideas just weren't coming:

> The nature of creative work fits well with a flexible schedule. There are days when you're not creative and nothing comes to you. There would be pressure on the designers in an office to get things

ready in eight hours. With Marie I'll schedule a week of work; which gives me the freedom to start on something, go away from it, and come back to it when I've got more ideas. Instead of one 12-hour day, I can spread the 12 hours out over three days; 12 good hours, not 12 hours in one day, some are good and some are not.

Dionne argued that this structure created savings for customers. Because the client gets billed only for hours of actual work, a lot of wasted time that pads the bills of large agencies doesn't end up on the bills received by clients of The Aspect Group.

Members of The Aspect Group described Bohm's leadership as participative and demonstrating great respect for the professional opinions of others. Bohm saw a benefit of giving a lot of autonomy to professionals:

I have the expertise in many areas, so I could meddle in everyone's work. But that would cause several problems. Delegating the tasks cleanly shows respect, increases job satisfaction, creates better time management for me, and creates clear lines of responsibility. I'm not a responsible manager if I meddle and interfere with their process! I'm also happier because the list of what's my job doesn't grow.

Yet as Vicki Sanderson described, Bohm provided guidance when it was needed to meet project goals and deadlines:

For example, we'll have some copy for a brochure that's 99.9 per cent there, but there's one little thing to look at. Bohm will say something like, "Vicki, can we just look at the last sentence on the third page." Being the creative person, I'll say something like, "I have a new idea, let's redo the whole thing." She'll say, "well, let's just look at this one sentence." She's good at keeping projects on track."

BUSINESS DEVELOPMENT AND GROWTH

Business needed to be generated constantly and consistently for The Aspect Group to thrive. Thanks to the high quality of their work and

stellar reputation for providing reliable service to customers, The Aspect Group had 90 per cent to 95 per cent of its proposals approved by potential clients. The environment can get tough, however. The third year in, which was a slow period for the industry as a whole, The Aspect Group had no work at all. Bohm said, "At the time, I didn't have a huge line of credit, so financially, it was very hard. I really had to look at my priorities and ask, are these really my priorities? There were opportunities to go into a 70-hour a week agency job."

Business cycles create a feast or famine, and being self-employed means riding that roller coaster without the benefit of a steady salary and benefits. Bohm emphasized:

That's definitely not the fun part. But I choose this type of being tough rather than the other type of being tough—being the employee who is able to tough out the 70-hour work weeks. I don't view it as any less secure. Agencies face business cycles too, and they downsize, and it's not up to the employee who leaves and who stays. This way, I control my own fate. How much business is initiated and how much the client base is built is all up to me. I have control over my own fate, my own time, and my own location. The sacrifice is the lean times, but I prefer that to the sacrifices I'd make as an agency employee.

Other factors can also arise, "It's also scary when you cannot do the work because you become ill or for some other reason. I can trust my team to keep doing their parts, but business development and sales is up to me. I was very ill for four weeks last year, and that was frightening."

To maintain a strong foundation for her business, Bohm capitalized on every success as much as possible:

For example, I took purchase orders to the bank to show them my success in order to argue for a higher credit line. As a single mom with a business, the bank treated me like I was an alien. It seemed like they'd rather give money to a teenaged boy. So, twice a month, I do the books. I have a profit/loss statement available at all times. I sold myself to the bank and started with a $5K line of credit. I tried to work with that bank for a number of years, but their intransigence sent me elsewhere. I waited for a large influx of business and took the results to another bank, and got a much larger credit line. Every time I get a great project, I showed it to the bank. Now at six years out, I have a client roster, I have a record, I have a balance sheet. The larger credit line makes it much easier to ride out the lean months.

Another problem faced by small business is collecting payments from recalcitrant clients, "I spend a lot of time chasing down money, 90-day late payments, tens of thousands of dollars. I lost a whole month of business development during my peak season this year because I had to run after these people." And the situation can sometimes get nasty. Bohm described one particularly difficult episode:

A problem developed with a particular client. There were no problems on the project, he raved about the work, gave compliments all the time. But payment was not forthcoming. Every time I'd see him, I'd say, "so the check's in the mail, right?" He lied to me about it for a month.

Unable to reach the client directly, Bohm continued communicating with him through voice mail and e-mail. The project reached the point of going to press with 30,000 menus, and Bohm had to decide whether or not to continue the project. She decided to carry forward. She sent a payment schedule listing the services that would be rendered upon receipt of each payment. The tactic worked at first, and the client complied with all payments except for the last one. He insisted that he would not send a final payment until he received digital files, so he was withholding the final payment.

After some negotiations, the client sent two postdated checks for two-thirds and one-third of the final payment. By this time, Bohm didn't trust him and so she checked with his bank. Sure enough, he had put a stop payment on the final check. So, Bohm called him and said she would not send him the digital files until he paid her. Calling back, the client left a voice mail saying, "You should think before you talk, you shouldn't say these things to a client . . ." and he threw in some four-letter words.

Things got worse. A person Bohm had done business with but whom she had not worked with for a few years had sent this client Bohm's way. The client had told this person only his side of the story, and the person started phoning and harassing Bohm. He threatened to call several of her clients and tell them what a "bitch" she was. He'd leave phone messages at night that terrorized her. Bohm told the client about the harassment, but he refused to talk to him about it, "I've had to let other clients go due to harassment issues. Probably many small business owners have these problems with clients, but choice of language and tactics seemed to be directed at me because I'm a woman."

Growing The Aspect Group by bringing on another project manager with a strong personality seemed like one way to strengthen her position against client harassment:

Jason Recker is my designer of choice right now. We've talked about business development and project management and will work on a few projects together and see how it goes. He's like a California surfer dude; he wants a reasonable environment, evenings and weekends to himself. I got a sense from him that when I mentioned my 9 to 5 attitude, that was what really sold him on working with me.

PARTNERING OPPORTUNITIES

Bohm was determined to grow The Aspect Group, and 2005 was a good time to do it. The business environment was strong, and business was coming in. Bringing Recker on board would help her deal with the increased volume of work. Also, Lisa was in high school now, and Bohm would soon need money for college tuition. Once Lisa moved on to university, Bohm would have the time to take her business to the next level, and in order to do that, the time to start building was now.

One possibility was to contract with a large agency to do specialty work, something many boutique agencies did. The benefit of such a partnership would be help with business development. A large agency could provide a steady stream of business with larger clients. A potential downside would be the pressures an agency would bring to bear. The experiences Bohm had endured as an employee of a large agency— working long hours, meeting impossible dead-lines and jumping to meet unreasonable client expectations—were not burdens she wanted to place on the members of The Aspect Group.

A few interesting partnering opportunities had arisen, which might avoid the downside risk of contracting with a large agency. One possibil-ity was to create a relationship with another small London firm with similar values of quality and balance, "It seems like the perfect fit, with good chemistry and the right energy." Adding the firm to The Aspect Group's network would allow the business to grow beyond the number of projects Bohm could juggle at one time as the lone project manager. Bringing on Recker would help, and together, the two groups could take on considerably more projects and larger, more complex ones. Importantly, with all members having home-based businesses and sharing the values of quality and balance, this connection would allow The Aspect Group to retain its core value of providing a humane workplace and flexibility for members.

Another opportunity presented itself at about the same point in time. A prestigious boutique agency in Toronto was also sending out feelers to explore the possibility of joint projects with The Aspect Group. The benefit of partnering with the agency was high visibility and prestige. Nothing Bohm could do in London would give The Aspect Group the immediate credibility boost that partnering with the agency on a series of projects would create. She worried, however, about the agency's organizational culture and values. Unlike the London group, the agency had an office front to maintain. Its work was high quality, but she got a sense that the atmosphere was more high-pressured and intense than she wanted for herself and the other Aspect Group members. On the other hand, the agency would be able to provide a steady stream of the types of interesting projects members of The Aspect Group enjoyed, as well as a steady source of income for everyone.

NOTES

1. London, Ontario, is a city of about 350,000 people, located about 200 kilometres (120 minutes) southwest of Toronto.
2. *Marketing Magazine,* June 21, 2004.
3. Eve Lazarus, "True believers [Small advertis-ing agencies that put creative above all else]," *Marketing Magazine,* November 26, 2001, p. 41.
4. Noreen O'Leary, "Old dogs, new tricks," *Adweek,* January 13, 2003, p. 14.
5. Eve Lazarus, "True believers [Small advertis-ing agencies that put creative above all else]," *Marketing Magazine,* November 26, 2001, p. 41.
6. Ibid.
7. Ibid.

THE PURCHASING CO-OP

Prepared by Professor Larry J. Menor
under the supervision of Professors M. Leenders and J. Erskine

Version: (A) 2000-09-25

In May 2000, Margaret Warren, owner and manager of M-Powered Ideas of St. Thomas, Ontario, reflected upon the successful perfor-mance of the small business owners purchasing co-operative she had helped organize four months earlier. Margaret was considering how the co-op, which she used to purchase essential oils used for the production of her Utopia Soap products, should grow and what membership benefits to promote.

Margaret Warren and M-Powered Ideas

Margaret started M-Powered Ideas in January 1997 to offer small-office desktop publishing services. In addition, M-Powered Ideas faxed newsletters and announcements for the Western Ontario district of the Purchasing Management Association of Canada. Prior to starting M-Powered Ideas, Margaret was employed as a professional purchasing agent for Victoria Hospital in London, Ontario.

During the summer of 1997, Margaret visited an herb farm in California and came across a handmade-soap maker with whom she spoke at length. Intrigued by the chemical blending and creativity involved in the soap-making process, she purchased several books on soap making and immediately began experimenting with soap formulations that were produced in one-pound batches. Margaret shared her creations with family and friends who kept returning, even offering to pay for more soap. Soon after, she began to show and sell her line of fragrant hand-made soaps outside of this group of family and friends. Margaret created the brand name "Utopia Soap" for her product and produced it under the umbrella name of M-Powered Ideas.

Utopia Soap

As sole operator of Utopia Soap, Margaret opened a workshop in her backyard where all soap production took place. Her soaps started with a special combination of coconut, olive and palm oils—the base oils; the blending of additives and fragrances resulted in numerous soap blends. For example, one standard soap produced and labelled "Jasmine Dream" contained an infusion of dried calendula blossoms in olive oil. Other standard blends were likewise descriptively labelled (e.g., "Seabreeze," "Winery Weekend," "Berry Fresh" and "Manly") and were typically offered on a year-round basis. In addition to these standard blends, Margaret offered specialty products such as an emu oil soap and custom blended soaps. The average production cost per bar of soap was $1.[1]

Sales of Utopia Soap for 1999 amounted to $10,000. Approximately 70 per cent of annual sales were for standard soaps. Additionally, 40 per cent of annual sales came from Ontario retailers such as gift shops, craft stores, health-food stores and bed and breakfasts as the soaps were primarily viewed as gift items or skincare products. All soaps were sold to retail and wholesale customers for $2.99, with retailers typically selling the product with a $1.00 mark-up (Margaret also retailed a small percentage of Utopia Soap herself at $3.99). Despite the relatively small volume of soap sales, Margaret anticipated a 25 per cent growth in sales during the current year with a goal of reaching $100,000 in annual sales at the end of the next three years. Based upon the past two years of sales, Margaret planned for 80 per cent of this year's soap business occurring between mid-April and mid-November.

Handmade Soap Production and Materials Purchasing

The production of standard and custom handmade soap involved melting base oils to a temperature ranging between 100° F to 150° F. Concurrently, sodium hydroxide was mixed with water, and this combination was eventually blended with the melted oils at a temperature of 100° F. Color, fragrance and other additives (e.g., ground oatmeal, dried flowers, etc.) were next added and the mixture poured into molds. Producing a typical batch of soap (approximately 20 pounds) took three hours. After spending 24 hours in an insulating chamber, the molds were removed and allowed to rest at room temperature for three days. The soap was then removed from the molds and allowed to rest for an additional 24 hours. After cutting, the soap cured for 24 hours,

Category	Percentage
Base oils	60
Essential and fragrance oils	30
Labor	4
Packaging	1
Overhead	5

Exhibit 1   Production Cost Break-Down by Category

Source: Margaret Warren, owner.

was trimmed and then air cured for four weeks. A typical batch yielded 75 soap bars.

Given that sales growth projections were constrained by the current production capacity, Margaret was investigating the potential upgrade of her "low-tech" production process (e.g., she currently melted the oils using an electric heating element and a pot) by purchasing heating equipment with precise heating controls and a custom-made cutter. The use of this equipment would increase the batch size up to 100 pounds.

Materials used in the production of standard soap, such as base and essential oils, were typically purchased every five weeks. Base and essential oils accounted for approximately 90 per cent of soap production cost (see Exhibit 1). Given that a 467 millilitre bottle of essential oil, for example, might cost $100, Margaret's material purchases averaged $200 an order with average shipping costs of $10. Shipping lead times from vendors averaged two to three days. On average, she kept approximately eight weeks of finished goods inventory on hand of standard soap products. Materials for custom soaps were purchased once orders were confirmed.

THE PURCHASING CO-OPERATIVE

Operations on the scale of Margaret's Utopia Soap typically lacked purchasing clout when dealing with materials suppliers. The production quantities of MPI's typical materials orders were too small to meet purchasing discount volumes, and some vendors were quite unresponsive from a service standpoint to requests, for example, for detailed product information and expedited shipments. Owners of small businesses such as Utopia Soap typically were craftspeople or artisans lacking the business experience and savvy to deal with vendors. The tasks of arranging purchases and understanding purchasing terminology, let alone finding and reaching vendors, while necessary, were considered non-value added activities.

Margaret recognized in the fall of 1999 that one way to quickly gain purchasing clout with vendors would be through the formation of a purchasing co-operative. Members join a co-operative for the benefit of the services it renders. Margaret's own experience with purchasing co-operatives started with the London Public Purchasing Co-op. This consisted of publicly funded agencies collaborating to purchase commodity type items ranging from copier paper to electrical and plumbing parts. Some of the co-op contracts Margaret packaged and negotiated ran into the million-dollar range. While nothing on that scale would be needed, Margaret approached members of the Local Business Women's Association (LBWA) in November 1999 to pitch the formation of a purchasing co-operative for commodity items like essential and fragrance oils. Looking at the industry representation of LBWA members (see Exhibit 2), Margaret identified several individuals who sold products in retail locations similar to these where she sold Utopia soap (i.e., those with similar raw material needs) and convinced five other small business operators of the benefits in forming a purchasing co-operative. These five LBWA members included an emu farmer, a rhea farmer, an herb gardener, a jam and preserve maker, and a skin care products producer. All co-op members agreed to aggregate their monthly purchases into a single order with the first, for essential oils, placed in January 2000. Since then, monthly co-op orders have ranged between $800 and $1,000 with a $15 shipping charge shared among members.

Articulate Books	McDonald Organic Farm
Aussie Rhea Farms (rheas and related products)	Memorable Collectibles (specialty gifts)
Blueberry Fields (farm produce)	Michelle's (makeup and beauty consulting)
Brady Securities, Inc.	Museums of Art
Camp Shady Grove (vacation pet minding)	Ontario On My Mind (specialty gifts)
Carol's Better Home (gift shop)	Outfitters (clothing)
Certified Holistic Health Practitioner	Paradise Valley Farms (farm produce and gardening supplies)
Chuck Wagon Ltd.	
Cliff's Ceramics & Craft Boutique	Pat's Perennials & Dried Flowers
Closet Warehouse (consignment clothing and gifts)	Peterson Accounting & Tax Service
Country Hair Design	Port Stanley Orchard (farm produce)
Duds (clothing shop)	Profitable Investment Planning
Eveready's Rustic (gifts)	Promising Scholarships Consultants
Farrell's Seat Upholstery Service	Reminders & Responsibility (scrapbooking and accounting services)
Harris Farms (goat milk soaps and related products)	Stephanie's Gifts (candles and holders)
Harris House (gift shop)	Stepping In (clothing shop)
Health and Holistic Services	The Balloon Shop (balloon-o-grams etc.)
Hidden Valley Company (farm produce)	The Chop Shop (restaurant)
International Health (food supplements)	Tidy Bowl Trading Co.
Jammin' (jams and preserves)	Trisect Group (investment consulting)

Exhibit 2   Local Business Women's Association Membership*

Source: Local Business Women's Association.

*Where needed, a brief business description is noted parenthetically.

While specific cost savings for all co-op members were not regularly collected, Margaret estimated that the co-op members each had reduced purchasing-related costs by about 20 per cent. More important for the co-op members was the recognition that while their combined ordering volumes allowed for some purchasing discount volumes to be achieved, the materials vendors they had dealt with since the co-op's origin appeared more responsive to servicing specific member requests. On one recent order, a fragrance oil vendor, atypically, charged the co-op for a litre but re-distributed the product into two half-litre bottles for the two co-op members using the oil.

Margaret recognized the knowledge of materials management practices, production techniques and the local retail market that co-op members were now sharing. She liked the fact that each member was willing to share responsibility on an agreed-upon rotation basis in the management of the co-op's primary activities of obtaining price quotes, aggregating ordering needs, planning case splits, placing orders, paying vendors, invoicing co-op members and making delivery arrangements. The current co-op members were considering the possibility of extending the type of materials purchased collaboratively (e.g., currently oils and packaging) to photocopying services, and the printing of brochures and business cards—all applicable to the needs of the members. Margaret mulled over how the purchasing co-op she had organized should grow.

NOTE

1. All amounts in Canadian dollars unless otherwise stated.

RUBENESQUE

Prepared by Patrick Leu under the supervision of Professor Michael R. Pearce

Version: (A) 2002-04-10

INTRODUCTION

As Rubenesque, a consignment store specializing in women's plus-size fashions, celebrated its third birthday in July of 2000, Shawnda Walker, part owner of the retail enterprise, examined the performance of the business to date. While the Toronto-based business had grown and become profitable, the store was still not achieving its potential. To extend the marketing reach of the business and to better communicate with customers, Rubenesque was in the process of developing a Web site. In considering the Web site design, Walker wondered how and to what extent she should establish an online community.

An important marketing strategy utilized by Rubenesque was that of developing a community of customers. Walker felt that there were tremendous opportunities for the store to create relationships with women of size who were underserved by retailers. These customers shared similar concerns, and a Rubenesque community could open up a forum to share ideas, resources and experiences. There were some ways by which the store could access its target market. For example, there were social organizations and online chat rooms and Web sites that focused on larger women. Walker wondered if Rubenesque should take a lead role and form its own community, both online and offline, or simply participate in existing ones. She provided her thoughts on the role of a Rubenesque Web site:

> First and foremost, I want the Web site to sell clothing—whether it be online or by making consumers aware of our store. I also want content and stimulation that will bring people back. I also want it to be a place where people can read things or do things that make them feel good about themselves and their size. The Web site provides me an opportunity to give back to the community on the knowledge that I have about events and information in Canada relating to size issues.

PLUS-SIZE MARKET

Data suggested that plus-size women were highly underserved by the retail fashion industry.

Marketdata estimated the total plus-size apparel market in the United States to be over $28 billion in 2000. NPD Group measured women's plus-size sales at $23.7 billion in 1999 or about 25 per cent of the total women's clothing market. This ratio represented a low proportion of the total market, considering that the average woman wore a size 14 and that almost half of the population wore plus-sizes. Further, Marketdata cited industry observers who predicted that more than half of U.S. women would wear a size 16 or larger by 2002.[1]

The plus-size category in women's fashions encompassed clothing sizes of 14 or greater. Standard plus-sizes ranged from 14 to 28 with sizes 14 to 16 accounting for approximately 45 per cent of the total plus-size market. Sizes 18 to 28 represented about 35 per cent of the total. Sizes greater than 28, commonly referred to as Super Size, represented about 20 per cent of the plus-size market.[2] The industry lacked standards in sizing for plus-sizes which provided challenges for women in finding the right outfit (see Exhibit 1 for an approximation of plus-size measurements). "Regular" sizes were women's fashions ranging up to size 12. Other specialty categories included Petite for heights up to five feet four inches, Tall for women at five feet nine inches or greater, Maternity for expectant mothers, and Junior or Missy were fashions for teens. The combination of Petite Plus-Sizes, Tall Plus-Sizes or Junior Plus-Sizes were also distinct categories that were recognized as being underserved in the marketplace.

Despite the fact that almost half of North American women were plus-size, the majority of retailers and manufacturers of women's apparel offered clothing in the regular sizes only. Walker, a person who wore plus-sizes all her life, was all too familiar with the three complaints commonly heard by larger women: lack of retail selection, lack of stylish fashions and premium prices.

Lack of Retail Selection

Beyond a few independent specialty stores, the retail alternatives were very limited. Major retailers such as Banana Republic, The Gap, Mexx and Club Monaco did not carry plus-sizes. The Yorkdale Shopping Centre, recognized as one of the major fashion centres in Toronto, listed 52 retailers (excluding department stores) that specialized in women's fashion or offered both women's and men's fashions. Of the 52 stores, only four carried plus-size apparel.

Many Canadian women simply had difficulty finding clothes in their size. Because the retail industry in the United States had recognized the market discrepancy to a greater extent, more shopping alternatives existed there. For example, Lane Bryant, the 800-store plus-size concept owned by The Limited, was considered by many to be the leading American retailer serving this segment. Other American fashion forward

Women's Size	Comfort Size	Bust*	Waist*	Hips*
14	L	38 < 40	30 < 32	40 < 42
16	L	40 < 42	32 < 34	42 < 44
18	1X	42 < 44	34 < 36	44 < 46
20	1X	44 < 46	36 < 38	46 < 48
22	2X	46 < 48	38 < 40	48 < 50
24	2X	48 < 50	40 < 43	50 < 52
26	3X	50 < 52	43 < 46	52 < 54
28	3X	52 < 54	46 < 48	54 < 56

Exhibit 1 Sample Plus-Size Mesurements

*Measurements in inches.

retailers, such as Nordstrom, offered plus-size apparel. Due to the limited selection in Canada, some women purchased their plus-size clothes in the United States. Many others were simply not aware of the retail alternatives in the United States or were not able to travel there frequently and thus relied on the offerings in Canada. Rural areas were particularly underserved with plus-size options.

Lack of Stylish Fashions

Plus-size fashions often lacked style or did not exhibit the latest seasonal trends in designs as seen in regular sizes. As a result, many larger women were often limited to clothing that was baggy, drab and dull. Walker commented, "First and foremost, the biggest challenge is actually finding fashions, particularly finding plus-size fashions that are also trendy."

Most major design labels, including Guess and Esprit de Corps, who manufactured fashion forward designs for the masses, did not offer their products in plus-sizes. Yet, large-bodied teens and college students desired to wear the same fashions as their thinner friends. Plus-size professional women needed stylish careerwear. Because of the inability to find stylish fashions, larger women in many cases did not have the wardrobe they desired. Consequently, these women were often stereotyped as unattractive and lacking fashion awareness. Some believed this stereotype may be a reason why major designers disregarded the plus-size segment.

Premium Price

Because there was a significant demand combined with a limited supply of fashionable clothes in plus-sizes, prices were at a premium. It was not uncommon that a dress in a plus-size would retail at a 30 per cent price higher price than that of an identical dress in a regular size. Walker noted that women were prepared to pay this premium:

The plus-size woman is willing to pay whatever it costs to get something that she likes, something that she considers fashionable, that she looks and feels good in. Price doesn't seem to be a huge issue as it would with a thinner person who has more choices and thus can be more selective. A plus-size woman doesn't have many choices.

Nevertheless, the fashion industry was making progress in addressing the discrepancy in the marketplace. Some American retailers specializing in plus-sizes were flourishing. Lane Bryant and Avenue were well-known destinations. Department stores such as Macy's reported plus-size clothes represented a significant growth area in their fashion aisles. Designers were beginning to recognize the market gap as well. In the 1980s, Liz Claiborne was one of the first major labels to offer a line in plus-sizes which was named "Elisabeth." Since then, some other major labels have followed suit including Jones of New York, Anne Klein, Dana Buchman and Ellen Tracy. Thus, in the United States, the number of outlets for plus-sizes was increasing and the level of trendiness offered by designers was improving. Nevertheless, the discrepancy was still significant when compared to the offerings in regular sizes. This gap was believed to be more considerable in Canada.

PLUS-SIZE RETAILING IN TORONTO

Mainstream specialty chain stores primarily consisted of three players: Addition-Elle, Cotton Ginny Plus and Penningtons Superstore. Most department stores have added women's plus-size fashions to their showrooms in recent years. A few high-end independent boutiques existed as well (see Exhibit 2 for a listing of specialty retailers).

While the standard store retailed new apparel, a growing category was the consignment store which retailed used items. The consignor, a person with a used clothing item to sell, would bring the item to a consignment store to be priced and placed on display. If the item sold,

Chains

	Type	Toronto Area Locations	Categories	Pricing Position
Addition-Elle, A.E. & Co. Sport	Mall Chain	15	Casual, Business, Formal, Lingerie	Medium
Cotton Ginny Plus	Mall Chain	25	Casual	Medium
Penningtons Superstore	Plaza Chain	17	Casual, Business	Low-Medium
Laura II	Mall and Plaza	4	Casual, Business	Medium

Independent Stores

	Type	Toronto Area Locations	Categories	Pricing Position
The Answer	Independent	1	Casual, Business, Formal	Mid-Premium
Toni Plus	Small Chain	4	Casual, Business, Formal	Premium
Village Shop Plus	Independent	1	Casual, Business, Formal	Premium

Consignment Stores

	Type	Toronto Area Locations	Categories	Pricing Position
Rubenesque	Independent	1	Various	Medium

Exhibit 2   Plus-Size Specialty Retailers in Toronto as of July 2000

then the consignor would earn a proportion of the selling price—typically about half. If it did not sell, then the consignor would not earn money and she could take the clothing back.

The consignment model possessed cash flow advantages which were beneficial for small business owners. First, a store could carry thousands of dollars worth of merchandise that was entirely supplied by consignors. Second, money was owed to the consignor only after the item sold. The business had use of this money for its operations until the consignor picked up her cheque and thus, the money owing acted as an interest-free loan.

In Toronto, a local chain of four consignment stores called Ex-Toggery retailed clothing of all types for men, women and children. The growth in popularity in the 1990s of Ex-Toggery confirmed acceptance of the consignment store among mainstream shoppers. Previously, resale shops were considered places where people of lower income shopped for their needs. The stigma was lifted and the general public now shopped at resale stores for quality goods at a significant discount. While one could find some plus-size clothes at Ex-Toggery, the selection was usually very limited.

Big Time was a family-operated consignment store that had been in business for several years.

Because it was the only consignment store in Toronto that specialized in plus-sizes, it had developed a loyal clientele. Walker commented on Big Time:

> Someone told me about a plus-size consignment store in Toronto which was probably only 10 minutes away from my home. Having grown up in Toronto and being large all my life, I was quite shocked that there was such a place that I didn't know. I felt that as far as plus-size stores were concerned, I was very knowledgeable of all of the retailers. The first thing that I thought about, being in the marketing support business, was "why didn't I know about this?" Big Time had done a poor job of communicating its existence.
>
> I went in and was very disappointed. It was a mishmash of clothes with very little attention to detail. The clothing was good, but the presentation was horrible. It felt very much like a thrift store. Afterwards, I felt that this was a simple business concept that I could do much better. I thought about some of the consignment stores that I had seen in Vancouver that had a more tasteful presentation, and I decided I would start a retail business.

RUBENESQUE

In early 1997, Walker approached a friend to join her as a business partner. The two would pool their talent and resources to start the retail venture. The store was to be named Rubenesque. The term was derived from the 17th century painter, Peter Paul Rubens, who was renown for his works which often featured nude, voluptuous women. The term Rubenesque had come to describe an attractive, larger woman.

To carve its own place in the marketplace, Rubenesque would position itself as a high-end consignment store of women's plus-size fashions. The business was anticipated to be a success because it would address the three common concerns of larger women:

1. Retail Selection: Rubenesque provided a retail option that specialized in plus-sizes.

2. Style: The store would endeavor to merchandise high-quality, stylish fashions.

3. Price: Because the clothes were previously worn, they would retail for approximately half of the original price.

Staff would need to be particular about clothes that were accepted on consignment to ensure that merchandise for sale fit with the store's desired image. Clothing items would be required to be less than two years old and in mint condition. Unfortunately, some clothes would be turned away because they did not suit the store image, but the end result was an inventory of much-sought-after plus-size apparel. Walker commented on the clothing selection:

> We carry a little bit of everything, but our focus has been businesswear. It's a large ticket item. Trendy clothes, particularly those in style for the current season, are hard to find in plus-sizes and are the most desired items which move very quickly.

To further enhance this high-end consignment positioning, the store interior was designed with large, comfortable change rooms, bright lighting and elegant display fixtures. A high-traffic street-front location with nearby parking and access to major highways was secured in North Toronto. Unique shops and other consignment stores were also in the area. When Rubenesque opened, Big Time was within a 10 minute drive.

Walker discussed her vision of the store:

> I really wanted to make it appear more like a mainstream store as opposed to a consignment store. So I wanted our store displays to be neatly organized by apparel type—not just a bunch of clothes thrown on a rack. It was really important to me that customers would not come in and see a mess and spend an hour trying to find exactly what they wanted (as with most consignment stores). It could not look like a thrift store—it had to be appealing.
>
> I really wanted the store to be perceived as a new place to find trendy, fashionable clothing at reasonable prices. We also wanted to make it a nice experience for the plus-size shopper. The employees would be educated on plus-size fashions and knowledgeable about the community for the larger woman. We would have information on events in

the large-size community or on health for people with weight. The goal was to set out a size-friendly destination.

Walker felt she had put together a sound business concept. Rubenesque's focus on stylish fashions would provide a badly needed source of trendy apparel for larger women at reasonable prices. The cash flow advantages would allow Walker and her partner to create and operate a business with limited capital. Because of the resale aspect of the business, there was no major threat from any well-subsidized retail chains to enter the segment. The business was relatively easy to operate and would be run on a day-to-day basis by part-time employees. This was important since Walker and her partner each held full-time careers and Rubenesque was a side business for both of them.

For both consignors and clothing purchasers, Rubenesque would target young, middle-income businesswomen between the ages of 25 to 45. In the end, the concept of the store appealed to a broad range of women because of the lack of alternative plus-size clothing retailers.

In July 1997, Rubenesque opened its doors for the first time. Sales were initially slow but gradually grew year over the year. The business broke even in its second year and sales continued to grow 15 per cent in the third year. Over time, the store expanded its resale offerings which included casual, business and formal wear, as well as wedding gowns. In addition, the company purchased new inventories of swimwear and lingerie which were considered hard to find in plus-sizes. In 1998, Rubenesque was able to form a relationship with a wholesaler of plus-size clothing who agreed to place new clothes on consignment in the store. This provided another useful source of clothing inventory. Once the business developed a solid financial situation, management intended to examine purchasing new inventories of business and casual wear directly from manufacturers.

Shortly after the opening of Rubenesque in July 1997, Big Time, the store's sole direct competitor, announced that it would close for one week to undergo store renovations. In 1999, Big Time announced that it would be closing permanently. Rubenesque became the only player in its niche category of plus-size consignments in Toronto.

RUBENESQUE MARKETING

Because plus-size shops were scarce but in great demand, Rubenesque management decided that marketing should be about informing people that the store existed. Costs were a consideration for a small business like Rubenesque. The owners attempted to be creative within a low budget in their promotions.

Once the store was operational, Walker set out to target the local media for free publicity. Press kits were assembled and targeted at specific journalists. To the fashion and lifestyle reporters, Rubenesque was positioned as the answer to the problems faced by larger women who represented half of the population. To business reporters, Rubenesque presented an innovative small business story. In every case, Walker acted as the store spokesperson. Articles appeared in newspapers describing the need for retailers to offer plus-size apparel. One article in the fashion section of the *Toronto Star* featured Rubenesque and resulted in over 50 phone calls from excited consumers, which subsequently resulted in a sales increase. The response encouraged Walker to take out advertisements in the *Toronto Star.* Walker noted that, "Our advertising has been more focused on mainstream media." Rubenesque became a fixture in *Toronto Life Fashion Magazine*'s semi-annual listing of specialty size retailers. A press release announcing the new store was transmitted by Canada Newswire (see Exhibit 3). Some local newspapers and news services such as Reuters published the release.

From the beginning, Walker worked towards developing relationships with some of the established local journalists. She found that many reporters kept files of various contacts, and Walker would occasionally be enlisted for a quote

September 9, 1997

NO SMALL SIZES HERE - RUBENESQUE ANNOUNCES STORE OPENING

TORONTO, Ont. - Let Calvin Klein worry about dressing the Kate Moss's of the world for on September 18, resale clothing store Rubenesque celebrates the voluptuous woman with its much-anticipated grand opening.

Located at 1751 Avenue Road in the heart of Toronto's resale fashion district, Rubenesque specifically caters to women sizes 14 and up who are so often neglected by the city's mainstream clothing stores. "Fashionable clothing for the larger woman is difficult to find," explains store owner Shawnda Walker, speaking from personal experience. "While a significant part of the population is wearing plus-size apparel, the majority of retailers only provide clothes for the slim person."

However, Rubenesque provides larger women with more than just plus-size fashions at discounted prices. Recognizing that women are fashion-conscious at any size, Ms. Walker is careful to add to her collection only those pieces of the highest quality and latest style. Gone are the days of grungy cotton sweats and monochrome tees for Rubenesque carries designer labels such as Jones of New York, Louben and Brian Bailey.

Obviously not your typical consignment store, Rubenesque continues to defy categorization by acting as a one-stop clothing shop. Customers are free to choose from its assortment of dress shoes, costume jewellery and fashionable accessories that would compliment any of the store's designer outfits.

But most importantly, Rubenesque provides a comfortable atmosphere for plus-size women who often feel out-of-place in non-specialty stores and plain out-of-luck in dingy thrift shops. Along with its spacious change rooms, tasteful decor and display of informative magazines, Rubenesque offers a sense of community to its clientele of fashion-savvy plus-size women who are more concerned with competitive prices than competing with Kate Moss.

For further information, please contact: Shawnda Walker
Store Owner
Rubenesque (416) 787-8893

Rubenesque 1751 Avenue Road, Toronto, ON M5M 3Y8 (416) 787-8893

Exhibit 3   Rubenesque Grand Opening Press Release

if an article were written on specialty fashions. Walker commented on gaining media exposure:

> When we put our attention on working with the media, we often focused on the challenges of plus-size fashions since it's a very topical subject. If we have a good story idea, the media really has been supportive and willing to talk about it and work with us. They understand that a significant proportion of their readers are large-sized.

The owners were successful in organizing a plus-size fashion show for a nationally televised program on the Life Network and for a morning news and information program called Breakfast Television at a Toronto television station. Special events were held in the store including a grand opening ceremony and fashion show. A plus-size lingerie show held in advance of Valentine's Day also raised free publicity for the store— particularly by the *Toronto Sun* newspaper. Also, Walker's business partner was occasionally found handing out coupons in parking lots.

When the closure of Big Time was announced, Walker made contact with the Big Time owners and was successful in purchasing their customer mailing list. The store staff was also encouraged to ask customers to join the Rubenesque mailing list. Over 9,000 mailing addresses and 1,500 e-mail addresses of plus-size shoppers had been assembled over three years. Walker, with a graphic artist, developed professionally designed newsletters which were sent to her mailing list once a year. The newsletter included a description of the store, information on consignment, fashion tips, and a $10 coupon (see Exhibit 4 for a sample newsletter). Each quarter, Walker sent e-mail reminder messages to customers of new season merchandise and end-of-season sales.

The market need for Rubenesque was evident. Word of mouth was a significant factor in the development of new customers as women enthusiastically recommended Rubenesque to their friends. People from as far away as Windsor travelled to Toronto specifically to shop at the store. Consignment inventory was rarely in shortage as the concept proved to be an easy way for people to earn money. Many customers had earned hundreds of dollars selling their clothes at Rubenesque.

RUBENESQUE WEB SITE

Walker decided to utilize the Internet as a marketing tool. The company listed a coupon on FabulousSavings which was a Web site that offered savings at local businesses for consumers. Also, Walker was successful in listing her store on various Web sites that provided information on specialty plus-size retailers. As the Internet continued to grow and become a valuable information resource, Walker felt that it was necessary for Rubenesque to have its own Internet presence:

> We started the Web site to gain more awareness for the store. At some point, I knew we eventually wanted to startup e-commerce. But it's quite a challenge to implement e-commerce because of the time requirements.

Walker expected the Rubenesque Web site to contain information about the store as well as the consignment process. It was hoped that e-commerce would provide an additional form of revenue and allow the store to reach potential customers outside of Toronto. In many ways, Walker viewed the Web site as an extension of the store:

> When we opened the store, we were very cognizant of making the store a better shopping experience. We often used the word boutique—not only to describe the way the store looked but also its level of service. Employees knew people's names and had developed relationships with these customers. We had information to pass on about where to shop, social events and things like that. We really strived for this in the store. This is something that I really want to accomplish with the Web site. I want it to be more than just somewhere to shop but a place to get more information and resources— just as in our real store.

As Walker considered the many features that could be incorporated into the Web site, she wondered to what extent concepts of a community should be incorporated. By developing an online community, would there be an opportunity to develop customer loyalty?

Walker felt all women of size shared similar concerns. Not only did they have difficulty finding retailers who had a broad offering of stylish clothes at reasonable prices, larger women shared the pressures imposed on them by a thin-obsessesed society. Most had experienced taunting and discrimination because of their size. Over time, communities for larger people had been established and as a result, the size acceptance movement was born.

(Text continues on page 223)

Rubenesque News

PLUS SIZE FASHIONS
ON CONSIGNMENT
SIZES 14+

Fall/Winter 1999
Volume 3

Plus-Size Specialty Store Draws Customers From Across Southern Ontario

Shawnda Walker, Owner of Rubenesque

TORONTO - People from as far away as Guelph, Barrie, Oshawa and even Windsor regularly make the trek to trendy North Avenue Road to visit Rubenesque, a plus-size clothing boutique.

Located at 1751 Avenue Road between Highway 401 and Lawrence, Rubenesque has made a big splash in the retailing sector since opening its doors just over two years ago. In this short time, the store has been regularly featured on television and in major daily newspaper fashion sections.

So what draws clients from so far away to this specialty shop?

"Plus-size fashions are hard to find and quality at a good price is even harder," explains Shawnda Walker, owner of Rubenesque. "This is the rationale behind our business. As a plus-size shopper, I understand how difficult it is to be a fashionable, voluptuous woman, considering the lack of selection from the mainstream retail outlets."

Indeed the clothes are fashionable. Rubenesque specializes in high quality resale outfits that are in mint condition, yet cost almost half the price as a new item. Famous brands such as Elizabeth, Louben and Brian Bailey are among some of the more popular items that are in the store.

"We are very particular about the items that are for resale at Rubenesque," comments Walker. "We only offer clothes to our shoppers that are stylish and in nearly new condition. Unfortunately, we have to turn away items that do not meet our standards, but in the end, it's our selectivity that brings people back to the store."

In fact, the sales from Rubenesque has netted some customers thousands of dollars in spending money, in exchange for placing their plus-size fashions for sale in the store. Walker sees it as a "win-win" situation.

"On the one hand, we have a client who walks away with some extra cash, while on the other, we have another client who has purchased a quality outfit at a discount."

The offerings are diverse. The selection ranges from casual wear, to business suits, to formal gowns and even hard-to-find plus-size wedding dresses. To meet the growing demand from shoppers, Rubenesque has further expanded beyond its resale roots by also offering brand new end-of-line fashions, swimwear by Christina and sexy lingerie.

Thanks to Rubenesque, today's B.B.W. (Big and Beautiful Woman) can dress stylishly without paying the premium normally associated with plus-size clothes. In fact, most out-of-town customers declare that it's worth the drive to Toronto!

How to get to Rubenesque:
North of St. Germain on the east side of Avenue Rd.

STORE HOURS

Mon. – Wed. . . . . . .10 a.m. – 6 p.m.

Thur. . . . . .10 a.m. – 8 p.m.

Fri. . . . . .10 a.m. – 6 p.m.

Sat. . . . . .10 a.m. – 6 p.m.

CONTENTS

Fabulous Reading 2
Consignment Policy 2
Letter from the Owner 3
Suiting Up 3
Diana Rojas 4

Rubenesque, 1751 Avenue Road, Toronto, Ontario, M5M 3Y8, (416) 787-8893

Exhibit 4   Rubenesque Newsletter—1999

(Continued)

Fabulous Reading...

Over the last few months, a number of fabulous books have been released that relate to women of size and their stories. Here are a few reviews:

Wake Up, I'm Fat! *Camryn Manheim*

FEATURE BOOK

"Emmy Award-winning actor Camryn Manheim is a Goddess! She shares with us a painfully honest account of growing up as an outcast fat girl in our obsessed society. The first biography I've read that I could completely relate to. A refreshingly funny and inspiring read."

"A wonderful book. Cheerful, engaging, honest, funny, and (of course) confrontational. It will make you feel better no matter what your size. Our society's bigotry against fat doesn't do anyone any good, with the possible exception of the diet and 'health' club industries."

"This book is never boring; I read it in one and a half sittings, and it would have been one if I could have possibly found the time. I felt grief at her sorrows, anger at her injustices, and elation at her well deserved success. A wonderful story with a happy ending that anyone with a shred of open-mindedness will enjoy."

Sexy at Any Size *Katie Arons*

"Sing it sister Arons! Go yell it from the mountain tops, your wise message of personal acceptance. I would like to hug this author. After reading this fabulous book I felt wonderful. Ms. Arons follows in the footsteps of Delta Burke's "Delta Style" and Teri Poulton's "No Fat Chicks" in teaching plus-size women how to love themselves. She doesn't preach or condemn because she's been there. Buy the book and learn how to love yourself at any size. This is a must read, and not only for the larger women but for their loved ones."

Rubenesque Consignment Policy

- The selling price is discounted according to the following schedule:

Season	Accepting	25% Discount	50% Discount	Pick-Up Date
Winter	Nov. - Jan.	Jan. 1	Feb. 1	Mar. 1 - 15
Spring	Feb. - April	April 1	May 1	June 1 -15
Summer	May - July	July 1	Aug. 1	Sept. 1 - 15
Fall	Aug. - Oct.	Oct. 1	Nov. 1	Dec. 1- 15

- All merchandise brought in on consignment must be less then 3 years old, freshly laundered and in an almost new condition.

- Your account will be credited 45% of the selling price, once the article has been sold.

- All monies owing from the sale of merchandise can be claimed 7 days after the sale of the item. It is your responsibility to call in or drop by to check the status of your account.

- You may pick up monies owed to you anytime. Please feel free to call us prior to coming if you wish to check your account balance.

Exhibit 4   Rubenesque Newsletter—1999   *(Continued)*

LETTER FROM THE OWNER

Wow ... it is hard to believe that as I write this we are well into our third year of business! Where does the time go?

Well, this year has brought on lots of change for us. We have expanded our line of new clothing, started to manufacture a few basics and are hoping to launch a web site by the end of this year. Another event that has, and in the future will, certainly impact our business is the closing of Big Time. This store has been a long time friend to the plus-sized female. It provided a fabulous outlet for women to not only find clothing but also to sell items that they no longer had a need for! We are sorry to see our friendly competitors go, but we welcome all the new consignors and shoppers.

We are accepting fall clothing and I am very excited about what I have seen coming in over the past few short weeks! Lots of business wear ... and the labels! Jones, Della Spiga, Ellen Tracy, Elizabeth, Dana Buchman, Brian Bailey ... the list is endless, I have had a hard time holding myself back (so, maybe I have purchased a thing or three!).

As always, I encourage you to let me know what you think of the store or any great ideas that you may have. I can be reached by e-mail at shawnda@total.net or by calling the store at 416-787-8893. I look forward to hearing from you.

Shawnda

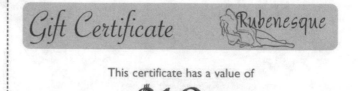
suiting up

Even though many offices today are going business casual, there is nothing more essential to the business woman than her "power" suit. But, there is more to that suit than its incredible colour, its notable label or its luxurious fabric.

Suits show their best when they are on the body type that is meant for them. Just like our bodies, suits come in all shapes and sizes. The new longer jackets that were introduced last year are out in full force this season, giving a full waisted woman a shapely silhouette. And, when it buttons higher and slightly flares at the bottom, it covers a multiple of sins around the middle section. This jacket looks great with a long straight skirt and even better with a straight legged pant paired with a pair of fashionable boots.

Petite women are being told to throw out all the rules this fall. Lengthen your skirts to the mid calf, add a pair of heels for a longer look. Pair this with a mid-thigh jacket to elongate the look. Choose a jacket with smaller lapels and a flat front to compliment your petite frame. A jacket that buttons higher will equalize a well endowed woman and help balance out broad shoulders.

Hour glass figures can indulge in a double breasted jacket that have buttons set close to the breast to draw the eye in. Wide lapels enhance your shoulders.

If you are unsure of your body type or if you want an expert opinion regarding what type of suit will "suit" you, come into Rubenesque and our staff will be more then happy to help you. There are many different types of suits in store waiting to dress you up!

3

Exhibit 4 Rubenesque Newsletter—1999 *(Continued)*

DIANA ROJAS

plus-sized custom designs

Rubenesque is excited to announce that Diana Rojas has joined us as our in-house designer! She will be designing custom made garments and wedding gowns exclusively for Rubenesque.

The Diana Rojas Plus-Size Collection is a culmination of her ten years of design experience creating plus-size garments. Her commitment to carefully customed pieces that embrace full figured bodies with comfort and beauty is a new approach to plus size dressing.

Diana's designs target the full figured woman who is looking for more "zing" in her wardrobe. She draws inspiration from trendy European fashions for regular sizes.

Diana has created unique separates that are a welcome and versatile update to every full figured woman's wardrobe.

Her design philosophy is lifestyle rather than age, size or profession. She designs for the full figured woman who appreciates the finer things in life and can afford to indulge in clothes that reflect her lifestyle and her personality.

The styling of each piece is distinctly Diana Rojas. To book an appointment please call Rubenesque at (416) 787-8893, or drop by the store to see her portfolio at 1751 Avenue Road in Toronto.

Exhibit 4   Rubenesque Newsletter—1999

SIZE ACCEPTANCE MOVEMENT

The purpose of the size acceptance movement was to provide equal opportunity for "fat" people wherever obstacles or discrimination existed. For example, "fat" people were discriminated against in employment, education, access to public transportations, and access to adequate medical care. Further, they were stigmatized for their size. Walker commented, "People do not respect the fact that large people get hurt by snide remarks. It's hard dealing with day-to-day issues relating to their size." Non-profit human rights organizations, such as NAAFA, the National Association to Advance Fat Acceptance, were formed to address these issues. To achieve its goals, NAAFA utilized public campaigns, legislative processes and education to combat discrimination and to dispel stereotypes. It was a significant political voice and held conventions throughout the United States. The International Size Acceptance Association was another well-organized network.

To illustrate the magnitude of the "fatphobia," a 1999 study of British and Canadian female smokers aged 11 to 18 found that most of them, despite knowing the health hazards, smoked to curb their appetites to stay thin.[3]

A common stereotype was that "fat" people were at fault for their size. In fact, one's larger size was often a product of genetic anatomy and a history of "yo-yo" dieting.[4] Another misconception was that fat was perceived to signify poor health. Research showed that 95 per cent to 98 per cent of all diets failed, and that health risks were not due to weight itself but actually attributable to yo-yo dieting. People of size who exercised and ate sensibly could live very healthily. Thus, size acceptance attempted to communicate the realities associated with larger size.

COMMUNITIES AND RESOURCES FOR LARGER WOMEN

As awareness of the challenges of living with a large body became more prevalent, thanks to celebrities such as Oprah Winfrey, numerous businesses and organizations had formed to serve larger women. A small but growing number of companies were selling plus-size apparel online (e.g., www.alight.com). Plus-size fashion magazines, particularly *Mode Magazine,* depicted women in more average sizes and provided fashion tips specifically for plus-size consumers.

Most major cities in North America had social and dating organizations that held events for BBWs (Big, Beautiful Woman) and their admirers. Probably the most famous was a nightclub called Goddesses located in New York City. The Internet had provided many opportunities for people to meet and date. There were numerous community Web sites and chat rooms on MSN and Yahoo as well as various BBW chat rooms on Internet Relay Chat[5] (e.g., #BBW-CANADA on the DAL Network). Walker provided her observations on the social aspect of the Internet:

> There is a large dating scene online. There are women who go there who know they are going to find men who are attracted to larger women. Some of these groups even get together and have social events.

The Internet had also served as a central means for larger women to connect. Chat rooms

and bulletin boards allowed women of size to meet and discuss size-related issues. Also, there were numerous informational Web sites where women could learn to live healthily with their weight or to obtain fashion tips (e.g., www.plusstop.com, www.sizewise.com, www.onlyreal.com). Walker noted:

> It has really opened up a forum for large people to group together. I think the attraction, first and foremost, is that they can get together and talk with people who will not discriminate. I've heard many people say that they believe size discrimination is the last acceptable form of discrimination in society today. So I think that a lot of people join these groups simply for acceptance, to be in a comfortable environment online.

> They will get together to talk about the challenges facing the large-size person whether it be personal, in the workplace, or in their family. They discuss different things that they would come across in their day-to-day lives that they want to share with someone who really understands.

Walker wondered if there was an opportunity for Rubenesque to tap into these networks to increase its presence or even to form its own community. Walker's personal discussions with other large women, including store customers, led her to believe that most women were not aware that such services or networks existed.

RUBENESQUE ONLINE COMMUNITY

Shawnda Walker believed that her customers had a deep appreciation for Rubenesque because it was one of the few businesses serving their segment. Further, the business had been operated by treating customers with respect and with an understanding of the issues relating to size and fashion. Her goal was to cultivate this sort of loyalty on the Web site too. Walker recognized some of the challenges:

> I would love for our store to become a wonderful resource within the plus-size community. Realistically, it is going to be very difficult considering the

lack of time commitment that I and my partner can devote to managing a community. The commitment would have to be so much larger on my part because of my understanding as a plus-size woman and as the store's spokesperson.

In addition, the business had limited funds and thus, could not afford to develop an elaborate Web site since much of the budget was reserved for the development of the e-commerce site.

Walker pondered whether an online community would make sense for the Rubenesque Web site.

NOTES

1. "Segmenting the plus-size market," *Marketing to Women,* Volume 13, Issue 10, p. 10; Oct 2000, Anonymous.

2. Ibid.

3. "Two views on fat acceptance: hip to be hippy?," Lynn Welburn, *Flare,* v.21(4), April 1999, pg. 79–80.

4. "Yo-Yo" dieting was the phenomenon whereby people repeatedly, but temporarily, lost weight through unsuccessful diets.

5. Internet Relay Chat (IRC) consists of networks that allow people to communicate in real time with others around the world. For more information, see htttp://www.irchelp.org.

GROWTH, STRATEGY AND SLOTTING AT NO PUDGE! FOODS, INC.

Prepared by Professor Chris Robertson

Copyright © 2003, Northeastern University, College of Business Administration   Version: (A) 2003-07-28

Call us skeptics, but we didn't believe homemade fat-free brownies could match the addictive flavor of the gooey, traditional kind. That was before we tried moist and fudgy No Pudge! Brownie Mix.

—Fitness Magazine

Lindsay Frucci was at a crossroads. Her seven-year-old fat-free brownie mix company, No Pudge! Foods, Inc. (No Pudge!), was just starting to take off, and she was considering a number of options for the future. She was seriously thinking about expanding into fat-free muffin mix. This would break tradition from her narrow, but strong, line of four fat-free brownie mix flavors. She also had an opportunity to develop a ready-made fat-free brownie for fast-food franchises such as Subway. Yet there was still plenty of unfinished business in the brownie world. The

U.S. Midwest and Southeast looked extremely promising. Perhaps going international was another viable, yet complicated, option.

THE BIRTH OF THE FAT-FREE BROWNIE MIX

In January of 1995, a New Hampshire brownie-aholic with minimal business experience decided to start a company that would revolutionize the brownie world. Although Lindsay Frucci had tasted various fat-free style brownies in the past, she was enormously displeased with the bland, at best, taste. After a month or so of whipping up experimental batches of different fat-free brownie mixes, she finally came up with a mix that was fudgy, chewy and delicious: everything that a brownie lover looks for in a brownie, but with *no fat.* With the recipe intact, and validated by friends, relatives and the local community, Frucci sailed forward into uncharted waters. Her mission: to take these tasty treats to the general public. Specifically, she wanted to target, "upscale, educated consumers, primarily females between the ages of 20 and 60." Her instinct was to initially go after health-conscious people who wanted to minimize the fat intake in their diets.

Fortunately, while seeking help from a local SCORE[1] (Service Corps of Retired Executives) office, she connected with some key people who would guide her through the arduous process of establishing a viable business and getting her product onto supermarket shelves. Jay Albert, a retired chief executive officer (CEO) of Blanchard and Blanchard (a condiment producer) in Vermont, and Bob Fox, the former associate chief counsel of General Foods, walked Frucci through the multitude of decisions that had to be made to get the firm up and running. Stuart Pompian, a retired venture capitalist, jumped in to carry No Pudge! to the next level. All of the time and effort of these retired executives was complimentary, and none received compensation from No Pudge!

Finally, in August of 1995, the first bags of the No Pudge! Original Fudge Brownie Mix hit the shelves of a few local New Hampshire stores. Less than seven years later, No Pudge! Foods, Inc. offered four different mixes in 48 states (all but Alaska and Hawaii) and Canada (see Exhibit 1 for media quotes about No Pudge!).

GROWING PAINS

In 1995, revenues at No Pudge! totaled a mere $6,000.[2] After experimenting with a number of alternative brownie mix flavors, and testing them out on a local mothers' ski group, Frucci decided to introduce the cappuccino- and raspberry-flavored mixes in March of 1996. Gradually, 1996 sales climbed to $42,000, though a profit had yet to be seen. In 1997, Frucci decided that she must be more aggressive if this venture were to survive. She pursued distribution at a fervent pace. Her efforts paid off, and Trader Joe's Company, a successful national supermarket chain with close to $2 billion in sales, agreed to put No Pudge! products on the shelf. As a result, 1997 sales jumped to $250,000. The mint-flavored mix was also introduced in 1997.

In 1998 and 1999, growth was steady, due to the addition of two distributors, with sales of $325,000 and $450,000 respectively. No Pudge! products were gradually finding their way onto more supermarket shelves. By the end of 1999, No Pudge! was offered by three distributors and was on numerous store shelves in eight states. Despite the positive trend, No Pudge! was still financially teetering between the red and the black. Production costs were extremely high, and margins were slim. Frucci was quickly finding out that the only way to turn a solid profit was to increase revenues substantially.

In January of 2000, Frucci decided to attend the National Food Distributors Association annual meeting and present her product to numerous national distributors. Her efforts paid off. In the next year, an additional 23 distributors agreed to sign on and offer No Pudge! products. Revenues in 2000 blossomed about 70 per cent to $750,000, and then rose to $1.5 million in 2001. A slim profit was finally realized in 2001. By April of 2002, sales were well ahead of the prior year, and if the trend continued, Frucci expected between $2.3 million and $2.5 million for the year.

OPERATIONS AND STRATEGY

Staffing was a concern for No Pudge!, as the growth projections came in. Initially, the firm was a one-woman show, with Frucci working out of her home in Hopkinton, New Hampshire. Manufacturing was outsourced from the beginning by using a "co-packer," Concord Foods (Concord) of Brockton, Massachusetts. Concord managed the entire manufacturing process and shipped orders directly to distributors nationwide. Supermarkets and specialty stores then placed their orders with their local distributor. This left Frucci primarily with sales, strategy,

"... all you add to this No Pudge! mix is vanilla yogurt. The best part of the quick and easy process is a fudgy, chewy brownie that has only 90 calories."

Muscle & Fitness Magazine

"Very satisfying."

Good Morning America

"Love the taste of brownies but hate the fat? We recommend No Pudge! Fudge brownie mix."

Self Magazine

"The Brownie of Your Dreams"

Weight Watchers Magazine

"... simply combine the mix with fat-free yogurt, and the end result is thick, moist and truly delicious brownies."

Chocolatier Magazine

"My expectations were low, I must admit. . . . I was surprised at seeing an end product closely resembling the full-fat versions. . . . In my book, they were a winner."

Kankakee Daily Journal

"No Pudge! Brownies, the best fat-free treat we've ever tasted."

Teen Magazine

"But the ease of preparation is second to the wonderful smell as the brownies bake, and their rich, moist, hard-to-believe-they're-not-sinful taste and texture"

Boston Sunday Globe

"You have to try this product. . . . I'm telling you, these are good."

Hartford Courant

"While fat-free brownies may seem like the ultimate oxymoron, skeptics beware: No Pudge! makes a thick, tender, fudgy brownie that can stand up proudly and be judged with its peers."

Boston Globe Food Section

"... thick, rich, chewy brownies. With just 100 calories each and no fat, preservatives or artificial ingredients, this dessert definitely qualifies as spa cuisine."

Spa Magazine

Exhibit 1   Quotes From the Media About No Pudge! Fat-Free Fudge Brownie Mix

---

marketing and financial duties. A bookkeeper was hired in 1996, and by 2002, the headquarters staff, including Frucci, totaled a mere four employees: three full-time and one part time. With continued growth, staffing changes would clearly be necessary.

Ninety-two per cent of sales were realized through the strong distributor network. The remaining eight per cent were essentially online orders placed through the NoPudge.com Web site. Frucci also chose to outsource the bulk of the work related to online orders. An answering service in New Hampshire took down the orders and passed the requests on to No Pudge! No Pudge! staffers then processed credit card authorizations and forwarded all orders to a fulfillment house in Connecticut that managed all distribution and delivery.

The original mix accounted for roughly 65 per cent of sales, with the remaining 35 per cent spread somewhat equally across the cappuccino-, raspberry- and mint-flavored mixes. Direct competition in the fat-free brownie mix category for No Pudge! was virtually nonexistent. While major producers such as Betty Crocker and Duncan Hines offered reduced-fat mixes (with five grams of fat), the only other totally fat-free mix was Krusteaz. The uniqueness for No Pudge! was in the just-add-yogurt concept. The distinctively styled No Pudge! box (see Exhibits 2 and 3) also differentiated the product from other mass-produced, generic-style mixes. From a price-point perspective No Pudge! products were usually offered at retail stores in the $2.99 to $3.79 range, which was about $1.00 over the standard price for the reduced-fat mixes.[3]

Frucci believed that online consumers could be extremely helpful in her "guerilla marketing" campaign. Along with every order, she also sent a 50 cent coupon and a "SIRF." A SIRF was a "special item request form" that No Pudge! advocates could deliver to their local grocer if the product was not on the shelf (see Exhibit 4). If enough SIRFs ended up on a store manager's desk, there was a good chance that an order would be placed for the requested item. Frucci went a step further than other SIRF users by listing all of her distributors on the back of the card. This made it much easier for the grocer to identify where to place the order. SIRFs were enormously helpful in No Pudge!'s rapid geographic expansion.

While Frucci's primary target market was the health-conscious consumer, she also targeted overweight individuals, specifically weight-loss groups. According to some experts, more than 40 million U.S. adults were more than 20 per cent above their desired weight.[4] While there were strict laws about sending promotions and samples to groups such as Weight Watchers, Frucci found out that if members or instructors initiated a request, then it could be fulfilled. The use of SIRFs helped stimulate interest and requests from weight-loss groups.

THE SLOTTING BLUES

One barrier to entry that Frucci continued to wrestle with was the industry norm of charging slotting fees in exchange for shelf space. This was a clever, profitable method for retailers to put new products on the shelf at no cost. It took the financial risk out of new product offerings for retailers. Slotting occurred in two forms: direct cash disbursements and free fill.

Generally, cash slotting fees ranged from $2,500 to $25,000 per new item. With all of the large supermarket chains, a slotting fee was a given (see Table 1 for a list of the top 20 U.S. supermarkets). This made obtaining shelf space extremely difficult and costly for small firms like No Pudge! Nevertheless, No Pudge! managed to gain entry into 16 of the top 20 chains. Big-time manufacturers such as Kellogg and Kraft spent close to 14 per cent of their revenues on various shelf-space costs. A 2001 accounting adjustment by Kellogg for shelf-space costs totaled $1.3 billion.[5]

Free fill was a request for a free shipment of the first order per store in order to earn the right to shelf space. Major chains such as Stop and Shop had 300 stores, which made free fill, *at each store,* incredibly costly. In 2002, the U.S. government and Federal Trade Commission had begun an investigation into whether paying for shelf space was anticompetitive.[6]

When first confronted with the slotting issue, Frucci knew that there was no way her firm could survive if she agreed to play by industry rules. Eventually, she came up with a barrage of arguments that she presented to retailers: first, her product was unique; second, No Pudge! was a small firm and if it paid slotting fees, there would be no money left for coupons or demos; third, No Pudge! was a Certified Woman Owned Company (by the Women's Business Enterprise National Council). In addition to these arguments she still had flocks of No Pudge! fanatics delivering their SIRFs to store managers.

Her hardball tactics paid off, and she avoided paying slotting fees. The only free fill she agreed to deliver was for new store openings. Nevertheless, retailers found other ways to dip into No Pudge!'s profits through charge-backs for advertising, reclamations (the return of damaged

Exhibit 2   Print Advertising

Source: Company files.

NO PUDGE! Fat Free Fudge Brownie Mixes are the only brownie mixes that make rich, fudgy REAL brownies with NO FAT. Our mixes are made from the finest natural ingredients using no artificial flavors, colors or preservatives, are low in sodium and contain no cholesterol. They are unique in that the only ingredient that the consumer adds to the mix to make the brownies is fat free vanilla or french vanilla yogurt. This provides a significant benefit to the consumer because they are adding a healthy, natural ingredient that they can feel good about. This is a significant benefit for the retailer as well because for every bag of mix that a consumer buys, they buy a container of yogurt as well. But the very best thing about NO PUDGE! Fat Free Fudge Brownies is the remarkable taste and texture. Weight Watchers Magazine told their readers that our mixes make "The Brownie of Your Dreams" and TEEN Magazine called them the "Best fat free treat we've ever tasted".

BROWNIES WITHOUT GUILT!!
Don't you love it?!

Original Fudge Brownie Mix makes traditional thick, fudgy brownies. Great for folks who don't want anything but a rich, all-chocolate taste.
Raspberry Fudge Brownie Mix captures that delectable combination of sweet, juicy raspberries and dark, fudgy chocolate. A treat that, quite simply, is not to be missed!
Cappuccino Fudge Brownie Mix combines our trademark rich, fudgy chocolate with real Brazilian Dark Roast coffee and a hint of all natural sweet vanilla. A coffee and chocolate lover's dream!
Mint Fudge Brownie Mix combines the dark, fudgy decadent chocolate of our Original Fudge Brownie with the mouth tingling zing of mint. If you like chocolate and mint you are going to LOVE these brownies!!

PRODUCT DESCRIPTION	UPC		
		Unit Size: 13.7 oz	
Original Fudge Brownie Mix	7 08758 00101 9	**Unit Dimensions:**	3.5" × 2.5"w × 7.5"h
Raspberry Fudge Brownie Mix	7 08758 00102 6	**Case Dimensions:**	7.25" × 7.75"w × 7.7"h
Cappuccino Fudge Brownie Mix	7 08758 00103 3	**Case Pack:** 6	**Case Weight:** 6 lb
Mint Fudge Brownie Mix	7 08758 00104 0	**Case Cube:** .25	

NO PUDGE! FOODS, Inc.
159 Clarke Lane   Hopkinton, NH 03229-2027   1-900-730-7547   Fax 1-800-730-1726
E-mail: lindsay@nopudge.com   www.nopudge.com

Exhibit 3   Product Descriptions

Source: Company files.

No Pudge! Foods, Inc.
Fat Free Fudge Brownie Mixes

SPECIAL ITEM REQUEST FORM

To the Store Manager:
As a regular customer of your store I would like to ask you to stock No Pudge! Fat Free Brownie Mixes. Please see the back of this paper for a list of distributors that stock No Pudge!. Thank You!!

Your Name: _____

City: _____   Zip: _____

Phone: _____

Date: _____

Store Name/Location _____

Associated Buyers	Kehe
Blooming Prairie	Lomar
Davidson	Millbrook
DPI-Colorado	Nikol Foods
European Imports	Northeast Coop
GAF - Great Lakes	Peter's Imports
GAF - Mid Atlantic	Peyton
GAF - North Central	Tree of Life MW
GAF - Southeast	Tree of Life/GAF N. Calif.
GAF - Southern California	Tree of Life NE
GAF - South Florida	Tree of Life SE
Gourmet Specialties/UWG	Tree of Life SW
Haddon House	Tumbleweed
Hannaford/Progressive	UNFI

Exhibit 4   Special Item Request Form (SIRF)
Source: Company files.

goods) and broker-paid commissions on net invoices. She felt lucky to survive in such a hostile environment for small businesses. As her firm continued to grow, the pressure to pay slotting fees also began to increase dramatically.

LOOKING AHEAD

As Frucci considered the many options for No Pudge!'s future, she kept thinking about her target of $15 million in revenues. If she were able to grow the firm to that level, then she would seriously consider selling the firm to one of the major food purveyors such as Kraft. The big question was how could No Pudge! grow that much more without further product extension and new product development? The opportunity to make ready-mix fat-free brownies for a franchise like Subway could produce a huge jolt in revenues. She had already developed fat-free muffin mixes in four flavors (corn, bran, lemon poppy and banana) that could make it to the market by late 2002.

Table 1 The Top 20 U.S. Supermarket Chains

		Sales ($mil)	Stores	NP	Headquarters
1	The Kroger Co.	50,098	3,600	Y	Cincinnati, OH
2	Albertson's, Inc.	36,762	2,400	Y	Boise, ID
3	Safeway Inc.	34,301	1,770	N	San Francisco, CA
4	Ahold USA, Inc.	27,023	1,475	Y	Chantilly, VA
5	IGA, INC.	21,000	4,000	Y	Chicago, IL
6	Publix Super Markets, Inc.	15,370	700	Y	Lakeland, FL
7	Delhaize America, Inc.	14,913	1,200	N	Salisbury, NC
8	Fred Meyer, Inc.	14,878	1,300	Y	Portland, OR
9	Winn-Dixie Stores, Inc.	12,903	1,150	Y	Jacksonville, FL
10	The Great Atlantic & Pacific Tea Company, Inc.	10,973	750	Y	Montvale, NJ
11	Meijer, Inc.	10,000	150	Y	Grand Rapids, MI
12	H. E. Butt Grocery Company	8,965	295	Y	San Antonio, TX
13	The Stop & Shop Companies, Inc.	7,748	300	Y	Quincy, MA
14	Ralph's Grocery Company	5,487	450	Y	Compton, CA
15	The Vons Companies, Inc.	5,407	330	Y	Arcadia, CA
16	Giant Food Inc.	4,780	180	N	Landover, MD
17	Giant Eagle Inc.	4,435	145	Y	Pittsburgh, PA
18	Shaw's Supermarkets, Inc.	4,100	185	Y	West Bridgewater, MA
19	Pathmark Stores, Inc.	3,963	140	N	Carteret, NJ
20	Hy-Vee, Inc.	3,900	210	Y	West Des Moines, IL

Source: www.hoovers.com.

NP = Chains that sell No Pudge! Products.

Table 2 Regional Breakout of 2001 Sales

Region	% of Sales
Northeast	46.82
Southeast	10.65
Midwest	15.76
Southwest	3.91
West	21.13
Canada	1.73

Geographically, No Pudge! sales were still lagging in various regions of the United States, and more work was needed in those areas to bolster sales (see Table 2). Although she had only just begun to explore expansion to Canada, she recognized that this would be a venerable entrance into international trade. Going international would require additional staffing as well, but might enhance No Pudge!'s perception as a potential acquisition target. All of these options looked viable, and Frucci realized that she needed to maintain a consistent standard, no matter how difficult, with regards to securing shelf space, if her firm were to survive.

NOTES

1. SCORE is a division of the U.S. Small Business Administration.

2. All financial figures are approximate and based on interviews with L. Frucci.

3. Typically, distributors added on a 27 per cent markup, and retail stores added a markup between 25 and 40 per cent.

4. Obesity: The World's Oldest Metabolic Disorder, by Michael Blumenkrantz, M.D. http://www.quantumhcp.com/obesity.htm

5. Julie Forster, "The Hidden Cost of Shelf Space," *Business Week*, April 15, 2002, p. 103

6. Ibid.

ENGLISH CENTER FOR NEWCOMERS

*Prepared by Ewa Borzecka under
the supervision of Elizabeth M.A. Grasby*

Version: (A) 1999-09-29

"One more exam and I'm done! I can hardly wait to start setting up my business," Dona Ronaldson, an English major at Baruch College, New York, U.S.A., exclaimed. In order to enhance her skills, she had enrolled also in a business course and on graduation, she was planning to turn her knowledge of English and business into a profitable operation.

Ronaldson had done extensive market research in preparation for opening her own school of English in New York City. She wanted to at least break even in the first year and achieve a small profit of $10,000 to $20,000 in the second year. However, she wondered whether her project was feasible and her goals realistic. If she decided to go ahead, she had to act quickly in order to have her English Center for Newcomers ready for September 1998.

THE STUDENTS

Ronaldson had identified four major student group markets: immigrants to the United States, refugees, foreign visa students, and local youth.

Immigrants

The first student group was immigrants. To improve their current employment situation, they took English as a Second Language (ESL) courses at different levels of difficulty, depending on their English language proficiency. Immigrants with good writing skills but limited ability to speak English took courses focusing on spoken English, while others who could speak English well but had trouble with writing, sought written English courses. However, most immigrants, particularly those at the beginner and intermediate levels, needed both of the spoken and written English skills that were taught in a typical ESL course. Immigrants close to and at advanced levels were occasionally interested in specialized ESL courses related to their professions. Most immigrants took ESL courses to increase their chances of employment, to improve their current employment situation, or just to "get started" in a new country. They relied on recommendations from others, and shopped around looking for bargains and a class schedule outside of work hours. They appreciated getting advice (for example, on legal matters) and help with translating their documents.

Refugees

There was also a segment comprising refugees (people forced to flee their homeland—usually due to political persecution). Their language needs were similar to those of immigrants; however, their education was usually paid for by the U.S. government once they had been granted refugee status.

Foreign Visa Students

Foreign visa students came to the U.S. on student visas arranged from their home country or they applied for a student visa after arriving in the U.S. To attract these students, some schools offered help with obtaining a student visa. Depending on their proficiency, foreign visa students took different ESL courses as well as English courses, such as American literature, history, and culture. Sometimes, taking classes at an English school was their first step before attending an American college or university.

Local Youth

The fourth student group was made up of local youth who needed remedial ESL and/or English courses in order to get accepted to a college or university or for advancement.

Since the immigrant segment was the largest and, therefore, most attractive of the four groups, Ronaldson further researched this segment and its related issues.

THE U.S. IMMIGRATION POLICY

In general, there were two groups of immigrants: legal and illegal. The former encompassed the newcomers to the country, whose status as immigrants was sanctioned by a legal process before or after their arrival in the U.S., and who, therefore, had the right to remain in the country.[1] Between 1981 and 1993, most immigrants came from countries in North-Central America (many from Mexico and the Caribbean), and a smaller number came from Asia. However, the statistics were reversed in the mid-1990s when Asia (headed by the Philippines, Vietnam, China, and India) contributed 37 per cent of the total legal immigration to the U.S., followed by North-Central America (32 per cent), Europe (18 per cent), South America (six per cent), and Africa (less than six per cent).[2]

Illegal immigrants were people who remained in the country illegally according to the U.S. laws. This included those who stayed beyond the visiting dates on their visas or who crossed the U.S. border illegally. In 1997, it was estimated that there were five million undocumented immigrants living in the U.S.[3]

Over the past decade, the Congress of the United States had sharply reduced its federal aid to immigrants, pushing the costs of supporting legal immigrants more and more onto the individual states. In 1996, the U.S. government increased the number of guards on the U.S. borders, tightened asylum rules and made it tougher for illegal immigrants to become legal. At the same time, the numbers of immigrants had risen to their highest levels in American history.[4] The foreign-born population of the U.S. had been steadily rising, reaching 24.5 million in 1996. In 1997, 9.5 per cent of all U.S. inhabitants were born outside the United States. Two states had the highest immigrant population: 25 per cent of Californians were born outside the U.S. (in Los Angeles, this figure was close to 40 per cent), while 16 per cent of the New York state population was foreign-born (33 per cent in New York City[5]).

In the mid-1990s, public polls indicated rising hostility by Americans towards immigrants in the U.S. The earlier consensus that immigrants provided a source of hard-working, cheap labor had eroded and many Americans believed that even legal immigration should be reduced.

THE NEW YORK CITY MARKET

New York City, known as "the big apple," was one of the most robust American cities. It was made up of five distinct divisions known as boroughs, only one of which—The Bronx—was situated on the North American continent. The island of Manhattan was the central borough whereas Brooklyn (largest in population) and Queens (largest in area) were located in the western part of Long Island (which itself stretched miles into the Atlantic). These four boroughs were well connected by the local transit system of subway and bus lines. The fifth borough was Staten Island situated near the state of New Jersey. Every year, New York City attracted thousands of tourists, as well as immigrants, from all over the world. Most visitors to New York were struck by its extremes of wealth on the one hand, and poverty on the other.

Nearly 15 per cent of the U.S. immigration influx in both the 1980s and early 1990s was to New York City. During 1990 to 1994, 563,000 legal immigrants settled in the City, representing an annual average of 112,600 (compared to some 86,000 per year in the 1980s) immigrants. The majority of immigrants were from the Caribbean, followed by the former Soviet Union, and then China. Thirty-five per cent of all immigrants to New York City in the 1990 to 1994 period settled in Brooklyn, with another 30 per cent settling in Queens, 20 per cent in Manhattan, 14 per cent in the Bronx, and two per cent in Staten Island. The greatest increase in immigration during this period was observed in Washington Heights and Chinatown and vicinity in Manhattan, and Gravesend–Homecrest in Brooklyn.[6] Recent immigrants to New York were much younger than the general population, the median age being 27 years, compared to 34 years for the general population. (See Exhibit 1.)

THE ENGLISH CENTER MARKET

Ronaldson decided to concentrate on three boroughs: Brooklyn, Manhattan, and Queens (Exhibit 2). She considered the Bronx dangerous and, although the Bronx represented over 16 per cent of New York's total population in 1990, its foreign-born population made up only 13 per cent of New York's foreign-born inhabitants.[7] She deemed Staten Island's socioeconomic and demographic data unsuitable.

Although the number of vehicles per household had increased over the years, Ronaldson knew there were still many families with no car, especially in Manhattan where there was an excellent transit system. She realized that accessibility to a good transit system would be one of the factors affecting her choice of the location for the center.

THE COMPETITION/OTHER ENGLISH CENTERS

English centers were numerous in the three boroughs. Although some centers exited the market from time to time, the overall number of centers had been growing and no single center dominated the market.

The English Language Institute Inc.

The English Language Institute, Inc., located in Manhattan, was the least typical of the schools because of its unique strategy. It targeted immigrants, refugees, students, business people, and visitors. The school had operated since the early 1960s, offering training in both ESL and American culture and literature, in an informal and relaxed setting. Participation in classes depended on two kinds of basic memberships: a six-month basic membership, which cost $125, and a 12-month for $150.[8] The basic membership entitled students to attend any of the forty-two English group classes taught by a volunteer instructor, under the supervision of an ESL teacher (Exhibit 3). Although classes were taught at three different levels of difficulty (high beginner, intermediate, and advanced), most group classes were open to all members on a walk-in basis. The group size was limited to the number of seats in the classroom. The 12-month membership entitled students to purchase additional one-to-one programs: a 16-hour conversation partnership (one hour per week for 16 weeks) cost $80, 32 hours of grammar lessons cost $160, and a 12-hour mentoring program was $80; the cost of materials was included in the fee. Student-members had access to a library, listening lab, and a lounge, as well as to a resource center providing information and referrals for jobs, housing, and college application. The English Language Institute, Inc. organized workshops (topics included job-search techniques, computer skills development, and immigration issues), social and cultural events (holiday celebrations and international festivals featuring food, dance, and music from around the world), forum discussions, trips and tours, and more.

International Schools

The International Schools in New York was located in Manhattan close to the United Nations building. The International Schools in New York offered ten levels of ESL, from basic to the most advanced levels, as well as some advanced specialized courses. The school did not offer

(Text continues on page 240)

Exhibit 1   New York City Neighbourhoods

1. "The Newest New Yorker 1990–1994: An Analysis of Immigration to NYC in the Early 1990s," *New York City Department of City Planning,* 1997, P. 55

NEW YORK CITY (All five boroughs)	1980		1980		Change 1980–1990	
	Number	%	Number	%	Number	%
Total Population	7,071,639	100.0	7,322,564	100.0	250,925	3.5
Nativity						
Foreign-born	1,670,199	100.0	2,082,931	100.0	412,732	24.7
As a percent of tot. population	23.6		28.4			
Year of Entry						
1980 to March 1990	N/A	—	953,449	45.8	—	—
1970 to 1979	669,892	40.1	502,850	24.1	(167,042)	(24.9)
1965 to 1969	268,963	16.1	199,778	9.6	(69,185)	(25.7)
1960 to 1964	147,970	8.9	116,381	5.6	(31,589)	(21.3)
Prior to 1960	583,374	34.9	310,473	14.9	(272,901)	(46.8)
Language Spoken at Home[2]						
Persons 5 years of age and over	6,606,223	100.0	6,820,456	100.0	214,233	3.2
Speaks a language other than English at home	2,342,299	35.5	2,793,773	41.0	451,474	19.3
Does not speak English "very well"	1,195,598	18.1	1,361,746	20.0	166,148	13.9
Per Capita Income (1989 constant $)	$12,190		$16,281		$4,091	33.6
Brooklyn						
Total Population	2,230,936	100.0	2,300,664	100.0	69,728	3.1
Nativity						
Foreign-born	530,973	100.0	672,569	100.0	141,596	26.7
As a percent of tot. population	23.8		29.2			
Year of Entry						
1980 to March 1990	N/A	—	313,692	46.6	—	—
1970 to 1979	227,995	42.9	171,844	25.6	(56,151)	(24.6)
1965 to 1969	85,385	16.1	61,993	9.2	(23,392)	(27.4)
1960 to 1964	41,445	7.8	32,919	4.9	(8,526)	(20.6)
Prior to 1960	176,148	33.2	92,121	13.7	(84,027)	(47.7)
Language Spoken at Home[2]						
Persons 5 years of age and over	2,056,856	100.0	2,124,614	100.0	67,758	3.3
Speaks a language other than English at home	723,436	35.2	844,374	39.7	120,938	16.7
Does not speak English "very well"	367,314	17.9	410,338	19.3	43,024	11.7
Per Capita Income (1989 constant $)	$9,642		$12,388		$2,246	28.5

Exhibit 2   New York City Population[1]   *(Continued)*

	1980		1990		Change 1980–1990	
Manhattan	Number	%	Number	%	Number	%
Total Population	1,428,285	100.0	1,487,536	100.0	59,251	4.1
Nativity						
Foreign-born	348,581	100.0	383,866	100.0	35,285	10.1
As a percent of tot. population	24.4		25.8			
Year of Entry						
1980 to March 1990	N/A	—	164,801	42.9	—	—
1970 to 1979	145,868	41.8	91,339	23.8	(54,529)	(37.4)
1965 to 1969	55,003	15.8	38,552	10.0	(16,451)	(29.9)
1960 to 1964	32,763	9.4	25,609	6.7	(7,154)	(21.8)
Prior to 1960	114,947	33.0	63,565	16.6	(51,382)	(44.7)
Language Spoken at Home[2]						
Persons 5 years of age and over	1,359,838	100.0	1,409,243	100.0	49,405	3.6
Speaks a language other than						
English at home	496,277	36.5	549,149	39.0	52,872	10.7
Does not speak English "very well"	265,972	19.6	271,394	19.3	5,422	2.0
Per Capita Income (1989 constant $)	$18,074		$27,862		$9,788	54.2
Queens						
Total Population	1,891,325	100.0	1,951,598	100.0	60,273	3.2
Nativity						
Foreign-born	540,818	100.0	707,153	100.0	166,335	30.8
As a percent of tot. population	28.6		36.2			
Year of Entry						
1980 to March 1990	N/A	—	323,653	45.8	—	—
1970 to 1979	212,837	39.4	170,729	24.1	(42,108)	(19.8)
1965 to 1969	91,646	16.9	71,045	10.0	(20,601)	(22.5)
1960 to 1964	53,033	9.8	40,869	5.8	(12,164)	(22.9)
Prior to 1960	183,302	33.9	100,857	14.3	(82,445)	(45.0)
Language Spoken at Home[2]						
Persons 5 years of age and over	1,781,488	100.0	1,833,315	100.0	51,827	2.9
Speaks a language other than						
English at home	616,285	34.6	805,411	43.9	189,126	30.7
Does not speak English "very well"	309,238	17.4	404,669	22.1	95,431	30.9
Per Capita Income (1989 constant $)	$12,652		$15,348		$2,696	21.3

Exhibit 2 New York City Population[1]

1. Exhibit prepared by Ronaldson on the basis of the information compiled from "Socioeconomic Profiles: A Portrait of New York City's Community Districts From the 1980 & 1990 Censuses of Population and Housing," Department of City Planning, Richard L. Schaffer, Director, March 1993, pp. 9–37.
2. English-speaking proficiency of those persons who spoke a foreign language at home was measured in terms of those who spoke English "very well," "well," "not well," or "not at all." The category shown in the table is the sum of the last three items.

Pronunciation

Pronunciation	Mon.	4:00-4:55	Rm. 3	Beg.*
Sounds Great	Mon.	6:30-7:45	Rm. 1	Int.*
Pronunciation	Tues.	2:30-3:25	Rm. 1	Beg.
Funny Thing About English	Wed.	1:00-2:00	Rm. 2	Int.
Pronunciation and Then Some	Thurs.	3:00-3:55	Rm. 2	Beg.

Vocabulary/Idioms

Basic Idioms	Tues.	11:30-1:00	Rm. 2	Int.
Contact in U.S.A.	Tues.	4:00-5:00	Rm. 2	Beg.
Word Power	Thurs.	10:30-11:30	Rm. 1	Int.
Idioms and Vocabulary	Thurs.	4:30-5:30	Rm. 3	Adv.*
Idioms	Fri.	1:00-3:00	Rm. 2	Int.
Vocabulary Through Slides	Fri.	3:00-4:25	Rm. 2	Beg.

Conversation/Discussion

Problems in Conversational English	Mon.	11:00-1:00	Rm. 1	Int.
Speak Out	Mon.	3:00-4:00	Rm. 2	Adv.
Conversation	Tues.	3:00-4:00	Rm. 2	Int.
What's Buzzing?	Tues.	5:00-6:00	Rm. 2	Int.
Talking Pictures	Wed.	10:30-12:00	Rm. 2	Int.
Conversation	Wed.	2:00-3:30	Rm. 1	Int.
Interactive Conversation	Wed.	6:30-7:50	Rm. 2	Int.
Conversation	Thurs.	11:00-12:55	Rm. 2	Int.
Drop In	Fri.	2:30-3:45	Rm. 3	Beg.
Plain English	Fri.	5:00-6:00	Rm. 1	Beg.
Words, Words, Words	Sat.	10:00-11:55	Rm. 3	Int.

TOEFL

TOEFL	Wed.	2:00-2:55	Rm. 2	Adv.
TOEFL	Wed.	3:00-3:55	Rm. 2	Adv.
TOEFL Practice	Thurs.	10:30-12:25	Rm. 3	Adv.
TOEFL	Sat.	3:00-4:25	Rm. 4	Adv.

Grammar

Intermediate English Grammar	Wed.	10:30-11:25	Rm. 3	Int.
Everyday Grammar	Wed.	4:45-6:00	Rm. 3	Int.
Troublespots in Grammar	Thurs.	3:30-4:30	Rm. 3	Adv.

* Beg.   Beginning
  Int.   Intermediate
  Adv.   Advance

Writing

Practical Writing	Wed.	10:00-12:00	Rm. 1	Int.

Literature

Literature	Mon.	5:30-7:55	Rm. 3	Int.
American Short Stories	Fri.	3:30-5:00	Rm. 1	Int.
Literature	Sat.	12:00-2:55	Rm. 4	Adv.

Specific Subjects

How to Use the Classifieds	Mon.	2:00-4:00	Rm. 1	Int.
Reading *The NY Times*	Tues.	11:00-11:55	Rm. 3	Int.
Media Chat	Tues.	12:00-1:30	Rm. 3	Adv.

Exhibit 3   English Group Classes by Subject *(Continued)*

The World of Jazz	Tues.	5:00-5:55	Rm. 3	Int.
Food, Kitchens, Cooking	Thurs.	12:00-1:55	Rm. 1	Int.
Television	Tues.	1:00-2:00	Rm. 2	Int.
Great Decisions	Thurs.	6:00-7:25	Rm. 1	Int.
U.S. History, Government, & Laws	Fri.	5:30-6:45	Rm. 4	Adv.
New York City History	Sat.	10:00-11:55	Rm. 4	Int.

NOTES: Open English Group Classes are not structured classes.
Levels indicated are guidelines only—members may attend any group.
Registration is not required for these classes.
If a leader is absent, a sign will be posted on the classroom door.

PLEASE COME TO THE CLASS AS CLOSE TO THE STARTING POINT AS POSSIBLE!!

Exhibit 3   English Group Classes by Subject

additional activities for students and had strict requirements and policies (Exhibit 4). Students had to pay a $50 non-refundable registration fee and could choose from either day or evening classes. One hundred class hours taken during the day cost $595. Evening classes were taught three days a week (three class hours per evening) for eight weeks at a cost of $425. The daytime ESL courses were also offered during the summer. In its promotion, the school emphasized its authorization under the Federal Law to enroll non-immigrant foreign students. The school was also certified by the New York State Department of Education.

The English Language School

The English Language School, a smaller school with which Ronaldson expected to compete, was located in Greenpoint, Brooklyn. Ronaldson believed that the school's location was one of the major factors contributing to its success. It was located close to the subway, in an area densely populated by immigrants who were the primary students of the school. Since no Green Card or passport was required during the registration process, the school attracted both legal and illegal immigrants. Like International Schools in New York, The English Language School in Greenpoint did not organize any after-school events for students. The school offered eight levels of ESL from beginners to advanced. Students

could choose from daily evening courses running for four months from 8 p.m. to 9:30 p.m. Monday through Friday (at $260), daily intensive courses running for one month between 9:30 a.m. and 1:30 p.m. Monday through Friday ($365), Saturday morning and Saturday afternoon courses, as well as Sunday morning and Sunday afternoon courses. Combined Saturday-Sunday afternoon courses were also available. Weekend courses were most popular among students due to the fact that many of the students worked during the week. The maximum number of students per group was fifteen. Every course ended with an exam.

Other Schools

Ronaldson counted over twenty schools of English listed in the Queens Yellow Pages alone and worried that English courses were becoming a commodity. An increasing number of schools offered their students free access to computers and free computer classes in order to stay competitive.

CENTER OPERATIONS

Staffing

Ronaldson considered hiring either one full-time or two part-time teachers initially. Since there was a numerous supply of qualified

We offer ten levels of English, from the very basic to the most advanced levels. A one-hour placement test is given at the time of registration to determine the student's entry level.

An Introductory Level (0)
This level emphasizes the basic elements of the language for students who have little or no previous exposure to English.

Beginning Levels (I, II)
The beginning classes emphasize the simple tenses through spoken English and listening comprehension. Reading comprehension and writing skills are also introduced at these levels.

Intermediate Levels (III, IV, V, VI)
The intermediate levels involve the difficult but necessary perfect tenses, modals, passive voice and subjunctive mood. Spoken English with idiom practice, listening comprehension, reading comprehension, writing skills and vocabulary building are all emphasized.

Advanced Levels (VII, VIII, IX)
The advanced levels take the student to increased proficiency in both spoken and written English. Vocabulary building is continued through reading and listening comprehension.

Advanced Specialized Courses
Courses are also available in TOEFL, conversation, reading and vocabulary building, writing, fluency development and explorations in American culture. For further information, please contact the school.

Entrance Requirements
The following items must be presented to the school at the time of registration:

All students

1. One recent passport-sized photograph
2. Passport or Green Card

and for *Student Visa (I-20) students*

3. One xerox copy of your high school or college transcript or diploma
4. One xerox copy of your affidavit of support, and/or bank statement

and for *Student Visa (I-20)* requested for *students coming from abroad*

5. $95 deposit + $5 handling charge

All students issued an I-20 from International Schools in New York must attend day classes.

Day Schedule	Evening Schedule
Monday - Friday	Monday, Tuesday and Thursday
Each level: 4 class hours per day 5 weeks 100 class hours	Each level: 3 class hours per evening 8 weeks 72 class hours
Morning classes: LEVELS V - IX 9:00 a.m. to 1:00 p.m.	All levels 6:15 p.m. to 9:00 p.m.
Afternoon classes: LEVELS 0 - V 1:30 p.m. - 5:30 p.m.	

Exhibit 4   International Schools in New York   *(Continued)*

Fees: ALL FEES PAYABLE IN ADVANCE

Registration	$50	Registration	$50
Tuition (1 level - 5 weeks)	$595	Tuition (1 level - 8 weeks)	$425

MASTERCARD and VISA accepted

Refund Policy:

1. The registration fee is not refundable.

2. If the student cancels this agreement 24 hours before instruction begins, the school will refund all tuition fees paid.

3. If the student withdraws or is discontinued after instruction has begun, the student will receive as a refund no less than

   a) 100% of tuition paid if termination is during the first 2 days of the course.
   b) 75% of tuition if termination is after completion of the first 2 days, but during the first 20% of the course.
   c) 50% of tuition if termination is during the second 20% of the course.
   d) 25% of tuition if termination is during the third 20% of the course.
   e) 0% of tuition if termination is after completion of 60% of the course.

Any monies paid to the school in excess of the sum due to the school by the student who cancels, withdraws, or is discontinued will be refunded within thirty (30) days of such action.

Exhibit 4   International Schools in New York

candidates, she did not think she would need to pay more than $30,000 annually, including benefits, for one full-time position. She wondered what qualities she should look for when selecting the teaching staff. As an English major herself, Ronaldson was planning to teach some classes, in addition to handling administrative responsibilities. Although she expected to work long hours, Ronaldson decided to draw a minimal salary of $25,000 a year until the center was financially stable.

Location

One of the most important decisions Ronaldson had to make was the choice of location. Commercial real estate in Manhattan was the most expensive of all three boroughs. She could lease 1,200 square feet in the Washington Heights neighborhood of Manhattan for $2,200 per month (other Manhattan areas were more expensive). Her real estate agent had also told her about an 1,100-square foot space at $2.20 per square foot a month in the Bensonhurst area of Brooklyn, located close to the subway. Since the Brooklyn location was located in a "hot" market, Ronaldson had to make her decision quickly.

Other costs and conditions were similar for the two leases. Both Manhattan and Brooklyn locations could be converted to three classrooms and required about $5,000 worth of leasehold improvements in order to make the spaces suitable for classrooms and an office. A one-time fee equal to one month's rent had to be paid to the agent. A lessee was usually expected to sign at least a five-year lease; however, favorable agreements as to the breaking of the lease could occasionally be negotiated with the landlord. When comparing the two sites, Ronaldson recalled, however, that Washington Heights already had one well established English school. She also wondered if she should not try to find a location in Queens where one square foot of commercial space cost on average from $1.80 to $1.90.

	School Furniture & Equipment, Inc.	Office Products
Student's table	N/A	$40 – $45
Student's chair	N/A	$20 – $25
Teacher's desk	N/A	$225
Chalkboard	4' × 4' $160 4' × 6' $180	4' × 6' lowest priced model: $120 best steel frame model, with a life-long guarantee: $225
Corkboard	4' × 4' $125	4' × 4' $85
Display case	2' × 3'	2' × 3' $185 – $200
	• 3-week lead time • will customize to suit customer's needs	• delivery costs included

Exhibit 5   Comparison of Prices Charged by School Equipment Providers

Equipment

Ronaldson identified a few school furniture and equipment providers (Exhibit 5). She planned to have up to fifteen students per class, sitting at their own desks. She also considered buying used furniture and equipment which she estimated would save her from 10 to 20 per cent.

Promotion

Since Ronaldson could not afford an experienced marketing manager, she had to develop the center's marketing strategy. Smaller players, like The English Language School in Greenpoint, advertised in some of the local ethnic daily newspapers. Rates differed depending on the newspaper; for example, placing a small print ad in Polish Daily News cost $10 per day if the ad appeared in the Monday, Tuesday, or Wednesday issue, $12 on Thursday or Friday, and $14 on the weekend; the weekly rate was $50 while a four-week placement cost $185. Another newspaper, the Daily News, however, charged about $100 per day for a small print ad. Ronaldson wondered in how many ethnic newspapers she should advertise and with what frequency. Should she advertise in more upscale newspapers, like the New York Times, or on the radio or TV? She also had to decide what these advertisements would say and look like.

Other marketing costs Ronaldson considered were related to the use of the telephone and advertising in the Yellow Pages. For a 1-800 number, Bell Atlantic (a telephone company) charged a one-time service fee of $56, rental fee of $10 per month, and $12 per hour of use. A regular business phone cost $19.73 per month per line, plus the cost of local and long-distance calls. Although Ronaldson was not sure whether she should go ahead with the 1-800 number, she knew that placing the information about her school in the Yellow Pages was crucial. The closing date to submit an ad differed within each borough; to have a business listed in the Queens Borough Yellow Pages, the ad had to be in by the end of July; in the case of Brooklyn Yellow Pages, it was June; and for the Manhattan Yellow Pages, February. Should she place her ad in all three boroughs' Yellow Pages? (See Exhibit 6 for Yellow Pages advertisement costs.)

	Queens	Brooklyn	Manhattan
Regular listing: small print business name, address, and phone number	$4.25 / month	$4.25 / month	$4.25 / month
Regular listing: bold business name and phone number; small print address	$27 / month	$29.75 / month	$31.75 / month
Display: 1/16 page (2" × 2.5")	$311 / month	$351 / month	$375 / month
Yellow background and black ink	(Ronaldson's estimate)		(Ronaldson's estimate)
Display: 1/8 page yellow background and black ink	$603 / month	$702 / month	$754 / month

Exhibit 6   Yellow Pages Pricing[1]

1. Exhibit compiled by Ronaldson presents prices charged by Bell Atlantic for Yellow Pages listings. Ronaldson learned also that when requesting a display ad, a business owner received help from Bell Atlantic. A sales representative discussed the design and needs of the business and worked with the business owner on the design.

Finance

In addition to the costs mentioned previously, Ronaldson estimated that another $4,000 to $5,000 would be needed for office and classroom supplies (chalk, sponges, paper, etc.), utilities, licensing fees, registration of the business, and miscellaneous costs. She could only invest $20,000 from her savings; however, her boyfriend offered to lend her $15,000 at no interest, repayable at her convenience. She also believed that she could secure some financing from her bank with a solid business plan.

DECISION

Ronaldson looked back at all the research she had done and wondered how many levels of ESL and what kind of policies should be implemented in order to ensure full enrollment; how to schedule classes to satisfy students' demand and maximize the center's capacity at the same time; and how many students she needed in order to break even on all the costs. Ronaldson wondered how she could differentiate her school from the rest. If she decided to open the center, she wanted to have the right strategy in place and have developed a solid business plan.

NOTES

1. The premise for the legalization of their stay could have been an application for a political asylum, marriage to an American resident or citizen, sponsoring by family or work, etc.

2. "Statistical Abstract of the U.S. 1997"; *The National Data Book,* 117th Edition, U.S. Department of Commerce, Economics and Statistics Administration Bureau of the Census, Washington, D.C. 1997, p. 11.

3. Wirpsa, L., "Immigrants Uncertain as Deadline Nears," *National Catholic Reporter,* Oct. 17, 1997.

4. Almost ten million immigrants arrived in the U.S. in the 1980s.

5. Sources: "Turn of the Tide? Immigration," *The Economist,* Sep. 27, 1997, and "The Newest New Yorker 1990 - 1994: An Analysis of Immigration to NYC in the Early 1990s," *New York City Department of City Planning,* 1997.

6. "The Newest New Yorker 1990–1994: An Analysis of Immigration to NYC in the Early 1990s," *New York City Department of City Planning,* 1997, pp. xi, xiii.

7. Information based on "Socioeconomic Profiles: A Portrait of New York City's Community Districts from the 1980 & 1990 Censuses of Population and Housing," *Department of City Planning,* Richard L. Schaffer, Director, March 1993, pp. 8, 14.

8. All dollar values given in the case, including the exhibits, are given in U.S. currency unless otherwise stated.

About the Editor

Alison M. Konrad is a Professor of Organizational Behavior and holder of the Corus Entertainment Chair in Women in Management at the Richard Ivey School of Business, The University of Western Ontario. Previously, she was Professor of Human Resource Administration at Temple University's Fox School of Business and Management, where she taught for 15 years. She received her Ph.D. from the Claremont Graduate University in 1987 and held a 2-year postdoctoral fellowship at Stanford University from 1986 to 1988.

Professor Konrad was Chair of the Academy of Management's Gender and Diversity in Organizations Division in 1996–1997 and President of the Eastern Academy of Management in 1997–1998. She is the 2003–2007 Editor of *Group and Organization Management,* a ranked journal in the fields of management and applied psychology. She is an Associate Editor of the journal *Gender, Work and Organization* and a past editorial board member for the *Academy of Management Review.* She has published more than 40 articles and chapters on topics relating to workplace diversity in outlets such as the *Academy of Management Journal; Administrative Science Quarterly; Gender, Work and Organization; Group and Organization Management; Human Relations; Psychological Bulletin; Sex Roles;* and the *Strategic Management Journal.*

Professor Konrad's forthcoming book, the *Handbook of Workplace Diversity* (coedited with Pushkala Prasad and Judith Pringle), is an international edited collection of conceptual perspectives on the topic of diversity within the field of organizational studies. Her current work focuses on organizational diversity and inclusivity initiatives, job retention among former welfare clients, and the links between individual preferences and career outcomes for women and men.